Spatial Orientation

Princeton Series in Neurobiology and Behavior

ROBERT R. CAPRANICA, PETER MARLER, AND
NORMAN T. ADLER,
Editors

Spatial Orientation

THE SPATIAL CONTROL OF BEHAVIOR IN ANIMALS AND MAN

by HERMANN SCHÖNE
Translated by CAMILLA STRAUSFELD

Princeton University Press   Princeton, N. J.

Published by Princeton Univerty Press,
41 William Street, Princeton, New Jersey 08540
In the United Kingdom: Princeton University Press,
Guildford, Surrey

All Rights Reserved
Library of Congress Cataloging in Publication Data
will be found on the last printed page of this book
ISBN clothbound: 0-691-08363-0
ISBN paperback: 0-691-08364-9

This book has been composed in Linotron Baskerville

Clothbound editions of Princeton University Press books
are printed on acid-free paper, and binding materials are
chosen for strength and durability.
Paperbacks, although satisfactory for personal collections,
are not usually suitable for library rebinding

Printed in the United States of America
by Princeton University Press, Princeton, New Jersey

First published in German as *Orientierung im Raum
Formen und Mechanismen der Lenkung des Verhaltens im
Raum bei Tier und Mensch* by Wissenschaftliche
Verlagsgesellschaft mbH (Stuttgart, 1980)

Dedicated to the memory of my teacher Erich von Holst

Contents

3. Particulars of the Sensory Modalities   149

Preface

This century has witnessed a metamorphosis in the way we regard orientation behavior. The first comprehensive attempt to explain this behavior causally was the tropism theory of Jacques Loeb. It led to a purely mechanistic conception of orientation, as a simple chain of physicochemical transformations working toward an equilibrium between two antagonistic systems. Alfred Kühn proposed a classification of orienting responses, founded partially on Loeb's system, that formed the basis of Fraenkel and Gunn's system, still the most complete summary of directed movements.

Around 1950 orientation began to be viewed as part of the whole structure of behavior instead of just a reaction. This is reflected in the work of von Frisch, Griffin, von Holst, and Kramer. Erich von Holst, using simple means in ingenious ways, instigated a new way of looking at the structure of orientation and behavior systems. Some of his discoveries about the mechanisms of gravity orientation, stimulus weighting, central disposition, and the central organization of "drives" [358, 365, 366], although in part forgotten, still represent the latest state of the art.

New methods of analysis arose with the cybernetic theory of Norbett Wiener. Similarities in the mode of operation of the systems "man and machine" inspired a comparative study of technical and biological causal systems. Since then, systems analysis has assumed an increasingly central role in the formulation of research problems. How do the components of a system intermesh, how does this give rise to the orientation behavior, how are "multimodal" systems connected, and above all, what are the operational principles? Although a little is already known and much is currently under investigation, large areas remain "underdeveloped." The accomplishments in receptor and neurophysiology are notable, but other areas are still largely untouched. This book draws attention to many of the unanswered questions. Not the least of its intentions is to encourage their elucidation.

The focus of this book is on the analysis of the system as a whole: the physiology of the orientation behavior. We shall look at mechanisms from the stimulus-response relationships and the determination of the central reference value to the structure of interaction within the whole system, e.g., to human spatial perception and to space constancy. Sensory physiology is covered where it is necessary for the understanding of the orientation itself.

Although I have tried to limit the use of specialized terminology, I could not do without it completely. Most of the terms are listed and explained at the beginning of the book; others are defined where it is necessary to use them. The concepts of taxis and kinesis appear sparingly. A few new labels are used, like array process, bisensor system, and indirect orientation, but they are only names for new ways of looking at familiar relationships.

This book is meant to provide an overview of the entire field of orientation, as well as to give some detail. For some readers coverage may appear too extensive, for others, too restricted or perhaps even too speculative. In addition to firmly established theories, explanations are included that have the character of working hypotheses. The expert may find that the chapter on his subject is too sparse or unbalanced in the treatment of its various aspects. From his point of view he may be right, but this book is not intended only for him. It can also be read by the interested—and not entirely uninformed—lay person, especially by students and teachers of biology in high schools and colleges. Researchers in the field of orientation will also find ample material for discussion.

I would like to take this opportunity to express my gratitude to all who contributed directly and indirectly to this book, who allowed me to pester them with questions and problems, and who were ever ready to discuss a point for its clarification. These include, above all, my colleagues in Seewiesen: E. Gwinner, F. Huber, E. Kramer, M.-L. Mittelstaedt, H. Mittelstaedt, D. Schneider, G. Wallraff, T. Weber, and G. Wildgruber. My thanks go also to many others for their critical review of individual chapters: N. Bischof, G. S. Boyan, C. Fitger, M. Lindauer, H. Nyborg, R. Preiss, J. Rheinlaender, K. Schmidt-Koenig, F. J. Verheijen, G. Wendler, and I. Würdinger. In particular I would like to thank J. S. Kennedy for taking the time and trouble to write lengthy epistles that contributed substantially to the clarification of the taxis and kinesis concepts.

Special thanks go to Renate Alton for her tireless assistance in all the technical aspects of preparing this book: for the multiple retyping of the manuscript, the painstaking gathering of the literature, the systematic arrangement of the citations, and above all, the careful execution of the drawings. I would also like to thank Jürgen Schiller for typing the English manuscript.

Hermann Schöne

Key to Symbols

Equivalent or comparable variables are represented by the same symbol except in a few figures where the symbols used by the author of the original paper were kept.

Several of the symbols for the angle relative to stimulus direction are standard, such as α for the direction to gravity, β for the direction to light, and θ for the direction to sound.

In the circuit diagrams all variables referring to the same angle are represented by the same symbol. Different "functions" are indicated by the subscript, e.g., β_i for the "internal" signal of angle β supplied by the sensory input. External variables are represented by arrows below the level of the boxes (see horizontal lines in Fig. 2.4/10); internal variables, above the level of the boxes.

The primary axes and planes, as well as the degrees of freedom of movement, are illustrated in Fig. 1.3/2.

(a) Angle between animal and stimulus direction

α	Sense organ/body–gravity
β	Sense organ/body–light
β	Sense organ/body–visually perceived object
β_s	Sense organ/body–sun
β_o	Sense organ/body–optokinetic pattern flow
μ	Body–magnetic field
σ	Body/body part–substrate
θ	Sense organ/body–sound

(b) Other angles

γ	Stimulus direction–stimulus direction (e.g., gravity–light)
δ	Body–body part
ϵ	Course–north
ϵ_s	Sun–north
κ	Body/body part–stimulus direction (not directly detectable by senses, e.g., arm–gravity)

λ Visual object–stimulus direction (e.g., illuminated line–gravity)
τ Substrate–gravity
β_{so} Sun–pattern flow direction
ω wind direction–north

(c) Indexes

c command signal of the variable to the motor apparatus
d disturbance of the variable
i internal signal of the variable
m motor change in the variable
r reference value (controlling variable)
s with respect to the sun
o with respect to the optokinetic direction (pattern flow direction)
w with respect to the wind direction
h horizontal
v vertical

Introduction

Insects fly into a flame, birds beat their wings at lighthouse windows, fish are drawn to the glare of fishing lanterns—eye-catching behavior, seemingly pointless, even dangerous for the animals. Why do they do it? The old question "why" crops up whenever we are faced with something new and puzzling.

But this curiosity may have different roots. When one person asks why, he may be asking what the behavior is for. What purpose is served when an animal seeks out the light? Another person means something else when he asks why. He is not concerned with the purpose but wants to know what causes the behavior. What makes an animal in the dark move toward a light? How does the process work?

The first question, what is the behavior for, is directed at its biological significance. An example of this kind of interpretation is the "trapping effect" proposed by Verheijen [875]. A spot of light in a dark surround is like an opening in an enclosure in which the animal is trapped. The animal moves toward the light in an attempt to escape. This kind of approach can be applied at various levels. At the species level it may refer to an advantage for the species, such as survival value and selective advantage. (According to more recent sociobiological theory the site of action of natural selection is the unit of replication, the gene, and not the species [see the introduction to chap. 2].)

However, the question "what for" can also be asked at the level of the organism. What purpose does this behavior serve within the physiological framework? Let us postpone until section 2.4 the question of whether an organism possesses the capacity for purposeful action. Here we just want to establish that the accomplishments of a system are a consequence of the way it functions. This brings us back to our second question, how does it work?

An explanation of this kind was offered by Romanes in 1885 [719] for the behavior of animals flying into a light. He wrote: "There can be no doubt that the flame is mistaken for a white flower or something similar. This behavior is due to the animal's curiosity, its urge to investigate the unfamiliar." Romanes' suggestion that curiosity is the driving force for this behavior is not as farfetched as might at first appear. Curiosity is well known in modern ethology [191].

Every causal analysis begins with this kind of question and answer. It leads to further observations and finally to a working hypothesis that can be experimentally tested. For example, the investigation of a light orientation involves questions such as how the sense organs register light direction, how the animal uses this information to adjust the position of its body, and how, if necessary, it changes its direction. The major portion of this book deals with the study of these processes, the physiology of orientation.

We begin by defining and discussing the terminology of orientation. This is followed by a look at orientation from "the outside," in order to get acquainted with its external manifestations. We shall investigate and describe the "morphology" of the orientation phenomenon, without delving into its physiological interrelationships. Afterward we practice some "functional morphology" by asking how the orientation is put to use. What is its role within the behavioral framework? This leads us to physiological considerations: What are the sensory mechanisms of direction measurement, and how is the orientation direction adjusted and changed? What is the nature of the causal interactions in higher-order orientation systems? Separate chapters are devoted to the questions of space constancy and to human spatial orientation.

There is no need to discuss the concepts of taxis and kinesis in great depth since these are well covered by Fraenkel and Gunn in their standard work on orientation [230]. Gunn [287] himself wrote: "Most of the system that Fraenkel and I put forward in 1940, on the basis of Kühn's system, has simply gone into the language as a set of useful terms. It deals with types of spatial manoeuvre and does not pretend to describe physiological mechanisms; these may be brought in as evidence for or against the feasibility of types of manoeuvres." Nowadays the physiological aspects of these concepts are hardly discussed.

As for the "useful terms": Specialized terminology is necessary for the precise and comprehensible characterization of processes and relationships. Special terms facilitate the task of describing and conveying specialized information, but only when they are understood correctly. Unless there is general consensus as to their meaning, heated discussions may arise. As Fraenkel and Gunn so aptly put it, "Names should be convenient tools and nothing more."

Spatial Orientation

1. Orientation: Its Meaning and Scope

1.1 DEFINITIONS

Colloquially, to "orient oneself" means to acquaint oneself with a situation. Orientation commonly refers to an adjustment to the spatial aspects of a situation, i.e., spatial orientation. This is reflected in its etymological derivation. The word *orientation* stems from the Latin verb *oriri*, which means "to arise from" or "to originate in." The word *oriens*, which originally referred to the daily rising of the sun, came to be used for the direction of its rising—the east—and finally for the lands that lay at that compass point, "the East" or the "Orient."

Opinion has differed over the years about the meaning of spatial orientation and what should be included within the scope of this concept. Loeb regarded all movements of living organisms as responses directed toward external stimuli. According to this view, animal behavior consists almost exclusively of orienting movements. In contrast, Fraenkel and Gunn emphasize that the subject of their book, *The Orientation of Animals*, comprises only a small portion of animal behavior [230].

Brun [96] gives the following definition: "In its broadest sense, orientation is the ability of organisms to position their bodies (or parts of their bodies) in a particular way with respect to stimuli or to relate their locomotion in some way to them." Fraenkel and Gunn also include both a stationary and a locomotory response in their definition: "We include under the term orientation not only those reactions which guide the animal into its normal stance, but also reactions which guide it into its normal habitat or into other situations which are of importance to it" [230]. Since orientation into the normal stance is, as a rule, always present, they call it "primary" orientation. Other directional reactions are superimposed on the normal stance and are termed "secondary" orientation.

In contrast Kühn [480] excludes locomotion from his definition and limits orientation to the act of adjustment: "The active positioning of an organism with respect to a particular spatial direction ... we call its orientation." Koehler [459] and Tinbergen [856] similarly restrict the concept to orientational turning (see 2.5).

In the *Handbuch der Psychologie*, Bischof [64] expands the scope of spatial orientation to "the act of relating to a spatial reference system." He distinguishes between two separate categories of human spatial orientation: motor orientation, which is concerned with motor activity, and perceptual orientation, which refers to perceptions that may or may not lead to motor activity. The definition given by Jander [405] encompasses only motor orientation. He writes: "Spatial orientation is the ability of motile organisms to maintain or to alter their activity and position relative to their spatial environment." He explicitly excludes "coordinating movements . . . which merely change the spatial relationships between the body and its parts."

Perceptual orientation has been studied primarily in humans (see 2.9). Animal studies have concentrated more on motor orientation, i.e., on the motor aspects, since it is difficult to demonstrate perceptual processes in animals.

We use spatial orientation to refer to *all* movements and states that are, or were, actively ordered in space. The concept describes the ability of animals (including humans) to relate the position and movement of their bodies, body parts, and even foreign objects to spatial cues (see 2.2). This ability includes the establishment of a spatial relationship, as well as its maintenance and perception.

1.2 ORIENTATION, BEHAVIOR, AND ECOLOGY

Orientation refers to the spatial organization of movements. Since movements are elements of behavior, orientation and behavior are intimately associated with each other. It is unnecessary here to go into a thorough discussion of what constitutes behavior. Let us simply define behavior as any overt manifestation of life by an animal, especially one that takes the form of movements. A behavior pattern is the unit of behavior and is defined as a sequence of movements characterized by a specific configuration of time and space. This underscores the special significance that spatial organization has for behavior. Every behavior is oriented in some way. Whether an animal walks, grooms, catches prey, or interacts with a social partner, "where" or "in which direction" is an indispensable feature of its behavior pattern. Thus, we can define orientation as the process that organisms use to organize their behavior with respect to spatial features.

For an animal and its behavioral organization the abstract concept of space has a very concrete meaning, namely, its environment—the ground upon which it walks, the sun toward which it turns, the blossom to which it flies, the child it approaches. An organism's behavior is finely tuned to environmental conditions. The constant interactions of an animal with its surroundings, its ecological embedment, as it were, are essential for its survival. Orientation processes have to do with the spatial aspects of these interactions.

The specific orientation systems of an animal correspond to the particulars of its environment. The hermit crab *Coenobita* of the coastal regions of Somalia occupies a habitat extending from the moist beaches, across the dunes, into the dry bush regions. Several orientation systems guide these animals through their ecologically different habitats [873, 874]. They use a system that is probably based on substrate slope to find their way from the beach up to the dunes and back, landmark orientation to find shelter during the hot hours of the day, and a sun compass system to guide them in the bush region.

A special orientation system makes the heterogeneous life cycle of the cockchafer, *Melolontha vulgaris*, possible. The larvae live in the earth of open fields; the beetles feed in wooded areas. The freshly emerged beetle must first find its way to feeding grounds, then the female must find its way back to the open field to deposit her eggs. A combination of landmark and compass orientation makes this feat possible (3.1.5).

The habitat of plankton poses completely different demands. Plankton live in particular water layers. Many species move from one layer to another according to a daily cycle. This vertical migration is guided by an orientation complex in which gravity, light, and hydrostatic pressure all play a role (2.7.1).

Many animals migrate according to seasonal changes in the conditions of their habitats. Migratory birds fly great distances twice a year between their summer breeding grounds and the warmer southern regions where they overwinter. When the autumn storms begin, the Caribbean lobsters migrate in long chains from the shallow coastal regions into deeper waters (Fig. 1.2/1).

Other animals such as salmon change their habitat only twice in their lifetime in connection with their reproductive cycle. One-year-old salmon (smolts) move from the heads of rivers, where they hatched, to the ocean. Adult salmon return to the same breeding grounds to spawn. These migrations are guided by a sun compass and the characteristic odor of the home waters (Fig. 2.8/9; 3.5).

Some freshwater fish families that spend much of their time in murky water have developed a very special orientation system. They produce electric fields, which are altered by objects in their surroundings. These perturbations are registered by electroreceptors and enable the fish to get their bearings within their environment (3.3).

Before we investigate the capability and performance of orientation mechanisms within the framework of behavioral-ecological systems (1.4), let us first look at the geometrical aspects of spatial processes.

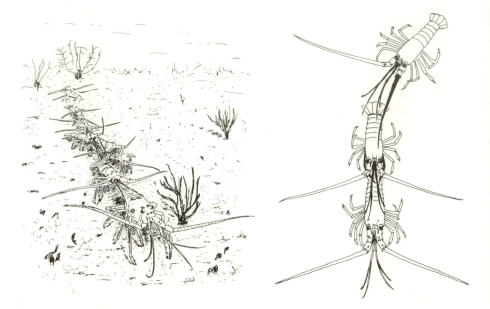

Fig. 1.2/1 Each fall thousands of spiny lobsters, *Panulirus argus*, migrate in chains of 20 or more animals, each keeping physical contact by touching the one in front of it with its antennules, forelegs, or antennae. (In the illustration on the right, those parts in contact with the preceding lobster are blacked in.) The queue shown on the left has been disturbed by a diver (not shown). Normally the chains form a straight line. (Left drawn from a photograph; right from a drawing kindly supplied by W. Herrnkind)

1.3 THE SPATIAL STRUCTURE OF ORIENTATION MOVEMENTS

The act of orientation can be categorized according to the geometrical structure of its movement in space. Jander [405] has already pointed out the importance of spatial geometry for the analysis of orientation behavior.

1.3.1 Rotation and Translation

Physics distinguishes between two basic movements: rotation, or turning in place, and translation, or change of locus. A body can be either rotated or translated, and a spatial change can consist of one or both of these elements.

Consider a butterfly on a flower as it turns to expose its opened wings

Fig. 1.3/1 Translation: The butterfly
changes its location in space. Rotation: It
turns in place to face the sun.

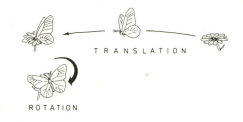

to the sun (Fig. 1.3/1). This is an example of a rotatory movement, i.e., a
change in direction, which can be expressed in terms of angles.

After the butterfly has basked for a while in the sun, it flies to another
flower. This translation not only bridges two points separated by a certain
distance in space, but it also has a direction. Translatory movements thus
can be seen to have a directional and a distance component. If the direction
remains constant, the movement forms a straight line. If it changes in a
regular fashion, the path is a circle.

Since a translatory movement consists of both direction and distance, it
can be expressed as a vector. It can also be described in terms of a Cartesian
coordinate system (compare 1.3.3).

1.3.2 The Degrees of Freedom of Movement

In free space, animals have three dimensions at their disposal (Fig. 1.3/2).
A fish can move forward or backward, to the left or right, and up or down.
These directions are the basic lines of locomotory translation and can be
consigned to the three main body axes. The longitudinal, or rostro-caudal,
axis is the X axis; the transverse, or left-right, axis, the Y axis; and the
vertical, or dorsoventral, axis, the Z axis. Thus, the X, Y, and Z axes represent the three degrees of freedom of translatory movements.

The three axes also determine the three degrees of freedom of rotatory
movements. Rotation around the X axis is called roll; around the Y axis,
pitch; and around the Z axis, yaw. Roll is a sideways leaning around the
longitudinal axis taking place in the transverse plane; pitch, a tilting up
and down of the anterior or posterior part of the body around the transverse axis in the medial plane; and yaw, a sideways swaying around the
vertical axis, in the horizontal plane.

In total there are six degrees of freedom for movement in space, three
translatory and three rotatory. Very few animals have all six at their disposal. No flying or swimming organism can perform translatory movements
with equal facility in all three basic directions. Many fish swim well forward
or backward (along the X axis), but must usually turn their body to move

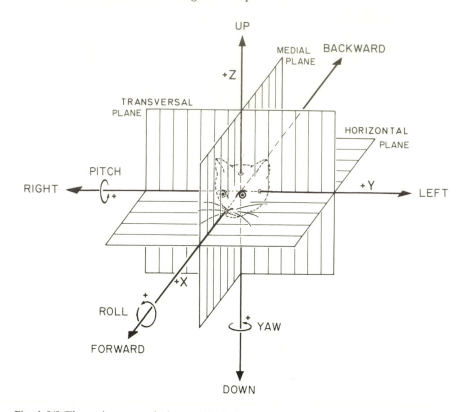

Fig. 1.3/2 The main axes and planes with their corresponding movements. The + signifies: right side first for the X axis (roll); ventral side first for the Y axis (pitch); and left side first for the Z axis (yaw). (Definitions from [284, 343])

sideways or up and down. Most fish perform rotatory movements equally well around all three axes, i.e., they can roll, pitch, and yaw.

Flying organisms such as birds can fly forward and ascend or descend during flight (translations along the X and Z axes). However, only a few species can fly sideways along the Y axis. One of these exceptions is the hummingbird as it hovers from side to side in front of a flower. Hover flies can also fly sideways. Birds can roll and yaw. Pitch occurs only occasionally, as when a hawk starts to plunge toward its prey.

Animals that move about in only one plane are usually limited to three degrees of freedom, backward and forward or sideways translations, as well as rotation around the Z axis (yaw). A mole moving in its tunnel has only two degrees of freedom, translation along the X axis and roll.

1.3.3 Graphic Representation

The methods used to describe and depict spatial relationships depend on the type of mechanisms and the particular questions being dealt with. Take, for example, the flight of a honeybee to a food source (Fig. 1.3/3). This situation can be described by coordinate systems in which the hive is the origin and the axes are based on either the points of a compass, the direction of the sun, or the direction in which the hive is facing. All three of these graphic representations are space-constant since their coordinates refer to the external world (sun, hive, earth). The situation can also be represented as animal-constant by making the bee the origin of a coordinate system where the primary axis coincides with the flight direction.

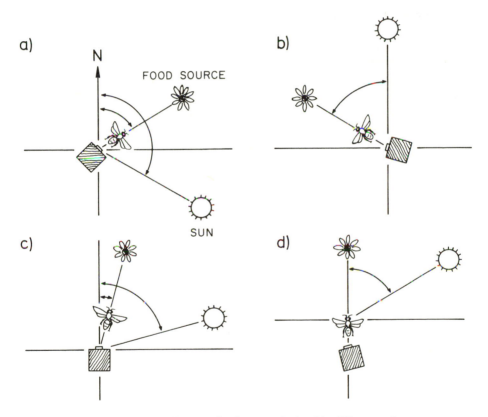

Fig. 1.3/3 The flight of a honeybee to a food source depicted in different reference systems. The angles are given relative a) to north ("geographical" representation), b) to the sun, c) to the hive, and d) to the flight direction. In a)–c) the hive represents the origin; in d), the bee.

Rotatory movements around the primary axes, i.e., in one of the primary planes, can be depicted relatively simply by placing the plane of movement in the plane of the paper. The conceptual representation becomes more difficult when the turning possibilities must be shown in two or three axes. Figure 1.3/4 gives an example in which the three primary axes of a fish (X, Y, Z) are fixed to a sphere that can be moved relative to the spatial reference, gravity. The rotatory movements of the fish relative to gravity can be represented by the two angles α_x and α_y.

Translations that take place in one plane can be transferred directly to paper using the appropriate scaling. In a bicoordinate system a locus is defined by two values (x and y) (Fig. 1.3/5). The grid of a map is a good example of this, where x and y correspond to the values of longitude and latitude, respectively. Calculation of values for direction and distance of translation is derived in Fig. 1.3/5.

Polar coordinates can also be used to describe translation. Direction is given by the angle to the main axis and distance by concentric circles around the zero point. A particular location is defined by one value for direction and one for distance.

1.3.4 Geometry of Orientation

An orientation movement is characterized by its specific geometrical relationship to a stimulus. We see this immediately when an animal moves toward a light, approaches an olfactory source, or maintains a horizontal

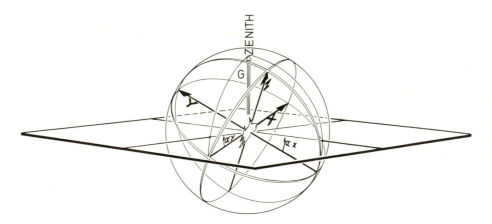

Fig. 1.3/4 The coordinate system of an animal within the framework of a reference system based on gravity (G) and the horizontal plane. The position of the fish is defined by the angles α_x and α_y, formed by the X and Y axes with the horizontal plane.

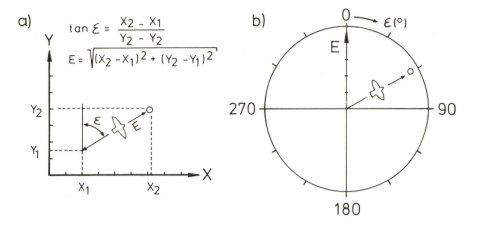

Fig. 1.3/5 Change of location according to direction (ϵ) and distance (E) in two forms of graphical representation: a) Cartesian coordinates and b) polar coordinates.

position with respect to gravity. Since these spatial relationships are much more obvious than their underlying mechanisms, orientation movements are, for the sake of convenience, labeled according to their spatio-geometrical associations. Positive or negative phototaxis or geotaxis are examples of this kind of labeling, as are compass orientation and course orientation. In the following we want to collect these labels and categorize them according to the basic processes of rotation and translation. For pure rotatory orientation movements, i.e., turning on the spot, we have various labels, such as rotational, angular, directional, and positional orientation.

The expression compass orientation is used for both rotation and the directional component of translation. It emphasizes the spatial reference of a directional orientation (e.g., the sun). A compass is an instrument for measuring direction with respect to a spatial reference. A magnetic compass, for example, gives directions relative to the earth's magnetic field.

An animal can control its translation according to either distance or direction or both. The term vector orientation applies when both distance and direction are used. When only the distance component is oriented, it is called distance orientation. Jander [405] also used the term "elasis" as the converse of "taxis," which in this context means rotational orientation. (Chmurzyński [130] originally proposed "elasis" for the directing of locomotion, i.e., the rotatory component of translation, and reserved the term "taxis" for turning in place.)

Course orientation is used if only the direction of a translation is oriented. When a ship "holds its course," it maintains its direction and moves forward in a straight line. This expression contains no information as to what cues are used or in what direction the course lies. It can, for example, be a compass course. A bee flies a compass course using the sun as its reference point, i.e., sun compass course orientation (in short, sun compass orientation). In both these examples the reference is external, but an external reference is not a requisite for course maintenance. An animal can hold a course by just continuing in the same direction and not turning. In such a case, the animal uses internal information about the direction of its locomotion. Course maintenance according to internal cues is called idiothetic course orientation. We shall discuss the difference between external, or "allothetic," and internal, or "idiothetic," spatial information later (see 2.2.2, 3.11).

A special type of translation occurs when locomotion takes place in a medium that itself moves or flows, such as streaming air or water. Both the movement of the animal and that of the medium are superimposed, resulting in a change of location in space (see 2.8.1). The resulting translation relative to the ground can be represented as vector addition (Fig. 3.8/2). In this context the word *course* has several uses. It may refer to the direction of movement with respect to the ground or, especially in aviation, with respect to the medium. The path a vehicle takes over ground is called the track. The situation for locomotion on a substrate is simplified by the fact that course and track are identical. When substrate is both carrying medium and spatial reference, only the term course is used.

Two rotations can occur in compass course orientation, that of the body and that of the direction of locomotion. They can change together or separately (Fig. 1.3/6). In the first case the animal changes course by changing the direction its body is facing. This is called course orientation with course-constant body alignment. In the other case the animal changes its course without turning its body. The body alignment remains constant relative to space. Only the direction of leg movement relative to the body

Fig. 1.3/6 Course orientation with course-constant body alignment (left) and with space-constant body alignment (right). β is the angle between stimulus direction and the body; δ, between direction of locomotion and the body; and κ, between course and stimulus direction.

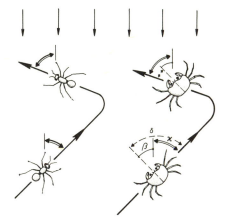

changes, as in a switch from a forward to a sideways walk. This is course orientation with a space-constant body alignment (for more detail, see 2.8.1.1).

1.4 THE FUNCTION OF ORIENTATION

Orientation processes are the means by which an animal adjusts its behavior to the diverse spatial requirements of its environment. There are three distinct classes: (1) placing the body into a particular preference position, (2) directing the behavior toward a particular goal or target, and (3) stabilizing body position in a given alignment. Classes (1) and (2) are equivalent to the primary and secondary orientations of Fraenkel and Gunn.

The first class, positional orientation, applies to rotatory processes. The second class, goal orientation, refers to translatory processes, which can be controlled by mechanisms of distance, course, and landmark orientation. In contrast to the first two classes, the third class, stabilization, is not concerned with assuming a certain direction in space, but rather with securing and maintaining a given spatial situation. In principle the other classes do this also: however, stabilization mechanisms perform this task exclusively.

1.4.1 Positional Orientation

Some examples of preference position are normal position, equilibrium position, and resting position. Most animals are characterized by a certain normal position of their bodies in space. For instance, the dorsal side is often on top, especially in terrestrial animals but also in most swimming and flying animals, The normal position for two-legged animals like humans is an upright stance with the body perpendicular to the ground. Gravity is the usual spatial reference for orientation of the normal position. Light is also used as a reference by many aquatic animals. Animals also orient their normal position with respect to their substrate. If more than one reference stimulus is used, they may give conflicting positional information. In this case an animal often assumes an intermediate position, e.g., a fish between gravity and light (see 2.7.1).

Balance or equilibrium is a special case of normal position. Gravity exerts its force on the body mass, which must be supported and prevented from falling over. This is particularly critical for terrestrial animals that balance their bodies on long legs over a relatively small base. The balance mechanisms try to keep the center of gravity over the base formed by the feet. Gravity receptors, stabilizing sense organs such as the semicircular canals, and sensory systems that register the pressure on the body parts contacting the substrate, all participate in these mechanisms.

When an animal is not engaged in an activity, i.e., is resting or sleeping, it often assumes a particular resting position that usually is especially "comfortable."

The position of a butterfly sunning itself is another example of a preference position. It turns its wings and body so that the rays of the sun strike them directly. Caterpillars also take up certain preference positions just before pupation.

1.4.2 Goal Orientation

Goal orientation includes all orientation behaviors that lead the animal to a previously determined place, either near or far away. To reach distant or hidden goals an animal must employ orientation mechanisms whose spatial references are not directly associated with the goal. This may involve intervening or interposed systems. Brun [96] called this type of goal orientation "indirect" orientation. Today the term distant orientation [898] is more commonly used.

The goal can be a narrowly localized area such as a nest, habitat, or territory, or it can be an extensive area such as a wintering ground. It may also be a zone that is unbounded in one or even two dimensions. Such is the case for the beach flea *Talitrus*. Its orientation goal is the beach, practically an infinitely long strip for this small arthropod. The goal area for planktonic species is planar and thus unlimited in two dimensions. These organisms live in particular water layers. Many species migrate between different depths according to the time of day. At night they linger just beneath the surface of the water. During the day they reside in deeper waters (see 2.8.4).

Nearby goals are usually directly perceived by the sense organs. The relevant cues originate from the goal itself, and the behavior is guided by these cues. Brun [96] called this "direct" orientation. Today we use the term proximate orientation [898]. Chmurzyński [128] makes a distinction between proximate and immediate orientation. He uses the nest-finding behavior of the digger wasp to illustrate the difference. When a wasp is several meters away from its nest, it uses proximate orientation to find the general nest area. As the wasp nears its nest entrance, it switches over to immediate orientation.

The goal orientations that we have mentioned up to now involve more or less extensive locomotory activity. In another kind of proximate orientation the goal is attained by a single brief motor action. This is called target orientation. Many prey capture behaviors in which the body or body parts are flung at a target come under this heading, like the pounce of a predator onto its prey, or the plummeting of a hawk onto a mouse. Frogs, toads, and chameleons snatch up prey with their tongues. Dragonfly larvae impale their victims with a thrust of their mouth parts (labia). The praying mantis strikes at, and captures, prey with its forelegs. Many mammals also use their forelegs to seize food or objects. Birds peck at food with their head and beak. Target behaviors are also important for social activities, such as sexual interactions, feeding of offspring, or territorial fighting.

Target orientation requires a precise assessment of both the direction and distance of the goal. Accuracy is especially critical when the object must be hit on the first try, as in prey capture.

The preference of animals for particular sites also falls under the heading of goal orientation. These sites are marked by their distance from a reference point. In a social structure the distances between members of the same species (interindividual distance) play an important role. The distance between individuals in herds, schools of fishes, and flocks of birds always remains within certain boundaries. Pair bonding is often expressed by the attempts of the partners to remain near each other. A particular distance is maintained—neither too near nor too far. The distance that an animal tries to keep between itself and a potential attacker also belongs to this category (flight distance).

1.4.3 Stabilizing Systems

Stabilizing systems serve to maintain or precisely alter a given position in space whether the animal is at rest or moving about (course control). We shall discuss three such systems: the optomotor mechanism, inertial systems, and idiothetic mechanisms.

The "optomotor response" is commonly used to investigate the acuity or movement detection of visual receptors. Animals are placed in the middle of a cylindrical drum that has a test pattern such as vertical stripes on its inner surface. As the drum is rotated, the animal tries to follow its movement. This response is a corrective movement produced by an orientation mechanism that stabilizes and actively controls an animal's position or change of position relative to its surroundings (2.9.2, 3.1.6).

The mammalian semicircular canals and similar systems (3.10) also perform stabilizing functions. The octopus and decapod crustaceans possess receptor systems comparable to the mammalian labyrinth. All these systems are inertia sensors. The physical principle of their stimulation is based on inertial mass. When the animal turns, the canal fluid remains stationary due to its inertia and stimulates the sense cells. The "pendulating" head of the dragonfly works on the same principle. The head is suspended so that it turns easily about its center of gravity. When, for example, the body is turned suddenly by a gust of wind, the head does not turn with it. This is recorded by special sensory bristles on the neck whose signals lead to corrective movements for aligning the body. The halteres of dipteran insects also have a similar function (see 3.10). In flies they detect high angular acceleration leading to compensatory head movements [1011].

Kinesthetic (idiothetic) control mechanisms can also lead to course stabilization. One example is the corrective behavior that has been investigated in running arthropods (insects, myriapods). Such mechanisms enable an animal that has been forced to make a detour to correct to its former course (3.11).

2. Physiology of Orientation

For the whole must needs be prior to its part.—Aristotle, *Politics*

Physiology, the study of structure and function in living organisms, is concerned with the way living systems work. Each organizational level of physiology can be seen as a network of interactions governed by certain basic principles. At the lower levels such as membrane, cell, and organ physiology, these interactions take place chiefly within the organism. External influences take on an increased importance at the higher levels. The effect of environmental factors on an organism and the reciprocal effect of the organism on its environment are fundamental processes of behavior. Behavioral physiology is concerned with the way these processes intermesh.

The field of sociophysiology treats conspecifics (members of the same species) or other living organisms as environmental factors. This discipline focuses on the interactions within and between social groups. All social systems, from a colony of *Volvox* or termites to a tribe of baboons or humans, are operational structures subject to certain laws. For the causal analysis of a structure it is not necessary to know how they have developed (ontogenetically and phylogenetically) or whether they contain genetically determined (inherited) or learned components.

Sociobiology is primarily concerned with the selection mechanisms involved in the evolution of social structures. It is in the midst of a conceptual revolution that is challenging one of its basic tenets, the selective advantage for the species. In the new sociobiology [942] the unit of evolutionary selection is not the species, but the gene—the replicator. The genes "try" to assert themselves. They "use" the individual as a vehicle for their own advancement, i.e., for their being replicated and passed on. The concept provides a productive approach for the investigation of social mechanisms such as altruistic behavior, which were previously difficult to explain. The more closely individuals are related, the more genes they have in common. Behaviors and adaptations that are advantageous for the relatives are favored (altruism), since they also serve to further the genes in question ("kinship selection"). Sociobiology is also starting to ask physiological questions, such as how the causal organization of a social grouping is constructed. Such investigations, which encompass the field of orientation, have been made on colony-building insects like ants [941, 349, 352, 354].

Structures are made up of components. The laws of one structural level presuppose those of the lower levels, but the converse is not valid. The fundamental laws governing the higher levels cannot be derived from knowledge of the lower levels. The realization that an organism does not behave like the arithmetical sum of its parts dates back to Aristotle (see introductory quotation) and has been emphasized time and again [107, 708, 710]. "The behavior of a complex system, composed of many elements, cannot be easily understood in terms of a simple extrapolation of the properties of its components. New properties appear and their understanding requires an independent approach which is as fundamental in its nature as any other" [692, p. 313].

It is immediately obvious that the social structure of a group cannot be deduced from the behavior of its individual members. But also the spatio-temporal structure of a single behavior can never be clarified by separate analyses of its components. No matter how careful and comprehensive the analysis of sensory, motor, and central nervous systems, it cannot lead to an understanding of how they cooperate within the structure of the orientation mechanism. This structure has its own functional principles.

Our topic, the physiology of orientation, pertains to the areas of sensory and ecological behavioral physiology. Two methodological pathways are available for the study of systems in behavioral physiology. One goes right to the inner workings. It intervenes in the mechanism: amputates, separates, isolates components and measures their energy expenditure, oxygen consumption, and nervous activity. The alternative approach observes and measures the whole system or larger components of the system from the outside. The external influences and their consequences are investigated in the form of input-output relationships. In this way it is possible to penetrate deeply into the tangle of interwoven processes and throw considerable light on the operational structure without destroying the system.

The control center of an organism is its central nervous system, including the brain (CNS). At present two of the main study areas in behavior are neuroanatomy and neurophysiology of central structures. Findings from these areas suggest possible or probable ways of information processing.

Electrophysiological methods consist of measuring the electrical processes that reflect the excitation of a nerve or neuron. The signals are picked up by electrodes, amplified, visualized on the screen of an oscilloscope, and stored on paper or magnetic tape. These signals can be elicited by natural stimuli or by electrical stimulation. Both kinds of stimulation can be used to release particular behaviors.

These techniques are the foundations for the study of the operational structure of the central nervous system. With the aid of anatomy we can trace the connections between the receptors to the highest centers and from there down through the nerve cord to the effectors. We know now how nervous signals arise and how they are transduced in the synaptic regions.

We recognize that certain neuronal processes are analogous to simple arithmetical computations like addition, subtraction, or multiplication.

In comparison, our understanding of how these elementary processes interact with each other to shape higher levels of organization is incomplete and for the most part hypothetical. In this light the goal proposed by Werner and Whitsel [923, p. 678] seems very ambitious: "The ultimate goal is to find a particular way for characterizing neural responses in quantitative terms ... such that the functional relation between stimulus and neural response is of the same form as the relation of stimulus to 'sensation,' measured in an independent psychophysical or behavioral experiment."

Systems analysis is having considerable success in the study of causal structures. The relationships between input and output provide quantitative results. However, there is an enormous gap between this kind of understanding and that of neurophysiology. What is the outlook for bridging this gap? Bullock has expressed doubt that "our present physiology of neurons, extrapolated, can account for behavior" [107]. Roeder wrote: "Effective use of neurophysiological information in describing the mechanisms of behavior is hampered less by an insufficient knowledge of intra- and interneuronal events than by our preoccupation with concepts associated with the analytic method and our consequent failure to arrive at novel viewpoints useful in the assembly of neurophysiological information" [710, p. 107]. We have to ask not only "How does the component system work?" but also "How does it contribute to the operation of the whole system?" [710]. Analysis is not enough; synthesis is also necessary.

2.1 WHAT DETERMINES THE ORIENTATION?

The orientation stimulus alone is still a far cry from the actual orientation. It is only one of the prerequisites of an orientated behavior. The bee registers the direction of the sun; the shrimp, the direction of the force of gravity. The course taken by the bee or the shrimp relative to their reference stimuli is determined by the central disposition of the animal. The specific central nervous state of an organism prescribes its behavior and thereby determines the orientation direction of this behavior. For some orientation responses the central disposition is variable; for others it is fixed (compare 2.5). Kühn [480] pointed out that a specific central disposition is a precondition for a taxis. The animal must be in the "mood" or disposed toward this behavior. Jennings [407] emphasizes that "the reactions to external influences depend on the internal state" (p. 449). Nowadays we use terms like motivation, readiness to react, drive, and mood to characterize the specific state that determines a particular behavior. This state itself depends on a profusion of other factors. (Fig. 2.1/1).

Fig. 2.1/1 The central disposition that is necessary for the orientation depends on internal and external factors. Orientation cues enter via the sensory system and together with the internal conditions make the orienting behavior possible. This behavior can, in turn, influence the external situation (e.g., the stimuli) and thus have an effect on itself.

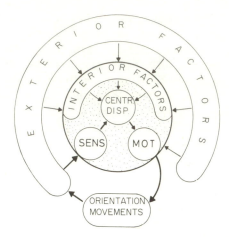

2.1.1 Releasing and Directing Stimuli

When a chicken hawk appears in the skies, chickens scurry for cover. The bird of prey releases escape behavior that is oriented in the direction of the nearest thicket. The hawk provides the releasing stimuli; the thicket, the stimuli toward which the orientation is directed. Tinbergen [856] makes a sharp distinction between "releasing and directing" stimuli.

The releasing and directing processes of a behavior can be combined in various ways with respect to the stimulus transmitter and the sensory modality: (a) They can be transmitted from different sources but received over the same sensory channel, as in our example of the hawk and the chicken. Other possible combinations are (b) different sensory channels and different transmitters, (c) same transmitter and different sensory channels, and (d) same transmitter and same sensory channel.

An example of combination (b) is provided by many plankton forms (larvae of fish and decapod crustaceans, mysids, etc.). An increase in hydrostatic pressure causes them to swim upward against the force of gravity. In this case a change in pressure releases an orientation to gravity (see 2.7.1). The escape behavior of some nocturnal moths is another example of combination (b). Flying moths respond to the high-frequency sounds emitted by bats with aerial acrobatics characterized by plummeting toward the ground [709, 712]. One moth family, the Choerocampinae, possesses hearing organs in which the morphology excludes directional sensitivity [716]. Since the moths are unable to determine the direction of the sound (see 3.6), they cannot orient their escape behavior to it. The cries of a bat release only escape movements that are directed, usually downward, by another reference, presumably the force of gravity.

The prey capture flight of the hunting wasp, *Philanthus triangulum*, is an example of (*c*), same transmitter and different sensory channels. This wasp captures honeybees and brings them back to its nest to feed its larvae [857]. The wasp lies in wait for its prey. When a bee approaches, the wasp leaves its post and hovers downwind of the bee. As soon as the wasp catches the bee's scent in the wind, it pounces on the bee. This pounce is chemically released and visually directed. Butterflies flitting from flower to flower present another example of combination (*c*). The blossoms emit odor stimuli that release approach and visual stimuli that direct it. When the releasing and directing components are separated experimentally, butterflies fly to colorful paper flowers (scentless) only if a certain floral scent is dispersed in the experimental chamber (Ilse, from [856]).

Combination (*d*), in which releasing and directing stimuli have both the same transmitting and the same receiving channel, is often found in prey-catching behaviors. The frog's turning movement is released, as well as directed, by a fly. However, even in this case the stimulus parameters that release and those that direct are not identical. Release depends on the physical properties of the stimulus itself, whereas orientation depends on its spatial properties. These processes will be discussed in conjunction with the concepts of identification and localization (2.3.1).

2.1.2 The Role of External and Internal Factors in Determining the Reference Value

The stimuli in our examples do not trigger just any behavior. They set a very specific behavior in motion and direct it in a very particular way. The appearance of a hawk causes chickens to flee for cover. The releasing cue aligns the animals in a specific direction with respect to the orientation cue. The particular value of an orientation is called its reference, or index, value (*Sollwert*). The alignment does not necessarily involve a movement toward or away from the stimulus. Experiments have shown that the sun compass orientation of spotless fall webworm larvae, *Hyphantria textor*, is temperature dependent [910]. At 26° C the larvae crawl almost directly toward the sun (Fig. 2.1/2). As the temperature increases, the course direction deviates more and more from the sun's direction. At 31° C the larvae crawl almost directly away from the sun. An endogenous variable, the larvae's state of hunger, also influences the course determination mechanism (curve *B*). Another example of the temperature dependence of light orientation is found in the beetle *Blastophagus* [662, 663]. Humidity influences the sun compass setting in *Talitrus saltator*. Low humidity, fresh water, or dilute salt water causes them to move from land toward the beach. When the salt

Fig. 2.1/2 The sun compass course (β) of *Hyphantria textor* caterpillars as a function of substrate temperature and hunger. Curve A (closed circles) = well-fed animals. Curve B (open circles) = animals deprived of food for 48 h. (Modified from [910])

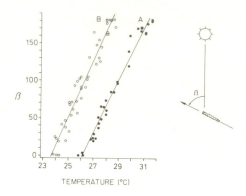

content of the water reaches a certain level, the beach fleas head in the opposite direction (Fig. 2.1/3), [737]).

Light intensity is another important factor in the determination of the reference value. Many aquatic animals, which are attracted to a light, turn around and swim away from it when its intensity is increased [655]. Since light intensity and direction can be changed separately, they can be treated as independent variables. Intensity determines the index value, whereas, incident direction provides the reference for the orienting process.

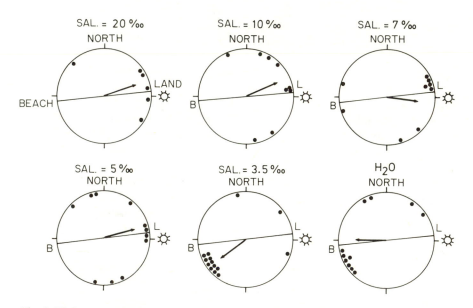

Fig. 2.1/3 Sun compass directions of *Talitrus saltator* in seawater of varying salinity. The arrows represent the vectorial means. In 20% solution the beach fleas move in the direction of land (upper left); in fresh water they move in the opposite direction (lower right). The direction change occurs between 5% and 3.5%. (Modified from [737])

Hydrostatic pressure plays a similar role in the vertical migration of many plankton forms. Plankton moves upward if pressure increases and downward if it decreases. These vertical migrations are oriented with respect to gravity and to light direction (for the functional mechanism, compare 2.7.1).

The orientation processes released by social influences are a special case. Bees communicate the sun compass direction of an abundant food source to other members of their hive by a special dance (see 2.7.2). Orientation and social communication are even more closely interwoven when ants recruit fellow colony members and lead them to a food source. The recruiter ant arouses the others by specific nudges or scents. These stimuli provoke the others to follow it either by maintaining direct body contact as it returns to the source or by following the scent trail it deposits (compare 3.5).

Behavior can also be "spontaneously" initiated, i.e., without direct external instigation. For example, an animal can suddenly begin to search for food without any overt cause. This behavior has been "released" by endogenous changes called internal releasing factors. A dytiscid water beetle larva changes the direction of its underwater swimming with respect to light after being submerged for a certain length of time. It moves obliquely toward the light until it reaches the water surface, sticks the tip of its abdomen into the air, and starts to breathe. The angle of upward swimming depends on the degree of oxygen debt (Fig. 2.1/4). If a larva is held underwater for a longer period than usual, its upward swimming angle is steeper than normal. Apparently its respiratory state modifies the reference value of its light orientation. The control of light orientation in lepidopteran larvae is also purely endogenous. Young caterpillars crawl toward a light

Fig. 2.1/4 Swimming direction of water beetle larvae to light. Upper diagram: a) breathing position, b) normal downward swimming, c) escape swimming, d) horizontal swimming, e) normal upward swimming, f) upward swimming during increased oxygen debt, and g) backing into breathing position.
Lower diagram: The angle (β) formed by the swimming course to the horizontal plane for positions b), c), e), and f) from *Acilius sulcatus* (A) and *Dytiscus marginalis* (D). Means from (n) animals. (Modified from [770])

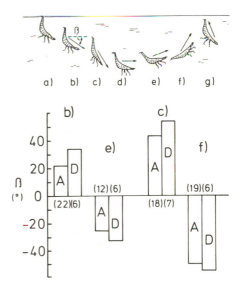

source, but caterpillars that are ready to pupate seek out dark places. These processes are correlated with the level of developmental hormones in the blood of the caterpillar (Fig. 2.1/5; 2.11.1.1).

2.2 COMPONENTS OF AN ORIENTATION

The reference value has been set; the orientation is performed. What does it consist of? What does an animal do when it orients? The bird flies back to its nest; the cow in the meadow presents its hindquarters to the wind; the monkey reaches for a banana. Two things can be distinguished in each of these orientation processes: (1) Something is oriented, and (2) this orientation is made with respect to something else, bird-nest, cow-wind, hand-banana. One is the oriented object; the other, the orientation or reference cue.

The last example illustrates a further point. If the monkey's hand is the oriented object, then the monkey that is guiding its hand is the orienting subject. In both of the other examples the object and subject are the same: the bird moves itself to its nest, the cow turns itself away from the wind.

2.2.1 What Is Being Oriented?

The animal may orient itself as a whole or only parts of its body: the giraffe lowers its head to the hay; the horse turns its ears back toward the shouting coachman. In addition, an animal may orient objects that are not part of its body. A bird always builds its nest with the bowl right-side-up, orienting its construction with respect to gravity. Bees [503] and hornets [396] orient their combs with respect to gravity. The larva of the neuropteran insect *Neuroclepsis bimaculata* orients its net in the direction of water flow [88]. When we straighten a picture on the wall, we are orienting it with respect to gravity. These are examples of motor orientation of foreign objects.

Fig. 2.1/5 Light-negative orientation of last instar caterpillars of *Smerinthus ocellata* after injection (arrow) of ecdysone (triangles) and neotenine (open circles) compared to controls (closed circles). Ecdysone increases the percentage of light-negative responses; neotenine decreases them. (Modified from [40])

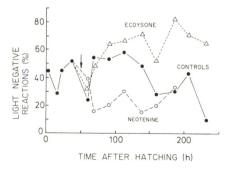

They are preceded and accompanied by perceptual orientation. In the absence of motor activity perceptual orientation is easily demonstrated only in humans. But we can also assume that animals are perceptually oriented when, for example, a bird lands preferentially on a horizontal branch. Monkeys also notice how a tree stands with respect to gravity, for they direct long leaps only at vertical trunks [622].

Orientation of foreign objects is comparable to orientation of body parts (Fig. 2.2/1). To orient an arm with respect to gravity (angle κ) a person needs to be able to register the direction of gravity (angle α) and the position of the arm with respect to the body (angle δ). To straighten a picture on the wall (angle λ), the direction of gravity (α) and the position of the picture with respect to the body (angle β) must be known. These systems are discussed in more detail in 2.7.5 and 2.9.

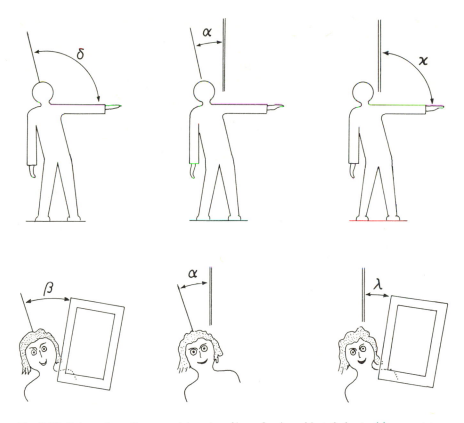

Fig. 2.2/1 Orientation of an arm (above) and/or a foreign object (below) with respect to gravity. Left: angle between body part or object and body (δ or β); middle: angle between body and gravity (α); right: angle between body part or object and gravity (κ or λ).

2.2.2 Orientation with and without External Directing Stimuli

The ant sets its course according to the sun; the shrimp, according to gravity. Sunlight and gravity are external reference cues. Orientations can also be based on spatial cues that do not come from outside of the body. In a familiar environment a person can move around without vision or hearing kinesthetically. If I wish to go from the table to the door, I stand up, turn slightly to the left, walk forward a few steps, stretch out my hand and grasp the doorknob. I can do this in the dark or with my eyes closed and even with my ears covered. I can move from my desk to the door without any exogenous cues to direct me. Many animals are capable of similar orientation processes. These processes seem to depend on the ability to follow a motor program that precisely covers the way from start to finish. This type of orientation is called kinesthetic or, more recently, idiothetic orientation. In general terms kinesthesia means the perception of one's own movements.

Kinesthetic orientation processes do not fit into the classical scheme of orientation, which viewed oriented movement as a reaction to external stimuli. Heusser [338] saw these orientation movements as "spontaneous turns similar to taxes." Jander [405] pointed out that these movements do not necessarily depend on any of the senses, i.e., on sensory processes. Rather they "are guided by spatial cues which are stored within the organism" [405]. The origin of this information is crucial. Does it come from "without" or "within"? Jander proposed the terms exokinetic and endokinetic orientation to replace the "antiquated" term kinesthetic orientation.

Recently Mittelstaedt and Mittelstaedt [598] critically surveyed this area of orientation with the aim of precisely defining the criteria for endogenous and exogenous origin of spatial information. The concepts they proposed, allothetic and idiothetic, have gained wide acceptance. Orientation is allothetic when the spatial cues "arise from the position of the animal relative to spatially ordered physical factors that are independent of the physiological state and the behavior of the animal." The organism's response does not have to occur immediately, i.e., the exogenous data may be centrally stored for a period of time. It is the external origin of the information that is critical.

Orientation that is based on information produced by the organism itself is called idiothetic. The spatial cues are "drawn from signals which have been produced by the organism itself and which are coupled to its body position or changes thereof, e.g., motor commands, proprioceptive signals stemming from motor activity, or the stored values of these signals." According to this definition neither stored information derived from exogenous cues nor genetically fixed information is idiothetic. Jander's definition of endokinesis, however, includes both of these sources of information. The motor program for moving from table to door in the above example is based on idiothetic information that is acquired upon becoming "familiar" with the spatial situation. Further examples of idiothetic orientation processes are discussed in detail in 3.11.

As the Mittelstaedts' definition implies, idiothetic spatial information can be acquired in various ways. Proprioceptive processes, for example, have a sensory origin. Another source, which is often overlooked, are the motor commands. All motor activity is controlled by motor commands, which in themselves contain the information about how a movement is to be executed in space. For instance, the command "turn to the right" contains the spatial information "to the right." If such data are stored as an efference copy, a program based on this copy can control the whole motor performance of an idiothetic orientation (see 3.11).

Where a receptor is located on the body (sensor-site label) and from which direction it receives stimulation (sensor-direction label) also belong to the conceptual domain of idiothetic spatial information (see 2.3.2.3). The signal of the position of a movable sense organ with respect to the body can be thought of as "produced by the organism itself." Even when the sense organ is firmly anchored in the body, the central processor receives idiothetic information about the spatial relationship of the receptor to the body axes.

An orientation without an external directing stimulus is still oriented to the "external" space. The animal finds its goal or reassumes its former direction in space. This orientation to the external space is possible because the idiothetic motor program is linked to the external environment at its starting position (in some cases, also at intermediate stations via allothetic contacts). The starting position of the animal must be "correctly" oriented in space. If not, the animal will move "incorrectly." An experiment on geckos [181] illustrates this point nicely. A gecko is placed on a turntable in the middle of an arena. When it is disturbed, it flees to its shelter by the wall of the arena. If the turntable with the gecko on it is rotated without the gecko's noticing, its subsequent flight direction is "wrong" by the exact angle of rotation (Fig. 2.2/2). This could not happen with allothetic ref-

Fig. 2.2/2 Idiothetic orientation by a gecko fleeing from a turntable (W) in the middle of an arena to its shelter (S) whose opening is not visible from the turntable. Each point represents the flight direction of a single trial. a) Turntable not rotated; b) turntable (with gecko) rotated 90° to the right. (Modified from [181])

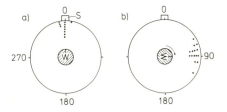

erence cues, since the direction would then be given by the external stimulus.

2.3 INFORMATION ABOUT THE SPATIAL REFERENCE

How do animals acquire information about their external reference cues? What processes are involved in determining the direction of the spatial reference or in measuring the distance of a goal? What are the physiological mechanisms for localization? Such questions emphasize the system's input, i.e., the reception of the reference stimuli and their conversion into spatial information.

Two kinds of localization are possible. When an organism relates the direction or distance of a stimulus to itself, the process is called absolute localization [65]. However, an organism can also spatially relate one or more stimuli to another, as in the case of straightening a picture with respect to gravity. This is relative localization (see 2.2.1, 2.7.5). Only absolute localization is discussed in this section.

2.3.1 What and Where Is the Spatial Reference? Identification and Localization

The "correct" reference stimulus is a requisite for every orientation. An organism needs to be able to determine what and where this reference stimulus is.

A bee given a choice of colored hives heads directly for the blue one. Blue is the color of its "home" hive and is the cue that the bee uses to recognize it. A female cricket approaches a singing male of the same species because she recognizes the pattern of his song (see. 3.6). An orientation stimulus is characterized by its physical, or identification, properties (blue, song pattern) and its spatial properties (the spatial coordinates of the hive or the male cricket). The determination of the former is identification; of the latter, localization.

The identification parameters used by the toad, *Bufo bufo,* in prey orientation have been investigated in detail [205]. When a stimulus is moved around it, the toad turns to follow the movement, stops, and turns again. The number of orienting turns the toad makes per minute is a measure of the effectiveness of a particular prey characteristic (size, shape, height versus width, contrast to background, movement). Figure 2.3/1 shows the number of turns/min as a function of the diameter of a black disc. The response increases with disc size until the disc subtends a visual angle

Fig. 2.3/1 a) Turning reactions of a toad following a moving disc. b) Number of turns per min toward the disc (closed circles) and away from disc (open circles) as a function of disc diameter (β).

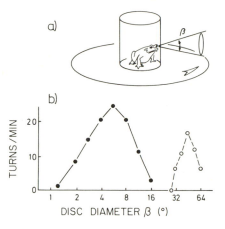

of 4°–8°; then the turning response decreases. At a visual angle of about 30°, instead of turning toward the stimulus, the toad turns away from it. This response reaches a maximum between 32° and 64°. These experiments show that identification is not an all-or-nothing process. The quality of effectiveness of a stimulus parameter is graded and has a certain optimum.

This gradation of stimulus quality, however, does not affect the actual process of localization. Each response is carried through to completion whether it is released by a good or inferior prey characteristic. These and other experimental findings indicate that the identification of the orientation stimulus, is controlled by different mechanisms than the localization of this stimulus (see 3.1.8.3). Two subsystems can be distinguished both anatomically and functionally in the mammalian auditory system; one is thought to be for detection of acoustic patterns, the other for sound localization [199].

Identification processes operate not only for reference cues with conspicuous features (e.g., prey) but also for those as simple and uniform as the sun. For the sun compass orientation of the bee the critical physical characteristic is the light intensity pattern around the sun. Light intensity must decrease gradually as the radial distance from the sun increases. If the sun is represented in an experiment as a sharply defined spot of light in a dark surround, the bee flies into the "light" [875]. Many animals behave this way when shown a light source in a dark background. Sea turtles, *Chelonia mydas*, which have just hatched in the night, walk in the direction of bright lights or a light patch of evening sky [699]. In general animals do not maintain a compass course to a spot of light surrounded by dark. Such stimuli often release light-directed responses and provide the physical cue for a "positive phototaxis."

When more than one stimulus is available as a reference, an organism needs a selection mechanism for the correct one. A special mechanism is unnecessary if there is only one stimulus for an orientation system, as in the case of gravity and gravity receptors. Here the sensory component of the system acts as the selecting filter since it responds to only one reference cue.

Earlier we discussed the pair of concepts, release and direct. How do they relate to identification and localization? Release and direct specify output subprocesses, i.e., the act of orientation. These behavioral components presuppose the input operations of identification and localization. Release is, in fact, based on the identification of the releasing stimulus. The directing mechanism depends not only on the physical identification of the reference cue but also on its spatial properties.

2.3.2 Stimuli and Receptors

2.3.2.1 Stimulating Agents and Stimulation

In this book, when we refer to the reference stimulus we are talking about the stimulating agent, i.e., the source of stimulation. Stimulating agents are chemical, physical, or physicochemical events that originate from a stimulus source. Stimulation is the process by which these events affect the receptors of the sense organ, resulting in excitation.

A stimulus (stimulating agent) may possess several parameters. For example, a light stimulus can be defined by its intensity, wavelength, direction of polarization, and its direction in space; gravity, by its magnitude and direction.

When both intensity and direction of a stimulus are important, it is represented as a vector. A scalar quantity is used when only the magnitude is relevant, as for background light intensity.

2.3.2.2 Reference Stimuli

Reference stimuli can be classified according to their arrangement and distribution in space. Particular forms of orientation are associated with each of these classes:

1. Fields of parallel stimuli (usually of uniform intensity)
2. Fields of graded intensity (gradients)
3. Fixed points (landmarks)
4. Trails

1. The sun, gravity, and magnetic field of the earth provide an animal with a constant spatial reference of fields of parallel stimuli, having the same direction no matter where the animal is. An animal can adjust its

body position or set and maintain a compass course relative to these fields. (In the case of the sun it may be necessary to temporally compensate for its daily passage across the sky, see 2.8.1.2). The parallel field structure of these stimuli is a result of the size and distance of the source relative to an organism living on the surface of the earth (for particulars on the earth's magnetic field, see 3.4).

2. When the intensity of a stimulus decreases gradually as the distance from its source increases, it forms a gradient. The stimulus source, a scent gland, for example, is usually within the activity range of the animal. When stimulus intensity decreases by the same amount in all directions, the gradient is radially symmetrical and comprised of concentric rings (or spheres) of equal intensity (Fig. 2.3/2). The gradient is steepest, and the distance to the source shortest, in the radial direction, i.e., perpendicular to lines of equal intensity. This determines the direction of the gradient. In most cases orientation consists of finding and following this direction. Over greater distances radially symmetrical gradients do not play a significant role in orientation to chemical stimuli. Under normal conditions the stimulus-carrying medium (e.g., water or air) is moving and flows past the stimulus source. This flow distorts the radial symmetry of the gradient into a longitudinally extended odor plume (Fig. 3.5/7).

3. Landmarks or markers are localized and usually distinctive stimulus

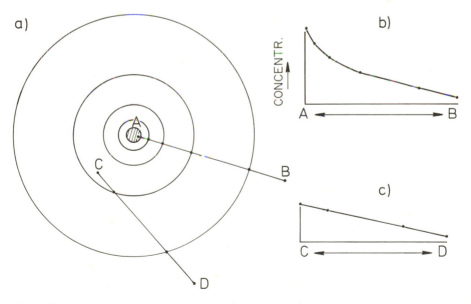

Fig. 2.3/2 Concentric gradient a), as viewed from above. The line B–A leads straight up the gradient: D–C cuts tangentially across it. The concentration profiles along b) A–B and c) C–D.

sources, which are used as reference points. The bee uses conspicuous features of the landscape like a solitary tree or the edge of a forest as a landmark to find its way about the countryside. Migratory birds are guided by prominent geographical formations like single mountains, mountain ranges, the course of rivers, or coastlines. Animals frequently orient to the pattern formed by several landmarks instead of to a single one (see 2.8.3, 3.1.5).

4. Orientation to trails is related to landmark orientation. A trail can be thought of as a series of markers strung together in a row and often conveys specific information about its maker (see 3.5).

2.3.2.3 Sensors, Sense Organs, and Sensory Apparatus

A sense organ is an anatomically definable unit composed of one or more receptor elements often associated with some kind of screening structure. Sensory apparatus is a more comprehensive term and includes the central nervous structures that process the excitation of the sense organs. In the terminology of cybernetics the sensory apparatus constitutes the input of the system. The output is represented by the motor apparatus, which includes the muscles and the motor centers of the CNS (Central Nervous System).

The receptor signals that are conducted centrally over the nervous pathways are called afferents. Nervous impulses flowing from the CNS to the periphery are called efferents.

Receptors that are normally stimulated by external events are called exteroceptors; those excited by events occurring within the organism itself are called proprioceptors. The crucial difference between them is the origin of the adequate stimulus, the class of stimulating agents for which the receptor is specialized. In gravity reception the stimulation is generated inside the organism by the movement of body parts (e.g., statoliths, or appendages of insects) relative to the body. However, the adequate stimulus for the sense organs is gravity, which obviously has an external origin. Thus, the gravity sense organs must be classified as exteroceptors.

Four properties of a sensory system are important for localization: (1) sensitivity to stimulus intensity, (2) sensitivity to stimulus direction, (3) the ability to measure and evaluate the time intervals between one stimulus and the next, and (4) positional information such as where the sensor is on the body (sensor-site label) and in which direction the sensor is pointing (sensor-direction label). Central mechanisms are required for the measurement of time intervals. Properties (1) and (2) are both differential sensitivities. Receptors with differential sensitivity can distinguish between stimuli because they are stimulated to different degrees depending on the intensity or the direction of the stimulus.

The direction from which the stimulus comes determines the degree of excitation of the direction-sensitive receptor. Its differential sensitivity may result, for example, from the fact that the sense organ is embedded in a body cavity that has an external opening in only one direction like the ear of a mammal. Funnel-shaped appendages like the auricles intensify this effect. The curve showing receptor excitation as a function of stimulus direction is called a directional characteristic. A simple photoelectric cell in a light beam can be used to illustrate how a directional characteristic is determined. If the disc-shaped photocell is first placed sideways in a beam of light, no light falls on the excitable surface and the photoelectric current is zero. As the disc is turned to face the light, its receptive surface catches more light, because it crosses a larger section of the beam. The section increases with the sine of the angle that the photocell is turned from its original position, resulting in a sinusoidal directional characteristic. Either Cartesian or polar coordinates can be used to plot a directional characteristic (Fig. 2.3/3). When given in polar coordinates, a sine function results in a heart-shaped, or cardioid, figure.

The sensor-site label and the sensor-direction label provide topological information to the CNS about the location of the stimulus on the body and the incidence sector of the stimulus relative to the body axes. These positional labels are of a qualitative nature and are not discernible in the firing pattern of the afferents. They correspond to the "specific sensory energy" as discussed by Johannes Müller [611, 612], which is defined primarily by its effect on, or connections within, the CNS and not by any neural quantity.

When the sensor is rigidly fixed on the body, the circuitry of the CNS determines the values for sensor site and direction. For movable sensors these values arise from signals giving the position of the sensor with respect

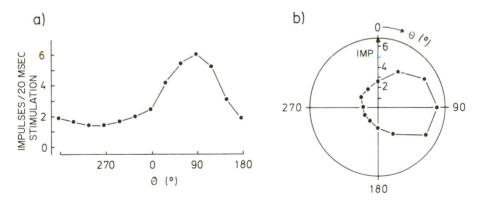

Fig. 2.3/3 The directional characteristic of the ear of the bush cricket, *Decticus verrucivorus*, to a sound of 25 kHz and 75 dB in a) Cartesian and b) polar coordinates. The response is given as the number of impulses/20 msec of stimulation. (Modified from [695])

to the body. These idiothetic (see 2.2.2) specifications of the sensor enable central mechanisms to relate the stimulus to the body coordinates, making a meaningful orientation of the body to the stimulus possible.

The significance of the sensor-site label can be experimentally demonstrated by crossing the antennae of a bee. Normally if the right antenna is more excited by an attractant than the left antenna, the bee turns to the right. The central circuitry is organized so that the motor system executes a right turn. If the antennae are crossed and the right antenna is stimulated, the bee still turns to the right, away from the attracting odor. It behaves as if its right antenna were still on the right side of its body [563, 821]. A similar phenomenon can also be shown in a fly when its head is twisted around its flexible neck so that the right eye is on the left side of the body and the left eye on the right. When normal flies are placed in the center of a rotating drum, they turn in the same direction as the drum. Flies with twisted heads turn in the opposite direction (compare 2.4.3.1).

Sensor-direction and sensor-site labels can differ from each other. For example, the medial facets on the right eye of a dragonfly point toward the left. Thus, the sensor-site label indicates "right," whereas the sensor-direction label indicates "to the left."

The term sensor is used here for receptors or groups of receptors that have the same sensor-site or sensor-direction labels. Thus, organs having the same directional characteristics comprise a single sensor.

2.3.3 Direction Determination

Direction determination is basic to most orientations. The acquisition of spatial information can also be termed localization. In the psychology of perception, localization denotes the sensory-perceptual acquisition of spatial information even though the "contribution of the motor orientation is . . . not completely excluded" [65]. This points out that localization is not always a purely sensory process. When an animal moves its head back and forth to get a fix on a stimulus source or canvasses a gradient to determine its direction, sensory and motor activities are closely intermeshed. Such interactions can persist for the duration of the orienting act so that localization and orientation practically coincide with each other. We include these mixed forms under localization since the sensory registration of spatial information often cannot be segregated from the motor activity either behaviorally or physiologically.

In Table 1 localization mechanisms have been divided into two classes according to what the system does: (I) measurement of the direction of stimulus incidence and (II) determination of gradient direction. Direction-sensitive sensors, i.e., those with directional characteristics, are essential for

Table 1. Mechanisms of Localization

Function	Type of Process	No. of Sensors		Mode of Operation
Measurement of direction of stimulus incidence	Ia Array	More than two		The sensor-direction labels of those elements in the array that are maximally stimulated by a stimulus determine the signal of its incident direction.
	Ib Bisensor	Two		The difference in stimulation of two directionally sensitive sensors determines the signal of stimulus direction.
	Ic Unisensor	One		The difference in successive stimulations of a single sensor in different positions relative to a stimulus determines the signal of stimulus direction.
	Id Time interval	Two		The time interval between the stimulation of two sensors by a stimulus determines its direction.
Determination of gradient direction	IIa Bisensor	Two		The difference in excitation and the sensor-site labels of two sensors, which simultaneously measure intensity at two gradient loci, determine the signal of gradient direction.
	IIb Unisensor	One		The difference in excitation and the idiothetically registered spatial locations of a sensor at two successive sampling points in the gradient determine the signal of gradient direction.
	IIc Indirect unisensor (kinesis)	One		Changes in stimulus intensity elicit idiothetically oriented responses, which are not related to stimulus direction but which still lead to oriented movement in a gradient.

The fourth column spans the upper group with the label "Direction-sensitive sensors" and the lower group with "Intensity-sensitive sensors."

determining the direction of incidence; intensity-sensitive receptors, for the direction of a gradient.

These two functional classes can be further subdivided according to the number of sensors and the measuring process they employ: (a) systems with many sensors (multisensor system, array), (b) systems with two sensors (bisensor system), (c) systems with one sensor (unisensor system), and (d) systems that measure time intervals between stimulations. An animal's orientation system often employs more than one of these mechanisms either simultaneously or sequentially with gradual transitions from one to the other.

2.3.3.1 Measurement of Incident Direction (Class I)

All four types of systems, array (Ia), bisensor (Ib), unisensor (Ic), and time interval (Id), can be used to determine the direction from which a stimulus is received.

Arrays (Ia). Array organs are composed of many sensors (Fig. 2.3/4). An organism's directional field is divided into as many sectors as there are sensors. The greater the number of sensors, the smaller the receptive sector of each individual one. In the ideal array the resolution is so high that the sensor-direction label of the maximally excited sensor corresponds exactly to the direction of stimulus incidence. If a single stimulus excites several sensors due to their overlapping directional characteristics, the excitation pattern of the array has a peak. The sensor-direction label of this peak then gives the stimulus direction (compare 2.6.2.2).

Many arrays possess foveas, or fixation areas, which usually point in the preferred direction of stimulus reception, e.g., forward. Stimuli that lead to an orientation response are brought into this region, i.e., they are fixated. Usually the fovea is more densely packed with receptor elements, providing finer resolution and higher direction sensitivity in this area.

Simultaneous excitation of several array elements by different stimuli allows an animal to spatially relate these stimuli to each other. This kind of mechanism makes pattern recognition and image formation possible.

As a rule the projection areas of the array in a particular central nervous structure are topographically organized (= central maps). This means that for each point in the sensory field there is a corresponding point in the area to which that sensor projects. In vertebrates the visual field of the retina is mapped onto the roof of the midbrain (tectum, superior colliculus) and onto the visual cortex (see 3.1). The electroreceptors of electric fish project topographically onto the subtectal region of the torus semicircularis (see 3.3). Somatotopic projections are mapped onto the superior colliculus and the cortex (see 3.9). Sensory elements from the fish utricle project onto the vestibular nuclei (see 3.10). In insects the structure of the medulla reflects the geometry of the compound eye (see 3.1).

Bisensors (Ib). In bisensor mechanisms the directional field is encompassed by two sensors with overlapping directional characteristics (Fig. 2.3/4). Bisensor systems are in principle just one extreme of a multisensor system.

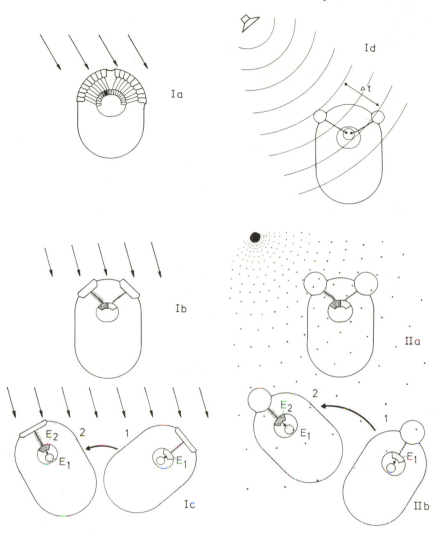

Fig. 2.3/4 Mechanisms of direction determination. Ia–Id measure the direction of stimulus incidence using a) a receptor array, b) simultaneous bisensors, c) successive unisensor, and d) time intervals separating stimulations. IIa and IIb measure gradient direction by a) simultaneous bisensor and b) successive unisensor sampling. E_1 and E_2 are excitations arriving successively at the central processing site.

The major difference is that in the ideal array the stimulus direction is given directly by a single sensor. In the bisensor system the receptive sector of each must cover a much larger range of directions. A single stimulus excites each of the two sensors according to its directional characteristic, and the stimulus direction is computed from the difference in sensor excitation. Figure 2.3/5 illustrates schematically how this process works. The directional characteristics of the two sensors in this example are shifted 180° relative to each other as in the utricular statolith organs of vertebrates. Subtraction of one characteristic from the other results in a difference curve that determines the direction of the orientation. Sinusoidal directional characteristics supply equal values for two directions (see arrows in Fig. 2.3/5). How each system arrives at an unequivocal value for the stimulus direction must be clarified for each individual case.

Difference curves corresponding to bisensor mechanisms have been found for interneurons in the acoustic system of the bush cricket, *Decticus* (compare Fig. 3.6/22) and for eye movement during gravity orientation of shrimps (compare Fig. 3.10/5c with Fig. 3.10/12).

Unisensors (Ic). In a unisensor system a single direction-sensitive sensor samples the sensory field from two or more positions. Because of the sen-

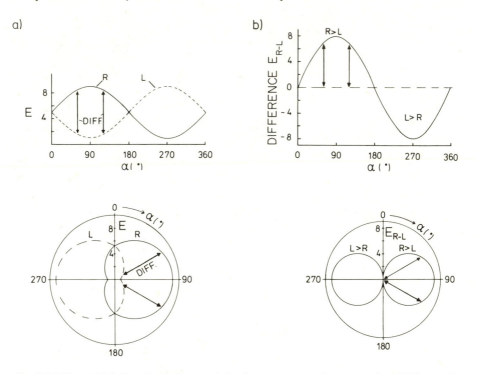

Fig. 2.3/5 Sinusoidal directional characteristics for two sensors that are excited 180° out of phase, such as the right (*R*) and left (*L*) vertebrate utricles during roll (3.10). The upper diagrams are in Cartesian coordinates; the lower, in polar coordinates. The curves for each sensor are shown on the left a) and for their differences on the right b). α is the angle between stimulus direction and the animal; *E*, the excitation in arbitrary units. The representation of a sine curve in polar coordinates yields a cardioid figure (left) and a double circle (right).

sor's directional characteristic its excitation is different at each position. The incident direction of the stimulus is then computed from these multiple readings and idiothetic data on the position of the sensor. Often the sensor is adjusted to the position of maximal stimulus reception. The outer ears, or pinnae, of many mammals are quite flexible and point reflexively in the direction of the sound (Preyer's reflex). The pinnae twitch back and forth until reception is optimized. Then the idiothetic information on pinnae position is used to calculate the sound direction relative to the body.

Maggots use a unisensor mechanism for light orientation. They follow a zigzag route as they crawl away from a light source. The angle of each turn depends on light intensity, but the side-to-side alternation is based on idiothetic cues.

Time intervals (Id). This type of mechanism computes the stimulus direction from the time intervals separating the stimulation of two or more sensors. The sensors themselves need not be direction sensitive. The interval duration depends on the direction, the spacing between the sensors, and the propagation speed of the stimulus. In sound orientation, for example, the time interval (Fig. 2.3/4, Δt) is greatest when the sound comes directly from the side. As the animal turns toward or away from the sound source, the interval decreases. When the source is directly in front of or in back of an animal, the sound waves reach both ears simultaneously and the interval is zero. The farther apart the ears are, the greater the time interval and the higher the differential sensitivity of the system.

2.3.3.2 Determination of Gradient Direction (Class II)

A gradient is comprised of stimuli that are spatially ordered according to intensity. Lines of equal intensity (isoclines) form a particular pattern that the sensors scan to determine the gradient direction. Three mechanisms with intensity-sensitive sensors are used in gradient orientation: bisensor (IIa), unisensor (IIb), and "indirect" unisensor (IIc). Theoretically, an array mechanism in which many sensors simultaneously register many loci of a gradient is also possible. The pattern of positional labels would give the intensity distribution from which the gradient direction could be derived. Some orientations to vibration appear to employ this type of mechanism (see 3.7).

Bisensors (IIa). Bisensor mechanisms measure stimulus intensity simultaneously at two loci of a gradient (Fig. 2.3/4). The site labels of the sensors give the spatial relationship of the sampled loci. For example, a bee entering an attractant odor gradient with the odor source on its left turns toward the source (gradient upward) because the chemoreceptors of the left antenna receive more stimulation than those of the right. In ants the degree of turning depends on the difference in stimulation of the two antennae.

When an ant with only one antenna enters an odor field, it turns toward its intact side. The stronger the odor, the more it deviates from a straight course (Fig. 2.3/6).

Simultaneous sampling is possible only when the gradient is steep enough to excite the two sensors differently. The required steepness depends on the differential sensitivity of the sensors and the distance separating them. Both parameters have been quantitatively studied in bees [563]. When a gradient is too shallow to be scanned by a bisensor mechanism, the bee switches over to successive sampling, i.e., it uses its sensory apparatus as a unisensor system.

Unisensors (IIb). When one antenna is removed, a bee can still determine the direction of a gradient by rapid side-to-side movements of the remaining antenna [563]. If this single antenna is fixed rigidly to the head, the bee moves its whole body to and fro to find the gradient direction, just like intact bees in a very shallow gradient.

The regular side-to-side alternation is usually based on an idiothetic program that instructs the animal to turn left following a right turn and vice versa. The stimulus directly influences only the angle of the turn or the distance between turns and not the side toward which the animal turns.

In both successive and simultaneous sampling the animal turns to the side that is more strongly stimulated. The two methods differ, however, in how the side is determined. In a bisensor mechanism the choice of side is based on the site labels of the two sensors; in a unisensor system the idiothetic information from the positioning of the sensor or the body determines the turning direction. Bees and other insects (see 3.5) can utilize either sampling method depending on the gradient steepness. There are even indications that both mechanisms can operate at the same time. An animal responding to simultaneously registered differences can also take successively registered stimuli into account during a single orientation behavior (see 3.5.2).

Fig. 2.3/6 Turning tendency of ants with only one antenna in a scent field. The turning tendency is expressed as the ant's change in course directly after entering the scent field from a corridor. Scent concentration is given as the number of rectal ampullae used to impregnate the walking surface. Each data point is the mean of 200 trials. Note that in an odorless field, the ants turn to the side on which the antenna is missing. (Modified from [298])

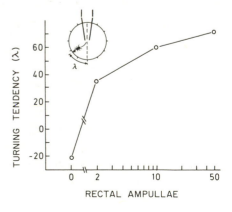

Our understanding of the details of these systems, such as the switch from simultaneous to successive sampling, the concurrent use of both sampling methods, or the acquisition of idiothetic signals and their relationship to sensor excitation, is still very incomplete.

Indirect unisensors (IIc). This mechanism employs a single intensity-sensitive sensor whose positional information has no bearing on the response. In contrast to all the other localization mechanisms so far discussed, the spatial relationship between body and stimulus does not directly affect the response, i.e., the response is not oriented to the stimulus. The stimuli, however, influence the animal's movements in a way that leads to orientation in a gradient. Such orientations are called kineses [230].

Let us consider two examples of this type of mechanism. When a mosquito flies from a humid room into a dry one, it exhibits a "startle reaction" in which it randomly changes its course ("phobotaxis") (Fig. 2.5/4). This course change is controlled only with respect to the previous course, i.e., it is idiothetically oriented. Since the preceding course was in the direction of the repellent source, the ensuing course change must lead away from it. In this way the summed responses lead down a repellent gradient. Attractants, on the other hand, have the opposite effect. The movements of some bacteria are characterized by periods of straight swimming interrupted by random changes of direction that have an endogenous origin. When the bacterium swims into an area of higher attractant concentration, its turning tendency is suppressed. This results in its swimming for a longer time in the direction of the stimulus source and indirectly orients the response up an attractant gradient.

In both cases locomotion is indirectly oriented with respect to a gradient by the effect of a stimulus on idiothetically oriented movement. When release of the movement is favored, the organism moves down a gradient; when it is suppressed, the organism moves up a gradient. Such orientations are treated in more detail in 2.5.4.

Orientation is said to be direct when the size or direction of a turn depends on the stimulus. When the stimulus affects the idiothetically controlled behavior instead of the individual turn itself, the orientation is indirect.

2.3.4 Distance Determination

A digger wasp reaching its nest, a toad catching a mealworm, and a migratory bird arriving at its wintering grounds are all examples of goal orientation. An animal needs to know not only in which direction its goal lies but also how far away it is (see 1.4.2). This discussion is limited to proximate orientations, especially those in which it is critical for the animal to reach its target on its first try. Distant orientations are discussed in 2.8.

Six mechanisms can be used to assess the distance to a directly perceived goal.

1. Converging angles or triangulation. The distance to the target can be determined from a triangle whose base is formed by a line connecting two points at which the angle (δ) between the line and the goal is measured (Fig. 2.3/7a). The angles may be simultaneously measured with two sensors, or successively, as is the case when the body is moved from one end of the base to the other. The distance between the sensor sites defines the length of the base D. Idiothetic signals from the movement provide the D value for successive measurements. Locusts appear to use the successive method of triangulation, shifting their bodies from side to side ("peering") before they pounce on an object [892].

2. Accommodation. An image can be focused on the retina either by adjusting the focal length of the lens to the distance of the visual object or by changing the distance between the lens and the retina. Either of these processes can be used to measure the distance to the visual object.

3. Lateral disparity. The lateral disparity of images on the two retinas [346] contributes to depth perception (relative depth localization). During binocular fixation the image of the object falls on the so-called corresponding areas of the two retinas (Fig. 2.3/7b), and its images fuse to give a single visual perception. Images of objects in front of or behind the fixated object fall on adjacent areas and are thus laterally disparate. The degree of lateral disparity can be used to calculate the distance and depth of objects.

4. Stereoscopic vision. Distance can also be determined from processes of stereoscopic or binocular vision. The two eyes view an object from different angles. The nearer the object is, the greater the discrepancy between the images seen by the two eyes and the more pronounced the three-dimensional impression.

5. Echolocation. Bats use echo orientation for distance localization (see 3.6). The distance is estimated from the time interval between sound transmission and the reception of its echo, rebounding from the orientation

Fig. 2.3/7 Mechanisms of distance determination. a) Converging angles or triangulation. δ is the angle between the body axis and target direction; E, distance to the target; D, distance between the two measuring sites. b) Lateral disparity. The cross is fixated on a particular retinal locus. Objects lying in front of (triangle) and behind (circle) it are registered by laterally disparate loci on the retina. Lateral disparity furnishes a measure for spatial depth.

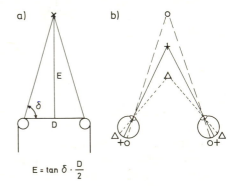

$$E = \tan \delta \cdot \frac{D}{2}$$

object. Training experiments by Simmons [812] have shown that this method can be amazingly sensitive. Bats can differentiate between objects that are only a few millimeters apart from about 30 cm away.

Echolocation also contributes to the orientation ability of blind people [139]. The blind can acoustically probe or "sound out" their surroundings from the reflection of sound off of objects in their environment. Frequencies above 10,000 Hz are especially important, and the Doppler effect may also play a role in this orientation (see 3.6).

6. Apparent size or intensity. In several sensory modalities the apparent size or intensity of a stimulus can be used to gauge how far away it is. A visual object subtends a larger angle when it is near than when it is far away. The praying mantis uses apparent size to estimate the distance of a prey object and strikes only when the object subtends a certain visual angle [551]. The male hover fly determines the distance to a female it is pursuing from the size of her image on its compound eye [138]. In the dark a truck driver estimates how far in front of or in back of him the next vehicle is from the spacing between the two taillights or headlights. We can approximate how far away a noise is from its loudness.

2.4 ORIENTATION AS A SYSTEM OF INTERACTING COMPONENTS

An orientation can be examined from various viewpoints (2.1). Tropisms and taxes treat it as a reflex chain that starts with the stimulus. The orientation is merely the consequence of receptor excitation (see 2.5).

As has already been mentioned, a particular central state is as essential for a response as the stimulus. The recognition of the importance of this central state led to the development of the reafference principle by von Holst and Mittelstaedt [363] and the concept of corollary discharge by Sperry [821]. These ideas cast a new light on the orientation problem by incorporating response and stimulus in the framework of a central state.

We can depart even further from the viewpoint of orientation as reflex and consider orientation behavior as if the stimulus were only the means to an end. That is, the animal uses the stimulus for a particular orientation process so that it can arrive at a certain goal. For example, an ant "makes use of" the sun to maintain a course in order to find its nest. This makes it sound as if an ant could plan ahead and appraise the results of its actions, which is unlikely. As yet, such rational behavior has been observed only in a few highly developed animals like the apes. As far as we know, an ant lacks insight into the consequences of its behavior. The apparent functionality and purposefulness of an animal's actions need not be based on insight. They may be merely due to a mechanism that operates according to a prescribed program. Take the case of a refrigerator, which turns on with the "purpose" of lowering the temperature when it is too high. Its function of maintaining a certain temperature is built-in. This is also the case for the functional operation of animal systems that have been adapted throughout the course of a long period of evolution to perform certain tasks. This has resulted in mechanisms that are governed by programs working toward particular ends.

The expression "teleonomy" has been proposed to denote the purpose-fulness of biological processes [669, 574]. "The purposefulness of a tel-eonomic process or behavior is the consequence of a control program" [575, p. 207].

The investigation and elucidation of such programs and control systems are the goals of a relatively young science, cybernetics. The name reflects its Greek root, *kybernetos* which means helmsman. Norbert Wiener, the father of cybernetics, characterized it as the study of "control and com-munication in the animal and the machine" [930]. Cybernetics attempts to describe an event in terms of the causal relationships of all the participating factors and to determine the fundamental principles of information trans-fer on which these interactions are based.

Cybernetic analysis attempts to trace the information flow that constitutes the way a system works. It is aimed at unraveling the network of intercon-nections and investigating the functions of the component systems. Such investigations often center on the association between the input and the output of a system, for example, the quantitative relationship between stimulus parameters and an orientation process.

Mittelstaedt and Hassenstein [586, 587, 589, 591, 312] were the first to apply the cybernetic approach to orientation systems. Today the body of literature on this topic has grown so large that it is not feasible to single out individual investigations for mention here.

2.4.1 Reaction and Action

We may have movements and changes of movements without immediate changes in the environment—S. O. Mast

In the tropism theory of Jacques Loeb behavior is no more than an oriented reaction. Living organisms are viewed as automatons that react to a stimulus by reflexively executing oriented movements (see 2.5). Although Alfred Kühn [480] incorporated this idea into his taxis concept, he also took into consideration the possible variability of the effect of the stimulus. He pointed out that the ability of an animal to respond to a stimulus did not necessarily mean that it would respond. A "certain physiological state" or "mood," as Kühn expressed it, is a prerequisite for each oriented reaction (taxis). Kühn was, thus, an early proponent of the idea that the orientation response is contingent on a specific central disposition, which depends on endogenous and exogenous factors other than the stimulus. Modern ethology uses the expression "readiness to react."

The supporters of the reflex viewpoint were also aware of the variability of a taxis, for instance, the variable geotaxis of the comb-jellies [99]. These radially symmetrical ctenophores have an apical gravity organ that directs the organ of locomotion via a very simple mechanism (see 3.10). A comb-jelly swims upward in an arc from a sideways position, unless it is disturbed, e.g., by vibrations, whereupon it swims downward from the same starting position. Such a reversal in response can be attributed to reflex reversal or change of mood [373].

A change in the central disposition can cause an unresponsive animal to suddenly respond to a stimulus (see 2.1.2). This spontaneously initiated behavior is an oriented "action," in contrast to the "reaction" of Kühn's concept of taxis. The description of an oriented reaction (or taxis), as shown in Fig. 2.4/1a, starts with (1) a stimulus exciting a sense organ (S), which (2) transmits an afference to the center (C), where (3) it elicits an efference to the motor organs (M), which (4) execute orientation movements. These

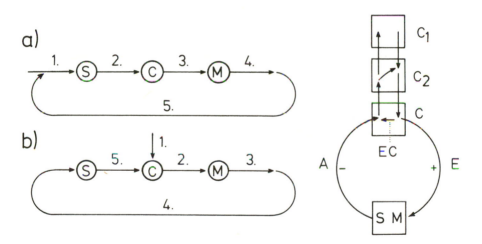

Fig. 2.4/1 Left: The causal sequence of a), a reaction, starting with (1) stimulation of a sense organ (S), which (2) transmits an afference to the center (C), where (3) it gives rise to an efference to the motor apparatus (M), which (4) carries out a motor action and (5) thereby changes the stimulus situation. The causal sequence of b), an action, is the same but starts with a change in the central signal at C.

Fig. 2.4/2 Right: The reafference principle. C_1, C_2, and C represent higher centers; EC is the efference copy; E, the efference; A, the afference (reafference); $S\,M$, the sensory-motor transformation of efference into afference [363].

movements influence, in turn, the orientation of the animal to the stimulus and thereby (5) alter the stimulus situation.

An oriented action or spontaneous change in orientation is described by the same events but starting at a different point in Fig. 2.4/1b. The causal sequence begins with (1) a change in the specific central disposition (C), (2) proceeds over the efference to (3) the orientation movement, which alters the (4) stimulus situation and the (5) afference.

In both reaction and action the interplay between the central disposition and the excitation by the stimulus is crucial. This insight led to the reafference principle.

2.4.2 Interaction between Efference and Afference

In their reafference principle, von Holst and Mittelstaedt [363] formulated a conception of orientation in which the specific central disposition is a concrete variable. Von Holst described the process of a spontaneous orientation (Fig. 2.4/2): "A command from a higher center brings about an activity change in a lower center which itself conveys a very specific efference to the effector. This change in the lower center, which represents, as it were, a central image of the motor signals, I want to call for the time being, the efference copy. When the effector is set in motion, the receptors associated with it are stimulated and bring about a specific reafference which returns to the lower center, encounters the efference copy and erases it" [361, p. 340]. Figure 2.4/2 emphasizes the effects of efference and afference in the reafference mechanism. The motor and sensory apparatus are represented as a single conversion site where the efference is transformed into the afference.

Sperry developed a similar concept based on his investigations on fish in which he had experimentally manipulated the eye positions [821]. The severe perturbations in the orientation of these fish led Sperry to conclude that the sensory excitation produced by an active movement affects subsequent movements. He proposed that the motor commands to the muscles also branch off to the visual centers ("corollary discharges"), where they compensate for the retinal excitations caused by the movement.

The term "reafference" was coined by von Holst and Mittelstaedt to emphasize that this afference is a repercussion of the oriented action. Its converse is exafference, i.e., the afference of the usual sort, which is based on stimulation imposed by external influences. As von Holst and Mittelstaedt clearly demonstrated, reafferent signals play a vital role in the control of behavior. The continuous regulation of motor activities by these signals ensures the smooth progression of a behavior. The relationships between reafference mechanisms and feedback control systems are discussed at the end of 2.4.3.1.

An important consequence of the reafference principle is that it provides an explanation for how an animal distinguishes between a change in stimulus situation that it has actively brought about and one that has been imposed upon it. Active changes do not lead to a response because the reafference is canceled by the efference copy. When a change of stimulus is imposed on an animal (= passive stimulation), there is no efference copy, so the animal responds to the stimulation. A passive stimulation is caused either by a passive movement of the animal with respect to the stimulus or by a change of the stimulus with respect to the animal as, for instance, by the movement of the surroundings about the animal. Thus, Gibson's [258] suggestion that a movement of the surroundings corresponded to a passive movement of the animal (compare 2.10.1) in no way contradicts the reafference principle.

Jander's [401] compensation theory of orientation is based on the tropotactic concept of excitation symmetry in the CNS (see 2.5.1). The "basic orientation," i.e., the position of symmetry with respect to the stimulus, reflects the central balance of excitations. A deviation from the basic orientation stimulates the sense organs whose afferences produce "turning excitations" in the CNS. These are transformed into motor commands leading to movements that bring the animal back into the basic orientation. An animal can spontaneously alter the direction in which it is oriented via changes in its central state called "turning commands." The movements produced by the turning commands turn the animal out of its basic orientation and thereby stimulate the sense organs. This stimulation generates turning excitations which, however, do not effect a response since they are intercepted by the turning command. When turning command and turning excitation are equal, they cancel each other out, and an equilibrium is reached. The system has adjusted itself to a new direction, which deviates from the basic orientation. This process closely resembles the reafference mechanism. A turning command corresponds to a change in the central disposition. The resulting response brings about sensory excitations (reafference, turning excitation) which are counterbalanced by the central events (efference copy, turning command).

2.4.3 Cybernetic Description

An orientation consists of processes (stimulation, afference, efference, movement) that are linked to each other by transformation sites (sensory apparatus, CNS, motor apparatus). The interconnections and causal relationships are often easier to comprehend when presented in diagram form (e.g., flow chart). The most common form of graphic representation is the block or circuit diagram. Figure 2.4/3 shows block diagrams describing the transformation of the body's angle with respect to gravity (α) into a

Fig. 2.4/3 Block diagram representing the transformation of the input variable α into the output variable α_i. The transfer function can be given as a) an equation inside the block, b) an equation next to the output variable, or c) in diagram form.

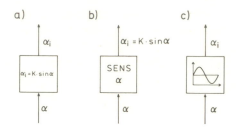

nervous signal (α_i). The transformation site (the gravity organ) is symbolized by a block. The arrow entering the block represents the input variable (α), and the arrow leaving the block, the output variable (α_i). The diagram also includes the mathematical equation according to which the transformation is made, the transfer function. For the gravity organ of vertebrates and crustaceans the nervous signal α_i varies proportionally to the sine of the angle α (see 3.10).

When the transformation is a simple addition, its site can be symbolized by a circle divided into four sectors instead of by a block. Blacking out one of the sectors denotes subtraction of the effect arriving at that sector (compare Fig. 2.4/5).

Figure 2.4/4 illustrates the three basic forms of control patterns: loop, chain, and mesh [586]. In the loop, the flow of effects forms a closed circuit in which the output of the system affects the input. This effect is called the feedback. In contrast, chain and mesh are open systems, i.e., their function is open-loop control. Behaviors under open-loop control cannot be revised once they have been released because there is no feedback and thus no possibility of correction. In the mesh form, a single variable bifurcates and influences two different elements of the system, whose outputs are then processed together.

A circuit diagram represents the effects and their transformations only as quantifiable processes and does not, as such, say anything about the physiology or morphology of these processes. The special construction of the sense organs, the kind of nervous connections, the muscle system, and the form of motor propulsion need not be taken into consideration. On the other hand, the proposed linkage should not contradict what is already known about these component systems.

Fig. 2.4/4
Basic forms of
circuit diagrams:
a) loop,
b) chain,
c) mesh.
(Modified from [586])

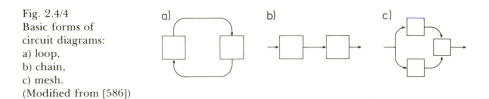

Although circuit diagrams are valuable for depicting complex relationships and causal networks in a clear and graphic form, they usually represent no more than working hypotheses [597]. The more complicated, the
more hypothetical. This applies also to the flow diagrams presented in this
book. Alternative representations are possible for most of them, especially
the more complex ones.

2.4.3.1 Feedback Control Systems

In an orientation, the processes going on within an organism are linked to
external processes by events like the stimulation of the sense organs or the
change in orientation to a stimulus by the animal's motor activities. The
two conversion elements, the sensory and the motor apparatus, may form
a closed loop in which the sensory signal influences the motor apparatus,
which affects the direction and thereby the sensory input.

In Fig. 2.4/5a the orientation system is depicted as a single box in which
two inputs, the sensory excitation α and the central disposition α_r are transformed to the output variable α_m, the oriented movement. In Fig. 2.4/5b
the effect of the movement on the sensory event is completed by an arrow
leading back onto the input α. Up to now we have not yet looked at what
is happening in the box. As long as the processes taking place there are
unknown or unspecified, it is referred to as a "black box." Figure 2.4/5c,d
illustrates a way of casting light on the contents of the black box. It contains
two transformation sites, the sensory and the motor apparatus. The input
α to the sensory apparatus can be influenced not only by the oriented
movement α_m but also by an outside disturbance α_d. When the animal makes
a movement of $\alpha_m = 10°$ and at the same time the stimulus source is
transposed by $\alpha_d = 5°$, α_m and α_d add to give $\alpha = 15°$.

The continuous regulation of the orientation direction is made possible

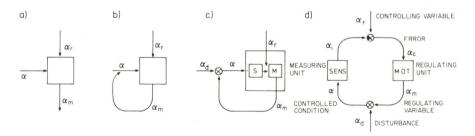

Fig. 2.4/5 Development of a circuit diagram. a) The input variables, stimulus direction α
and reference direction α_r, are transformed into the motor orientation angle α_m. b) The
output variable α_m feeds back onto α. c) Opening up the "black box": α enters via the sensory apparatus (S) which, along with the controlling variable α_r, influences the motor apparatus (M). d) Diagram c) is expanded and labeled with cybernetic terms.

by feeding back the output variable α_m onto the input variable α. Feedback control keeps a quantity constant by continuous measurement and correction of deviations. The temperature inside a refrigerator is regulated by feedback control. Warmth from the outside gradually increases the temperature ("disturbance"). When the sensor that measures the internal temperature reaches a certain upper limit, the cooling system switches on. The temperature sinks until the thermometer registers the "correct" value and the cooling system turns off.

Certain technical terms are used to denote the quantities and values of a feedback control system. The quantity to be regulated (temperature) is called the "controlled condition." Its value, which is measured by a sensor (thermometer), is called the "actual value." The value that the actual value is supposed to match is the "reference value" (desired temperature). The reference value can be reset by changing the "controlling variable." (In a refrigerator the controlling variable is set by turning a knob to the desired temperature.) Comparison of the actual value with the reference value determines the "error," which in turn controls the "regulating unit" (cooling system). This produces the "regulating variable," which readjusts the controlled condition (see Fig. 2.4/5d).

In an orientation feedback loop, the direction with respect to the stimulus (α) is the controlled condition. The angle that is registered by the sense organ is the actual value. The actual value (α_i) is compared centrally with the reference value of the controlling variable (α_r). The difference, or error, specifies the motor command α_c to the muscles. Their activity (regulating variable α_m) affects the controlled condition α. This last event is the feedback.

In feedback control, deviations from the reference value are corrected by reversing the deviation. The temperature increase in a refrigerator is corrected by a temperature decrease; an error in alignment to the left is corrected by a movement to the right. This means that the arithmetic sign of the feedback is opposite to the sign of the input. This kind of control pattern, therefore, is called a negative feedback loop. In the simplest case this process can be treated as a subtraction (see Fig. 2.4/5). The actual value is subtracted from the reference value. For example, the reference value of an ant's course direction with respect to the sun is 30° to the right. A disturbance suddenly displaces the ant 10° farther to the right into a new course of 40°. The reference value minus the actual value gives 30° − 40° = − 10°. This error dictates a 10° turn to the left and brings the ant back to its previous course of 30° to the right.

As yet we have only dealt with the correction of an error caused by disturbance. The control mechanism, however, works the same way when the controlling variable is changed. For example, our ant "wants" to change its course relative to the sun from 30° to 35° to the right. The difference between the new reference value (35°) and the actual value reported by the eyes is 35° − 30° = +5°. As a consequence, the ant makes a right turn of 5° and reaches its desired course of 35° to the right.

The above examples demonstrate that a feedback control mechanism can perform two tasks in orientation: (1) correction of directional deviations and (2) resetting of direction. Corrections make it possible to maintain a position or a compass course for an extended period of time. Both functions are based on the same process: comparison of actual and reference values to determine the error, which is then eliminated by an orientation movement. For a disturbance, the error results from a change in the actual value; for resetting the direction, it results from a change in the reference value.

Feedback control mechanisms can be investigated in a number of ways. The input-output relationship can be quantified for loop input, the controlling variable, or the disturbance. Also, one can intervene directly with the mechanism by blocking the feedback or reversing its sign.

The effect of disturbance on sun compass orientation can easily be observed in ants in an arena. The ants carry pupae placed in the middle of the arena to their nest at its edge. If the position of the sun (a lamp) is changed while an ant is on its way back to the nest, it immediately alters its course according to the shift in the sun's direction.

The controlling variable is more difficult to manipulate. Ants can be trained to a particular sun compass course by making them search for and find their nest. At first they err in the direction of the sun, but their course becomes more accurate with each successive trial. The controlling variable has also been altered in light compass experiments on water beetle larvae, which are described in detail in 2.6.3.

Direct intervention in a feedback loop mechanism was achieved in experiments on flies whose heads were twisted around their necks so that the right eye was on the left side and vice versa [584]. This meant that when the fly turned toward the left, the eyes reported a right turn. The sign of the feedback was reversed from negative to positive. Since in a positive feedback loop the actual value is added to the reference value, the corrective movement was amplified. This led to more positive feedback and to a more pronounced corrective movement. As the process snowballed, the fly turned in an ever tightening spiral until it was twirling around on the spot.

Feedback control systems are comparable to the mechanism of the reafference principle as described by von Holst: "When the reafference and the efference copy exactly cancel each other out, the action is over. However, if the afference is too small or missing entirely, something must remain of the efference copy and vice versa. . . . These remainders generate new impulses . . . which modify the movement" [361, p. 340]. As Mittelstaedt [594] has pointed out, the original formulation of the reafference principle suggested two alternatives for afference compensation: the efference copy circuit and the feedback loop circuit. In the efference copy mechanism (Fig. 2.4/6b) the sensory signal intercepts a branch of the efference, the efference copy. In contrast, in the feedback loop mechanism (Fig. 2.4/6c) the sensory message is processed directly with the central quantity which produces the efference. Both versions are based on a comparison of the afferent sensory signal with the efferent motor command (Fig. 2.4/6a).

2.4.3.2 Open-loop System

Fast orientation processes, like prey capture, are often too brief to allow time for sensory control and regulation. The strike movement of the mantis forelegs lasts only 30 ms (Fig. 3.1/14). This is not long enough for a visual feedback. The control pattern of the strike is a chain or open loop. Another example of an open system is found in hover flies (syrphids, *Syritta pipiens*).

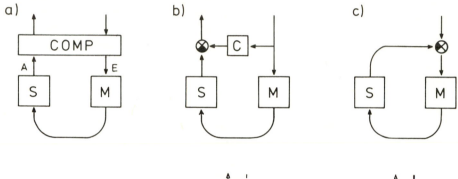

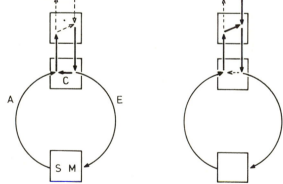

Fig. 2.4/6 Reafference principle flow diagrams in modern (upper) and classical (lower) renderings. a) Basic scheme showing comparison (*COMP*) of efference (*E*) and afference (*A*). b) The sensory signal collides with a branch of the efference, the efference copy (*C*). c) In the feedback loop the sensory signal is processed directly with the central quantity that produces the efference. (Upper a–c, modified from [594]; lower, from [363])

Flying males make rapid turns (saccades) to face in the direction of other hover flies. When its orientation target is sitting still, the male hover fly flies rapid side-to-side arcs around it, keeping its body axis aimed directly at the target. Neither these sideways flights nor the saccades are feedback-controlled [138].

An open-loop system has been elegantly demonstrated for the control of the prey fixation response of jumping spiders, *Metaphidippus harfordi* ([486], Fig. 2.4/7). The spiders were attached dorsally to a rigid object and given a paper ring to hold between their legs. Normally, when an object enters the spider's lateral visual field (lateral eyes), the spider turns its body to fixate the object. In a rigidly fixed spider the legs turn the ring instead of the spider. Although there is no fixation movement of the body, the angle of the turn corresponds precisely to the visual angle with which the spider views its prey, i.e., the response does not depend on feedback. The prey fixating movement of a toad is also a chain system (see 2.3.1). If the releasing stimulus is removed during the fixating movement, the toad still completes the movement.

Mittelstaedt [588] analyzed the prey capture movements of the praying

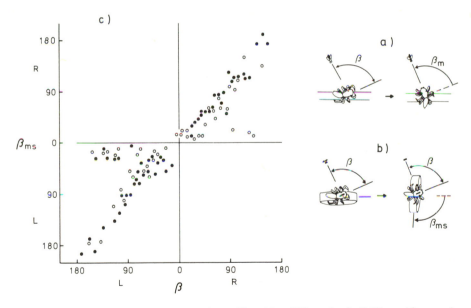

Fig. 2.4/7 Prey orientation of the jumping spider, *Metaphidippus harfordi*. The spider sees its prey at angle β and turns toward it. a) An unrestrained spider turns through the angle β_m toward its prey. b) A restrained spider turns the paper ring between its legs by an angle of β_{ms} (β_{ms} corresponds to β_m). c) A plot of β_{ms} as a function of β. Closed and open circles indicate turns in opposite directions. Note that the angle of the spider's turn (β_{ms}) is the same as the angle under which it sees its prey. (Modified from [486])

mantis in terms of how the direction of the prey is transmitted from the movable head to the body, which bears the striking legs (Fig. 2.4/8). Let us suppose that the mantis sees a fly at an angle β (head axis-fly direction). If the mantis turns its head directly toward the fly, then β becomes zero and the angle formed by the head and body (δ) is equal to the angle between fly and body (ρ). The information used for the head movement δ could then be used by an open-loop system to aim the strike (ρ_m). This presentation is somewhat simplified insofar as the head usually does not reach zero position with respect to the fly. There is some slip in the system that the transfer function of *MOT* ρ takes into consideration so that the striking legs are correctly aligned.

The prey capture mechanism of the mantis is an example of a system in which the sense organ that measures stimulus direction is movable with respect to the body.

2.4.4 Sensory Input onto a Movable Carrier

The sense organs of many animals are situated on body parts or appendages that are movable with respect to the body. In addition, some sense organs such as the vertebrate eye can be turned relative to the body part (e.g., head). Since it is usually the body that executes the orientation movements, the directional signals of these sense organs must somehow be related to the body. How is this accomplished? What does such a system of interactions look like? We have already seen how the mantis solves this problem. The spiny lobster has found a different solution [788, 774].

As in all decapod crustaceans, the gravity receptors, the statocysts, are located in the basal segment of the antennules (Fig. 2.4/9d,e). The antennules of the spiny lobster are very mobile relative to the body. A stretch receptor registers their dorsal and ventral movements, which simultane-

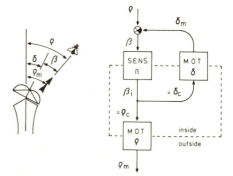

Fig. 2.4/8 Prey orientation of the praying mantis. Hypothetical flow diagram explains how the prey direction is transmitted from the sensors on the movable head to the striking legs on the body. The fly is seen at angle β. The signal of the angle between the head and the prey ($β_i$) gives rise to a motor command $δ_c$ to turn the head $δ_m$ and a motor command $ρ_c$ to align the forelegs with the body $ρ_m$ in preparation for the strike. (Modified from [588])

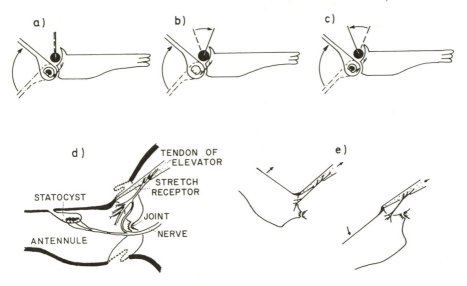

Fig. 2.4/9 Interaction of the statocysts and the antennule stretch receptors in the spiny lobster. Compensatory eye movements in response to antennule movement. a) When the statocysts and stretch receptors are intact, there is no response. b) When the statoliths are removed, the eyes move in the same direction as the antennules. c) When the stretch receptors are cut, the eyes move in the opposite direction as the antennules. d) Anatomy of the base of the antennule and its attachment to the body. e) Raising the antennule stretches the stretch receptor; lowering the antennule relaxes it. (Modified from [774])

ously stimulate the statocysts. The interaction between signals from the stretch receptors and the statocysts and its effect on compensatory eye movements were studied in a series of three experiments. In the first experiment the whole animal was tilted head-up so that only the statocysts were stimulated. The eye stalks moved in the opposite direction to compensate for the body tilt. Next, the stretch receptors were stimulated by moving the body tail-up against the immobilized antennules (i.e., antennules lifted with respect to body). The eye movement was in the opposite direction to that of the first experiment again compensating for the body tilt. Finally, the body was immobilized and the antennules were raised, stimulating the stretch receptors and the statocysts simultaneously. In this case, the eyes did not make any compensatory movements (Fig. 2.4/9a). Ablation experiments confirmed these results (Fig. 2.4/9b,c). These findings indicate that the signals from the statocyst and the stretch receptor are processed additively and that they have opposite signs. This mechanism ensures that corrective eye movements occur only when the body changes its position in space.

The control pattern of this system can be described by a mesh circuit diagram as proposed by Mittelstaedt [590] for systems in which "the sense organ must provide information on the spatial position of the animal's body, even when the organ is movable relative to the body." Movement of that part of the body on which the sense organ is located (antennule, vertebrate head, angle δ in Fig. 2.4/10a) has two effects. First, the movement furnishes data (α_i) on the position change of the sense organ in space (α), and second, it signals (δ_i) the position of the appendage with respect to the body (δ). Both signals α_i and δ_i combine to supply information (κ_i) about the position of the body in space (κ). The signal (κ_i) can then serve to control compensatory movements such as those of the spiny lobster eyes.

The signal κ_i can also be used to regulate the body position. Figure 2.4/

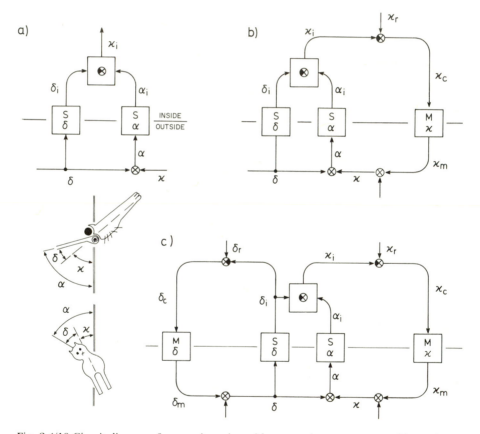

Fig. 2.4/10 Circuit diagrams for an orientation with sensory input onto a movable carrier. a) The angle of the carrier to the body (δ) and the angle of the stimulus direction to the sensory input (= carrier) (α) are processed together to give the signal (κ_i) about the angle stimulus direction-body (= position of the body κ). b) Feedback control of body position. c) Diagram b) is supplemented with a feedback loop to control the position of the carrier.

10b shows a possible circuit diagram for this control. κ_i is processed with the controlling variable κ_r, which determines the reference value of κ. Body position κ and appendage position δ sum to give the input variable α. In Fig. 2.4/10c a supplementary feedback loop has been added, which makes independent movements of the appendage (angle δ) possible.

2.5 TROPISMS, TAXES, AND KINESES

Tropisms and taxes treat an orientation as a reaction to a stimulus. It is often the oriented reaction that first catches the eye of an observer of animal behavior. A hawk swoops down on a mouse, a male baboon turns toward an approaching female, and a baboon youngster runs to its mother. It is easy to reach the conclusion that behavior is comprised of a chain of such reactions, in which animals are driven by external forces (stimuli). However, the observer soon ascertains that the hawk pounces on a mouse only when the hawk is hungry, and a baboon male is not always interested in a female nor the youngster in its mother.

The viewpoint that behavior is a reflex chain in which the CNS functions as a switchboard is no longer seriously advocated [439, 910a]. The significance of spontaneous central nervous activities (automatisms) vis-à-vis the reflex theory has been stressed repeatedly [357, 358, 523, 909, 856, 708, 910a, 108]. A particular orientation behavior can be elicited only when the appropriate constellation of internal factors exists. It has already been referred to as mood, readiness to react, or central disposition (see 2.4.1).

The central disposition is invariable for some orientation processes, such as many flight or startle responses or the orientation of lower animals like protozoans to chemical stimuli. A paramecium always exhibits a startle response to a CO_2 stimulus. For decades research in the field of orientation centered on this sort of "simple" stimulus-response mechanism. This chapter reviews and discusses the development and significance of the classical concepts of orientation.

As soon as experimental investigation into these processes commenced in the last century, special terms were introduced. Pfeffer [667] proposed the terms *tropism* for the directed growth processes of plants and other sessile organisms and *taxis* for the oriented movements of motile organisms. Pfeffer himself researched the chemotaxis of unicellular organisms such as protozoans and gametes. Since these organisms do not have organized nervous systems, their behavior was interpreted as the direct expression of a physicochemical system.

Jacques Loeb [518, 519, 520] attributed the oriented reactions of higher animals to similar mechanisms. According to Loeb, all stimulus-directed movements are based on tropisms. He described the processes as physicochemical reaction chains. "The morphological plane of symmetry is also the physiological and dynamic plane of symmetry, insofar as the tension of symmetrical muscles is the same and insofar as symmetrical organs on the body surface, e.g., the sense organs, have the same chemical composition and conversion rates. When the chemical reaction rate increases in one eye of an insect because that eye receives more light, the physiological symmetry between the two halves of the brain is disturbed and consequently that of the symmetrical muscles. A stronger tension builds up in the muscles of the side exposed to more light and in subsequent manoeuvres leads to a stronger reaction of the muscles that turn the head and body towards the light" [519].

2.5.1 Kühn's System of Taxes

Kühn was able to base his investigations on considerably more experimental data than his predecessors. It had become apparent that tropism theory could not account for many phenomena. Kühn systematically organized the facts and existing concepts, introduced new terminology, and brought them all together into a lucid and comprehensive whole [480]. He appraised his publication *Die Orientierung der Tiere im Raum* as "a short treatise in which I differentiated various orientation patterns for the first time and, not without qualms, introduced new terms to identify them."

Kühn agreed with Loeb about the reflex character of an animal's response to a stimulus. "The oriented reactions of multicellular animals ... are reflexes. The reaction is based on the nervous connections between particular sites of stimulus reception and particular elements of the motor apparatus" [480, p. 9]. In addition Kühn discussed the role of the central disposition as a determining factor for a taxis.

The concept of taxis encompasses not only the initial orienting maneuver but also the maintenance of the oriented state. Kühn explicitly excluded other simultaneously occurring motor activities such as locomotion from his definition of taxis. The various sensory modalities are indicated by prefixes such as photo-, geo-, chemo-, and phono-; the spatial relationship of the body to the stimulus is described as positive, negative, or transverse.

In accordance with Pfeffer's classification Kühn used *tropism* for the growth processes of sessile organisms and *taxis* for the motor reactions of motile organisms. He split taxes into two major subdivisions, *phobotaxis* and *topotaxis*. Phobotaxis denotes undirected turning movements released by a stimulus, as in the startle response of many unicellular organisms. A paramecium entering a zone of increased CO_2 concentration recoils, turns, and swims forward in a new direction. This pattern is repeated until the animal chances on a direction leading away from the stimulus (trial and error method). In contrast, topotaxes are reactions that are directed with respect to a stimulus. This is the largest group of taxes and includes tropotaxis, telotaxis, menotaxis, and mnemotaxis.

Tropotaxis and telotaxis represent two fundamental mechanisms of orientation. *Tropotaxis* incorporated the basic idea of Loeb's tropism theory: "Symmetrical adjustment reflects an excitation symmetry in the nervous system that leads to a symmetrical tension of the musculature. This excitation symmetry is the result of equal excitations in the sense organs of the right and left body sides, which flow into the nervous system and balance each other" [480, p. 13]. Asymmetrical stimulus incidence generates an unequal excitation, leading to unequal activity of the symmetrical muscles. The animal turns until the sense organs on both sides receive equal stimulations. This position is actively maintained by excitation flowing continuously from the right and left receptors into the respective brain centers. Thus, the maintenance of an oriented state represents the activity, not the inactivity, of the sense organs. Kühn compared a tropotactially adjusted animal to a team of horses driven with taut reins. Swerving to one side produces tighter tension in the opposite rein. This brings the team back on course and restores the balance of tension.

The idea of a physiological equilibrium did not originate with Kühn. Rádl [688] derived the physiological "internal" balance from the physical balance with respect to gravity.

Kühn did not limit tropotaxis to the left-right symmetry. With respect to the normal position of an animal he wrote "A balance of excitation prevails over all meridians of the receptive sensory area and of the muscles that carry out the orientation movements" [480, p. 18]. Kühn derived *autotropotaxis* from the tropotactic balancing of excitations. Autotropotaxes are elicited by proprioceptive stimulation and describe responses like those to semicircular canal stimulation or like the adoption and maintenance of the normal symmetrical position of body parts. Orientation with respect to several stimuli of the same or different sensory modalities is also based on tropotactic processes. The excitations of the participating receptor systems are balanced centrally.

The concept of *telotaxis* is original. It describes the processes of fixation and target orientation. The stimulus releases a turning response that aligns the animal with the stimulus. The turn depends on the site of stimulation and is concluded when the stimulus is brought into the fixation area, which is usually frontally situated. Corrective movements ensure that "the goal is retained in the fixation area" [480, p. 37].

Both tropotaxis and telotaxis align the animal with respect to the stimulus, either toward or away from it (positive or negative taxis). In contrast *menotaxis* brings the animal into asymmetrical orientations to the stimulus. Menotaxis is related to tropotaxis in that the animal maintains a particular distribution of right and left excitation. In menotaxis the distribution of excitation is "randomly determined." According to Kühn, this orientation is of a stabilizing nature, ensuring a straight line of advance.

Mnemotaxis is based upon experience and, thus, differs in principle from the other taxes. An animal "learns" its path by registering directions and changes of direction with respect to the stimulus in chronological order and storing them in memory. Later it orients according to the stored data. When the current stimulus situation diverges from the "memorized" pattern, the animal turns.

2.5.2 The System of Fraenkel and Gunn

Fraenkel and Gunn [230] adopted Kühn's concepts of tropotaxis and telotaxis. They emphasized that telotaxis requires receptors that independently register diverse stimulus directions. A telotactic turn is based on a reflex map of the eye that determines the particular degree of turning released by the stimulated elements.

Tropotaxis is supplemented by *klinotaxis*, which is based on a central comparison of successive excitations. For example, a maggot bends its body from side to side as it crawls away from a light, and light falls upon the receptors from one side, then from the other. Each stimulus affects the turn in the opposite direction. The turning angle depends on the stimulus intensity. By balancing successive excitations, the maggot pendulates into a course that is directed away from the light. This process is comparable to the simultaneous excitation processing in tropotaxis and is treated as such by Kühn.

Fraenkel and Gunn introduced a new class of orientation responses, the *kineses*. A kinesis is released by a change in stimulus intensity. Although not aligned with respect to the stimulus, it leads "indirectly" to an orientation in a stimulus gradient (compare 2.3.3.2). A differentiation between kinetic and directed responses had already been proposed by Mast [568], but at that time, kinesis only meant the activation of movement.

Fraenkel and Gunn distinguished between *orthokinesis* and *klinokinesis* according to how the stimulus affected the movement. Orthokineses are processes in which a change in the stimulus influences the activity or the rate of movement. In *klinokinesis*, on the other hand, the stimulus affects the rate or degree of turning. This is often expressed as the rate of change of direction (*rcd*). Since the responses that Kühn called phobotaxes belong to this group, the term phobotaxis and topotaxis have become obsolete.

Recent analyses of kinesis mechanisms have revised, as well as supplemented, the ideas of Fraenkel and Gunn. Detailed discussion of this important class of orientations is deferred to the end of this chapter.

A third class, the *transverse orientation reactions*, embraces responses that are defined by their geometry with respect to the stimulus and by their sensory modality. Light compass responses, dorsal light responses, and transverse responses to gravity all belong to this class. The term light compass response refers to all asymmetrical orientations to light. According to Fraenkel and Gunn, the mechanism may be either tropotactic, like Kühn's menotaxis, or telotactic, in which the light is maintained in a "temporary" fixation area. The dorsal light response is an orientation with the animal's back toward the light. This, too, can have either tropotactic or telotactic origins. Fraenkel and Gunn assume a tropomechanism for corrections about the longitudinal axis and a telomechanism for those about the transverse axis. Similar mechanisms may also underlie transverse responses to gravity.

2.5.3 Summary, Additions, and Discussion

Loeb's tropism theory was based on the idea of a rigid coupling between muscular activities and sensory excitation. This coupling makes the organism strive for an equilibrium between the excitations of symmetrically arranged sense organs and muscle systems. The tropism theory was one of the first attempts to analyze animal behavior from a strict scientific viewpoint, to account for it entirely in terms of physicochemical processes. Not surprisingly, Loeb's ideas were well received in his time. He offered a scientifically grounded explanation for orientation movements and for animal behavior itself. Until then, these processes had either been regarded as amazing and mysterious phenomena or had been interpreted anthropomorphically.

Loeb's conceptual edifice was seductive in its simplicity and clarity. Henke [329] has since characterized it as a "dangerously ingenious simplification." However, in Loeb's day hardly anyone noticed that his theory treated the CNS as a mere switching station where sensory excitations were converted into muscular activity. At that time the capabilities of the CNS were largely unrecognized. Little was known about its plasticity, its capacity to integrate internal and external factors, its programmability, or its learning ability. Equally little was known about the spontaneously arising nervous excitations (automatisms) and the significance of other physiological factors such as the humoral systems.

Kühn's tropotaxis resembled Loeb's tropism. Kühn originated the concept of telotaxis, an orientation process that differs in principle from the symmetry mechanisms of tropism and tropotaxis. Kühn also recognized the importance of the central disposition in determining a taxis (see 2.4.1). In the twenties and thirties, Kühn's system was the inspiration and basis for a profusion of experimental research.

Lorenz's theory of behavior control treated orientation in terms of "taxis and fixed motor coordination" [528, 527]. Behavior is based on a more-or-less fixed pattern of motor actions that are adapted to the spatial circumstances of the environment by orientation responses. Lorenz used Kühn's definition of taxis to describe the mechanism of this orientation.

Fraenkel and Gunn expanded Kühn's system. Their precise definitions of concepts and mechanisms with corresponding operational criteria have served as a useful point of departure for experimental investigations. In addition, they described kinesis, a large class of reactions that had been previously overlooked or whose significance had not been recognized. Many terms introduced by Fraenkel and Gunn are still in use today. Gunn's own assessment of his system of taxes and kineses was: "Most of the system that Fraenkel and I put forward . . . deals with types of spatial manoeuvre and does not pretend to describe physiological mechanisms" [287].

The terminology of Kühn and Fraenkel and Gunn has been revised repeatedly. Precht [679] presented a comprehensive and detailed classification of taxes, which has received little attention. Ewer and Bursell [207] have also revised the system of kineses and taxes. They distinguish between klinotaxis with lateral turning (old definition) and klinotaxis without lateral turning. Kennedy [441] referred to this in differentiating between *transverse* and *longitudinal* klinotaxis. In longitudinal klinotaxis the direction of locomotion is maintained when the intensity of an attractant increases, but changed when the intensity of a repellent increases. Ewer and Bursell also divided tropotaxis into two groups, one with bilaterally arranged receptors and one with an anterior-posterior receptor grouping. They treated startle responses, which they termed "titubant reactions," as a special kind of behavior and did not regard them as oriented reactions ([207], compare 2.5.4.2). Jander has also introduced some supplementary taxis concepts. *Astrotaxis* characterizes orientation to celestial bodies such as the sun, moon, and stars; *polarotaxis* refers to orientation to polarized light.

The tropism-tropotaxis concept. Why have theoretical considerations of orientation mechanisms attached so much importance to symmetrical adjustment? One reason is the assumption that symmetrical orientations express a basic mechanism because they are especially common. Their frequency of occurrence is, however, easily overestimated since symmetrical orientations are more obvious than asymmetrical ones. But, even if symmetrical orientations are more frequent than others, this is still no proof of a tropomechanism. Symmetrical adjustments can be based just as well on a telosystem.

Tropism and tropotaxis derive from the idea that the balancing of excitations in the CNS is a fundamental principle from which orientation mechanisms evolved. Such conclusions are easy to arrive at for bilaterally symmetrical animals. Should not the basic functions of the nervous system of such an animal also be symmetrically organized? One objection to this is that most animals orient not only around the axes of their planes of symmetry (X and Z), but also around the Y axis, i.e., they can pitch forward or backward. In this case, morphological and physiological symmetry is unimportant. Kühn postulated central tropotactic processes for such orientations. In doing so he distanced himself from the idea of a balancing process that was predetermined by anatomical symmetry.

Another objection is that telotaxis, the other fundamental orientation mechanism in the taxis system, does not function on the basis of excitation symmetry. The determining factor for telotaxis is the site of excitation on the body. Even lower organisms can give a directed response to tactile stimulation of localized body areas. It is just as conceivable that orientation mechanisms evolved on this basis (= array systems).

In summary, it is difficult to find convincing arguments for a basic mechanism of excitation symmetry.

The telo-tropo alternative. The idea of two major mechanisms, telotaxis, and tropotaxis, is still influential. Many earlier studies centered on the question of which of these two mechanisms was used by a particular system. Even today many scientific reports close with the indication that the orientation in question is either a telotaxis or a tropotaxis. This conclusion may hinder the discovery of further details by lulling the investigator with a fine-sounding name.

The differentiation is usually based on the operational criteria derived by Fraenkel and Gunn. Two of the most frequently applied criteria concern an animal's behavior toward two stimuli and its response after unilateral elimination of receptors. For example, in the so-called two light experiment an animal is presented with two light sources. A tropotactic mechanism should keep the animal midway between the two lights (excitation balance). In a telotactic system the animal has to choose one of the lights and ignore the other since it can fixate on only one of them.

If the animal moves in circles (circus movements) after unilateral elimination of sensory input, this indicates a tropotactic mechanism. It is assumed that unilateral loss of input disturbs the excitation balance, thereby leading to a continuous turning response. Since in a telotactic system a single eye can be used to fixate, this kind of intervention should not disrupt a telotactic mechanism. However, caution must be exercised in applying this reasoning to array systems. In an array the processing may correspond to vector addition of the excitation of all the array elements instead of to a tropotactic comparison of two excitations. The loss of some of the receptors leads to perturbations in excitation processing that are also expressed as circus movements. Thus, circus movements are not a dependable indicator for tropotaxis (see 2.6.2.1).

Furthermore, the operational criteria do not always provide the basis for a clear-cut decision. The hover fly *Eristalis*, for instance, moves midway between two lights (tropotaxis) when intact but heads for one of the two lights when one eye is blinded (telotaxis). In two-light experiments a bee may either walk along the midline or toward one of the lights. This shows that the two concepts need not be mutually exclusive [230].

Gravity orientation illustrates another limitation of the operational criteria of the tropotaxis and telotaxis concepts. Kühn cited crayfish gravity orientation as an example of a tropotactic system because after unilateral removal of the statocysts a crayfish tends to turn toward its defective side. However, crayfish with only one statocyst can recover the ability to orient to gravity [768, 774], as can fish [366] (see 2.11). This ability to orient to a stimulus after the loss of one sense organ is an indicator for telotaxis. Thus, according to the operational criteria, these animals can respond tropotactically as well as telotactically with the same system, a contradiction that von Holst first pointed out [366].

These inconsistencies stem from the inadequacy of taxis terminology for describing the details of how the system operates. In the gravity organs of crustaceans and fish, the sensory cells emit a resting discharge in the middle range of impulse frequencies even when the statoliths are missing (see 3.10). This frequency is modulated by stimulation caused by the statolith (see Fig. 2.11/4a,b). Gravity reactions depend on this modulation. Unilateral ablation of the whole organ eliminates the resting discharge, so there is no longer a signal to be modulated. This disrupts the central processing and leads to a turning response. Unilateral ablation also produces a turning response if all the statoliths are removed prior to ablation, i.e., when there is no gravity stimulation at all. On the other hand, unilateral removal of a statolith, leaving the sensory epithelium intact, does not result in a turning tendency. This sensory mechanism is difficult to fit into the tropotaxis-telotaxis scheme of Fraenkel and Gunn.

This critical evaluation can scarcely be summarized better than by quoting Mast [568]: "It would therefore seem to be much wiser to attempt to ascertain precisely what occurs in the organism in various physiological states, during the process of orientation under various accurately controlled conditions, than to attempt to ascertain whether the process of orientation in this or that organism should be designated thus or so."

Those aspects of the tropotaxis and telotaxis concepts that remain useful are made clear in a comparison with the mechanisms of localization (array, bisensor, unisensor). Several basic concepts of both systems are similar, even though a taxis encompasses the entire orientation process, whereas a localization mechanism emphasizes the sensory aspects (see 2.3.3). Telotactic adjustment depends on stimulation of a particular site on the receptor organ. This is conceivable only with an array system. Tropotactic adjustment, on the other hand, is associated with bisensor systems. If the tropotaxis definition is limited to a comparison and computation of two excitations resulting in a direction signal, it describes the common feature of the bisensor system of both classes, determination of incident direction with two direction-sensitive sensors (I) and gradient direction with two intensity-sensitive sensors (II). Klinotaxis, a response to successive excitation of a sensor, can be classified as a unisensor mechanism. The two unisensor systems of direction measurement (I) and gradient direction determination (II) are not differentiated by klinotaxis. Kineses correspond to "indirect" orientations (see 2.5.4.2).

2.5.4 Kinesis (Indirect Orientation in a Gradient)

Are kineses really orientation responses? A taxis is an alignment with respect to a stimulus. This clearly describes an orientation. Although a kinesis reaction is released by a stimulus, it is not aligned with respect to this stimulus. Strictly speaking, a single kinesis reaction is not an orientation response. However, the sum of the individual reactions that comprise a kinesis constitutes a directed movement in a stimulus gradient, so that kinesis as a whole can be regarded as an orientation process. We shall look more closely at this paradox that reactions that are not stimulus-directed nevertheless lead to a directed behavior (see also 2.3.3.2). But first let us survey the processes indicated by the kinesis terminology.

Dethier et al. [153] devised operational criteria for classifying the orientation responses, primarily of insects, to chemical stimuli. According to this scheme a moving animal may respond to a stimulus in the following ways: It may (1) continue its movement, (2) stop, (3) decrease or increase its rate of linear progression, (4) decrease or increase its turning rate (rcd), (5) orient toward the stimulus source, or (6) orient away from the stimulus source. Corresponding labels are assigned to stimuli according to how they affect the response: (a) arrestant when they decrease or stop the response, (b) stimulant when they increase or set it in motion, (c) attractant when they direct it toward the stimulus source, and (d) repellent when they direct it away from the source.

In the taxis terminology, classes (5) and (6) are taxes; (3) and (4) are kineses [440]. Class (3) corresponds to orthokinesis and (4) to klinokinesis. Kinesis is further subdivided according to the effect of an increase in stimulus intensity. If the response (rate of locomotion or of turning) increases with stimulus intensity, it is called *direct* kinesis; if it decreases, *inverse* kinesis [436, 437].

2.5.4.1 The Kineses

Orthokinesis. As soon as the fruit fly *Drosophila* enters a stimulant field, it begins to move about faster [226, 832]. Mosquitoes show similar behavior

[917, 440]. These are examples of direct orthokinesis. As an example of inverse orthokinesis Fraenkel and Gunn gave the sowbug, whose activity decreases as humidity increases, until it comes to rest in places where the humidity is relatively high (Fig. 2.5/1). The weevil *Sitona cylindricollis* [300] and the grass-grub beetle *Costelytra zealandica* [645] exhibit inverse ortho-kinesis when their movements slow down in the vicinity of a strong odor source.

Klinokinesis. Direct klinokinesis is shown by the female moth *Cidaria albulata* when she comes within a 50-cm radius of the plant on which she lays her eggs. Her random turns become more frequent, so that her flight pattern describes tighter loops and circles. Air collected from around the host plant affects this response in the same way [440]. The behavior of the flatworm *Planaria* in fatty acid mixtures is also a direct klinokinesis [566]. The flatworm's turning rate (*rcd*) increases with fatty acid chain length (Fig. 2.5/2). Fatty acid mixtures occur naturally when organic matter decomposes. Since fatty acid solubility decreases with chain length, a gradient of mixtures forms in which the proportion of short-chained acids increases with the distance from the source. At the margin of the gradient, flatworms move in wide loops (low *rcd*) because the short-chained acids predominate. The closer the planarians get to the source, the larger the proportion of longer-chained acids and the higher the animals' *rcd*. Their speed of motion also increases (= orthokinesis). Usually, direct orientation processes (= taxis) take over close to the source.

Under some conditions an inverse klinokinesis results in a translation up a gradient. This can be seen in the behavior of bacteria in a stimulant gradient [546, 467, 865]. Randomly distributed turnings, or "jerks," interrupt the straight or slightly curved pathway of the bacterium so that it tumbles back and forth. When the bacterium enters a higher concentration of stimulant, the frequency of jerks decreases. As a consequence, the animal swims longer stretches in this direction. The sum of all the inter-jerk stretches

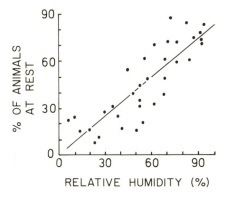

Fig. 2.5/1 Activity of the sowbug *Porcellio scaber* as a function of relative humidity. The animals come to rest in places with relatively high humidity. (The regression line was computed from the data points of the original figure.) (Modified from [230])

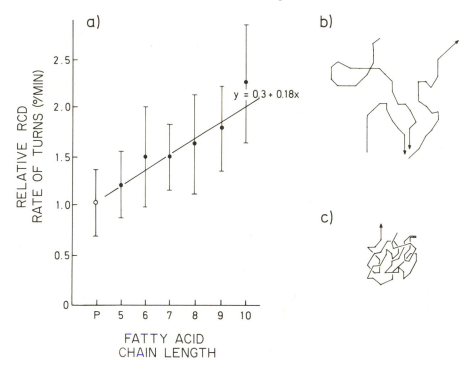

Fig. 2.5/2 Behavior of *Planaria* in fatty acid solutions. a) The relative rate of change of direction (experimental *rcd*/control *rcd*) as a function of fatty acid chain length. The equation is for the regression line. P = phosphate buffer. On the right are planarian tracks in b) pentanoic and c) decanoic acid solutions. (Modified from [566])

results in a translocation up the gradient. The male gametes of the fungus *Allomyces macrogamus* use a similar mechanism to find female gametes [674].

Examples of klinokinesis based on modalities other than the chemical senses are rare. Formerly, the much cited showpiece for klinokinesis was the behavior of planarians moving down a light gradient [872]. However, more recent studies have revealed it to be a directed response [827]. The animals react not to a gradient of light intensities but to directed light that reflects off particles in the water (scattered light).

Kinesis combined with taxis. An orientation behavior often consists of both kineses and directed responses. The foraging behavior of *Planaria* described by Koehler [458] is a good example of this (Fig. 2.5/3). When a flatworm first enters the chemical gradient produced by a food source, its locomotory speed increases (direct orthokinesis). Then the turning rate goes up (direct klinokinesis) and a directed response commences (tropotaxis). Either the animal makes a beeline for the source (using two sensors simultaneously = tropotaxis) or it zigzags toward the source, turning the

Fig. 2.5/3 The orientation of *Planaria* in the odor field of a food source (circle). After an initial search the planarian moves in a straight a) or zigzag b) path to the food source. In c) and d) the initial circling did not take place. (Modified from [458])

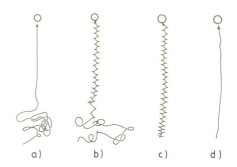

a)   b)   c)   d)

front part of its body from side to side (using successive gradient sampling = klinotaxis).

2.5.4.2 The Kinesis Paradox

Responses that interrupt locomotion in a straight line have recently received special attention [441]. These are responses such as the startle response of *Paramecium* to a repellent stimulus. Similar recoil responses are often observed in alternate choice chambers when an animal crosses the boundary dividing "nonstimulant" from "stimulant" [937, 703, 664]. Mosquitoes from an air column with favorable temperature, humidity, and CO_2 conditions turn when they encounter "neutral" air (Fig. 2.5/4, [149]). Fraenkel and Gunn classified startle responses as kineses, but Lorenz [526, 527] objected that they differ because the turns are not completely undirected. A change of direction implies that the turning directions are no longer randomly distributed since the former direction is exempt. On the average a direction change leads in the opposite direction.

A startle response and the inverse klinokinesis of bacteria and male gametes are not directed with respect to the stimulus but to the preceding direction of movement. This is the key to an understanding of the paradox that an undirected response can lead to a directed behavior. The reaction is related spatially to the preceding course direction. Spatial data on past movements are internally available and used to idiothetically guide sub-

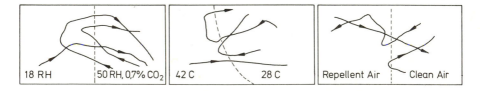

| 18 RH | 50 RH, 0,7% CO_2 | 42 C | 28 C | Repellent Air | Clean Air |

Fig. 2.5/4 Startle response of the mosquito *Aedes aegypti*. It turns around when it encounters less favorable conditions (on the left). *RH* = relative humidity. (Modified from [149])

sequent movements (see 2.2.2). In kinesis the stimulus biases the idiothetically controlled motor program toward movements that have a particular spatial relationship to the stimulus direction. This leads to an "indirect" orientation in a stimulus gradient ([442] see 2.3.3.2). If the velocity of locomotion is taken as an expression of idiothetic spatial orientation, orthokinesis also fits into this scheme. Note, however, that a change in velocity can only lead to an orientation when turns are interspersed in the course.

The klinokinesis of bacteria and male gametes resembles longitudinal klinotaxis (see 2.5.3). Kennedy [441] even spoke of an overlapping of the two concepts. The following definition demonstrates that a separation is not easy [994]: In klinokinesis the stimulus causes a change in the circular variance of the turning angle per unit time without, however, causing a change in the mean direction; in klinotaxis the stimulus elicits an alteration in the mean direction of the circular distribution of random turnings.

2.6 RESPONSE AS A FUNCTION OF STIMULUS DIRECTION AND INTENSITY

Stimulus-response relationships are not constant even when the stimulus parameters are fixed. As Kennedy writes: "The great variety of third variables intervening between stimulus and response cause so much apparent inconsistency" [439]. A source of this inconsistency is treated in the last section of this chapter. The emphasis of this chapter is on orientation responses to directed stimulation (see 2.3.3, Class I). These may depend on stimulus direction alone or on both direction and intensity. When the response depends on both parameters, the stimulus may be treated as a vector. The question arises whether the response also corresponds to this vector approach. Jander [404] has proposed the labels protaxis for the response to both direction and intensity and metataxis for a response to direction only.

In some cases, such as gravity organs that are stimulated by shearing forces, stimulus direction and intensity are physically combined by the stimulating event (see 3.10). Often, however, direction and intensity enter the system as separate signals, which may be combined later either in the sense organ or the CNS. For example, in array systems the sensor-direction label can be transmitted independently of the stimulus intensity. In bisensor systems, on the other hand, the response depends on the difference between the excitations of the two sensors. The excitations (and therefore their difference) are based on both direction and intensity, so that a purely directional response is impossible.

The relationship between stimulus and response is often expressed as a mathematical equation. Such formulations may serve as working hypotheses for further investigations but provide little insight into the physiological processes of the system.

2.6.1 Turning Tendency

Stimulus-response relationships are frequently measured as turning tendencies. The expression turning tendency describes central nervous processes that cause an animal to carry out a particular turning response. It is, thus, a central nervous variable that can be measured in the form of a response. Various parameters of the turning response can be used to quantify the turning tendency. Among these are measurements of torque, turning radius, angular velocity, turning angle, degree of influence of a second stimulus parameter (e.g., comparison of turning tendencies), and the distribution of turning responses in a group.

An experiment on the positional orientation of shrimp to light provides an example of the measurement of turning tendency. When a shrimp is forced out of its normal position with its back to the light, it uses swimming motions of its abdominal legs (pleopods) to try to turn itself around. Figure 2.6/1 illustrates how the turning force expended by the shrimp can be quantified. A shrimp is harnessed to a test tube, which has been slipped upside down over a pointed steel rod. A watch spring connects the mouth of the tube to the rod, and the turning force produced by the shrimp is measured directly from the spring extension as the torque (dyn × cm). Such measurements reveal that the torque changes proportionally to the sine of the incident light angle (β), resulting in a sinusoidal turning tendency curve (Fig. 2.6/1a). Each turning tendency curve applies to a particular illumination intensity. When this is changed, the shrimp responds to the same incident light direction with a different torque. Measurement of the response to all the incident light directions at different intensities provides a set of sinusoidal curves whose amplitudes are related to the logarithm of illumination intensity (Fig. 2.6/1b). These relationships can be summarized by the turning equation $D = L \times \sin \beta$, where $L = K \times \log B$, and K is a proportionality constant and B the intensity variable.

An example in which the turning radius is used to measure turning tendency is given later for light compass orientation of water beetle larvae (see 2.6.3). Since in a feedback loop system an animal turns until the reference value is reached, measurement of the turning angle is limited to open-loop orientations such as prey fixation in the jumping spider (Fig. 2.4/7). Orientation to two stimuli may provide insight into the turning tendency to single stimuli. This method of turning tendency comparison was introduced by Jander ([401], see 2.7.1), who also devised a method for

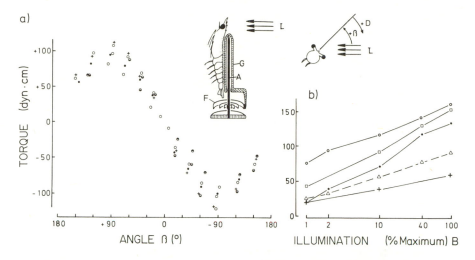

Fig. 2.6/1 Light orientation of the shrimp *Palaemonetes varians*. The shrimp is harnessed with its dorsal side to a glass vial (*G*), which is slipped over a pointed steel rod (*A*) and connected to its base by a watch spring (*F*). The plots show the shrimp's torque as a function of a) light direction β and b) illumination intensity. In b) the ordinate is given in terms of the difference between the maximum and minimum of curves like those in a). (Modified from [778])

determining turning tendency from a group. Ants trained to carry pupae from the middle of an arena to their nest opening at its edge walk a compass course relative to a light source. Shifting the light source while they are under way destroys their compass direction. By counting and scoring their subsequent behavior (right turn = +1, left turn = −1, straight ahead = 0), a weighted arithmetic mean can be calculated, which provides a measure for the turning tendency. For example: Out of 20 animals, 15 turned right, 3 left, and 2 walked straight ahead, giving a turning tendency value of $(15-3)/20 = +0.6$.

A turning tendency curve (also called direction response characteristic) gives the strength of the turning response as a function of stimulus direction. Such curves are often sinusoidal, as was found for the shrimp (Fig. 2.6/1). The curve is steepest to each side of the zero direction, the direction in which the animal "desires" to go. Since the turning tendency per degree is greater the steeper the curve, the system is most sensitive in the range bracketing the desired direction. This has the advantage of enabling quick and precise correction of small deviations. These parts of the turning tendency curves for flies, ants, and bees are even steeper than in sinusoidal curves (Fig. 3.1/13a, [741, 188]).

2.6.2 Orientation to Several Unimodal Stimuli

In gravity sense organs, gravity and centrifugal force interact physically at the statoliths to give a single resultant force. Since the sensory apparatus cannot differentiate the component forces, there is only a single stimulus and consequently only one direction signal to the CNS.

In other sensory modalities, however, different stimuli can excite the sensory elements separately. A visual array organ, for example, can monitor several stimuli independently, The processing of these stimuli is physiological.

2.6.2.1 *Vector Representation and Vectorial Processing of Stimuli*

When the response depends on both stimulus direction and intensity, a vector averaging comes naturally to mind. If the calculated resultant vector coincides with the behavior of the animal, the orientation mechanism may process the stimuli as vectors. The processing site remains obscure. The vector computation of a direction signal may occur in the sensory apparatus or at various sites in the CNS. It is conceivable that if the computation occurs just prior to the motor output, several turning tendencies arise independently and are combined in the motor event.

The use of vector diagrams (= triangles of forces) to represent orientation responses is not new. In 1903 Rádl [688] discussed the idea that a stimulus source emits very weak forces that affect the animal. Kühn [480] and Fraenkel and Gunn [230] presented the stimulus-response situation as a triangle of forces and discussed the possible physiological consequences in terms of tropotaxis. The model of stimuli working like forces on an animal is well known from the concept of tropotaxis. It is not quite as obvious when the signal processing is viewed as "mere" averaging.

An animal's orientation response of two stimuli often agrees with the calculated resultant vector. This can be demonstrated by representing the resultant direction as a function of the ratio of the two stimulus intensities: When the stimuli intersect at a right angle, this ratio is equal to the tangent of the angle formed by the resultant direction and one of the two stimuli (Fig. 2.6/5, Eq. 13). Figure 2.6/2 shows this relationship for light orientation of shrimp and *Acilius* larvae. The curves for fish and hover flies in this figure do not coincide with a "simple" resultant. However, if illumination intensities are plotted on a logarithmic, instead of a linear, scale these data also form a straight line. Thus, the resultant rule can also be applied to these cases.

When the response of two stimuli corresponds to the resultant vector, more than two stimuli are probably also processed by vector addition. As well as providing a localized stimulus, the sun delivers a field of irradiance

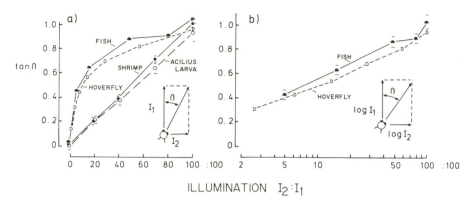

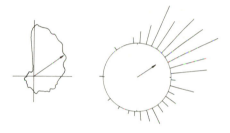

Fig. 2.6/2 Two-light orientation of the fish *Gymnocorymbus ternetzii*, the hover fly *Eristalis*, the shrimp *Palaemonetes varians*, and the water beetle larva *Acilius sulcatus*. a) The tangent of the angle β to the brighter light (I_1) as a function of the ratio of illumination intensities I_2/I_1. b) The data for fish and hover flies in a semilog plot. (Modified from [778])

Fig. 2.6/3 Light orientation of hatchling green sea turtles, *Chelonia mydas*, in a vertically striped drum. Starting with a white stripe at 12:00, each successive stripe is grayer until the circle is closed by a black stripe to the left of the white stripe. The diagram on the left shows the angular light distribution (ALD) and its mean vector (solid arrow). On the right is the distribution of walking directions of 192 hatchlings and its mean vector (solid arrow). (Modified from [878])

due to reflection and scattering with a peak in the direction of the sun [877, 699]. Similarly, under laboratory conditions an animal receives not only direct light from a light bulb but also scattered light according to the reflective properties of its surroundings. Verheijen termed this field of irradiance around the animal the "angular light distribution," or ALD. Sea turtles and starlings move in a direction corresponding to the resultant vector of the ALD (Fig. 2.6/3, [878, 876]).

Figure 2.6/4 illustrates how an animal with an array organ might compute the excitations (E) from an ALD comprised of five individual stimuli (R). Vector addition gives an excitation peak (E_R) in the array that supplies the direction signal for the orientation response. Normally this excitation resultant coincides with the ALD peak (R_1, Fig. 2.6/4a). In Figure 2.6/4b the animal is "correctly" aligned with the ALD peak (reference direction = light straight ahead). Covering the right eye shifts the excitation peak (E_R)

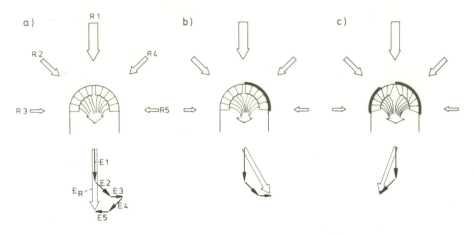

Fig. 2.6/4 Vector addition in an array organ of excitations ($E1$–$E5$) caused by stimuli ($R1$–$R5$) of an ALD. a) In a normal animal the excitation resultant (E_R) coincides with the intensity peak ($R1$). b) In an animal that has been blinded on its right, the E_R deviates to the left of $R1$. c) In an animal that can only see with the visual elements of the left eye that are directed toward the right, the E_R deviates to the right of $R1$.

to the left into the receptive field of the uncovered eye. The direction signal given by the array no longer corresponds to the reference direction. This discrepancy (= error) produces turning tendencies to the left. Note, however, that in Fig. 2.6/4c an uncovered eye element on the left side points to the right, so that the excitation peak is shifted to the right and the turning tendency is to the right. The determining factor is, thus, the receptive field direction of the uncovered elements, not the side of the body they are on.

In a uniform ALD these turning tendencies lead to circus movements; in an ALD with a maximum they lead to spiraling, as is often observed in animals that have been blinded on one side [230, 609]. As this is not a tropotactic mechanism, circus movements must be used with caution as a criterion for tropotaxis (see 2.5.3).

Experiments on the tectal projections of the monkey's visual field demonstrate that vector addition may also apply to "higher" orientation capabilities like directed eye movements ([706], see 3.1.8.2). Localized electrical stimulation of the tectum causes the eyes to move and fixate on a corresponding site in the visual field. If two tectal loci are simultaneously stimulated, the eye movement conforms to vector addition of the two stimuli.

2.6.2.2 Vector Addition and the Weighted Arithmetic Mean

Vector addition is direction averaging that is weighted according to stimulus intensity. A weighted arithmetic mean can also be used to average two directions. Figure 2.6/5 gives the procedures for calculating the sum of two vectors and the weighted arithmetic mean. For vector addition the two vectors A and B are drawn on a coordinate grid. Substituting the trigonometric relationships (2) into Eq. 1 gives a general equation for vector addition (Eq. 3). This can be supplemented for more vectors by adding the product of the vector length and the sine of the angle to the numerator and the product of vector length and cosine of the angle to the denominator. Setting τ to zero in Eq. 3 gives the simplified forms, Eqs. 5 and 6, which relate the resultant angle to the direction of the component vector A. Replacing γ by $(\alpha + \beta)$ gives Eq. 7, which can then be transformed into Eq. 9 by using the addition theorems of Eq. 8. Substitution of Eq. 10 into Eq. 9 gives Eq. 11, an important equation that we shall return to for the analysis of light-gravity orientation. If the two vectors intersect at an angle of 90° (Eq. 12), the relationship is simplified to a tangent equation (Eq. 13, compare with Fig. 2.6/2).

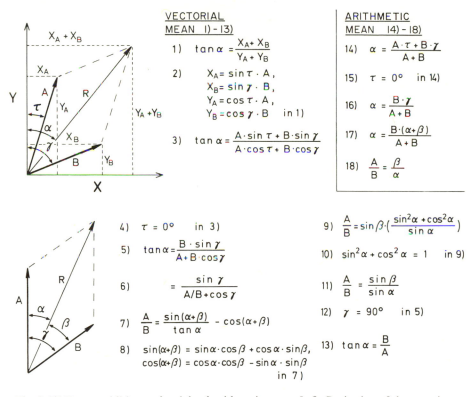

VECTORIAL MEAN 1) – 13)

1) $\tan\alpha = \dfrac{X_A + X_B}{Y_A + Y_B}$

2) $X_A = \sin\tau \cdot A$,
$X_B = \sin\gamma \cdot B$,
$Y_A = \cos\tau \cdot A$,
$Y_B = \cos\gamma \cdot B$ in 1)

3) $\tan\alpha = \dfrac{A \cdot \sin\tau + B \cdot \sin\gamma}{A \cdot \cos\tau + B \cdot \cos\gamma}$

ARITHMETIC MEAN 14) – 18)

14) $\alpha = \dfrac{A \cdot \tau + B \cdot \gamma}{A + B}$

15) $\tau = 0°$ in 14)

16) $\alpha = \dfrac{B \cdot \gamma}{A + B}$

17) $\alpha = \dfrac{B \cdot (\alpha + \beta)}{A + B}$

18) $\dfrac{A}{B} = \dfrac{\beta}{\alpha}$

4) $\tau = 0°$ in 3)

5) $\tan\alpha = \dfrac{B \cdot \sin\gamma}{A + B \cdot \cos\gamma}$

6) $= \dfrac{\sin\gamma}{A/B + \cos\gamma}$

7) $\dfrac{A}{B} = \dfrac{\sin(\alpha+\beta)}{\tan\alpha} - \cos(\alpha+\beta)$

8) $\sin(\alpha+\beta) = \sin\alpha \cdot \cos\beta + \cos\alpha \cdot \sin\beta$,
$\cos(\alpha+\beta) = \cos\alpha \cdot \cos\beta - \sin\alpha \cdot \sin\beta$
in 7)

9) $\dfrac{A}{B} = \sin\beta \cdot \left(\dfrac{\sin^2\alpha + \cos^2\alpha}{\sin\alpha}\right)$

10) $\sin^2\alpha + \cos^2\alpha = 1$ in 9)

11) $\dfrac{A}{B} = \dfrac{\sin\beta}{\sin\alpha}$

12) $\gamma = 90°$ in 5)

13) $\tan\alpha = \dfrac{B}{A}$

Fig. 2.6/5 Vector addition and weighted arithmetic mean. Left: Derivation of the equations for the addition of two vectors (A, B) in an X-Y coordinate system (Eqs. 1–3) and with respect to one of the vectors (Eqs. 4–13). Right: Calculation of the weighted arithmetic mean of two directions, giving the angle with respect to a set direction in space (Eq. 14) and to one of the two directions (Eqs. 15–18).

Equations for the weighted arithmetic mean of two angles are developed in Eq. 14 to 18 in Fig. 2.6/5. The mean direction α is calculated from two direction values, τ and γ, using the weighting factors A and B (Eq. 14). Setting τ to zero gives Eq. 16, which relates the angle to direction A. Substituting $(\alpha + \beta)$ for γ results in Eq. 18, the parallel equation to Eq. 11.

Equations 11 and 18 describe an animal's alignment when it assumes an "averaged" position between the incident directions of two stimuli. In the weighted arithmetic mean, the ratio of the angle values $\alpha{:}\beta$ is inversely proportional to that of the stimulus magnitudes $A{:}B$ (Eq. 18). The same applies for the sine values of the angles in vector addition (Eq. 11).

Since the two computation methods do not provide substantially different results if the angle (γ) formed by the two directions is 90° or less, the variance of the data must be very small before a decision between these procedures can be made (Fig. 2.6/6a,b). This condition is not fulfilled by the results of many earlier experiments, so that their conclusions that vector addition was used are doubtful. The results of experiments on crayfish light orientation suggest a vector addition (Fig. 2.6/6a–d); whereas light orientation in maggots [656] appears to be based on a computation of the arithmetic mean (Fig. 2.6/6e).

Other mathematical procedures cannot be excluded. Vector addition and arithmetic averaging are only two possible ways of describing the input-

Fig. 2.6/6 Orientation to two lights with different intensities separated by the angle γ in crayfish a)–d) and maggots e). α is the angle between the direction in which the animal is facing and the direction of the stronger of the two lights. The solid lines were calculated by vector addition; the closely dashed lines, by weighted arithmetic averaging. (a–d, modified from [807]; e, from [656])

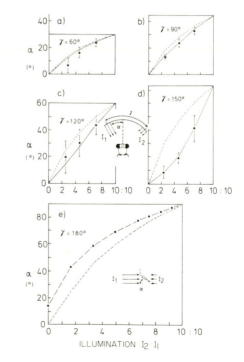

output relationships of a system and do not necessarily say anything about the physiological nature of the underlying mechanisms.

2.6.3 Alteration of the Stimulus-Response Relationship (Resetting the Reference Value)

Until now we have examined the response only as a function of the stimulus, assuming that as in many goal and target orientations, the reference value for direction and, consequently, the stimulus-response relationships are constant. However, in other systems, such as many compass orientations, an animal can align itself in various directions relative to the stimulus. To alter its orientation to a stimulus an animal must reset its reference value for direction. A change in the reference value means that quantitative relationships between stimulus and response must be changed. Turning tendencies must be reassigned to new stimulus directions, so that the new reference direction no longer generates a turning tendency and the old direction now leads to a turning response. What changes in the stimulus-response relationship produce the resetting of the reference value? Note that we are concerned here with how a new reference value is converted into an orientation direction, not with why the change arises (see specific central disposition, 2.1.2).

Four models have been proposed as reset mechanisms. They differ in the way the sensory signals are integrated with the centrally determined reference value. In the terminology of cybernetics, the turning tendency (D) depends on the difference (error) between the existing direction (actual value) and the desired direction (reference value, see 2.4.3.1). When they are equal, the turning tendency is zero, and the course direction is maintained. Any difference leads to a turning tendency.

As an introductory example let us examine the vertical light compass orientation of the larvae of two water beetles, *Acilius sulcatus* and *Dytiscus marginalis* [770]. Their entire behavior is spatially related to the incidence of light that falls on the surface of the pools and ponds that comprise their natural habitat. This is easily demonstrated by shining light through the bottom of a glass beaker containing larvae. Their orientation system is reversed so that they behave as if their world were upside down. Whether they are swimming "upward" to get a breath or horizontally on the lookout for prey, all their paths are related to the "light from below." (Vertical light compass orientation more aptly describes this circumstance than the usual expression, dorsal light response.)

Turning tendency curves can be determined for the reference directions of the diverse swimming behaviors shown by these larvae. Differences in the curves furnish insight into the mechanism of reference value reset. But first the animals must be brought into a situation where they show constant turns (= circling). Normally when light incidence and reference direction diverge, a larva turns until light impinges on the correct eyes. To prevent a larva from attaining this direction, the direction of light incidence was coupled to the animal. Part of the eye complex of a larva was coated with an opaque film, leaving a particular visual direction uncovered (Fig. 3.1/ 15). No matter how the larva turned, only the uncovered eyes received light. Under illumination from all sides this stimulation remained constant. Covering the "correct" eyes opens the control loop by blocking the feedback, so that an error cannot be corrected. This leads to a persistent turning tendency, and the animal swims in circles. The direction of circling (ventral or dorsal) gives the direction of the turning tendency; the circle diameters are inversely proportional to its strength (see 2.6.1).

When released from confinement, a larva always swims downward in a kind of escape response. The reference direction for this behavior corresponds to "caudo-dorsal light incidence." Rows a) and b) of Fig. 2.6/7 illustrate the results of experiments in which different eyes were covered prior to release. When only the rostro-dorsal eyes remain uncovered (a1),

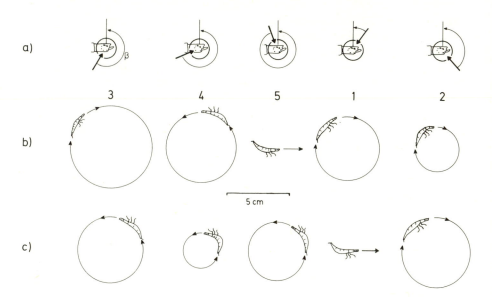

Fig. 2.6/7 Orientation of the water beetle larva *Acilius sulcatus* when its eyes are painted over so that it receives light only from the directions indicated by arrows in row a). The animals swim in ventral or dorsal circles trying to match the fixed incident light direction with a reference direction for b) normal downward swimming = light from the caudo-dorsal direction or c) upward swimming = light from the rostro-dorsal direction. Different reference directions lead to different turning tendencies for the same incident light directions.

the larva turns continuously in ventral circles (b1) in a futile attempt to bring the light into the caudo-dorsal eyes. If light is allowed to enter only via the rostro-ventral eyes (a2), the larva swims in even tighter ventral circles (b2). Ventral light incidence (a3) also leads to ventral circling (b3). Restricting light incidence to the more caudal eyes (a4) reverses the turning direction and results in dorsal circling (b4). When only the caudo-dorsal eyes are left uncovered (a5), the larva swims straight ahead (b5). The turning tendency is zero because this light incidence corresponds to the reference light direction for downward swimming. Analysis of the circles results in a sinusoidal curve for turning tendency (Fig. 2.6/8, upper curve).

The above experiments were repeated for another reference direction corresponding to "rostro-dorsal light incidence" (Fig. 2.6/7, row c). This is the upward swimming direction taken by a larva when it rises to the surface to take a breath, which can be experimentally induced by holding the larva underwater to increase its oxygen debt. Analysis of the results yielded the lower sinusoidal curve of Fig. 2.6/8. The analogous curve for horizontal swimming, i.e., dorsal light incidence, can be assumed to lie between and parallel to these curves (Fig. 2.6/8, middle curve).

In the transition of reference directions from caudo-dorsal to rostro-dorsal light incidence, all turning tendency values are shifted upward on the D scale by the same amount (Fig. 2.6/8). This parallel shift can be described by a simple superposition of the controlling variable (Fig. 2.6/9 and model a in 2.6/10). In this model, a turning tendency value is assigned centrally to each eye region according to its visual field direction (angle β). This stimulus-dependent turning tendency ($D_\beta = \sin \beta$) is, however, only part of the total turning tendency exhibited by the animal. The remainder is determined by the reference value $D_w = W$, and is independent of stimulus direction. We can combine these two turning tendencies in the equation, $D = W + K \times \sin \beta$, where K is a weighting factor (compare 2.6.2). In the experiments on water beetle larvae, K depended on illumination intensity, which was kept constant. Figure 2.6/9a illustrates how the turning tendency curve is computed from D_β and D_w. The scale was chosen so that the reference direction "30° to the right" is reached when $W = D = 2$. For example, when $\beta = +90°$, $D_\beta = -4$ and $D_w = +2$, so $D = -2$.

The flow diagram (Fig. 2.6/10a) is a simple feedback loop (see Fig. 2.4/5d). A positive direction value corresponds to a negative D value and vice versa, so the feedback is negative. This model of controlling variable superposition describes the gravity orientation of the grain weevil *Calandra granaria* [915]. On inclined surfaces, the weevils maintain a particular course relative to the shear direction (the component of gravity that pulls the weevil downward along the plane of the walking surface). The angle between walking direction and shear direction enters the computation as a sine value, giving the turning tendency equation $D = W + A \times \sin \beta$,

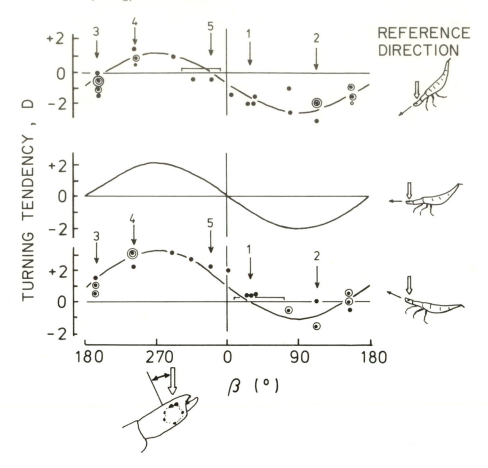

Fig. 2.6/8 Turning tendencies (*D*) of *Acilius* larvae as a function of incident light direction (β) for the reference directions "light caudo-dorsal" (downward swimming, upper curve) and "light rostro-dorsal" (upward swimming, lower curve). The middle curve is the extrapolated curve for horizontal swimming. *D* is given in terms of circle diameter with 0 = straight ahead, 1 = >11 cm, 2 = 7–11 cm, 3 = 4–7 cm. The smaller the circle, the greater the turning tendency. Dorsal circling is indicated by + and ventral circling by −. The numbered arrows correspond to Fig. 2.6/7, and the brackets over the abscissa indicate the range of swimming directions observed for normal larvae. (Modified from [770])

where *A* is the weighting factor of that portion of the turning tendency determined by shear. The orientation of the male silk moth *Bombyx mori* in an airstream loaded with female sex pheromone can also be explained by this kind of controlling variable superposition [468]. The weighting factor is given in this case by the sex pheromone concentration.

One drawback of the superposition model a (Fig. 2.6/10) is its instability

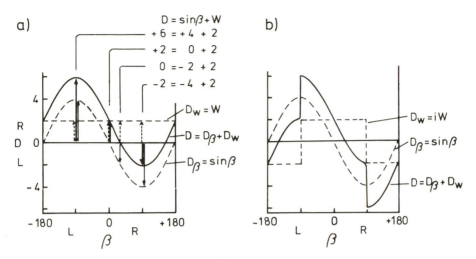

Fig. 2.6/9 Turning tendency D and its components D_β and D_W as a function of light incidence. a) Model a with numerical examples for different stimulus directions (compare Fig. 2.6/10). b) Model b.

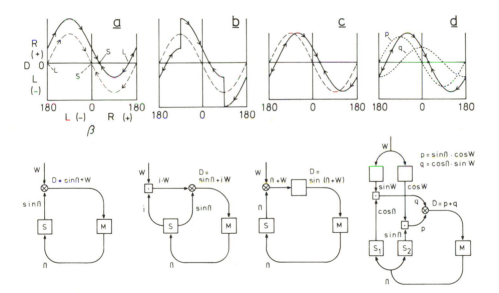

Fig. 2.6/10 Models of reference value reset. Upper row: Turning tendency curves. The dashed lines show the D curve for the reference value, $\beta = 0$; arrowheads indicate direction of turning tendency; S, stable point; L, labile point. Lower row: Flow diagrams for the a) simple superposition model, b) the superposition model with sign change at 90° effected by i, c) the angle hypothesis, and d) the bicomponent model.

at larger reference angles. The turning tendency curve has two zero intercepts. Until now we have considered only the reference or stable direction. The other intercept is called the labile direction because an animal is normally unable to maintain it. Like a ball delicately balanced on the highest point of a dome, the animal turns out of this direction at the slightest change in position. The turning tendency then brings the animal back into the stable direction. The labile direction is the second zero intercept in the curves of Fig. 2.6/8 and in Fig. 2.6/10a. As these diagrams clearly show, vertical shifts of the turning tendency curve move the stable and labile directions closer together. At reference angles near 90°, even small variations in direction can bring the animal from the stable into, or past, the labile direction. Since the turning tendency is reversed on the other side of the labile point, overshooting it causes the animal to circle until it "catches" again in the stable direction.

This instability can be circumvented by modifying the simple model so that the controlling variable is added for angles of 0°–90° but subtracted for angles of 90°–180° (Fig. 2.6/10b). This leads to steps at ±90°, and maintains the distance between stable and labile points. Such a model was considered for light orientation of walking flies (*Calliphora* [122]) and for wind orientation of a number of walking beetles [510]. Conceivably, the step at 90° is converted to a ramp in the physiological execution of such a circuit. The plus-minus switch at 90° must be controlled by the sensory input (signal i, Fig. 2.6/10b), and a similar switching process must be assumed for the controlling variable W.

In the next two models the controlling variable is processed in an entirely different way. These mechanisms shift the turning tendency curves horizontally along the base line. The equation for the simpler of the two models (Fig. 2.6/10c) is $D = \sin(\beta + W)$. Both the direction signal (β) and the reference value (W) are summed as angle values. Their total is then converted to a sinusoidally proportional turning tendency. In connection with an investigation by Howland [377], Edrich [188] called this model the angle hypothesis. Howland discusses it in terms of light orientation of fish, and Edrich in terms of the gravity orientation of bees.

In model c, sinusoidal direction signals such as those delivered by the gravity sense organs of crustaceans and vertebrates (see 3.10) cannot enter the computation process directly. Mittelstaedt [590, 592] proposed a solution that he termed the bicomponent theory (Fig. 2.6/10d). It is based on a transformation of the model c equation according to a trigonometric addition theorem: $\sin(\beta + W) = \sin\beta \times \cos W + \cos\beta \times \sin W$. In this model both the direction signal (β) and the controlling variable (W) are split into their sine and cosine. The two pairs of values are crossmultiplied, $\sin\beta$ with $\cos W$ and $\cos\beta$ with $\sin W$, giving two products, p and q. These two products (bicomponents) are added to give the turning tendency D.

In the turning tendency diagram of Fig. 2.6/10d, the two components of the D curve are represented as a sine curve (p) and a cosine curve (q). An important feature of the model is that the controlling variable reciprocally modulates the amplitude of the component curves p and q, amplifying one while attenuating the other. The D curve shifts in the direction of the component that is amplified. As in model c, a change in the controlling variable W leads to a horizontal shift of the D curve.

Although the bicomponent theory is tempting, it remains controversial [377]. The "simpler" angle hypothesis often satisfactorily describes exper-imental data. Findings such as those on shrimp [769], flatfish [772], and human [885, 791] gravity orientation are difficult to reconcile with the bicomponent theory. A thorough discussion of this model can be found in the literature [592, 593, 595, 596].

Jander's compensation theory (see 2.4.2) can be assigned to models b, c, or d. His own formulation corresponds to model b, with vertical shifts of the D curve in opposite directions for the anterior and posterior visual field of ants. However, these findings can also be explained by the angle hy-pothesis and the bicomponent theory, although the sine-cosine differen-tiations of the latter represent an unnecessary complication for a system in which the sense organs can furnish direct angle values.

Although the smooth curves of models a, c, and d are aesthetically more satisfying than the stepped curve of model b, there is no reason to assume that physiological mechanisms can be neatly described and pigeonholed. Central nervous processes may function in ways that cannot be attributed to any one of these models, but may be a combination of them or differ completely. In evaluating the pros and cons one should keep in mind that nature often prefers a functional "shortcut" to a mathematically elegant solution [1022].

Recently the idea has been revived that orientation is related to a pattern of stimulus distribution [187, 188, 740, 741] instead of to a single direction value. In 1911 Santschi (cited by Brun [96]) conjectured that the sun com-pass orientation of ants was performed on the basis of "the total arrange-ment of the illuminating zones." Models a–d are single-value models in that stimulus direction is registered and processed as one value. Scharstein [741] proposed an alternative model, the pattern comparison model, de-rived from his findings on ant sun compass orientation. The course direc-tion of ants that had been previously trained to orient to one light varied around two peaks when they were tested with two reference lights. Ap-parently the ants were unable to convert the two lights into a single direction signal, as would be predicted by a single-value model. The spatial reference that is compared with a central template is given by the spatial pattern of stimuli instead of a localized stimulus. This interesting hypothesis deserves to be tested further, theoretically elaborated, and delimited from other concepts such as computation of excitation peak (see 2.6.2.1) and landmark orientation (3.1.5).

2.7 MULTIMODAL ORIENTATION SYSTEMS

Most orientation behaviors involve more than one sensory modality. Many aquatic animals orient their body position and locomotion to both gravity and light. The positional orientation of substrate-bound animals including humans usually depends on both substrate and gravity. Multimodal systems are also found in distant orientation (2.8) and human spatial orientation (2.9). Chemical orientation in moving air (3.5) is based on a tight interweaving of chemosensory input and "optomotor" wind orientation (3.8). Ants simultaneously follow scent trails and align their locomotion with respect to the sun [96]. This was demonstrated experimentally by using a mirror to reflect sunlight onto the shadow side of an ant trail. Ants that were carrying pupae to the nest turned around as soon as they received sunlight from the other side, but those without pupae merely hesitated, then continued in the same direction along the scent trail. The ants carrying pupae probably could not easily sample the trail with their antennae and, therefore, were more dependent on cues from the sun. A cricket's course to a sound source is more precise if it can see its surroundings [1021]. Apparently, optokinetic course control contributes to the stabilization of acoustic orientation.

2.7.1 Orientation to Stimuli of Diverse Sensory Modalities

Positional orientation. In an aquarium near a bright window some fish assume a tilted position with their backs leaning toward the light. This occurs because these fish orient their normal position simultaneously to light and gravity. The light-gravity orientation of fish is one of the most extensively analyzed "composite" orientation systems [356, 366, 364, 795, 792, 73, 74, 76, 71, 826]. The pioneering experimental and theoretical work of von Holst and his colleagues in the 1950's not only elucidated how the statolith apparatus functioned, but also disclosed basic principles of the interaction between both stimulus inputs, light and gravity.

Figure 2.7/1 illustrates the experimental design for measuring the orientation of fish to varying light directions with respect to different magnitudes of "gravity" [366]. Gravity refers here to the resultant of gravity and centrifugal force (see 2.6.2, 3.10.1). The resultant alignment of the fish between light and gravity is a steady-state position which, as von Holst emphasized, is a "resting position." It can be described by the equation for

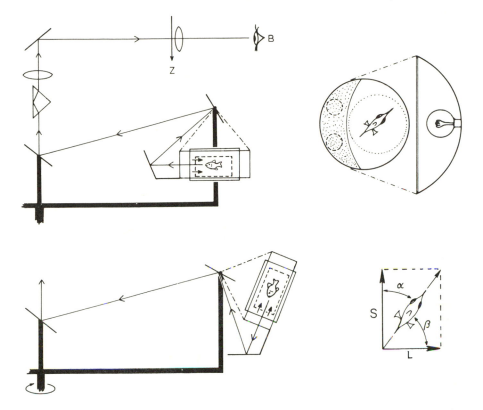

Fig. 2.7/1 Centrifuge for investigating the light-gravity orientation of fish. Upper left: The fish swims against the flow direction (small arrows); the experimenter (*B*) views the fish from the front over a system of mirrors, lenses, and a prism as shown on the right; the fish's tilt can be measured with the help of a pointer (*Z*) (angle α, lower right). Lower left: Even when the centrifuge is operating, the fish appears as a still image. The container swings freely into the resultant force direction so that the magnitude, but not the direction, of gravity is altered for the fish. Lower right: The vector diagram of the orientation between gravity (*G*) and light (*L*). (Modified from [366])

force triangles (vector diagrams, Fig. 2.6/5): $G \times \sin \alpha = L \times \sin \beta$, or $\sin \alpha/\sin \beta = L/G$, in which α and β are the angles of the fish to gravity and to light; *G* and *L*, the intensities of gravity and illumination. If the angle between gravity and light is 90°, the equation is simplified to $G/L = \cot \alpha$ (see Fig. 2.6/5, Eq. 13). When light intensity is constant, $G = \cot \alpha$. The linear relationship between $\cot \alpha$ and *G* (Fig. 2.7/2) demonstrates that fish assume a position corresponding to the vector resultant of gravity and light.

Course orientation. On an inclined surface many animals walk either upward or downward (negative or positive geotaxis). For their course orientation, only the gravity component parallel to the surface is critical. This

Fig. 2.7/2 Light-gravity orientation (α) of fish as a function of gravity magnitude for two different starting values of α (II, III). The insert on the right shows the curves from the main diagram in terms of cot α. Open symbols denote data points from *Gymnocorymbus ternetzii*; filled symbols, *Pterophyllum scalare*; and crosses, other fish. (Modified from [366])

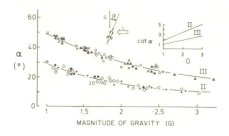

shearing force is maximal for vertical and zero for horizontal surfaces. For intermediate slopes the shear is proportional to the sine of the angle between the surface and the horizontal plane. Light from the side may cause an animal to deviate from its course. In ants and bees this new course depends on the angle between shear and light and on their intensities [401, 741, 188]. An ant's course can be described by the equation $\sin \alpha = \sin \beta$ (Fig. 2.7/3) and corresponds to the resultant of gravity and light (compare Fig. 2.6/5, Eq. 11).

To explain these results Jander introduced the concept "turning tendency comparison" which would occur whenever an animal oriented simultaneously to two stimuli (e.g., the light-gravity orientation of fish). The expression implies that both stimuli generate a turning tendency and that the animal turns until the two tendencies are equal. This is the idea of "counterbalancing forces." It is not as obvious if the orientation is viewed as a result of vector averaging of directions (see 2.6.2).

The direction signal for a multimodal system can arise from an external and an idiothetic cue, as well as from two external cues [512, 599, 600, 601]. For instance, if the horizontal walking surface of a millipede is tilted, the resulting gravity stimulus causes the millipede to deviate upward from its previous course. This course deviation releases a counterturn tendency, i.e., a tendency to regain the previous course on the basis of idiothetic signals (see 3.11.2.1). A compromise course results that corresponds to the resultant of both direction values.

Trimodal course orientation in vertical migration. The regulation of depth in the vertical migration of many plankton forms is an example of an orientation system based on three sensory modalities: gravity, light, and hy-

Fig. 2.7/3 Gravity course (α) of ants walking on a vertical surface as a function of incident light angle (β). The light is parallel to the walking surface. The insert on the right shows the dashed line of the main diagram in terms of the sine of the angles. (Modified from [401])

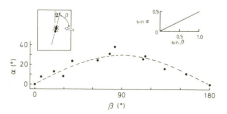

drostatic pressure. The habitats of many aquatic animals are limited to particular water levels. Many forms move regularly between different layers, remaining in the depths during the day and near the water surface during the night. The course directions are oriented to gravity and light, while pressure determines the target layer. Medusae, ctenophores, and the larvae of fish, squid, and crabs respond to changes in hydrostatic pressure with light- or gravity-oriented movements [700, 701, 839, 840]. An increase in pressure causes them to swim upward and toward light, while a decrease leads to the opposite responses.

These relationships can be represented by a circuit diagram consisting of two interlocking control loops [778]. In Fig. 2.7/4 the loop on the left controls the swimming course to light and gravity; the one on the right, the depth according to pressure. Pressure thus affects the controlling variables of the course angle with respect to light and gravity (α). Their direction signal α_i is compared with the reference value (α_r) to determine the swimming course that is executed by the effectors (α_m). Changes in course

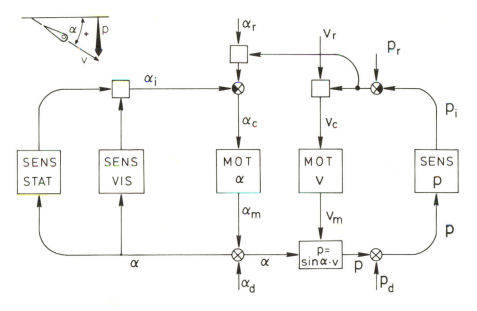

Fig. 2.7/4 The vertical migration of aquatic animals depends on three input variables: the direction to gravity and light (α) and hydrostatic pressure (p). It is controlled by two interlocking feedback loops. In the loop on the right the variables, swimming course (α) and velocity (V_m), determine the depth and thereby the water pressure (p). The pressure signal (p_i) is compared with the reference value (p_r), and the pressure error affects the controlling variables (α and V_r). In the loop on the left for regulation of the swimming direction, the course signal (α_i) is compared with the reference value (α_r), which is also affected by the pressure error.

angle (α) affect both the direction sensors and pressure reception (about which little is known). A downward course, for instance, leads into deeper water and thus increases the pressure. But pressure depends not only on the course angle but also on the swimming velocity (v) according to the equation $p = v \times \sin \alpha$ (see inset figure). Since swimming velocity is an independent motor variable, it is represented by a separate output. In crab larvae a pressure increase leads to increased swimming velocity [839, 840, 55].

The pressure signal (p_i) feeds back onto the controlling variable for pressure. When the animal reaches its "desired" depth, i.e., when the measured pressure p_i coincides with the reference value p_r, α_r and v_r are modified so that the animal remains at this depth. When p_r is changed by factors such as periodicity in illumination intensity, CO_2 content, or internal state, the animal leaves this water level.

2.7.2 Transposition

The conversion of the orientation from one sensory modality to another is called transposition. The sun compass angle flown by a bee to the food source is later transposed on the vertical comb into the same angle relative to gravity (Fig. 2.7/5). The bee accomplishes this by performing looping figures on the comb called dancing. In the waggle dance, for example, the bee moves in figure eights whose crossings are relatively straight and characterized by abdomen waggling. The angle of the straight part relative to gravity (α) is the same as the angle between the horizontal direction of the sun and the food source (β). If the bee's flight was 30° to the right of the sun's direction, the waggling stretch is oriented 30° to the right of the upward direction. Other bees follow the dancer and learn the direction. In this way a successful forager communicates the direction of a food source

Fig. 2.7/5 In the waggle dance a bee transposes the direction of its flight with respect to the sun into a direction with respect to gravity. St = hive, F = food source, β = angle of flight direction, α = angle of waggle dance to gravity.

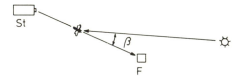

to the bees in the hive. This communication system was discovered by von Frisch [235]. Although there has been some controversy over von Frisch's findings [916], careful replication of these experiments by other investigators [273, 806] leaves no further doubt as to the accuracy of von Frisch's conclusions.

The ability to transpose a light course into a gravity course has since been demonstrated in many other insects [63, 399, 401, 403, 512]. Although the usual transposition code is that of the bee, with "vertically upward" equivalent to lightward and "right of vertical" equivalent to right of the light source, other codings can be found. For example, in a few insects downward movements indicate lightward, and left of downward, to the right of the light source. In some cases assignments are not rigid and can vary in a single individual.

2.7.3 Weighting of Reference Cues

Weighting is an expression of the intensity with which an animal responds to one stimulus relative to another. In the equation describing the position of a fish between gravity and light, $G/L = \sin \beta / \sin \alpha$, G and L are the weighting factors for gravity and light (= vector lengths in a vector representation; Fig. 2.6/5, Eq. 11). The ratio $\sin \beta / \sin \alpha$ gives the weighting in terms of the responses.

Investigations on fish show that the weighting of light is a complicated function of illumination intensity [73]. Both the retinal region (dorsal or ventral) and the adaptation state of the eyes play a role. L is proportional to the logarithm of illumination intensity only within a certain range of intensities.

Weighting and "change of mood." Two animals may respond differently to the same stimuli. For example, two fish can assume different positions under the same light-gravity conditions (Fig. 2.7/2, curves II, III). If fish A leans more toward the light than fish B, we say A weights the light stimulus more than B. If A's angle to light is smaller than to gravity, it weights light stronger than gravity. The weighting ratio for the same individual may also change. Thus, weighting factors like G and L include not only the effect of stimulus intensity but also that of other external and internal factors. Some of these were quantified by von Holst, who used the expression "change of mood." The weighting ratio of light to gravity is influenced, for example, by hydrostatic pressure and water turbulence. When hydrostatic pressure is increased, fish orient more toward gravity. In rough water they lean more toward the light. The "biological significance" of the first process may be that since less light is available in deeper water (= higher pressure), the fish must rely more on gravity. In turbulent water a fish is tossed about. The dependability of the labyrinth functions is diminished, so the system weights the light reference more heavily.

Keeping a fish in the dark for a longer period of time markedly decreases the relative weighting of light (Fig. 2.7/6b). Immediately after a dark period, a fish orients more to gravity than to side illumination. The light weighting increases with time until it reaches its predark-period value (Fig. 2.7/6b, curve 1).

The weighting of lateral light and gravity was also studied during prey capture (Fig. 2.7/6a). A fish temporarily changes its position in favor of light when it sees a morsel of food and snaps at it. At the moment of snapping, the fish is maximally tilted toward the light. If this experiment is preceded by a dark period, the fish at first does not notice the food, then just fixates it, and only after a few minutes snaps at it (Fig. 2.7/6b, curve 2). The tilt, i.e., the weighting of light, increases gradually to a plateau and then declines. The increase reflects the mood changing process observed after a dark period, and the decline has been attributed to increasing satiety of the fish. Feeding influences light weighting via chemosensory, as well as visual, input. When a fish in a resting position of 50° to gravity detects worm juice in the water, it tilts to 65°.

Lang [487] has shown that light-gravity weighting by guppies is subject to a moon phase periodicity. The same light stimulus has a stronger effect at certain phases of the moon.

The weighting of different reference stimuli is also important for human spatial orientation (2.9.4). Positional orientation (balance) and spatial perception depend on several reference cues, such as gravity and the visual spatial reference. Different factors enter into the weighting of the two:

Fig. 2.7/6 The weighting (U) of gravity and lateral light as a function of time in the positional orientation of fish. $U = 1$ means that the weighting is unchanged; $U > 1$, that the fish tilts more, i.e., that light is weighted more than before the test. a) Change of weighting ratio during prey capture. b) Curve 1, change of the weighting ratio following a dark period. Curve 2, maxima of U curves from prey capture experiments (see a). Triangles = no response to prey, crosses = prey fixated but not seized, filled circles = prey taken. The left-hand ordinate is for curve 1; right-hand, curve 2. (Modified from [359])

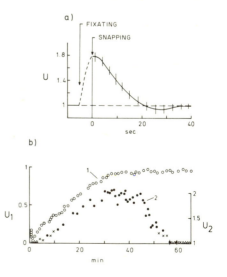

their physical characteristics, the transfer functions of the sense organs, and individual traits.

Weighting changes have also been demonstrated in transposition experiments. Jander [402] found that, in contrast to bees, trichopterans convert light angle into a gravity course according to a proportionality factor different from unity.

The information flow diagram of a hypothetical bimodal orientation is shown in Fig. 2.7/7. The weighting ratio of the reference stimuli (A/B) is the controlling variable. It arises from the stimulus-dependent components A_s and B_s and from the central components A_c and B_c. Stimulus directions (α, β) and intensities (A_e, B_e) enter separately. The ratio of the angle signals (β_i/α_i) is subtracted from the controlling variable A/B, and the difference (= error) determines the turning tendency (D). If the angle signals correspond to the sine values ($\beta_i \sim \sin \beta$, $\alpha_i \sim \sin \alpha$), the animal assumes the resultant vector. If they are proportional to the angle ($\alpha_i \sim \alpha$, $\beta_i \sim \beta$), the animal's alignment corresponds to a weighted arithmetic mean.

2.7.4 Bimodal Orientation of Turning Movements

The orientation of turning movements is often strongly bimodal. Angular acceleration is entered via the semicircular canals, optokinetic stimuli via the eyes. In humans, the labyrinth signals predominate during fast turning movements, and the optokinetic input predominates during slow ones (2.9.4.2).

A similar division has been found for the compensatory eye movements of crabs ([730], Fig. 2.7/8). When eye movements are optokinetically released by oscillating a striped drum around a crab, the gain approaches 1 as the oscillation frequency falls below 0.1 Hz. This means that the deflec-

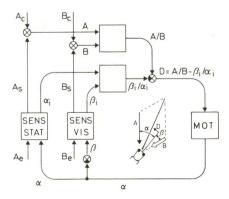

Fig. 2.7/7 Information flow diagram of positional orientation to gravity (angle α) and light (angle β). The weighting factors of gravity (A) and light (B) consist of sensory signals (A_s, B_s) and central components (A_c, B_c). The controlling variable is represented by the weighting ratio A/B. The difference between A/B and β/α_i (= error) gives the turning tendency (D). Equation D shows the angle ratio which can be determined by weighted arithmetic averaging; the angles are replaced by the sine values if vector addition is assumed. The input variables A_e and B_e are the stimulus intensities.

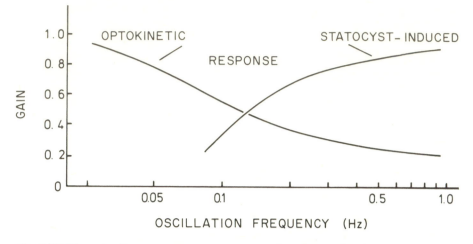

Fig. 2.7/8 The gain of compensatory eye movements in crabs as a function of oscillation frequency. The optokinetic response was elicited by oscillating a striped drum around the animal; the statocyst-induced response was obtained by oscillating a blinded animal on a torsion swing. Gain = eye movement amplitude/oscillation amplitude. (Modified from [730])

tion of the eyes is approximately equal to the turning angle of the drum. In contrast, if the crab is oscillated, the gain of the statocyst-induced eye movements is low at 0.1 Hz and approaches 1 as the frequency nears 1 Hz.

Neurophysiological investigations on vertebrates showed that both inputs are combined in the first sensory centers of the labyrinth, the vestibular nuclei (see 3.10). These nuclei contain neurons that are excited by labyrinthine, as well as optokinetic, stimulation (Fig. 2.7/9; [154, 133, 886]). The labyrinth excitation shows the typical time course of an inertial system:

Fig. 2.7/9 Normalized responses of neurons in the vestibular nuclei of *Rhesus* monkeys to rotation in the dark (squares) and in the light (open circles), as well as when a striped cylinder was rotated around the stationary monkey (filled circles). The abscissa gives the time after onset of rotation (Modified from [886])

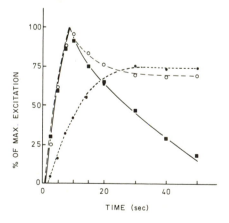

a steep increase during acceleration followed by a decline during continued turning at constant velocity. The optokinetically released excitation increases slowly during acceleration and reaches a plateau only after about 20 sec. The duration of the plateau depends on the length of stimulation. These findings show that the two inputs complement each other. The vestibular system responds to fast changes in movement, while the visual system is more responsive to slow ones. The curve for simultaneous stimulation of both modalities follows the labyrinth curve at the beginning of rotation, then changes over to the optokinetic response curve. Such a process is neither an addition nor an averaging but suggests a mechanism in which the more strongly excited system predominates ([886], compare with the model of integration of vestibular and optokinetic stimuli in 2.9.4.2).

The combined processing of optokinetic and vestibular turning signals appears to be important for normal execution of nystagmus. People with defective labyrinths show reduced optokinetic nystagmus [980].

2.7.5 Perception of How Objects Are Oriented in Space

We have as yet only dealt with single orientations involving one or more sensory modalities. Different modalities can also participate in different orientations, which are themselves coupled. For the perception of the spatial orientation of objects it is necessary to know and integrate (1) the orientation of the object relative to the body and (2) the orientation of the body in space. Why do we perceive a telephone pole to be vertical? The visual information about the pole's alignment to the body is related to information about the body's position with respect to the vertical. This furnishes information about the orientation of the pole relative to the vertical. The information on body position depends itself on two sensory inputs: gravity and the visual input on the structure of the environment. These perceptual processes are treated in 2.9 for humans. Here we shall look at comparable processes in animals.

To determine what cues were used to judge verticality, homing pigeons were trained to peck at a disc in the wall of an experimental chamber when the illuminated line on the disc was vertical. If the chamber walls were tilted sideways but the floor was horizontal, the pigeons pecked preferentially when the line was parallel to the walls (Fig. 2.7/10, left, [851]). If only the floor was tilted, pigeons tested in the dark preferred a line that was approximately perpendicular to the floor. However, when the chamber was lit, the pigeons regarded a line parallel to the walls as vertical (Fig. 2.7/10, right, [536]). Apparently, the subjective vertical of pigeons is determined primarily by visual and secondarily by substrate tilt cues.

In experiments on the corresponding perceptual system in octopus, Wells

Fig. 2.7/10 Homing pigeons were trained to peck at a vertical line on the wall of a chamber whose sides and floor could be independently tilted sideways. In the drawings, only the feet of the pigeons are visible. The diagrams show the percentage of correct responses as a function of the angle formed by the line and the floor (β_s) or the line and the bottom edge of the chamber (λ_s). The correct response rate is maximal when the line is parallel to the chamber walls (i.e., the visual vertical) no matter whether the chamber is tilted (by γ = 16°) and the floor is horizontal (left) or the floor is tilted (by τ = 24°) and the walls are vertical (right). (Left modified from [851]; right, [536])

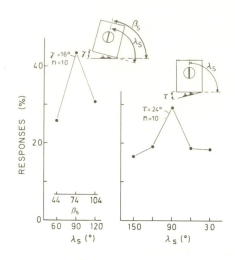

trained animals to grab prey only when a geometrical figure was in a particular orientation [911]. Normal animals (with statocysts) could distinguish the correct pattern from others (such as vertical from horizontal rectangles, Fig. 2.7/11). This ability was lost when the statocysts were removed. Analysis showed that the critical factor was the orientation of the pattern with respect to the eye. A normal octopus compensates for changes of position in space by moving its eyes so that the pupil slits are kept almost horizontal (Fig. 2.7/12, compare 3.10.2.2). In animals lacking statocysts the eyes always remain in the same position relative to the body. If the stimulus happens to be perpendicular to the pupil slits, the octopus grabs the prey. These results are compatible with the circuit diagram of a chain process (Fig. 2.7/13). A change in body position with respect to gravity (α) releases compensatory eye movements (δ). These influence the alignment of the object on the retina (β). Body position (α) also affects this alignment, since the eyes move with the body. The signal about the retinal position of the

Fig. 2.7/11 The effect of bilateral statocyst removal on shape discrimination of octopuses trained to attack a) vertical rectangles and b) black discs (positive signs). The closed circles show the responses to positive signs, the open circles to negative signs, statocyst removal at arrow. In a) each data point represents the mean of ten animals; in b), of five animals. Note that statocyst removal abolishes the octopuses' ability to discriminate between a vertical and a horizontal rectangle, but not a black and a white disc. (Modified from [911])

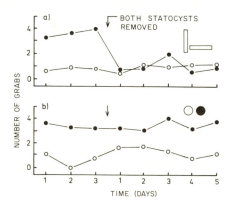

Fig. 2.7/12 Orientation of the eyes of an octopus before (upper) and after (lower) bilateral statocyst removal. After statocyst removal the slit pupil is always in the same position relative to the body regardless of the body position. (Modified from [911])

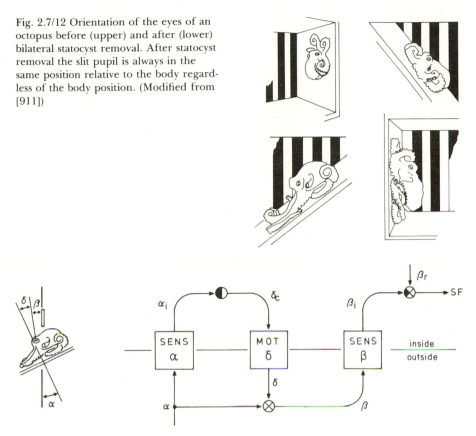

Fig. 2.7/13 Flow diagram of the visual perception of an object's orientation by octopus. The angle between body and gravity (α) is measured by the statocysts (*SENS* α). The position signal α_i causes a compensatory movement of the eyes (*MOT* δ; angle between eyes and body, δ). The orientation of the object to the eye (β) depends on α and δ. The visual signal β_i is compared with the reference value β_r to give *SF*, the signal that releases prey attack when β_i coincides with β_r.

object (β_i) is compared with the reference value (β_r). If the object is correctly oriented with respect to the eye, *SF* releases a grab.

2.8 DISTANT ORIENTATION

> The environment contains numerous cues that could give directional information to a migrating bird. Natural selection should favour the development of abilities to make use of all such information.—S. T. Emlen

Distant orientation in the sense of Watson and Lashley [898] leads an animal indirectly to a goal that is beyond the limits of direct sensory perception.

Actual distance is no criterion. The journeys of migrating birds, halfway around the world, and the search by an ant for its nest, a few meters away, both fall under this heading.

Understandably, it is the spectacular, extensive animal migrations that spark the imagination. Year by year they journey, often in the millions: over land—the caribou in Canada, the gnu and other herd animals in the African steppes, newt and toad to spawning ponds; in the seas—walrus, whale, salmon, eel, and spiny lobster (Fig. 1.2/1); and through the air—butterfly, migrating locust, and myriad bird species, from cranes to carrier pigeons specially bred since antiquity for sending messages over long distances.

Most migrations invariably follow the same routes, even over hundreds and thousands of kilometers. Nature lovers are fascinated by the mysterious feats of orientation, and in the last few decades science, too, has devoted much attention to them. The results can be found in many books and papers (in general [644, 750, 752]; birds [196, 280, 430, 571, 291]; insects [408]; fish [302, 850, 306]; and whales [445]. Their main theme is migration over great distances, so that we do not need to treat details here. Let us instead concentrate on the underlying mechanisms.

The methods for investigating these phenomena are best illustrated by those commonly used to study bird migration. One of the oldest field methods is to release birds marked with rings and to note the site of recovery. Recent technical developments allow tracking of swarms or individuals with radar equipment or small planes [643, 488, 195]. For laboratory studies of direction tendencies the registration of migratory restlessness in circular cages has proven valuable. The birds alight preferentially on perches in line with the migratory direction. Each perching is recorded, usually automatically. Light barriers can also be used to register the direction of movements in the cage. A device as simple as a paper funnel can also be used to determine direction tendencies. The bird stands in the middle of the funnel on an inked sponge, hops up onto the side of the funnel and slides back onto the sponge.

Griffin [277] made one of the earliest attempts to sort out the known orientation patterns of birds. He differentiated three basic forms: (I) search for familiar landmarks, (II) compass orientation, and (III) navigation. In an analysis and expansion, Schmidt-Koenig [750, 751] defined the concepts more precisely, and introduced the term "piloting" for (I).

Usually an orientation system combines several of these processes. As the introductory citation points out, animals have many resources at their disposal. We can assume that they will exploit them fully to meet the various demands and conditions that they encounter.

A consideration of distant orientation raises three questions: (1) Which direction will be taken? (2) How is this direction adjusted and maintained? (3) How is the goal recognized? As yet, there is no definite answer to the

first question. We can only infer how a migrating bird knows which direction to take. Many birds such as geese migrate as a family or flock, mostly
a mixture of adults and first-flight juveniles. By following the adults, the
juveniles might learn the way or gain experience that enhances their orientation abilities. This is supported by the results of displacement experiments such as Perdeck's starling experiment ([661], Fig. 2.8/1). The starlings usually winter from northern France to the south of England. Birds
in transit across Holland were caught and transported at right angles to
their direction of migration into Switzerland, where they were freed. Recovery of ringed birds showed that experienced adults and first-flight juveniles behaved differently. Juveniles resumed their original migration
direction and were eventually recovered in an area transposed from their
normal winter quarters by the displacement interval. The experienced birds,
however, were caught mainly in their "normal" winter quarters, so that
they must have altered their course in a northerly direction. The behavior
of the juveniles suggests an inborn component of migratory orientation,
and the behavior of the adults indicates the importance of experience.

In the reproductive season many species invariably seek out the same
places, frequently those where they themselves matured (cockchafers, toads,
salmon). They must have acquired the orientation values as juveniles on
their first migration. In several cases a direction tendency seems to be
genetically determined (beach fleas [653], see 2.11).

2.8.1 Compass Course Orientation

The beach flea hops only a few meters to the water's edge, whereas the
bee flies several hundred meters to a food source and the chiffchaff
migrates thousands of kilometers to its wintering grounds. They all utilize

Fig. 2.8/1 Starlings captured in Holland
(*H*) during their fall migration (shaded
arrow) were ringed and transported into
Switzerland (*S*) where they were released.
Experienced birds flew to their usual winter quarters (black arrow), but first-flight
juveniles (white arrow) were recovered in
an area (dashed line) that was displaced
from the normal winter quarters (solid
line) by the transport route. (Modified
from [661])

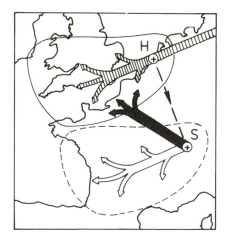

the sun compass to maintain their course. Other compass references are the stars, the earth's magnetic field, and even the moon [649].

Before we go into descriptions of these processes let us consider a geometrical complication of course adjustment. Course alignment and body alignment can be altered separately (compare 1.3.4).

2.8.1.1 Course-constant and Space-constant Body Alignment

Alignment of the body and of the direction of locomotion are two rotatory processes that can vary independently. This can be seen in the walking of the ghost crab (Fig. 2.8/2). In some of its course changes, the crab's body alignment follows the course (course-constant body alignment). In others only the legs change their walking direction, and the body remains pointed in the same direction as before the course change (space-constant body alignment). Course changes in which body alignment is space constant may also be oriented to external stimuli, such as the sun, even though the eyes always register the same stimulus direction.

Wehner found a similar form of course orientation in desert ants [901]. Foraging ants maintain a sun compass course by intermittently turning their heads toward the sun, apparently to get a compass reading. This is a case of space-constant head alignment, but for brief periods only. The ant's body maintains a course-constant alignment.

Jander [405] has proposed new terms for these two forms of course orientation. He uses "efferent" orientation when the body is kept space-constant, because only the motor or efference-guided activity is altered. "Afferent" course orientation occurs when the body is turned into the course direction, since the consequent alteration in the body-stimulus angle also changes the afferences. We should bear in mind, however, that affer-

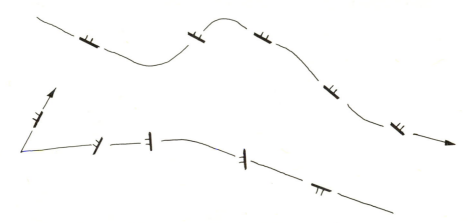

Fig. 2.8/2 Two walks of the ghost crab *Ocypode*, showing the alignment of its transverse body axis (bar) with respect to its course (arrow). (Modified from [147])

ences and efferences are involved in both cases. The spatial cues are taken into account, whether they stay constant or not.

A flow diagram that has the capacity for course-constant and space-constant course orientation is shown in Fig. 2.8/3. Two spatial cues combine to give a course angle (κ): the body-sun angle β inputs through the sensory apparatus, while the information about δ is idiothetic (= efference copy = branch of δ_c). For a course change in which the body alignment (β) is kept constant, a common control of the two variables κ and δ is necessary. This is represented by activating both controlling variables δ_r and κ_r. If β is to be changed, only κ_r is altered.

2.8.1.2 Sun, Star, and Magnetic Compasses

The sun, moon, stars, and the polarized light of the blue sky present natural cues for compass orientation. These forms are combined under the expressions astro-compass or celestial compass orientation. The earth's magnetic

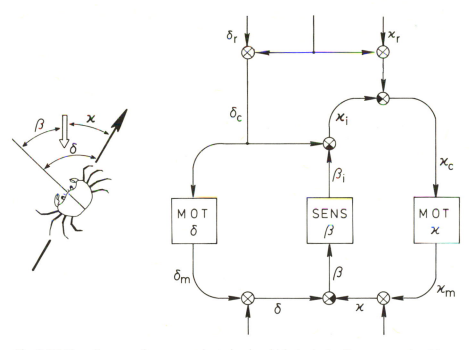

Fig. 2.8/3 Flow diagram of a course orientation in which the body alignment can be either course- or space-constant. The course angle (κ) relative to the reference (e.g., the sun, white arrow in inset) is controlled by two inputs: β, the angle of the body to the sun, and δ, the angle of the body to the course direction. Information about the latter is idiothetic, coming from motor commands for leg movement (δ_c). The motor output δ_m adjusts the alignment of the body relative to the walking direction, and the motor output κ_m, the walking direction relative to the sun.

field also provides an extensive and, unlike the celestial compasses, space-constant reference. Only a brief survey is given here (for more detail see 3.1 and 3.4).

Sun compass orientation was discovered almost simultaneously in birds by Kramer [472] and in bees by von Frisch [234]. Von Frisch found a further visual reference for course orientation, which was also dependent upon the sun's position—polarized daylight. This is especially useful at twilight.

Sauer initiated the study of star compass orientation [733, 734, 735, 736]. Several species of warblers were tested in circular cages, either under the open sky or in planetaria. They were disoriented under overcast skies, but oriented when stars were visible. Subsequent experiments have shown that birds need to see only the circumpolar stars ([193, 194] see 3.1.4). There are many indications that birds recognize star configurations independently of their placement in the sky. They may, for instance, be able to extrapolate north from a familiar constellation much as we find the North Star from the Big Dipper.

Experience seems to play a role in a bird's stellar orientation [948, 949, 950, 196]. In a series of experiments European robins were first shown an artificial "star" pattern in the absence of a magnetic field. Their migratory restlessness was not oriented. When the same birds were again exposed to the star pattern in the presence of a magnetic field, their activity was oriented in a magnetic northeast direction corresponding to their spring migrations. The birds maintained this direction tendency in a third experiment in which they were again shown the star pattern and shielded from the magnetic field. They had acquired the ability to orient according to the pattern, having learned its direction by association with the magnetic field. Apparently the direction of a constellation must be learned, whereas that of the magnetic field is genetically fixed [1027]. Wiltschko calls the former "secondary" and the latter "primary" orientation (see 3.4).

Compensation for the movement of celestial bodies. As early as 1913 Santschi (cited in [96]) suggested "that ants take the passage of time into account and shift the localization of the source of light on their compound eyes accordingly" (p. 16). It has since been shown that animals compensate for the sun's daily passage (e.g., bees [235]); and perhaps also for movement of the moon (*Talitrus* [649], *Orchestoidea corniculata* [197]).

Figure 2.8/4 illustrates the astronomical relationships of the sun's apparent movement across the skies. The earth is a revolving globe illuminated from the side by the sun. At a locus (*A*) on the northern hemisphere in the shadow of the sun, it is nighttime. If an inhabitant of this locus faces north, its left side is toward the west, and its right is toward the east, the direction into which the earth is turning. Dawn appears from the east when *A* turns into the light from the sun (A_1). Assuming that the earth has a

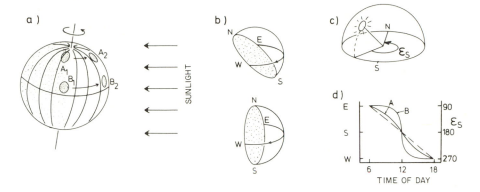

Fig. 2.8/4 Apparent movement of the sun across the sky. a) Globe with a locus in the north (A) and near the equator (B). At sunrise they (A_1, B_1) are on the boundary between the light (day) and the shadow (night) side; at noon they face the sun (A_2, B_2). b) The path of the sun in the sky over A and B. c) Position of the sun in the afternoon, showing the sun height (angle subtended by dotted line) and its azimuth (ϵ_s). d) Sun's azimuth as a function of the time of day for loci A and B.

rotation time of 24 h, 6 h ($=90°$) after dawn locus A is facing the sun. For an inhabitant of A the sun is directly to the south (A_2) and has attained its highest point in the sky, its culmination. At a point farther south (B_2) the sun's culmination is higher than at A: The height and course of the sun's arc through the sky depend on the geographical latitude of the point from which it is observed.

We can distinguish two components of the sun's position: its height over the horizon and its angular distance from north, its azimuth. Imagine that you are standing in the middle of a disc that is bounded by the horizon. The sun, like all celestial bodies, can be represented as a point on a dome that fits over the disc (Fig. 2.8/4b,c). The height of the sun is measured as the angle between the surface of the disc and a line joining you and the sun. If you project a line from the sun onto the horizon, the angle between this point on the horizon and north is the azimuth (Fig. 2.8/4c, ϵ_s). Since this establishes the sun's compass direction, directional compensation for the sun's apparent movement must be based on changes in the sun's azimuth.

This is accomplished by a compensation mechanism that continuously changes the course direction relative to the sun. For example, the eastward course of a flying animal is toward the sun in the morning and deviates more and more to the left as the day progresses. At noon it is flying 90° to the left of the sun, and in the evening, away from the sun. The compensation mechanism is based on an "internal clock." This expression encompasses the physiological systems that control various rhythmic processes such as alternating activity and resting phases. It is called internal because its controlling factors are rooted within the animal. However, since the period of the internal clock is seldom exactly 24 h, external influences (*Zeitgeber* = pacemaker) are required to reset the clock, e.g., to synchronize the internal period with the external day. This is reflected in the term *circadian* rhythm, which is derived from *circa*, approximately, and *dies*, day.

The natural light-dark cycle, or photoperiod, is an important external *Zeitgeber*, which synchronizes the internal clock with the sun clock. The internal clock can be reset by experimentally altering the photoperiod. This manipulation has been used to demonstrate the control of the sun orientation by an internal clock. Hoffman performed the first experiment of this kind [347] on starlings. Comparable experiments by Schmidt-Koenig [749] on homing pigeons provided similar results. Starlings that had been taught in an arena to walk east to get food were trained to a light-dark cycle that was shifted back 6 h from the normal day. The experimental "day" began at noon local time with the switching on of lights and ended at midnight when the lights were turned off. After they had adjusted to this new rhythm, the starlings were retested in the arena (Fig. 2.8/5). They moved directly toward the sun at noon, a time when prior to training they had sought food at 90° to the left of the sun. The starlings had set their compass direction according to their internal clock time.

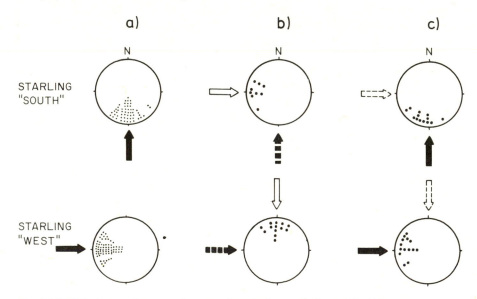

Fig. 2.8/5 Direction preferences of two starlings before and after a 6 h shift of their internal clocks. Starling "south" was trained to find food in the south; "west," in the west. a) Scores before clock shift, b) after clock shift, and c) after being retrained to local time (like a). Black arrows denote the original training direction; white arrows the direction expected after shifting the internal clock. (Modified from [347])

The sun's path through the sky depends on the geographical latitude (Fig. 2.8/4). In the latitudes of the moderate zones it is relatively shallow; near the equator, very steep. The average velocity of the sun is 15°/h, as can easily be calculated from the time it takes the earth to complete a rotation (360°/24 h = 15°/h). The azimuthal motion of the sun, however, approaches this value only near each pole where the sun moves along the horizon (Fig. 2.8/6). The closer one gets to the equator, the more arched the sun's path. Plots of the azimuth against the time of day are flat at their beginnings and ends (morning and evening) and steep around the middle of the day. This means that the azimuthal angular velocity is higher at midday than in the morning and evening. The steepness of the middle section of the curve increases toward the equator. At noon on the equator the curve jumps abruptly from east to west.

The sun compass orientation of many animals is based on a time program that is adapted to the local azimuthal motion of the sun (Fig. 2.8/7, [75, 77]). As a migrating bird flies from the northern to the southern latitudes, the sun's arc, which was inclined southward at the beginning of its migration, gets more upright from day to day. At the equator it is vertical. In the southern hemisphere it leans more and more to the north. Practically nothing is known about how a bird compensates for this continuous shift.

It appears from clock-shifting experiments [193, 194, 570] that stellar orientation is independent of time. Whether this applies to all cases is not yet settled [736]. If birds, as discussed above, can extrapolate north from the star pattern, then a compensation for the movement of constellations across the sky would be superfluous.

Compass orientation in birds is summarized in the flow diagram of Fig. 2.8/8. It consists of three feedback loops: sun, star, and magnetic compass, which all terminate on the mechanism for setting flight direction (ϵ_m). Three input signals converge on a single box that determines which compass system is to be used. The loop for the sun compass course (outermost) is

Fig. 2.8/6 The sun's azimuth in the northern hemisphere as a function of the time of day on March 31 or September 23 for different latitudes. 0 = Equator, 5 = Bogotá, 20 = Mexico City, 40 = Madrid, and 90 = North Pole.

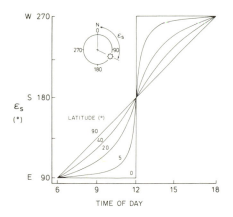

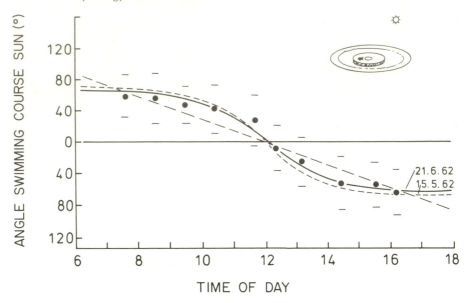

Fig. 2.8/7 Sun compass courses (closed circles) of fish as a function of the time of day. The fish were trained to find cover in the south when placed in an experimental tank (inset). The curves show the sun's azimuthal motion at the time and place of the experiments. (Modified from [77])

linked to a time compensator. A change in the sun's azimuth enters as a disturbance value and influences the sun compass angle (β_s). Its signal (β_{si}) is subtracted from the compensator signal (β_{sr}), which depends on the endogenous circadian rhythm and on an exogenous *Zeitgeber* (Z_e). The signal follows the same time course as β_s, keeping the result of the compensatory computation β_{sc} constant. This is directly transformed into ϵ_i, which gives the geographical course and is checked against the reference value ϵ_r. Errors lead to turning tendencies for course correction.

Compensation over longer time periods. The daily passage of the sun across the skies necessitates a circadian change in the compass angle if a geographic course is to be maintained. The compensation program of young salmon on their seaward migration differs from this in two respects. It extends over a longer period of time, and it must compensate for directional changes in the route instead of changes in the sun's position. The course of a salmon smolt is not constant but is determined by the geography of the river. Experiments on Canadian salmon [282] suggest that the direction-time program is endogenous. In the spring the smolts migrate from the sources of the rivers where they hatched and developed to the sea. Their routes are often quite complicated, through a labyrinth of rivers and lakes (Fig. 2.8/9). Some smolts were caught near their spawning grounds and held in

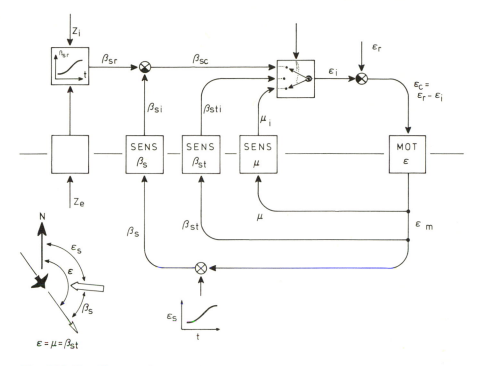

Fig. 2.8/8 Flow diagram of course orientation to sun, stars, and magnetic field with compensation for the sun's apparent movement. The angle of the course relative to the sun is β_s; to the stars, β_{st}; to the magnetic field, μ ; and to north, ϵ. ϵ_s is the azimuth of the sun; Z_i, the internal *Zeitgeber*, and Z_e, the external *Zeitgeber*.

tanks with an open view of the sky. Later, others were caught at sites farther down their seaward route. A close correspondence was found between the direction of the tank-held smolts and that of migrating smolts tested on the same day. The orientation appears to be controlled by a time program that quite accurately conforms to the seaward route.

A comparable mechanism guides the migration of the garden warbler [294] and seems to depend on an endogenous annual rhythm (Fig. 2.8/10, compare 2.8.4).

2.8.2 Navigation

Navigation is the theory and practice of charting a course to a remote goal. It includes finding and holding the "correct" direction at any time and place but not necessarily recognizing and reaching the goal.

The term vector navigation (also vector orientation), however, denotes

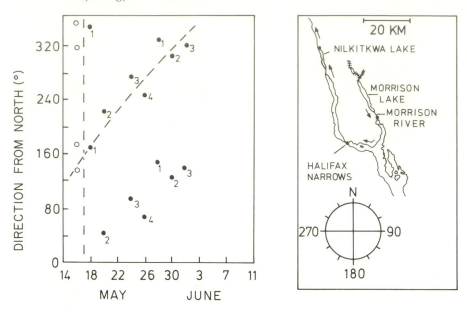

Fig. 2.8/9 Orientation of sockeye salmon from Babine Lake, Canada, during seaward migration in 1961. Salmon smolts from the tributary spawning grounds (cross-hatching on map) were netted in the Morrison River and held in open tanks under natural light conditions. The data points give their preferred direction at dusk (bimodal distribution 180° apart indicates orientation to polarized light); the numbers show how many animals are included in each point. Other smolts were netted at the same location, marked, and released. Some of them were recaptured 10–14 days later at Halifax Narrows and Nilkitkwa Lake. The route they were following corresponded to the directional changes of the tank-held animals during the same time period. (Modified from [282])

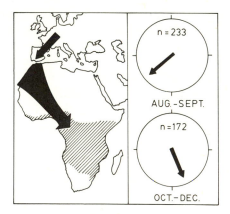

Fig. 2.8/10 Left: Migration directions (arrows) to winter quarters (shaded area) of the garden warbler, *Sylvia borin*. Right: The upper arrow is the mean heading of migratory restlessness shown by caged birds from August to September; lower arrow, October to December. The directional preferences coincide with the primary migratory directions for the corresponding time periods. (Modified from [294])

the ability to orient via both direction and distance to the goal (see 2.8.4). Note that it is not the same as the vector processing of stimuli (see 2.6 and 2.7). In vector orientation the routes, not the stimuli, are given as vectors.

Vector navigation is not limited to globe-spanning migrations. Jander [401] has used the term vector integration for an orientation process of ants. When an ant leaves its nest, the individual stretches of its route are assimilated as vectors: the directional components by a compass mechanism (sun or polarized light) and the length components presumably by a time measurement. The individual vectors are used to calculate the direction of the nest for the return trip. After a meandering excursion through the countryside, the desert ant returns straight to its nest by orienting to the pattern of polarized light of the sky ([902, 903, 1022], compare 3.1.2). The desert isopod *Hemilepistus reaumuri* uses the sun and (apparently) idiothetic distance information from its outbound journey to find its way back to its burrow (Linsenmair, personal communication). A spider also employs idiothetic and visual cues to return to its retreat (compare 3.11). Navigation on a purely idiothetic basis is also possible. Ghost and fiddler crabs can find their way home even if they are forced to make detours on the way out (Fig. 3.11/3).

At present two alternative theories are receiving widespread attention, inertial navigation and bicoordinate navigation.

Inertial navigation. Eugene Marais was probably the first to formulate a hypothesis about the homing ability of carrier pigeons (and related capabilities in humans). His experimentally based considerations led him to the conclusion that "every movement in space, every turn of the body around its axes is registered in the subconscious. An animal at the end of a journey, even one made in a box, possesses a complete psychic map of its route" ([553], from a posthumously published treatise; Marais died in 1936). Today his theories would be classified under inertial navigation, which is homing based on the turns of the outward journey as registered by inertia sensors. The return path is oriented according to a reconstruction of the outward path from these values and their intervening stretches. The inertia sensors of the homing pigeon are generally assumed to be the labyrinths; however, it has been shown that pigeons can still home even after ablation of the semicircular canals [893]. In fact, it is questionable whether pigeons use inertial navigation, since they are still capable of homing when transported to the releasing site under full narcosis [890] or continuous rotation [571]. A possible example of inertial navigation has been found in female gerbils, which seek out lost sucklings and carry them straight home [1003]. Experiments using defined stimulation of the semicircular canals suggest that the information about turns carried out during the search originates from the labyrinth.

Bicoordinate navigation. An animal's ability to determine its geographical location and the direction to the goal can serve as a basis for navigation. One possible means for location determination is derived from the way a map is partitioned into a bicoordinate grid of meridians and parallel circles. Coordinates such as longitude and latitude define a location on the globe.

The idea that birds employ bicoordinate navigation was first discussed by Kramer [472, 473] and has since won considerable support. According to this concept a bird fixes its location within the framework of a coordinate grid (= map) and sets its direction with the aid of a compass (concept of "map and compass"). Such a grid might consist of two transecting gradient fields, which do not have to be at right angles to each other. For example, in case A of Fig. 2.8/11 the gradient intensity increases from 2 to 4 as a bird flies in the direction of the y axis. In case B, locus S is defined by $y = 2$, $x = 2$; and the bird flies at a compass angle ϵ toward locus Z.

We can only speculate as to the geophysical nature of coordinate grids. Based on his investigations on homing pigeons in northern Italy, Papi [650] proposed that pigeons orient according to olfactory cues from their surroundings. The working hypothesis is that geographical regions are characterized by certain odor combinations that are carried by the wind. The pigeons learn these odors and associate them with compass directions relative to their loft. If they smell an odor combination at a releasing site that at home is carried by the north wind, they "know" that they are north of home and must fly south. This is supported by the results of experiments in which wind from one direction was conducted via a system of fans and corridors onto the pigeons from another direction [394]. The vanishing bearings of these pigeons' releases deviated from those of the controls by the angle with which the wind direction was changed (Fig. 2.8/12). In another experiment the wind at the home loft was deflected into another direction by large screens. These animals also showed a deviation from the controls that tended in the direction of the wind deflection [891].

Although similar studies in North America and Germany either did not lead to conclusive results or were interpreted differently [304, 651, 754], little doubt remains that olfactory cues affect pigeon homing [1019, 996]. These capabilities may be developed or utilized only in areas with "distinctive" odors. It is conceivable that the pigeon uses a kind of map whose

Fig. 2.8/11 Coordinate grid of two obliquely transecting gradients (x and y). Bird A flies in the direction of the y gradient; B flies from point S to point Z at an angle of ϵ to north.

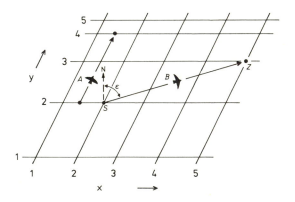

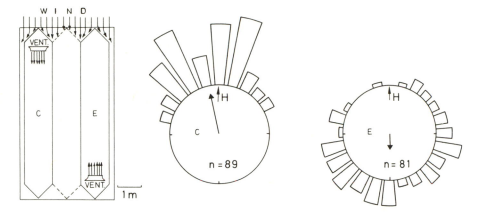

Fig. 2.8/12 Homing of pigeons in wind corridors. The experimental setup is shown on the left. Ventilators switched on as soon as the wind blew parallel to the corridors. Group C (left corridor) received outside air from the wind direction; group E (right corridor), from the opposite direction. Controls (middle corridor) received natural wind. The vanishing bearings for releases 20–290 km from the home loft are shown for C (middle) and E (right). H denotes the direction of the home loft. The length of each column is proportional to the number of vanishing bearings (n = total) in each 15° sector. The length of the mean vector is a measure for the significance of the data (radius = 1, Raleigh test). The control group (not shown) was similar to C; E tended in the opposite direction. (Modified from [394])

coordinate system is partially given by odor gradients carried by the wind.

Wallraff [894] has recently examined the theoretical prerequisites of the coordinate grid and its linkage with a compass system by computer simulation and compared them with the wealth of experimental data on pigeon homing. He relates the different homing performances of pigeons released at different distances from home (Fig. 2.8/13) to the structure of a coordinate grid. The improved homing perfomance at distances over 100 km may be due to the fact that gradient fields are stretched out over greater distances. At shorter distances the grid is too coarse for the pigeons to comprehend. In the familiar surroundings of the home region, other mechanisms such as landmark orientation may take over.

Still other orientation abilities may be important, as shown by experiments on pigeons whose vision was impaired by frosted contact lenses. Although they could distinguish only differences in brightness, they were able to return to the area of the home loft [745, 755, 753].

According to a third navigation hypothesis, *sun navigation* [569, 571, 660], a bird determines its geographical location by relating it to the sun's path. Height and azimuth movement over a given time span are characteristic for any particular location (compare Fig. 2.8/4). A bird might be able to determine from differences in the sun's path that it has moved from one

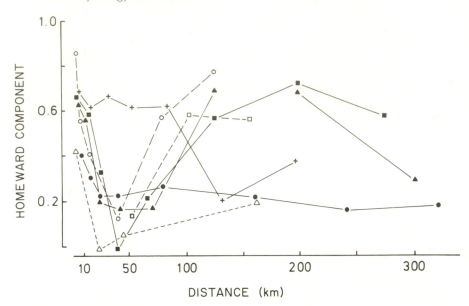

Fig. 2.8/13 Homing performance of homing pigeons. Each curve represents results from one experimental series. The homing component is computed from the deviation from the home direction and the standard deviation of the vanishing bearings [894].

geographical locus to another [660]. Matthews [569, 571] proposed that a bird extrapolates the noon height from segments of the sun's arc and compares them for different loci. This would require a very exact measurement of time and the sun's path, and it is unlikely that birds possess mechanisms with the necessary precision. As yet, experimental studies have proven negative, and the sun navigation hypothesis does not have many adherents [196, 291, 752]. Still another concept, the sun compass hypothesis, presumes exact data about latitude, time of day, and height of culmination of sun (Mittelstaedt, personal communication).

2.8.3 Landmark Orientation ("Piloting")

The previous section dealt mainly with astronomical navigation. Orientation by landmarks is a form of terrestrial navigation. Distant orientation encompasses only those landmark orientations in which the landmarks represent stations along the way to a goal. When the landmark is the immediate target of the orientation, it is classified as proximate orientation. Here we shall concentrate on the abilities of migratory birds to orient according to landmarks. The voluminous material on arthropods is treated in detail in 3.1.

Migratory birds appear to orient according to conspicuous geographical formations such as mountain chains, coastlines, and river valleys [196, 887, 95]. But we must take care not to jump to hasty conclusions. For example, many species of northern European birds migrate along the north face of the Alps and the wide Swiss valley bordered by the Alps and the Jura Mountains [95]. Apparently these birds do not use these mountain chains as direct visual landmarks. They follow the direction of the valley even when the mountains are not visible from the distance due to low-lying cloud cover or misty weather. As the valley is not in the main migratory direction, Bruderer [95] interprets this "detour" from the migratory path as an evolutionary adaptation to the geography.

When crossing the southern Alps, birds also follow mountain valleys and passes [95]. It is open to debate if they use such geographical features as path markers, or if they follow them out of physical necessity. Both may be the case.

Landmark orientation usually refers to the determination of course direction from familiar landmarks. But in a subcategory, "dead reckoning orientation," markers may merely stabilize a predetermined course such as a sun compass course (Vleugel, cited in [291]). If the sun disappears behind the clouds or the bird encounters a strong crosswind, it might set its sights on a landmark in front of it, with reference to one behind it, and fly a straight line between them [196]. Upon approaching the front target, the bird selects a new pair of reference points to fly between. Such a strategy would enable a bird to maintain a straight course over long distances.

2.8.4 Reaching the Goal

Direction finding alone does not bring an animal to its goal. There are several alternative strategies which an animal can use to eventually find it: (1) recognizing the physical characteristics of the goal, (2) measuring its distance, (3) following a motor program based on stored idiothetic or inertial data, (4) defining it in terms of a coordinate system, and (5) searching for it.

Alternative (1) has been thoroughly studied in bees. Form, color, and scent determine which flowers the bee will fly to within its goal area [235]. This is a proximate orientation since the bee orients to direct signals from the goal object.

Alternatives (2) and (3) are vector orientations (see 2.8.2). The ability of a bee to determine from its food reserves how far it must fly is an example of alternative (2). Before a bee leaves for a food source that it has learned about from another bee, it ingests only enough nourishment to reach its goal (Istomina-Tsvetkova, cited in [235]). As soon as it runs out of fuel, it starts to search for the food source. The migratory restlessness of birds may also provide a measure for distance [57, 58, 56, 294]. Under normal conditions it lasts just long enough for the birds to reach their winter quarters [294]. This is shown by experiments on warblers [292]. If the duration of migratory restlessness determines distance, it must be tuned to the velocity of migration. Migrating birds were caught in Germany, ringed, and released. Their velocity was calculated from the location and time of subsequent recovery. Multiplying the velocity by the duration of migratory restlessness measured on caged birds gives a distance that, when plotted along the migration route, coincides with the winter quarters (Fig. 2.8/14). Idiothetic homing is an example of alternative (3). A fiddler crab uses the sequence of movements it made on its outward journey to determine the direction and distance it must cover to return to its burrow (see Fig. 3.11/3).

The vertical migration of many aquatic organisms might be considered an example of (4). The pressure gradient serves as a coordinate system, and the goal water layer is defined by a particular pressure [839, 840].

Alternative (5), search orientation, is often used to supplement the other alternatives. The success of this strategy depends on alternative (1). A systematic search brings the animal close enough to perceive its goal so that proximate orientation can take over. A bee must sometimes circle its goal area several times before finding its food source. Ants returning home also begin search maneuvers if they do not come upon the nest opening right away [351]. Goal-finding mechanisms (2–4) are not always sufficiently precise to hit a small goal from relatively great distances on the first try. For this reason many species terminate "goal-directed" orientation just before they reach the place where the goal is supposed to be and initiate search orientation. Both the desert isopod *Hemilepistus reaumuri* [345] and the desert ant *Cataglyphis bicolor* [1025] discontinue their straight course a

Fig. 2.8/14 Breeding areas (lines slanted to the left) and winter quarters (lines slanted to the right) of the chiffchaff and the willow warbler. Dots indicate the end of migration as predicted by the product of duration of migratory restlessness and migration velocity (with standard error) for two groups of chiffchaff and three of willow warblers. (Modified from [292])

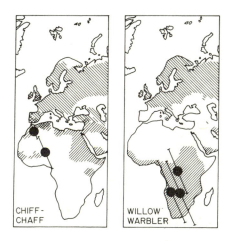

short distance before their burrows and start a crisscross pattern that normally soon brings them to their burrow entrances. If they do not find the entrance, their search encompasses more and more of the outlying area. This strategy ensures a high probability of success even if an animal misses the opening the first time.

2.9 HUMAN PERCEPTUAL AND MOTOR ORIENTATION OF POSITION AND MOVEMENT

Human orientation does not differ in any essential way from that of animals. However, some systems such as perceptual orientation are more easily investigated in humans because of our ability to analyze our perceptions and communicate them to others. Of the many known systems of human orientation [376], we shall consider only the positional orientations based on the detection of position and movement. This includes both the perceptual and motor orientation of the body and of objects.

2.9.1 Orientation to the Vertical

We perceive the position of our bodies in space. For instance, we know when we are lying on our side (perceptual orientation of body position), and we can change this position (motor orientation of body). In addition, we have a conception of directions in space such as up and down (vertical direction). This direction can be experienced purely introspectively or recognized from the things surrounding us (perceptual orientation of objects). We can also align objects with this direction (motor orientation of objects). Sensory information about the "vertical" is a prerequisite for all these orientations. This is provided by various sensory modalities. The statolith organs and the somatosensory receptors register the direction of gravity, and the eyes evaluate the alignment of structures in our visual field (visual standard, see 2.9.1.2).

2.9.1.1 Orientation to Gravity

The effect of centrifugal forces on spatial perception is apparent to anyone who is riding in a train as it speeds around a bend. If you look out a window on the inside of the curve, the world outside appears tilted. Telephone poles, chimneys, and trees seem to be leaning toward you. Centrifugal force and gravity interact at our gravity receptors. The resulting force is the stimulus for these receptor organs and the reference for our perception of space (3.10).

In 1875 Mach [538] had already suggested that during centrifugation the resultant force determines the vertical direction for human orientation. The centrifuge has since been used in many experiments to study the effect of gravity [87, 866, 259, 274, 635, 956, 410, 771, 884]. Perceptions described by these experiments are sometimes termed "illusions." This is misleading, since no sensory deception is involved. The perceptions are generated by real changes in the "gravity" vertical (3.10).

Orientation of body position. The effect of increased gravity on body position was investigated on experimental subjects in a chamber (gondola) that was attached to one arm of a centrifuge and could swing freely into the direction of the resultant force. For the subject, centrifugation changed the magnitude of gravity (number of G's) but not its direction. The subjects had been previously trained to maintain an upright sitting posture under normal gravity [791, 885]. When centrifuged, they had the feeling that they were leaning backward and tilted their bodies forward to compensate. In a further experiment they were trained to hold their heads tilted forward about 30°. Centrifugation had no effect on their position. In a third experiment, the head was bent even farther forward. These subjects felt as if they were tipped forward and tried to correct their position by leaning backward.

These and other results (subjective height of the horizon, see below) indicate that the utricles of the statolith organs mediate these perceptual processes. With the head bent 30° forward (neutral head position), the sensory surface of the utricle is horizontal, so the statoliths exert no shear and a change in the magnitude of gravity has no effect. In other head positions, the statoliths exert a shearing stimulus on the sense hairs, which is amplified by an increase in gravity; hence, these subjects register a change in their position.

An increase in gravity (or a decrease as in space flight) must thus affect the perception of body position. During takeoff an astronaut is exposed to strong acceleration, which presses him backward with several times the force of gravity. This shears his statoliths strongly backward, signaling a pronounced backward lean. When the space capsule stops accelerating, the backward shear vanishes, explaining why astronauts report a sensation of falling or staggering forward at this moment [261].

Orientation of objects. We relate objects and events in our environment to the vertical (or the horizontal). We can assess how an object is oriented by its look, sound, or feel, and we can, if necessary, readjust its position. The direction in which we perceive objects to be vertical is called the "subjective vertical" (*SV*). "Visual" *SV* or "tactile" *SV* connotes the sensory modality used for the assessment. Similarly, the "subjective height of the horizon" (*SH*) is where we judge objects to be in line with the horizon.

Experiments on human perception of direction often exploit our ability to judge and alter the orientation of objects. The object to be oriented may be reduced to a mere spot or line of light in a dark room. Such experiments have been performed in a centrifuge to test the effect of increased gravity on the visual *SH* [771, 773]. The subjects sitting in an upright position were first centrifuged in a lighted gondola with their eyes closed. When they opened their eyes, the front of the gondola appeared to be tilted upward, corresponding to their feeling of being tipped backward. The subjects were then tested in the unlit gondola and instructed to adjust a spot of light to coincide with the horizon. The results showed a linear dependence of the visual *SH* on the magnitude of gravity (Fig. 2.9/1). In the neutral head position (horizontal utricles), an increase in gravity had almost no effect, but the farther backward the head was inclined from this position, the greater the effect of gravity. This indicates that the subjective horizon depends on the shear on the utricles.

The *SV* and *SH* may be expressed in terms of their relation to the body (angle β) or to the true vertical or horizontal (angle λ, Fig. 2.9/2). The reference used depends on how the problem is formulated. When the question is whether the alignment is "correct," i.e., does the subjective vertical coincide with the true vertical, λ is used. An error is called the Aubert phenomenon or deviation [12] if the *SV* deviates from the true vertical toward the subject, and Müller phenomenon [610] if it deviates away from the subject. This frame of reference is relevant for considerations of space constancy (2.10.4). However, if the emphasis is on the physiological process underlying the perceptions, β is used because it is a direct

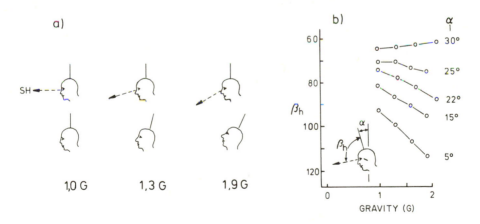

Fig. 2.9/1 a) The subjective height of the horizon (*SH*) (upper row) and the perceived body (= head) position (lower row) at different magnitudes of gravity. b) The *SH* (angle β_h) as a function of *G* for different head positions α. α = 30° approximates the position of the head at which the utricles are horizontal (indicated by dash behind the eye). (Modified from [771, 773])

Fig. 2.9/2 The subjective vertical (*SV*) as a function of body position relative to gravity (α) in terms of λ, the angle between the *SV* and the true vertical (upper curve) and in terms of β, the angle between the *SV* and the body (lower curve). The Müller phenomenon is when β > α; the Aubert phenomenon, when β < α.

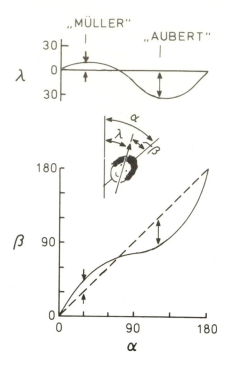

product of the adjustment mechanism (Aubert: β < α, Müller β > α, see Fig. 2.9/2). Whether or not the *SV* matches the true vertical has little bearing on the understanding of how the mechanism works.

An information flow diagram [65, 790] for setting a line to the *SV* is shown in Fig. 2.9/3. It applies also for the *SH*. Visual adjustment of the line relative to the body (β) depends on the sum of the two variables α and λ. The visual input furnishes a signal about the position of the line relative to the body ($β_i$), and the combined statolith and somatosensory input gives the position of the body with respect to gravity ($α_i$). Subtraction of these two provides a signal about the deviation of the line from the vertical ($λ_i$), which can be used directly to correct the alignment. This diagram can be supplemented to allow additional alignments by adding a controlling variable $λ_r$. Comparison of $λ_i$ with $λ_r$ results in $λ_c$, the command for adjusting the *SV* to the given reference value.

The sensory input α comprises two component systems, the statolith organs and the somatoreceptors. The effect of somatosensory input on the *SV* was investigated in subjects with normal and with defective labyrinths (no statolith cues) during centrifugation on land and immersion in a water-filled tank (no somatosensory cues). Centrifugation simultaneously altered the gravity direction by up to 30° and increased the magnitude to 1.15 *G*

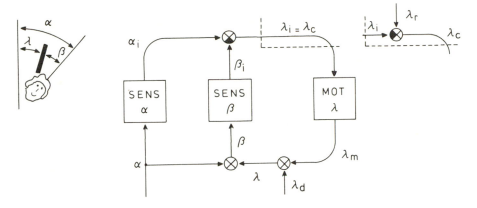

Fig. 2.9/3 Flow diagram for setting a line to the subjective vertical. The signal λ_i for the position of the line relative to the *SV* arises from the input signals α_i and β_i. The inset introduces a reference value for λ, so that the line can be adjusted to positions other than vertical.

[276]. The *SV* of both groups was affected more strongly on land than in water, demonstrating the role of somatoreceptors in the perception of body position with respect to gravity. The stronger responses of normals under both conditions reflect the influence of the statolith receptors on the *SV*. These two components of the gravity input seem to interact to give a weighted mean [495, 779].

Signals from the neck somatoreceptors are necessary to relate the position of the statolith organs in the head to the trunk of the body. Psychophysical studies on the *SV* suggest an additive process [217, 218, 883]. The effect of the neck somatoreceptors on the *SH* is shown in Fig. 2.9/4A. When only the head is tilted from 30° backward to 20° forward, the *SH* with respect to the head (β_h) shifts upward by 50° (left diagram). Since only 40° of this *SH* shift is due to statolith signals (right diagram, no neck stimulation), the remaining 10° must be due to the neck somatoreceptors. In addition, Fig. 2.9/4A shows that an increase in gravity has no effect on the neck receptors. The difference between 1 *G* and 1.6 *G* is the same for both conditions (left and right diagram). (The difference between the experimental curves and the diagonal lines give the deviations of the *SH* from the horizon that correspond to the Müller-Aubert deviations of the *SV*.)

A further somatosensory input may play a role in the adjustment of tactilely perceived objects. Centrifuge experiments showed that if the adjustment of a rod is performed by a relatively mobile body appendage like the hand, the downward pull of gravity directly affects the position of the hand [221]. This appears to furnish another cue about the up-down direction and influences the tactile (haptic) adjustment of the rod. Under-

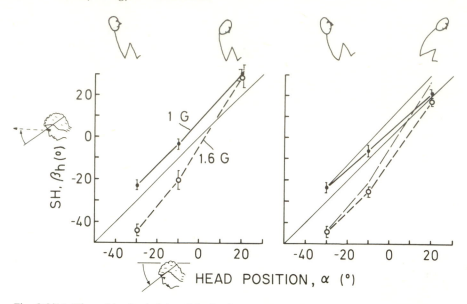

Fig. 2.9/4A The subjective height of the horizon (*SH*) as a function of head position at 1 G (closed circles) and at 1.6 G (open circles). The diagonals indicate adjustment to the true horizon. Left: Only the head is tipped forward (influence of neck receptors!). Right: The whole body is tipped so that the head is at the same angles as in the left diagram. The curves from the left have been included in the right diagram for comparison. (Modified from [773])

water experiments show that an increase in buoyancy (= decrease in gravity) affects the adjustment in the opposite direction.

2.9.1.2 The Gravity and the Visual Standard

The structure of the visual field provides an important spatial reference for our perception of the upright. Normally our visual surroundings are organized with respect to vertical and horizontal axes. This is reflected in our man-made environment by the preponderance of gravity-related contours such as walls, rooftops, windows, and doors. But even in nature the horizon and the vertical direction of plant growth dominate our visual impressions [65]. This vertical-horizontal dominance is a consequence of the laws of statics and, thereby, also an effect of gravity. In the final analysis, the visual standard also depends on the direction of gravity.

Orientation of body position. Amusement parks often have fun houses with rooms in which the walls and furnishings are all slanted in the same direction. When you stand in this room, you feel as if you were tilted. If you respond to this sensation you may lose your balance and fall down [454]. Similar rooms were used in experiments to determine the effect of the visual standard on the perception of body position [454, 954, 957]. Subjects sat in chairs that they could adjust until they felt they were sitting upright. In the tilted room they assumed an intermediate position between the tilt of the room (visual standard) and gravity (Fig. 2.9/16a).

Orientation of objects. Experimentally the visual standard may be given by a whole room, a field of parallel stripes, or a rectangular frame. Subjects are instructed to adjust a rod or a line in front of this field to the vertical. It was found that the inclination of a tilted room or of a striped field has a significant effect on the adjustment of a rod ([454], Fig. 2.9/4B). Witkin reduced the room to a rectangular illuminated frame within which a rod had to be adjusted to the vertical [954]. We shall return to this classical rod-and-frame test later.

A simple flow diagram (Fig. 2.9/4C) for such a system has two signals from the measurement of vertical, α_i for the gravity vertical and β_{oi} for the

Fig. 2.9/4B Alignment of a rod with the subjective vertical (β_h) as a function of the tilt of the experimental chamber around the Y axis (λ_h). Each curve represents the responses of a single subject when the room was tilted backward (r) or forward (v). (Modified from [454])

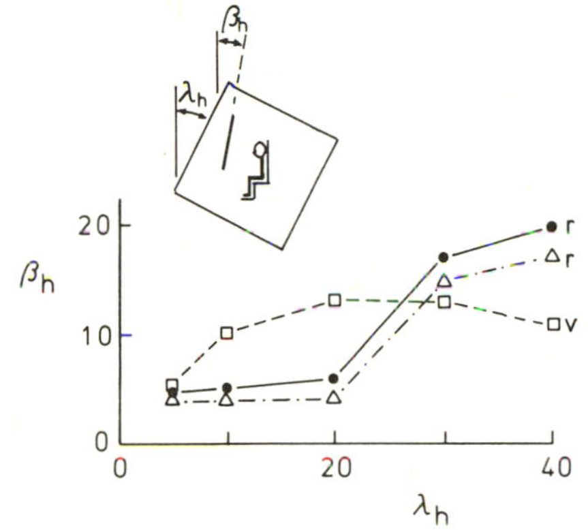

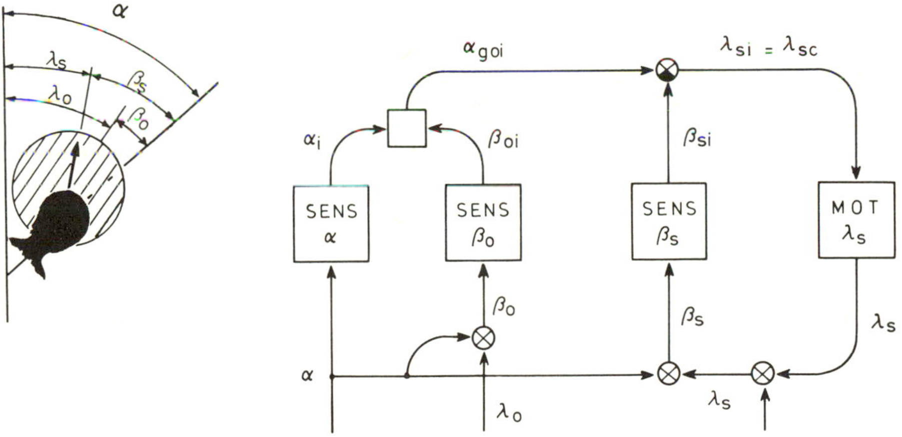

Fig. 2.9/4C Flow diagram for the adjustment of a line to the subjective vertical as a function of the true vertical and the visual standard (striped field) (compare Fig. 2.9/3). The angle of the body to gravity is α; of the head to the striped field, β_o; of the line to the head, β_s; of the striped field to gravity, λ_o; and of the line to gravity, λ_s.

visual standard. These combine to give a signal for the up-down direction (α_{goi}), which is compared with the signal for the object's direction (β_{si}). The difference can be used as a motor signal for the adjustment of the line to the vertical. The rest of the diagram continues as in Fig. 2.9/3. Experimental results indicate that the two input signals are averaged (weighted means, Figs. 2.9/10, 2.9/14).

As a field of parallel stripes slowly rotates (Fig. 2.9/5), it coincides twice with the gravity vertical ($\lambda_o = 0°$, 180°) and twice with the horizontal ($\lambda_o = 90°$, 270°). The strongest effect on the *SV* occurs when the stripes cross the vertical position. In the region 15° to each side of this position, the *SV* is pulled along.

Orientations to the vertical are influenced not only by the direction (= visual standard) but also by movement of the visual field (optokinesis).

2.9.2 Apparent Self-motion Induced by Optokinesis

We are familiar with the optomotor response from experiments on animals (1.4.3), which in a rotating striped drum try to turn with the drum. Do humans respond the same way? Let us first consider what happens when we are turned around inside a fixed striped drum. This stimulates both the visual and the vestibular systems, creating the sensation of self-motion. When we reach a constant speed, the vestibular stimulation ceases, leaving

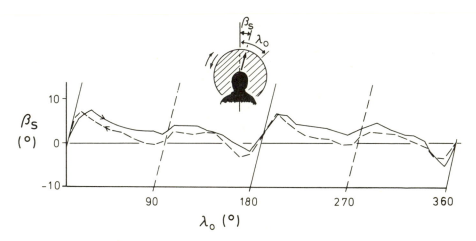

Fig. 2.9/5 The effect of a slowly rotating striped visual field on the subjective vertical. The angle β_s between the *SV* and the subject depends on the angle λ_o between the stripes and gravity. The field was rotated clockwise (solid line) and counterclockwise (dashed line). Each curve shows the mean of three measurements. (Modified from Bischof and Scherer, 1966, cited in [66])

only the movement of the visual surround across the retina. If we now close our eyes, the sensation of movement vanishes. Opening our eyes brings back the sensation of self-motion because the images of our surroundings again move across the retina. This is the same visual stimulus situation as in an "optomotor" experiment, when a striped drum is turned around a subject (Fig. 2.9/6A): Its image also moves across the retina. It is thus not surprising that after a few seconds the subject experiences an apparent self-motion or vection. The subject feels as if his surroundings were standing still and he was moving in the opposite direction of pattern movement.

A person can avoid the feeling of self-motion in this situation by turning with the pattern. This is exactly how animals behave in an optomotor experiment. If we assume that the concepts and principles of space constancy apply also to animals, their behavior must be an attempt to correct for a sensation of self-motion [258]. In his thorough analysis of this phenomenon Bischof [65] related apparent self-motion to mechanisms of space constancy. An organism assumes "a priori" that structures filling large portions of its visual field are space constant (reconstruction principle, 2.10). A relative shift of these structures signals self-motion to the constancy mechanisms, so an animal reacts as if it were being moved.

Apparent self-motion due to movement of the visual field has been the object of many investigations [326, 220, 288] since it was described in 1875 by Mach [538]. Duncker [186] used the term "induced movement." Recently, "circular vection," as proposed by Fischer and Kornmüller [220], has been readopted [85, 155]. This label is from the Latin and means riding in circles.

Vection can be induced by corresponding movements of the visual field

Fig. 2.9/6A In an optokinetic experiment a vertically striped drum is rotated around the subject, who soon experiences the feeling of self-motion, or circular vection.

in all degrees of freedom of spatial motion. If we consider only the primary axes, there are three rotatory and three translatory processes. An apparent movement around the X axis is induced by turning a patterned visual field in front of a person around this axis. This is called roll vection (Fig. 2.9/7). Accordingly, circular vection can also be called yaw vection (movement around the Z axis) and movement around the Y axis, pitch vection.

Of the translatory movements, apparent self-motion along the X axis has been studied in detail [59]. If striped patterns are moved along both sides of an experimental subject, either forward or backward, the subject experiences a "linear vection." If the pattern is moving forward, he has the feeling of riding backward and makes compensatory forward movements (Fig. 2.9/9, [498, 499]).

We experience similar translatory movements in our everyday lives, such as when we stare at flowing water (= waterfall illusion) or when we are in a train at the station and the train on the next track passes us.

Recently it has been discovered that apparent self-motion can be produced by arthrokinetic stimulation if a subject places his fingers on the wall of a rotating drum and lets its movement pull his arms along (3.9). Audiokinetic stimuli, like moving sound sources, can also cause a circular vection [484, 561].

2.9.3 Interaction between Perception of Position and Motion

2.9.3.1 Statolith Organs and Semicircular Canals

Positional changes usually stimulate both the statolith organs and the semicircular canals. A gymnast performing one grand circle after another on the high bar senses the actual motion of swinging around an axis. However, when an experimental subject in a water-filled tank is rotated with constant velocity (up to 60 rev/min) around an imaginary axis connecting his ears, he feels as if he were moving in vertical circles like those on a ferris wheel (Fig. 2.9/6B [835]). On land, subjects lying parallel to, and rotated around, a horizontal axis (barbecue rotation) experience rotation around the body axis at a constant velocity of 60 rev/min, but the ferris wheel illusion at a velocity of 180 rev/min [284].

It has been suggested that the subjects do not perceive their actual motion during rapid rotation because the statolith organs cannot respond quickly enough to follow position changes [284, 573]. However, the following explanation cannot be excluded. In the experiments, the rotatory cues from the semicircular canals, which are stimulated by changes in velocity, disappear as soon as the subjects reach a constant velocity. For the gymnast they are continuously present since his velocity is always changing. In the

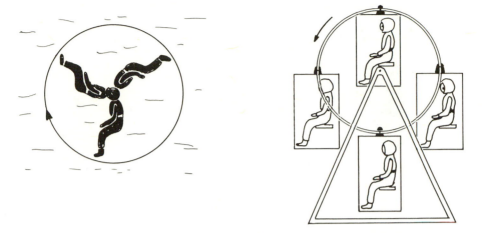

Fig. 2.9/6B Left: A person immersed in a water-filled tank was turned at a constant speed (0–20 rev/min) around an axis level with the ears (pitch). Right: The perceived motion was like riding around in circles on a ferris wheel. At higher angular velocities (20–55 rev/min) the motion seemed more and more elliptical, until at 55–60 rev/min it felt like a vertical plunging motion. (Modified from [835])

underwater experiments, rotatory cues from the somatoreceptors are also missing. Somatosensory stimulation appears also to be attenuated by faster rotation on land. We can, therefore, assume that the statolith signals dominate and turning signals are missing in the experiments in which the ferris wheel illusion occurs. The statolith organs must normally be able to register and correctly interpret linear accelerations in addition to that of gravity. For instance, they are also stimulated during jumping or when starting a car. Such linear accelerations are followed by the appropriate perceptions, although the stimulus process in the statolith organs is the same as for a tilt with respect to gravity. The critical difference is the absence of rotatory components and the corresponding rotation signals. We can thus assume that labyrinth signals that arise in the absence of turning signals (from the semicircular canals and from the somatosensory system) are interpreted as horizontal or vertical motion or a combination of both. The ferris wheel illusion is such a combination.

2.9.3.2 Position Signals from the Gravity Sensors Interfere with Vection

Since roll vection occurs in a vertical plane, it influences the perception of body position with respect to the vertical. Experimental subjects feel tilted in the direction opposite to pattern rotation and try to right themselves by leaning in the direction of pattern movement (Fig. 2.9/7). In doing so,

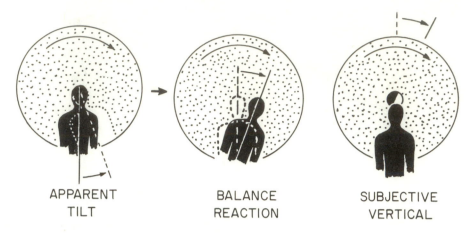

APPARENT   BALANCE   SUBJECTIVE
TILT   REACTION   VERTICAL

Fig. 2.9/7 The effect of vection on body position and *SV*. Left: A pattern of dots rotating in the frontal plane produces the sensation that the body is tilted in the opposite direction. Middle: The roll vection elicits balance reactions in the direction of rotation. Right: The subjective vertical is shifted in the direction of the pattern movement and the reactions.

however, they interfere with the positional signals from the statolith organs and the somatoreceptors, which indicate unwanted tilt. This usually leads to a compromise leaning position. However, reaction to vection can be so strong that it overrides gravity signals. In this case the subject may lose his balance and fall down. Such falling tendencies have been known for some time [220, 189, 84]. Alternating the direction of pattern movement elicits swaying of the body from side to side (Fig. 2.9/8, [158]).

When the subject is rigidly supported in an upright position and told to adjust a line to the vertical, the line ($=SV$) is shifted relative to the true vertical in the turning direction of the pattern (Fig. 2.9/7).

Movements of the visual field around the Y axis affect the perception of body position in a corresponding fashion. Pitch vection interferes with the position signals of the gravity-dependent systems, depending on head position (Fig. 2.9/12).

An illusion called the pseudo-coriolis effect [80] is apparently associated with the interaction between rotatory vections and the perception of vertical. If an experimental subject tilts his head during a circular vection, he feels as if he were moved diagonally in an arc in an awkward motion that he is unable to describe clearly. The term "pseudo-coriolis" was chosen because the illusion resembles perceptual effects that arise when the head is tilted during an actual rotation. Coriolis forces arise when parts of a rotating system are brought into another spatial arrangement relative to the axis of rotation. When, for instance, a person rotates in the horizontal

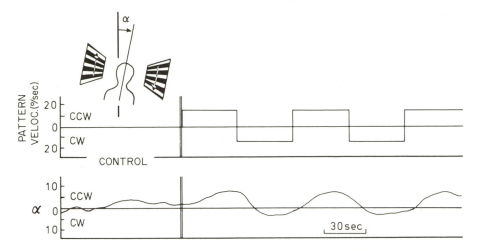

Fig. 2.9/8 The effect of roll vection on body position. A pattern of horizontal stripes on both sides of a subject alternates between clockwise (*CW*) and counterclockwise (*CCW*) movement (upper curve). The subject corrects induced tilting sensations by adjusting body position (lower curve). (Modified from [158])

plane with a normal head position, the vertical semicircular canals are in a neutral stimulus position perpendicular to the plane of rotation. Tilting the head brings them into the rotation plane, so they are stimulated and produce turning sensations.

When the head is bent (sideways or forward) during a vection, coriolis forces do not occur since there is no actual rotation. Tilting illusions are, however, not surprising if one considers that when the head is tilted, the subjective vertical deviates from the true vertical (Müller-Aubert phenomena). During a circular vection, tilting the head shifts the subjective vertical away from the axis of optokinetic stimulation (which no longer appears vertical). Tilting illusions must arise because the rotational axis of the visual field is subjectively not vertical as in the case of roll and pitch vections.

2.9.4 Input Weighting

A reference cue can have a greater or lesser effect on the orientation mechanism. This is particularly evident in the weighting ratio of two or more reference cues (2.7.3). Terms for the relative intensities of these effects are weight [777] and confidence factor [971]. The weighting of a signal depends on the characteristics of the reference cue and/or those of the sensory apparatus.

Fig. 2.9/9 Foot position as a function of the density of a checkered pattern moved at normal walking speed (4 km/h) along both sides of the subject and producing linear vection. κ is the angle between the position of the ankle during and after the stimulus. (Modified from [498])

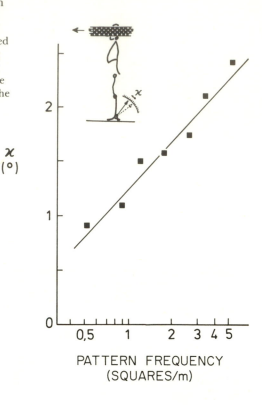

2.9.4.1 Differential Weighting

Gravity signals from the statolith organs. It has long been known that we experience great uncertainty about our position in space when we are upside down [686, 217, 218, 610, 92, 274, 771, 773, 65, 275]. The statolith organs apparently no longer furnish reliable position signals. The results of measurements of the *SV* can be interpreted in terms of this phenomenon. The variability of *SV* increases with increasing body tilt up to 180°, particularly in underwater experiments where the position signals of the somatosensory system have been largely eliminated (Fig. 2.9/11). This reflects an increasing uncertainty in the assessment of the *SV* with increasing tilt that can be attributed to a decrease in the weighting of the statolith signals.

The findings on interference of other sensory direction signals support this assumption. The influence of the visual standard on the perception of vertical increases as the head is tilted from the upright position (Fig. 2.9/10). The effects of somatosensory signals and semicircular canal signals (Fig. 2.9/11) also depend on head position, as do vections (Fig. 2.9/12, [156, 976]). Since the variability of the *SV* and the influences of other sensory inputs are at a minimum in the upright body position where the utricles

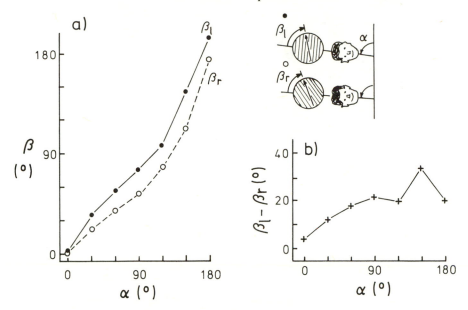

Fig. 2.9/10 The effect of a striped field on the subjective vertical (*SV*). The field is presented at a fixed angle to a line that is to be adjusted to the vertical. a) The *SV* (angle β) as a function of body position (α) for a stripe alignment to the left (β$_l$, closed circles) and to the right (β$_r$, open circles). b) The effect of the striped field (β$_l$ − β$_r$) increases with body position α. (Modified from [790])

Fig. 2.9/11 Parameters of the subjective vertical (angle β) as a function of body position (α). The variance of β (left scale) in experiments on land and underwater; β$_l$ − β$_r$ (right scale) gives the effect of a striped field (see Fig. 2.9/10) and of the semicircular canals. All curves show a decrease in weighting of statolith signals with increasing body tilt. (Modified from [790])

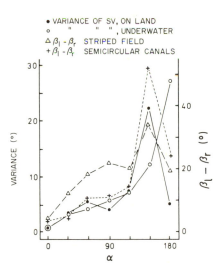

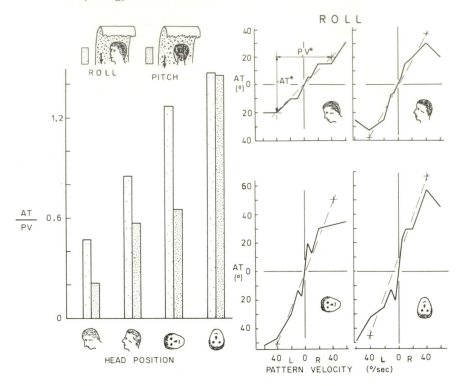

Fig. 2.9/12 Apparent tilt as a function of pattern movement around the X and Y axes (roll and pitch) for different head positions. Right: The apparent tilt (AT) as a function of pattern velocity (PV) around the X axis in the indicated head positions. The dashes on the head profiles indicate the orientation of the sensory surface of the utricles. Left: The change of AT per unit PV for roll and pitch calculated from the middle parts of curves like those shown on the right. Note that AT/PV is smallest for the neutral head position shown in the first column. (Data from [976])

are horizontal (= head tilted 30° forward, Fig. 2.9/12), the weighting of the statolith signals appears to depend on receptive properties of the statolith organs.

Visual signals. The properties of the receptor organs are also important in the weighting of visual signals. Figure 2.9/13 shows the weighting of different regions of the visual field for optokinetically induced changes in the SV (compare Fig. 2.9/7, right). Pattern movements in the peripheral field are more effective per unit area than in the foveal regions [155, 83]. This difference is observed in all optokinetic experiments and has been attributed to the two visual mechanisms of localization and identification. For localization the peripheral regions are most important; for identification, the foveal regions.

Experiments on the effect of stimulus properties demonstrate that the

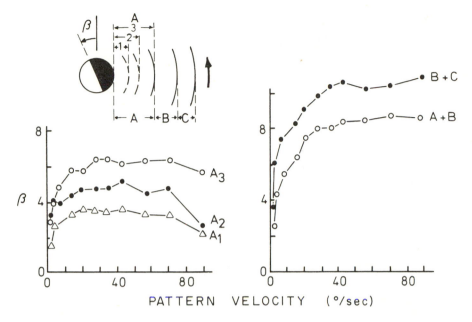

Fig. 2.9/13 The dependence of the subjective vertical on rotation velocity of different regions of the visual field. Concentric rings were rotated separately or in combination behind a stationary target divided into a black and a white semicircle. The line separating the two halves of the target was adjusted to the visual vertical, and its deviation from the vertical was measured (β). Rings A, B, and C subtended the same spatial sector. Left: β increases with ring area (A_1 to A_3). Right: Rings $B + C$, which subtend the retinal periphery, are more effective in inducing tilt of SV than those ($A + B$) subtending an area close to the fovea [323].

weighting of the visual vertical depends on the size of the visual field and the extent to which it is structured, e.g., number of contours [65, p. 393]. Subjects viewing a tilted, fully furnished room weighted the visual standard considerably more than subjects presented with a simple rectangular frame (Fig. 2.9/14, rod-and-frame test). Optokinetically induced vections also depend on stimulus parameters such as rotational velocity, stimulus duration, and size of the patterned field. Motor reactions induced by linear vection are a function of pattern velocity and density (Fig. 2.9/9). Circular vection is likewise influenced by pattern velocity. Up to velocities of about 90°/sec, only self-motion is perceived. At higher pattern velocities, a movement of the visual field is also registered.

2.9.4.2 Interaction and Weighting of Diverse Inputs

The function of sense organ or reference cue properties in weighting must be particularly evident in the interaction of different inputs. Bischof [65]

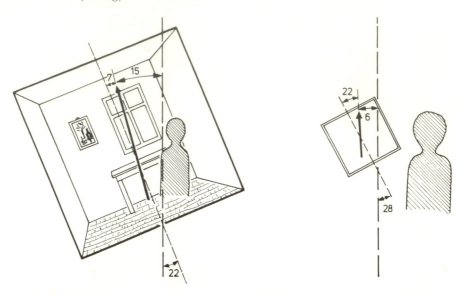

Fig. 2.9/14 Adjustment of a rod to the subjective vertical (*SV*) in a room tilted by 22° (left) and a frame tilted by 28° (right, rod-and-frame test) by a subject standing in front (shadow figure). The numbers give the mean angles of the *SV* to gravity and to the visual field direction in degrees for 76 (left) and 41 (right) subjects. (Data on right from [10A]; on left, from [959])

distinguished several procedures for taking two or more reference cues into account. Three of them are simultaneous solution, alternative adjustment, and averaging.

Simultaneous solution is when contradictory signals affect a response at the same time. An example is the adaptation to disturbance of the perceptual system as described by Kohler [461]. Subjects wearing inverting goggles reported that trees appeared upside down but that snow falling from these trees fell downward; the trees had not yet been inverted, but the movement of the snow had been (compare 2.11.4).

Alternative adjustment applies to cases in which the system considers only one of several contradictory signals. The occasionally observed perception of people in a tilted room comes under this heading. An individual may sometimes report that the room is tilted and sometimes that it is straight [454].

Averaging has already been covered in 2.6.2. All compromise positions between the gravity and the visual vertical belong to this category. In some cases this may be represented as a weighted averaging and in others as vector addition (2.7.1, 2.7.3).

A "conflict model" has been proposed for the situation in which visual and vestibular signals give contradictory information [977]. It was derived from experiments in which subjects were asked to adjust their positions until they no longer had a sensation of motion when they and their surroundings were turned randomly back and forth around the vertical axis. The superposition of vestibular and optokinetic signals gave a total turning signal that the subjects tried to correct. These corrective movements in turn affected both inputs. It was found that the vestibular signals dominate during fast movements, and optokinetic signals dominate during slow ones. This corresponds to results from behavioral (Fig. 2.7/8) and neurological (Fig. 2.7/9) experiments on animals. The conflict model states that when one signal is much stronger than the other, only this signal is considered. However, when the difference between the two signals is relatively small, the signals are averaged. This model can be viewed as either a combination of alternative adjustment and averaging or a weighted averaging in which the weighting ratio shifts so far toward one of the components that the other is ineffective.

Figure 2.9/15 shows a flow diagram for this model. Imposed rotations of the subject (ω_d) and the visual field ($\omega_{vis\,d}$) are entered as disturbances. Together with the corrective turn of the subject (ω_m) they determine the actual turn that is registered by the vestibular and visual inputs (ω_{vest}, ω_{vis}). The signals of these two input variables ($\omega_{vis\,i}$ and $\omega_{vest\,i}$) are combined to give a common turning signal (ω_i). This is compared with the reference value ($\omega_r = 0$ for no turning) to give the error signal that effects the counterturn (ω_m).

2.9.4.3 Group-specific and Individual Differences

Individual differences in weighting of gravity and light have already been discussed for the fish (2.7.3). The weighting of the visual standard plays a special role in the psychological literature. In the rod-and-frame test sub-

Fig. 2.9/15 Flow diagram of an experiment with randomly induced rotations of the body (ω_d) and of the visual field ($\omega_{vis\,d}$). Angular acceleration registered by the vestibular organs ($\omega_{vest\,i}$) and circular vection ($\omega_{vis\,i}$) combine to give the turning signal (ω_i), which is used to adjust body rotation to zero. The corrections (ω_m) sum to the disturbance inputs (ω_d and $\omega_{vis\,d}$). (Modified from [977])

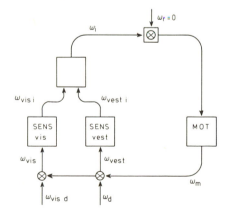

Fig. 2.9/16 The effect of the visual field on body position and the subjective vertical as a function of age and sex. Adjustment to the *SV* of a) the body (α) in a tilted room and b) a rod (β) within a tilted frame (rod-and-frame test). c) The righting response of children gazing into a rotating patterned hemisphere as a function of age and sex. Responses were graded according to: 0 = no response, $+$ = slight head and body tilt, $++$ = distinct tilt with body weight shifted to one side, and $+++$ = extreme tilt accompanied by balancing movements of the limbs and/or falling down. (a and b, modified from [957]; c, from [84])

jects in the dark are shown an illuminated frame that is tilted by 28° to gravity (see Fig. 2.9/14). A rod within the frame must be adjusted to the vertical. The deviation of the rod from the gravity vertical is used as a measure for the weighting of the visual field (= visual standard) and is referred to as field dependence. This is correlated with certain characteristics of the subjects, such as age and sex (Fig. 2.9/16b) and has also been claimed to be related to a number of personality traits such as I.Q. [961, 957]. For this reason the rod-and-frame test has been developed as a test for visual field dependence of humans and for experiments in clinical and developmental psychology [960]. Nyborg [641, 642] has revised and reinterpreted the entire complex of the rod-and-frame test in the light of physiological data.

Figure 2.9/16c [84] demonstrates how the effect of vection in young children changes with age. Rotating the visual field of a child leads to balance reactions due to roll vection. Children from 2–4 years of age orient more strongly to vection than younger or older children.

Fig. 2.9/17 The subjective vertical (β_v) as a function of body position (α) for two experimental groups. As body tilt increases over 90° the *SV* of group I diverges from the true vertical, whereas the *SV* of group III continues to coincide with it. Group III may place more weight on somatosensory signals, and group I, on statolith signals. (Modified from [493])

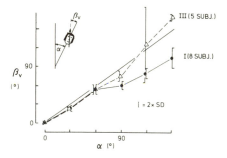

Individual differences in the relative weighting of statolith and somatosensory signals have been found in the perception of the subjective vertical, especially when the body is tilted more than 90° (Fig. 2.9/17, [493]). Presumably those subjects whose *SV* almost corresponds with the true vertical (curve III) rely more on somatosensory cues, whereas the others (curve I) place more weight on statolith signals.

2.10 SPACE CONSTANCY

As your eyes wander over your environment, its images move across the retina. Despite this movement your surroundings appear stationary. Although your sense organs register changes in direction, distance, size, and proportion, the objects around you retain their spatial properties. They are space constant.

The perceptual phenomenon of space constancy is fundamental to normal behavior. A meaningful interaction between animal and environment is inconceivable in a world that wavers and shifts whenever the animal moves. Constancy mechanisms indicate whether a spatial change that is registered by an animal's sense organs connotes a change in the environment or a movement of the animal itself.

In a comprehensive analysis, Bischof [64, 65, 66] brings together the psychological and physiological foundations of space constancy. A review of more recent theories on the visual perception of spatial coordinates during movement can be found in Richards [702].

For spatial orientation, the most important constancy phenomenon is direction constancy. A stimulus direction is operationally defined as space constant if a change in it does not elicit a corrective orientation movement. It is assumed that if the animal does not respond, it perceives the stimulus direction as "unchanged." For example, when an animal actively assumes a new orientation with respect to a reference stimulus, the spatial relationship between stimulus and animal is altered, but the animal does not react to this stimulation. The reference stimulus is perceived as space constant. "Spatial constancy is understood to be perceptual stability" [542].

But to meet the needs of an organism, a perception must not only be stable, it must also be reliable. A constancy mechanism must function in such a way that the perceived constancy is coincident with reality (2.10.4). Adjustment processes are often necessary to achieve this coincidence with reality (2.11).

How do constancy mechanisms work? There are three principles on which they could be constructed: reconstruction, correction, and compensation [64, 65, 66].

2.10.1 Reconstruction Principle

According to the reconstruction principle, "An organism bases its perceptual world on certain regularities (redundancies) that it 'expects' in the physical world" [65, p. 366]. Frequently recurring spatial features are marked as "space-stable" reference cues. This marking is rooted in the central nervous organization of the orientation mechanism. It is an adaptation to the structure of the environment, which has arisen either in the course of phylogenetic development or from individual experience. Optokinetic illusions such as circular vection (see 2.9.2) are based on such assumptions of constancy. An organism interprets the movement of many contours across the retina as self-motion [257, 991].

The "evaluation principle" developed by MacKay [539, 540, 541, 542, 545] has features in common with the reconstruction principle. In this concept the perceptual mechanism assumes that the external world is space constant. All shifts in the spatial relationship between environment and organism appear as motion of the organism. An organism maneuvers according to "a stored picture of organism plus world." The afferent signals, which result from the movement of the animal with respect to the environment, are used to evaluate the stored picture in terms of the external world. If they do not correspond to the spatial values used for the movement, the internal picture is revised "to keep the stable representation up to date."

2.10.2 Compensation Principle

Compensation and correction principles assume that perceived changes in the environment are "disturbances" to be eliminated. The reconstruction principle is often a prerequisite for compensation or correction.

According to the compensation principle an animal receives two pieces of information about the disturbance, a direct report of the disturbance (= disturbance signal) and a compensation signal. The latter is used to compensate the disturbance and maintain constancy. Two compensation operations are possible: (1) nervous and (2) physical compensation.

Nervous compensation. The disturbance caused by movement of the animal is compensated by the CNS. The compensation signal may stem from a second sensory channel ("afferent outside compensation," [65]) or from the motor commands for the movement ("efferent outside compensation"). The vertical constancy of human spatial perception is an example of compensation by a second sensory signal (2.9.1). When we lean over, objects maintain their alignment to the vertical even though the image of the object has shifted on the retina (i.e., is disturbed). This disturbance is compensated by body position signals from the statolith organs and/or from other systems that measure the vertical direction (2.9.1). When disturbance and compensation signals cancel each other out, the direction of the object is perceived as constant. In Fig. 2.9.3, β_i is the disturbance signal and α_i, the compensation signal. The signal λ_i indicates direction constancy (of line).

Wiersma and his colleagues [932] have found space constancy neurons in the optic nerve of decapod crustaceans. Regardless of the animal's position, these neurons are only excited when light strikes those eye regions that are directed upward with respect to gravity. Since space constancy is lost after statocyst removal, statocyst signals must participate in connecting the space constancy neurons to the upward-directed retinal regions.

Reorientation by reference value reset is an example of compensation by efferent signals (2.4.3). In the reafference principle and feedback control theory, the afferent signal produced by a change in direction is compensated by the efference copy or motor command. For example, if you jiggle your eyeball with a finger, the world appears to jump back and forth. Space constancy is lost. Yet when you move your eyes normally, everything stays in place because the visual movement signals are compensated by efference copies of the motor commands [363].

Physical compensation. The "disturbance" of the animal-environment relationship is compensated physically by a countermovement of the sense organ or the appendage on which it is situated. The compensation signal is used to control this countermovement to keep the sense organ spaceconstant. Almost all animals with movable eyes show compensatory eye movements. In many cases the signals for the countermovement stem from the statocysts or from the sensors that indicate body position relative to substrate (3.9).

More than one compensation signal may be used. For example, migratory locusts perform a peering behavior to judge target distance [137]. As the locust moves its body from side to side, the body pivots around the dorsoventral axis of the abdomen, and the head counterrotates with respect to the body. The compensatory neck movement that keeps head orientation constant depends on two signals. The signal for a "coarse" adjustment is derived from the motor program for leg movement (= idiothetic, "efference copy"). The "fine" adjustment is provided by an optomotor reflex, which prevents image slip over the lateral retina.

Nystagmic eye movements are also compensatory processes. As the head is turned, the eyes drift slowly in the opposite direction, holding the visual field steady. This slow phase is followed by a rapid jerk back into the starting position, followed by another slow drift. The signal used to move the eyes is derived from the disturbance signal itself ("afferent self-compensation,"

[65]). It is computed by "vector addition of the movement of all contours in the visual field" (reconstruction principle!).

Nystagmus-like ear twitching can be induced in rabbits by stimulation of the semicircular canals or optokinetic stimulation [739]. When the stimulation is due to rotation of the animal, these ear movements contribute to a constancy of the auditory field.

The compensatory movements of bees hovering in front of an object lead to spatial constancy of the head [900].

Course orientation with space-constant body alignment also results in the maintenance of the constancy of the visual environment (2.8.1.1). The compensation signal is given by the direction of locomotion relative to the body and may have either afferent (proprioceptors) or efferent (efference copy) origins. (In Fig. 2.8/3 the signal δ_c is represented as an efference copy.)

2.10.3 Correction Principle

A correction system is based on double checking. More than one reference cue furnishes information about the same spatial relationship. For instance, many aquatic animals orient their position according to gravity and light. Disturbances of one reference cue can be corrected from data provided by the other. In contrast to the compensation process, signals do not cancel each other out but work in the same direction. In humans, vertical signals are furnished by the gravity sensors and the eyes (2.9.1.2). In terms of the reconstruction principle the visual standard is a reference cue based on redundancy in the visual field. In the correction system these visual signals serve to correct possible "errors" of the gravity sensors, thus improving the coincidence with reality (veridicality) of the perceived constancy.

But how does an animal know which of several contradictory signals is "correct"? Physiologically, this is a question of evaluation or weighting of diverse reference cues (2.7.3, 2.9.1.2, 2.9.4). Bischof [65, p. 393] writes "the greater the probability that a signal is reliable, the heavier its weighting." Experiments on human perception have shown that the reliability of a visual reference increases with the area and complexity of the visual field ([958, 323], 2.9.4). A decrease in weighting of the gravity input, as occurs when the body is tilted sideways, increases the relative weighting of visual cues (2.9.4.1). Tilting probably decreases the gravity effect because the working range of the statolith organs is adjusted to the range of normal head positions, i.e., close to upright [65]. Considerations on reliability criteria and the origin of weighting "rules" are based on the reconstruction principle.

2.10.4 Direction Constancy and Coincidence with Reality

Clearly a compensation mechanism can only furnish a "correct" signal if the disturbance and compensation signals are equal. Otherwise, the disturbance is undercompensated or overcompensated [65]. For example, only when the gravity sensors report a body tilt corresponding to the retinal slip of the environment does the visual environment really remain stationary. Lack of agreement results in discrepancies between the perceived and the true vertical such as the Aubert or Müller phenomena. The former is an undercompensation for the tilt; the latter, an overcompensation. These phenomena depend not only on the degree of body tilt, but also on its duration and the preceding body orientation [773, 790, 494]. In the upright head position the subjective vertical deviates to the left of the true vertical if preceded by a tilt to the left, and to the right if preceded by a tilt to the right (hysteresis). These errors are presumably due to sensory adaptation of the statolith organs and the somatosensors.

Space constancy is often taken to mean coincidence with reality (= veridicality). However, the function of a constancy mechanism is to maintain perceptual stability, and perceptual stability does not necessarily include veridicality. An experiment on vertical constancy during tilting of the body illustrates when veridicality errors show up as loss of perceptual stability. If we lean more and more to one side while viewing an illuminated vertical line in the dark, the line appears to tip more and more to the side. The *SV* deviates more and more from the true vertical. We perceive a change in the *SV*, indicating a loss of vertical constancy. If the discrepancy between the *SV* and the true vertical were to remain constant, the veridicality error would go unnoticed, since the *SV* would remain stable. (The shift in the *SV* is probably due to erroneous indications of the gravity direction by the statolith organs, 3.10.1.1.4).

Tuning and calibration are often necessary for the sensory signal to coincide with reality. The motor execution of the orientation must also be correctly scaled. In many systems adjustment processes are taking place continuously to "keep the stable representation up to date." These are treated in the following chapter.

2.11 DEVELOPMENT AND RECOVERY OF ORIENTATION ABILITIES: THE EFFECT OF EXPERIENCE AND ENVIRONMENT

Developmentally determined differences, variability of orientation cues, compensation of perturbations, and tuning of the motor-sensory interaction appear at first glance to be quite heterogeneous topics. However, they are all concerned with changes in the orientation behavior. In particular, they deal with the effect of experience and environment on the form and operation of a system. Analyses of the mechanisms provide widely divergent solutions to the old controversy "heredity versus environment." The basic structure of an orientation contains numerous junctures where environmental influences may be critical. They extend from the formation of central nervous structures during sensitive periods to the learning of special features of an orientation cue, and from idiothetic storage of a movement sequence to continuous calibration of the motor-sensory interaction.

2.11.1 Development

2.11.1.1 Endogenous Factors

The disparate life styles of young and adult animals often call for different orientation behaviors. The needs of a caterpillar are obviously not the same as those of a butterfly. Differences in orientation behavior may even occur within one larval stage or from one stage to another. The response of caterpillars to light is a function of time after moulting (Fig. 2.11/1) and is correlated with the level of certain moulting hormones in the hemolymph (Fig. 2.1/5). Hormonal factors also appear to play a role in the development

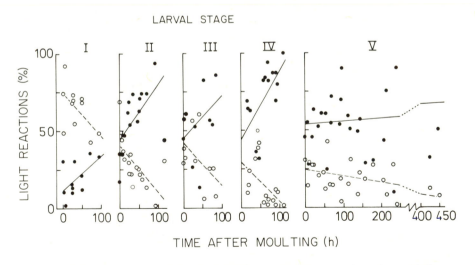

Fig. 2.11/1 Light orientation of the five larval stages of the eyed hawk moth, *Smerinthus ocellatus*. Open circles denote light positive responses; closed circles, light negative. (Modified from [726])

of acoustic orientation in crickets, *Acheta domesticus*. The species-specific song of a male, which attracts the sexually mature female, elicits avoidance behavior in the immature female [811].

The older larvae of many decapod crustaceans reside in deeper water layers than the younger ones (crabs, *Leptodius floridaneus* and *Panopeus herbstii* [839, 840, 55]). This segregation is a consequence of an age-dependent effect of hydrostatic pressure. Younger larvae increase their upward and lightward swimming speed (negative geotaxis, positive phototaxis) as hydrostatic pressure increases. Thus, as they enter deeper waters, their tendency to move upward increases. Older larvae are unaffected by pressure increase.

2.11.1.2 Exogenous Factors

An organism's ability to see and to orient visually depends on the visual impressions received during a certain sensitive period of its development [67]. Sensory deprivation during this time arrests the normal development of higher centers and leads to permanent damage. In cats this sensitive period starts at the end of their third week, at an age when kittens are beginning to explore their environment. The sensitivity starts to diminish after the sixth week, ending completely in the fourteenth. If one eye is covered during this critical period, it becomes irreversibly blind [935, 936, 384, 24]. The blindness is associated with degenerative changes in the lateral geniculate bodies and abnormal conditions in the visual cortex (3.1.8.2).

Even partial sensory deprivation can have devastating effects. Three-week old kittens with only one functioning eye were raised either in vertically or horizontally striped environments [69]. Those raised with only vertical cues later showed no reactions to horizontally aligned objects. The others did not react to vertical objects. Electrophysiological recordings showed that the visual cortex of each cat contained only cells of the orientation type corresponding to its behavior. More recent experiments [1014] show that the blueprint for the system of orientation columns is genetically determined, but the extension of the columns into the nongranular layers of the brain depends on experience. These findings suggest that all deficits caused by sensory deprivation can be accounted for by competitive interactions between intracortical pathways.

Similar deficits have been observed in kittens and people suffering from strabismus (cross- or wall-eye) [384]. In this condition the eyes do not converge properly, so that the retinal images do not coincide. In spite of this a cross-eyed person does not see double. One of the two images is suppressed centrally, and he sees only with one eye. In humans the sensitive period for development of normal binocular vision begins a few months after birth and reaches a maximum between the first and third year [19].

As in kittens, if this visual defect is not corrected early enough, the central structures do not develop normally.

2.11.2 Parameters of Orientation Cues

The identifying and spatial properties of an orientation cue (2.3.1) are not always equally affected by experience. A chicken can learn the identifying features of food objects, but the spatial values it uses to direct its pecking are uninfluenced by experience [335].

Identification parameters. The characteristics of both the calling song of a male cricket and the sexual pheromone of the female silkmoth are species specific and invariable. The recognition of these features by their prospective mates is genetically fixed. Even recognition of food objects may be inherited. When young snakes and lizards first encounter a prey odor, they show specific feeding reactions that are not elicited by control odors [120]. The spectrum of species-specific food preferences may also be constricted or broadened by learning additional features. Young toads [191], chicks [335], and goslings [968] learn the identifying features of the food at which they strike or peck. Chicks and turtles exhibit a kind of imprinting to the first food they eat, later preferring it [118, 119].

Learning identification parameters is very important when the orientation target may be quite variable. For example, the digger wasp memorizes the pattern of landmarks surrounding its nest entrance during its orientation flight over the nest area (3.1.5).

Spatial parameters. The direction and/or distance values of an orientation cue may be fixed or variable. They are inalterable for many target orientations. A chicken pecks only in the direction in which its beak is pointing. Hess put prism goggles on chicks so that they saw their food displaced to one side [335]. These chicks did not learn to readjust their pecks in spite of repeated misses. The direction of the stimulus and the pecking are strongly coupled.

The reference directions of many compass orientations are variable. Bees fly different sun compass angles depending on the direction of the food source (2.7.2). However, compass directions can also be genetically fixed. Beach fleas [653, 1013] use a sun compass to find their way to the beach from water or dry land, maintaining a course perpendicular to the coastline. When young beach fleas hatch in the laboratory from pregnant females captured on beaches with varying coast directions, their preferred directions correspond to the geographical orientation of the mother's home beach. This indicates that the intermingling of adjacent populations is so slight that the coastline direction can be genetically fixed.

2.11.3 Perturbations

2.11.3.1 Motor Perturbations

As a rule animals compensate quickly for the loss of an extremity by read-justing the coordination pattern. Insects can walk with as few as three legs, vertebrates with three or even two, and humans can hop along on one. Other kinds of perturbations are considerably more difficult for an animal to compensate. When the right and left forelimb buds of embryonic sala-manders are switched, the nervous connections formed by the healing leg buds correspond to their original positions [908]. Although the dorso-ventral axis remains the same, the front surfaces of the legs point backward. When the salamander tries to move a foreleg forward, the leg is thrust backward so that the front legs work counter to the hind legs. Although the animal is unable to move from the spot, it does not readjust its move-ments. Rats also cannot learn how to readjust the locomotor system if the insertions of the flexor and extensor muscles of a foot are switched [819]. Apparently, the development of locomotory behavior is to a great extent genetically determined (inherited coordination), and no allowance is made for the influence of experience.

The ability to compensate for this kind of perturbation first becomes evident in primates. A monkey, in which the insertions of the arm flexor and extensor muscles have been switched, is initially unable to correctly reach for a banana. However, after a period of days or weeks, it learns to brake the false arm movement and to visually guide its hand to the banana. The monkey learns to activate the extensor to flex its arm and the flexor to extend it. This is equivalent to the ability of humans to drive prosthetics with completely different muscles, as when an arm amputee uses chest muscles to move artificial fingers.

2.11.3.2 Sensory Perturbations

When a sense that is normally used for a behavior is lost, other senses may take its place. Blind people learn to find their way around by hearing and touch. People with auditory and labyrinth defects learn to rely on visual and somatosensory cues.

The consequences of unilateral ablation depend not only on the structure but also on the performance of the system. For instance, in array systems it affects direction localization differently than binocular determination of depth or distance.

Binocular performances. Unilateral blinding initially abolishes the ability to measure distance and depth. When one eye is blacked out, dragonfly larvae overshoot their prey [18]. In the predatory water beetle larva *Acilius sulcatus*, the no. 3 eyes are particularly important for estimating target distance (3.1.7). If one of this pair is covered, the larvae miss their prey. Their orientation system can, however, accommodate to the loss and an animal's aim gradually improves. One-eyed toads can also learn to catch prey [756]. Binocular fixation is replaced by a process in which the good eye approaches the prey in an arc-shaped path.

Array systems. Loss of one eye impairs direction localization, insofar as the visual field of this eye is missing. After unilateral blinding a destatolithed fish rolls toward its intact side [356]. The rotation decreases gradually as the fish compensates for the loss. After 6.5 hours only a tilt toward the intact side remains, which decreases with light intensity ([793], Fig. 2.11/ 2, left). Compensation progresses, so that after 13 days (right) the tilt is practically zero at the initial illumination intensity, and a decrease in light intensity causes the fish to tilt toward the operated side.

Compensation in *Acilius* larvae also appears to be tuned to light intensity. When the left eyes are covered, the larvae roll toward the right. The turning tendency diminishes if the larvae are allowed to swim around for a while under overhead lighting. A subsequent increase in illumination intensity increases turning [766, 767]. If the right eyes are also covered or the left eyes uncovered after a compensation has taken place, the larvae rotate to the left.

The dependence of compensation on stimulus intensity can be explained in terms of the vectorial processing of multiple stimuli (2.6.2, Fig. 2.6/4). Loss of array components leads to a turning reaction. Since compensation

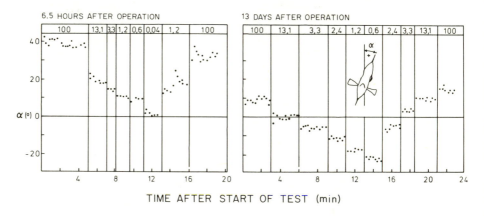

Fig. 2.11/2 Positional orientation of a one-eyed fish as a function of the intensity of light from all sides. The first row of numbers gives the intensity as a percentage of initial illumination. Left: 6.5 h after unilateral ablation of right eye. Right: 13 days after operation. (Modified from [793])

involves reestablishing the central balance of excitation that is required for the normal orientation to the stimulus field, the missing excitation vectors must be replaced. This central substitution must be calibrated to the excitation vectors that are still present and thus to the intensities of the stimuli causing these excitations.

Bisensor systems. Unilateral ablation also leads to turning tendencies in bisensor systems. The loss of excitation from one of the two sensors gives rise to a strong excitation difference between them (2.3.3). The resulting unisensor system can still be utilized for gradient orientation with successive sampling, as in bees and other insects with only one antenna (2.3.3, 3.5). However, in bisensor systems that respond to directed stimuli, such as gravity sensors, loss of one sensor causes conspicuous behavioral defects. Vertebrates lacking one labyrinth roll vigorously and continuously toward the damaged side (3.10.1.1). These rotations subside very slowly, and even after an animal has settled into a normal position, renewed turning can be triggered by disturbances such as threatening behavior by a conspecific [358].

Quantitative measurements of the time course of compensation in fish (Fig. 2.11/3) and frogs show that the turning tendency decays exponentially [792, 464]. In frogs it can start to decline as early as 5–10 min after the operation [464]. If the remaining organ is removed after complete compensation, animals resume turning at about the same intensity as after the initial operation, but in the opposite direction (mammals [543], fish [366, 792, 521], amphibians [464], crustaceans [768]). This turning is also compensated. The resumption of turning in the opposite direction is evidence

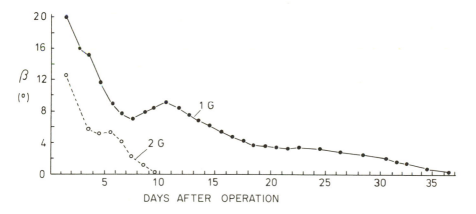

Fig. 2.11/3 Compensation for unilateral utricle ablation in the fish *Gymnocorymbus ternetzii*. The difference (β) between the tilt produced by light to the intact and to the operated side was used as the measure for compensation. Compensation proceeds faster under increased gravity (2G) than under normal gravity (1G). (Modified from [792])

that the first loss of excitation has been replaced centrally (compensation excitation). In cats and rabbits the primary sensory centers, the vestibular nuclei, of the defective side play a decisive role in these processes ([543, 824], 3.10.3). Removal of the vestibular nuclei from the intact side has no effect on the compensated state.

In crustaceans the turning compensation is reflected in the eye position. Directly after unilateral statocyst removal both eyes deviate toward the operated side. When an animal is turned around its longitudinal axis, eye position changes sinusoidally, but the whole curve remains above the zero line. As compensation proceeds, the sine curve drifts back to the zero line (Fig. 2.11/4, second row b,c). Crustaceans also compensate for excitation differences caused by unequal right and left statolith loads [768].

Figure 2.11/4 summarizes the compensation for statocyst removal in vertebrates and crustaceans. It may also apply to other bisensor systems such as that of cricket sound localization (3.6). The sensors are sinusoidally modulated by the stimulus. For the simplest case of a 0° reference direction, the turning tendency (D) is determined by the difference between the excitation curves of the right and left sensors. Removal of the left organ eliminates its afference. The turning tendency curve shows only rightward tendencies and is halved in amplitude. As central compensation excitation develops, the turning tendency curve sinks until it lies symmetrically around

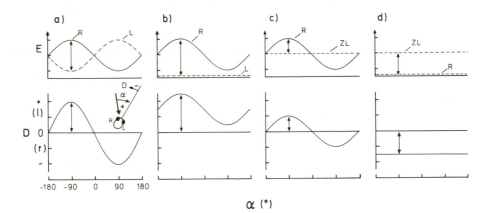

Fig. 2.11/4 Compensation in a bisensor system in which the sinusoidal direction characteristics of the sensors differ by 180°. Upper row: Excitations as a function of stimulus angle α. Lower row: Turning tendency (differences between curves in upper row) as a function of α. a) Intact animal. b) After loss of the left sensor its excitation becomes zero, leading to a continuous leftward turning, which is modulated by stimulus intensity. c) Central compensation excitation (ZL) takes the place of the excitation from the missing left sensor and brings the turning tendency curve back to the zero line. The amplitude of the D curve is half that of the normal one. d) Loss of the right sensor after compensation results in a (nonmodulated) rightward turning tendency.

the zero line. If the other organ is now removed, the compensation excitation causes turning tendencies in the opposite direction. When, instead of removing the whole organ, only the statoliths are removed, the stimulus-free side still receives resting excitation from the sense hairs. This situation resembles that of Fig. 2.11/4c, with ZL corresponding to L (= resting excitation).

What initiates compensation? What determines its course and its termination? In fish the central compensation of unilateral labyrinth ablation can proceed on its own, albeit slowly [359]. It is faster under normal gravity and is accelerated further if gravity is increased by centrifugation (Fig. 2.11/3). Visual input also seems to play an important role in this compensation [792].

The compensation time for unilateral labyrinthectomy in the tadpoles of *Xenopus laevis* depends on the developmental stage and whether or not they can see ([370], Fig. 2.11/5). The older they are, the longer they take to compensate. Blinded tadpoles no longer compensate, indicating that redundant signals contribute to the readjustment and reorganization of the orientation mechanism.

2.11.4 Motor-Sensory Adjustment

For a successful orientation the motor action must correspond to the spatial values given by the sensory signals. The performance of the movement and the resulting feedback play a crucial role in the organization processes. Often insights into the mechanisms can be gained by eliminating or distorting the sensory input.

2.11.4.1 Readjustment after Sensory Perturbations

Crossing the antennae of an insect or inverting the head of a fly reverses the sign of the direction signals. As a consequence, the animals turn in the

Fig. 2.11/5 Compensation for unilateral labyrinth ablation in tadpoles (*Xenopus laevis*) as a function of the developmental stage. The compensation time is defined as the number of days after the operation when 50% of the tadpoles can swim normally. Closed circles are for sighted animals. The open circle over developmental stage 46 denotes blinded animals. Beyond this stage blinded animals no longer compensate. (Modified from [370])

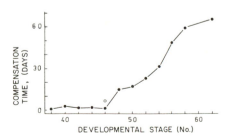

"wrong" direction. Flies are unable to compensate for head inversion. It is not known whether insects can correct for crossed antennae.

When their heads are fastened at an angle to one side, praying mantises cannot hit their prey (see 2.4.3.2). Even after seven days there is no sign of compensation [588]. However, after the nerves signaling head position are cut on one side, strike accuracy slowly improves.

Similarly, when its eyes are surgically fixed in a different direction, a fish leans at an angle that corresponds to the eye displacement (Fig. 2.11/6, left, [364]). Like the compromise position between gravity and light, this position is maintained (2.7.1). The fish does not compensate. However, if only one eye is displaced and the other eye removed, the fish compensates not only for the unilateral ablation (2.11.3.2) but also for the displacement of the eye.

In contrast, kittens do compensate for rotation of an eye. Nine months after the operation cats can visually track objects, bat them with their paws, and avoid obstacles [583]. Neurophysiological experiments indicate that the superior colliculus (tectum) plays an important role in this adjustment. Neurons are reassigned to new stimulus directions in accordance with the degree of eye rotation [143].

Experience in motor-visual coordination is crucial for readjustment. Young cats that have been raised without seeing their legs cannot hit objects with their paws [325, 319, 320]. Monkeys, *Macaca speciosa*, that have never seen their arms cannot guide their hands toward objects [321]. In both cases

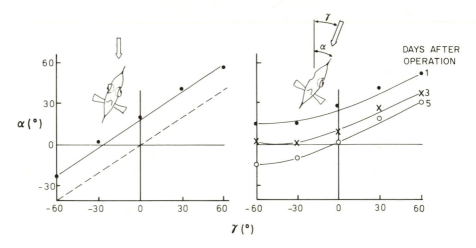

Fig. 2.11/6 Positional orientation of fish in which the eye positions have been surgically altered. Left: When both eyes were displaced about 28°, the fish behaved as if the light direction had been changed by 28°; no compensation took place. Right: When one eye was removed and the other displaced upward by 25°, the fish compensated for both operations. (Modified from [364])

this defect can be corrected if the animals are allowed to watch the movements of their limbs for a day.

Normal feedback from the motor activity is necessary for the incorporation of visual signals into the orientation process. This was evident in experiments where pairs of kittens were harnessed together so that only one could walk while the other was towed along in a basket by the first. In this way both kittens received the same visual stimulation, but only the active kitten could correlate this stimulation with its self-produced movement. After a total of about 30 hours in this apparatus the kittens were placed on a visual cliff, formed by a sheet of glass beneath which were two surfaces, one shallow and one deep. The active kitten avoided the deep side, and when lowered to a surface, it put out its paws as if to ward off collision. The passive kitten showed neither of these behaviors, but was able to develop them after a few days of running about in a normal environment. This emphasizes the role of practice in motor-sensory interactions. Sensory signals do not a priori elicit the correct responses. They must be coordinated with an active movement by an adjustment process that is subject to practice [325]. Experiments on humans confirm and supplement these insights.

2.11.4.2 Spatial Perception and Oriented Movement in Humans

Special goggles or prisms that make the world look upside down or shifted to one side have proven useful for the study of human motor-visual coordination [461, 376, 65]. It has been shown that when hand movements are distorted by a prism, a subject needs to watch only half an hour of self-produced movements under the prism to compensate for the displacement. However, if the experimenter guides the subject's hand through the same movement, no noticeable adjustment takes place [324].

Movements of the whole body can also be readjusted if active movement is permitted [322]. Experimental subjects wearing goggles that laterally displaced their line of sight were instructed to rotate a chair until a target was directly in front of them. They all erred by the angle of deflection. They were then given an hour to get accustomed to the goggles, but some were allowed to walk about freely while the others were rolled around in wheelchairs. In subsequent localization tests the walkers showed significant improvement, whereas the riders showed none.

Investigations initiated by Kohler [461, 462] have shown that inverting goggles interfere even more radically with visually guided movements and perceptual constancy [993]. Not only does the world look upside down; it moves in the opposite direction to what is expected during a self-produced body movement. For example, when the head is raised, the ground disappears upward. At first it is almost impossible to move about. However, after several weeks of practice and active movement, visual signals and body movements become associated in a way appropriate to the changed conditions. The world is no longer consciously perceived as upside down, and the movements of the surroundings are again felt to be correct. This perceptual adjustment mechanism may also explain why the world normally appears rightside up, even though the image of the environment is inverted on the retina.

Experiments on sensory deprivation show that adjustment is continuous. Several days of visual, acoustic, and somatosensory deprivation seriously impair a person's perception of constancy and ability to orient. Objects appear to drift and tumble about or move with the eyes. The capacity to conceptualize spatial relationships is undermined, and the stored picture of the outside world is strongly reduced [176, 331]. These results can be interpreted according to MacKay's evaluative principle (2.10.1). Man's perception of space is based on an image of the external world as registered by his senses and is continuously checked and stabilized by sensory feedback from his own activity.

Localization-identification. As we have already seen, the spatial and identifying parameters of a stimulus are taken in by different mechanisms (2.3.1, 3.1.8.3). It is, thus, not surprising that readjustment does not operate equally well for localization and identification. Disturbances of localization processes can be quickly and completely corrected by experience, whereas there is less leeway for correction of identification processes such as form perception. This has been demonstrated using a prism goggle that laterally deflected only the upper half of the visual field [461, 320]. After a few weeks the localization mechanism was fully readjusted. Objects that lay in the same direction in the two halves of the visual field were perceived as having the same direction. However, a single object occupying both halves appeared simultaneously to be whole and fragmented. A flagpole, for example, was perceived both as a single straight line extending from the upper to the lower half of the visual field and as two segments that were out of alignment.

3. Particulars of the Sensory Modalities

The differences between the senses depend on the physicochemical properties of the stimulus. In the evolution of organisms these properties have contributed to the development and formation of special receptor mechanisms, the sense organs.

The sensory modalities are categorized according to the stimulus: light, heat, electrical and magnetic fields, chemicals, sound, gravity, vibration, movement of currents, and touch. The last five are combined under the general heading of mechanoreception. This chapter discusses the most important physical properties of the stimulus for each modality, as well as the morphology and physiology of the sense organs involved. However, not every orientation refers to an external stimulus. The modality is not always allothetic and must not even have a sensory origin. Idiothetic orientations, i.e., those based on "internal" reference cues, are treated in the last section.

Since the discussions of most of the sensory modalities also touch on central processes, an overview of the basic structure of the vertebrate brain is included here (Fig. 3.0/1). The vertebrate brain represents an enlargement of the anterior end of the main dorsal nerve, the spinal cord. It can be divided into five general regions: (1) telencephalon, (2) diencephalon, (3) mesencephalon, (4) metencephalon, and (5) myelencephalon. The myelencephalon, or medulla oblongata, merges imperceptibly with the spinal cord.

The cerebrum (telencephalon) increases in size and importance as we ascend the vertebrate series (fish, amphibians, reptiles, birds, mammals). In humans it is enormously developed, overlying the rest of the brain. Its outer layer, the cortex, is folded into gyri, separated by fissures and sulci. This folding greatly increases the surface area. The brain of a cat, which is barely as big as your fist, has a surface area of about 2 m². The cortex can be mapped into areas according to their specific sensory or motor functions (Figs. 3.9/5, 3.10/28).

The diencephalon is a relay station between the forebrain and the rest of the brain. In mammals the lateral geniculate bodies of the thalamus are an especially important switching station of the visual system. The pineal gland (epiphysis) is situated on the dorsal surface of the diencephalon, and

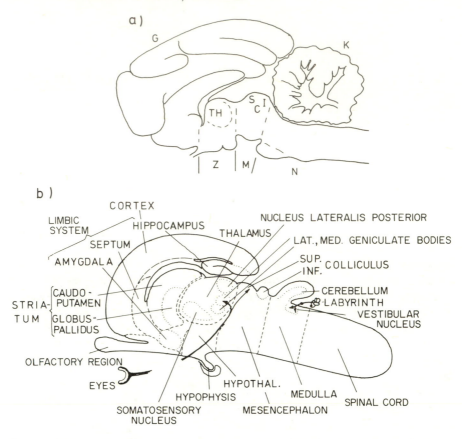

Fig. 3.0/1 Mammalian brain. a) Longitudinal section of a cat brain: G = telencephalon, Z = diencephalon, M = mesencephalon, K = metencephalon, N = myelencephalon, SIC = superior and inferior colliculus (dorsal surface of the superior colliculus = tectum), TH = thalamus. b) Schematic drawing of a longitudinal section showing major brain regions and nuclei. (b, modified from [623])

the pituitary gland (hypophysis) dangles from a stalk attached to its ventral surface (hypothalamus).

The mesencephalon, or midbrain, is an end station in the visual pathway. Visual fibers terminate on its dorsal surface, or tectum (also called the superior colliculus in mammals). Tracts from other sensory inputs end in deeper layers of the midbrain. The inferior colliculus is an important acoustic center.

The metencephalon is composed of the cerebellum and the pons. The cerebellum is a dorsal extension of the anterior part of the medulla and has a complexly folded surface. Its main functions are balance and motor coordination.

The myelencephalon (also rhombencephalon), or the medulla, is the entry point and relay station for information from several important sense organs. Afferent fibers from the labyrinth (vestibular organs, ear), as well as other cranial sensory nerves, terminate here. The sensory nuclei (groupings of nerve cells) and reticular formations of the medulla connect to all regions of the brain. It is also a relay station for part of the ascending and descending fibers from the spinal cord. Most of these nuclei and relay structures are concentrated in the brainstem, which is continuous with the ventral midbrain.

3.1 VISUAL ORIENTATION

3.1.1 Physical Properties of Visual Stimuli

Only a small portion of the electromagnetic spectrum excites the photo-receptors of living organisms (Fig. 3.1/1). Electromagnetic radiation that produces visual sensation is called light. It is conventionally described in terms of wavelength, given in Ångstrom units (1 Å = 10^{-10}m) or in nanometers (1 nm = 10 Å). Light occupies a range from approximately 360 to 780 nm. Many organisms can perceive qualitative differences within this range, i.e., they have color vision. For humans the short wavelengths (about 360 nm) are violet; the long ones (780 nm), red, with the other colors of the rainbow in between (blue, green, yellow, orange). In comparison, the visible spectrum of bees is shifted toward the shorter wavelengths. They can see ultraviolet light and use it to identify flowers [235], but their vision at the red end of the spectrum is not as good.

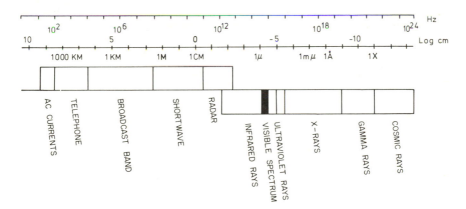

Fig. 3.1/1 Electromagnetic spectrum with frequency (upper scale) and wavelength (lower scale). (From [281])

The velocity of light is too fast to be measured by sense organs (300,000 km/sec). This excludes orientation mechanisms such as the measurement of time intervals between successive stimulations (2.3.3).

An incandescent light bulb emits a given amount of energy per unit time, the radiant flux. This power is measured in watts (J/sec). Most of a light bulb's radiant energy is emitted in the form of heat. Only a fraction of the total energy is in the form of light. This light portion of the radiant flux is called the luminous flux, measured in units of lumens (lm). Two other concepts bearing on the light emitted by a source are defined in terms of the luminous flux. They are luminous intensity and luminance. The luminous intensity of a source is the luminous flux in a given direction relative to the emitting source and is measured in lm/solid angle or in candela (cd) units. (The candela is 1/60 of the luminous intensity/cm^2 of a black body radiating at the temperature of the freezing point of platinum.) The luminance, or photometric brightness, gives the intensity per unit area of the viewed surface. The same luminance that is painful when radiated from a point source (e.g., welder's arc) is harmless if radiated from a piece of typing paper.

The above concepts describe light in terms of its source. Illuminance is defined in terms of the surface that is lit, i.e., the visual organ. It is used when one is concerned with the light that is received and that affects the orientation. Illuminance is defined as the luminous flux per unit area on a surface exposed to incident light. Its unit is the lux (1 lux = 1 lm/m^2). Since the greater the distance between receiver and transmitter, the smaller the cone of light impinging on the receiver, the illuminance is inversely proportional to the square of the distance. The spectral sensitivity of the photoelements in many measuring instruments is adjusted to human vision. Thus, the readings taken on another organism should be interpreted with caution. For example, when the meter reads 10 lux in red light, this applies only for humans; bees do not register any light.

The greatest natural source of light is the sun. It emits light in a mixture of all wavelengths, which we perceive as white. Different wavelengths appear to play different roles in the orientation systems of some animals (see below).

Polarization, another physical property of light, is used by many animals for light orientation. Elementary light waves oscillate at right angles to the direction of propagation (transverse waves). The plane of oscillation is characterized by an electrical (E-vector) and a magnetic vector. The polarization direction is commonly given in terms of the E-vector. A beam of light is composed of many elementary waves. When these all vibrate in the same plane, the light is polarized. Direct sunlight is unpolarized; its waves vibrate in all directions. However, as it travels through the earth's atmosphere, sunlight is scattered by minute particles so that the waves tend to vibrate in a specific direction at each point in the sky. The direction of polarization seen by an observer depends on the sun's relative position (Fig. 3.1/5). The *E*-vector is perpendicular to a surface described by a triangle between the sun, reflecting air particle, and observer. For the observer, different points on the celestial sphere have different degrees of polarization, forming a pattern in the sky (Fig. 3.1/2). The parts of the sky 90° away from the sun are the most polarized. At dawn and dusk this is the zenith region.

Seen from the earth, the sun is a tiny disc of less than 1° diameter. As a rule the distribution of light in the sky is critical for light orientation (ALD, see 2.6.2.1). Most animals orient to the brightest point in the sky, which is usually the sun. However, if the light distribution is asymmetrical, the region over which the animal integrates is crucial. Figure 2.6/3 shows that for a helical light distribution, the orientation direction corresponds to the resultant vector.

The pattern of illuminance can also serve as an identifying feature. When the sun contrasts sharply with its surroundings, it releases a positive phototactic response (2.3.1) instead of serving as a reference cue for compass orientation.

Daylight enters water through an "air window" (Fig. 3.1/3). When the water surface is smooth, the horizon formed by the surrounding land looks like the narrow rim of a round window. However, most natural water surfaces are rippled. They tend to be translucent and scatter light. Suspended particles in the water also have a light-diffusing effect, which increases with depth. The joint effect of these factors is that illuminance is maximal near the middle of the window, i.e., near the vertical. Light is thus a relatively reliable vertical indicator for aquatic animals.

Fig. 3.1/2 Polarization of the light of the sky when the sun is near the horizon (0°). Arrows indicate *E*-vector direction. Contours connect points with an equal degree of polarization (percentage of total light that is polarized at any particular locus). Maximum polarization is found in a band over the zenith region 90° away from the sun. (Modified from [235, 902])

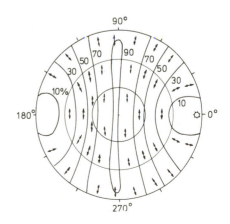

Fig. 3.1/3 The "view" from beneath the water's surface. Above: The "window" through which light shines from above. Below: Light hitting the surface of the water at a very shallow angle (point-dash line) forms an angle of 48.8° to the vertical and demarcates the window. Objects on the bottom are seen to the side of this window.

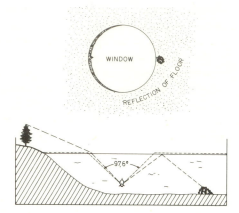

3.1.2 Photoreceptors and Direction Measurement

The eyes of most higher organisms are composed of many photosensitive elements and can serve as analyzing arrays (2.3.3). Vertebrates and higher molluscs, as well as jumping spiders and many insect larvae, have single lenticular eyes, which project the visual field onto an array of visual elements. Many arthropods like insects and the higher crustaceans are equipped with compound eyes.

In insects, receptor sensitivity differs for the various spectral regions and for light polarization (see 3.1.8.1). Bees are trichromatic, and ants are probably bichromatic [902]. Differences in chromatic sensitivity are associated with different orientation functions. The detectors for polarized light are part of the system of compass course orientation [183, 327]. The green receptors of bees mediate the optomotor response [416, 415] and make possible optokinetic orientation to the pattern of a green environment (3.1.6; presumably including the background pattern, comp. 3.8.3). White light is the primary stimulus for alignment with a light source (phototaxis, sun compass) (bee [417]). Color vision is also important for the recognition and identification of targets such as flowers, the hive, and landmarks.

The target orientation of many predatory animals is based on the localization of the prey object on the receptor array of the eye. The site of stimulation releases a turn (usually open loop), which brings the prey image onto the fovea and/or the animal into a favorable strike position. Orientation to landmarks necessitates a comparable sensory capability since individual markers must be localized.

Orientation to polarized skylight requires that the polarization direction (E-vector) be perceived and that an unambiguous value for the orientation be derived from the E-vector pattern. There are various hypotheses as to how these are accomplished [235, 447, 449, 182, 902, 1023, 1024]. The desert ant *Cataglyphis bicolor* uses only a small region near the upper rim of its eyes for orientation to polarized light (Fig. 3.1/4). If this eye region is painted over, the animals can no longer home. However, when only the lower regions are shielded, their navigational ability is scarcely impaired [182]. In bees the upper eye region is also important for orientation to polarized light [902].

As an insect scans the sky, it tries to match the perceived polarization pattern with a stored one that is based on a simplified master image of the sky (Fig. 3.1/5b). It encompasses only the highly polarized portion of the celestial hemisphere (= antisolar hemisphere) and is characterized by iden-

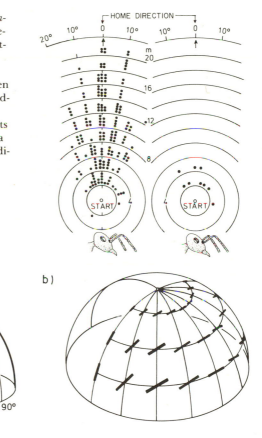

Fig. 3.1/4 Homing of the desert ant *Cataglyphis bicolor*. Each dot represents the recovery site of an ant released at the starting point. Left: Ants were still able to home with the rear third of their eyes (hatched area) painted over. Right: When the front two-thirds were covered (including the dorsal patch of ommatidia that perceive polarized light), most of the ants remained near the starting point. Only a few were found in sectors in the home direction. (Modified from [902])

Fig. 3.1/5 a) The axis of skylight polarization at a point on the celestial hemisphere is perpendicular to the plane of a triangle connecting the observer (*E*), the sun, and the point (*H₁* or *H₂*). b) Irrespective of the sun's elevation, the bee always refers to an internal stereotyped celestial map. (a, modified from [902]; b, from [1024])

tical E-vector distributions for all parallels of altitude. In relying on such a simplified master image, the insect need not resort to more complicated strategies, which may be mathematically elegant, but not amenable to an insect's brain.

Direction measurement has been categorized into array, bisensor, and unisensor processes (2.3.3). The above analysis of polarized skylight uses array organs. Optomotor orientation also requires a receptor array, which registers the spatial arrangement and movement of the pattern (3.1.6). Orientation to polarization pattern and to the sun are based on different central mechanisms [1023, 989].

The light orientation of maggots is a unisenor process. They zigzag away from light by turning the front part of their bodies from one side to the other. Each turn stimulates the photoreceptors in the pharyngeal skeleton of the head (which are shielded from the back by pigment and the body). Receptor excitation determines the size of the subsequent turn and thus the crawling direction. The right-left alternation is idiothetically controlled (2.3.3.1).

The orienting reactions of many unicellular organisms are also unisensor processes with direction-sensitive sensors. For example, the flagellate *Euglena* has spot of pigment, the stigma or eyespot, on one side of the light-sensitive base of its flagellum, the paraflagellar body. As a *Euglena* swims, it rotates around its longitudinal axis. When light comes from the side, the stigma casts a shadow on the paraflagellar body in the rhythm of rotation. This shadow changes the beating direction of the flagellum so that the *Euglena* turns until light stimulation is symmetrical [211].

Many dinoflagellates possess two sensory spots [297] and may use a kind of bisensor process. Others have many sensors, which may function as an array and may make form perception possible [990].

3.1.3 Positional Orientation and Vertical Course Orientation

The positional orientation of aquatic animals to light was first described by Rádl [688] in water fleas. Von Buddenbrock [98] found that shrimps lacking statocysts turned their backs to light from the side or from below and termed this the dorsal light reflex. Von Holst discovered a comparable process in fish, calling it optical equilibrium orientation, in analogy to the corresponding gravity orientation [356].

The terms dorsal light and ventral light reaction [230] clearly convey that positional orientations are involved; however, they are also closely associated with vertical course orientations. Fraenkel and Gunn showed in *Daphnia* that the actual orientation at any moment was due to a combination of dorsal light reaction and phototaxis [230]. Von Holst also understood optical equilibrium orientation to mean more than mere maintenance of body position [356]. He wrote, "In fish lacking labyrinths, up and down are determined solely by the direction of light incidence. When its tank is lit from below, a fish that wants to rest, swims to the water surface, not to the floor of the tank. A fish with oxygen debt seeks out the floor of the tank and not the surface." All movement is turned around by 180°. Such mechanisms determine not only body position in space but also the vertical direction for a compass course (Fig. 2.1/4). Vertical compass course orientation to light and the mechanism of direction reset have already been discussed for water beetle larvae (2.6.3). The old terms, dorsal light reaction and positive, negative, or transverse phototaxis, refer only to single reference values of this positional and course orientation mechanism.

Under certain circumstances body position is kept space-constant during up and down movements that may still be oriented to light and/or gravity (course orientation with space-constant body alignment, 2.8.1.1). This possibility is often overlooked.

Terrestrial animals also possess an optical positional orientation. One such mechanism has been investigated by Mittelstaedt [585] in dragonflies.

3.1.4 Horizontal Compass Course Orientation

In 1874 Lubbock ([533], cited in [96]) showed that ants could orient their locomotion to a light source. His discovery, however, went unnoticed until Santschi's [732] famous mirror experiment (Fig. 3.1/6). Santschi shielded an ant trail from direct sunlight and used mirrors to reflect sunlight onto the trail from the opposite direction. Ants entering the reflected light turned around and walked in the opposite direction. Since the ants' eyes maintained a particular light direction like a compass, Santschi used the term light compass.

Kramer also used mirrors to show that starlings can orient to the sun, taking its apparent movement into consideration (time compensation) [471, 472]. At about the same time, von Frisch independently found the same mechanism in bees (2.8.1.4).

Von Frisch also made the major discovery that bees could navigate by the polarized light of the sky. It has since been shown that many animals orient to polarized light (for a review, see [235]). For example, salmon smolts usually migrate at dusk, a time when the zenith region is highly polarized (until long after sunset). Experiments show that they can orient to polarized skylight ([282], see 2.8).

The Danish archeologist Ramskou has suggested that the Vikings used the polarization pattern of the sky as a navigational aid (cited in [902]).

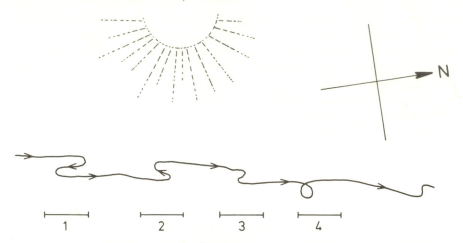

Fig. 3.1/6 Sun compass orientation of ants. In Santschi's [732] classical mirror experiment the ant's sun side was shaded from direct light, and sunlight was reflected onto the ant from the opposite side. When this was done at positions 1–4, the ant turned around and walked in the opposite direction. (From [235])

Nordic sagas describe a "sunstone" that may very well have been the birefringent crystal, cordierite, found along the coast of Norway. The direction of polarization of the sky can be determined with this crystal.

3.1.5 Landmark and Pattern Orientation

If you ask a child how he knows which way to go when he is walking to school, he might reply, "I just know the way. First the park is on my right, then I turn left at the next traffic light, go past the post office, and I can see the church steeple in the distance." The child's route is strewn with familiar landmarks whose sequence and relative positions he has memorized. This is landmark orientation. Other examples of landmark orientation have already been discussed in 2.8.4. Wehner [1022] has written a comprehensive review and analysis of landmark orientation in insects.

Landmark orientation was recognized much earlier than sun compass orientation. In 1863 Bates described the looping flights made by the digger wasp *Microbembex* after leaving its burrow "for taking notes of the locality" ([29] cited in [129]). All insects that orient to landmarks make such orientation flights [1022]. Visual markers are very important for the homing of many animals. On their way to a food source bees fly to conspicuous points like solitary trees or roofs as intermediate goals [235].

It is not surprising that landmark orientation has been so thoroughly investigated in the digger wasps [209, 854, 857, 16, 61, 390, 391, 392, 128,

129]. These hymenopterans of the family Sphegidae have a solitary life style, building their nests in the ground in open areas. The female hunts insects or larvae, which she paralyzes with her sting and carries back to her burrow to feed her young when they hatch. Some species, like *Ammophila campestris*, drag large caterpillars back on foot. When they run into dense plant growth, they put down their catch, climb a tall plant to use as a lookout tower, and continue in the direction of the burrow [16].

When the digger wasp *Bembix rostrata* leaves a nest containing its young, it sweeps earth over the entrance, rendering it practically invisible. *Ammophila* also plugs up its burrow entrance before departing. Closing the nest makes it more difficult for predators and parasitic flies or wasps to force their way in, but it must also make it more difficult for the burrow owner to find the entrance. To find the right spot a wasp needs a locating system that is precise to the centimeter. Usually the wasp lands right on target, shovels free the entrance, and disappears into the burrow.

Several ranges can be differentiated over which the wasp appears to use different orientation systems. Orientation in the far range comes under distant orientation, since the end goal cannot be directly perceived and the landmarks are only intermediate goals. The digger wasp *Bembix* can find its nest from a distance of up to 500 m [128]. Wasps that were transported over circuitous routes in closed containers and then released flew straight back to their nests (Fig. 3.1/7). They must, therefore, be able to recognize the terrain up to this distance. *Philanthus* may hunt as far a 1 km from its nest [858].

In the immediate vicinity of the nest (within a 4 m diameter for *Bembix* and *Philanthus*) proximate orientation sets in. The wasps orient to the nest entrance and to objects around it. The boundaries of the near range were determined by moving markers stepwise from the entrance until their displacement no longer elicited orientation flights [130]. The size of this region depends on the number of landmarks in the nest vicinity and the distance between them. The more numerous and closer to the nest, the smaller the near range. When some of the closest markers are covered, the near range expands.

The more often wasps fly to their nests, the more details they remember and the more precisely partitioned their perceptual field (*Philanthus* [857]).

In extensive field studies, van Iersel found that *Bembix* uses cues from areas near its nest up to the distant horizon. Not all areas, however, are equally important. The disturbance caused by introduction of objects into the nest area was determined from the duration of the search flights. It depends not only on the kind of object but also on its placement in the nest area. A rectangular bar behind the nest elicits longer search flights than one to the side of the entrance (Fig. 3.1/8). Although the proximate nest region is more heavily weighted, distant landmarks on the horizon

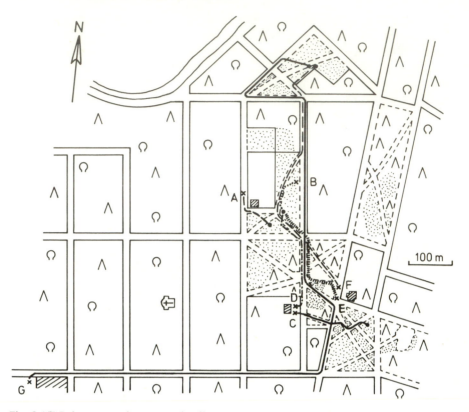

Fig. 3.1/7 Release experiments on the digger wasp *Bembix rostrata*. Wasps were removed from their nests (dots) and transported to different release sites (X) in closed containers (path shown by connecting lines). Wasps A–F flew straight back to their burrows, but wasp G (lower left) did not return to its burrow. The distances between release sites and burrows were: A = 75 m, B = 100 m, C = 150 m, D = 200 m, E = 265 m, F = 500 m, and G = 900 m. (Modified from [128])

also play a role. Digger wasps may even take into consideration whether the burrow faces good horizon landmarks when laying out their burrows [392].

Baerends [16] studied the significance of landmarks by aligning a row of shrubs with the burrow entrance of *Ammophila*. After the wasp had become accustomed to finding its burrow at the end of the row, he moved the whole row to the side. When the wasp returned, it searched futilely at the end of the row for its burrow entrance.

Tinbergen [854, 857] placed a ring of pine cones around the nest entrance of *Philanthus*. After the wasp had learned the initial layout, the ring was moved to the side of the entrance (Fig. 3.1/9). When the wasp returned, it flew to the middle of the ring even though the dark entrance was clearly

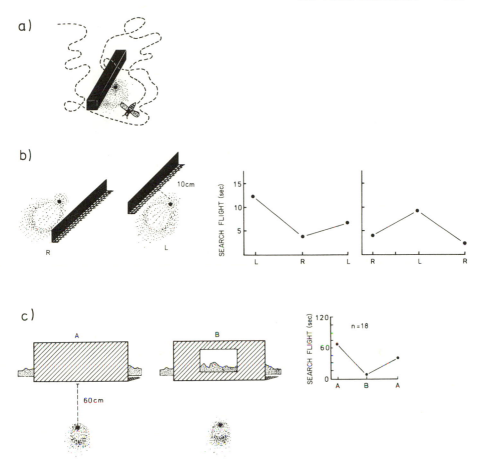

Fig. 3.1/8 Orientation of the digger wasp *Bembix rostrata* to its burrow entrance. a) The more extensively the nest area is altered while the wasp is away, the longer its search flight upon its return. b) The disturbance created by a new object often depends on its place-ment relative to the entrance. For instance, a cardboard strip elicits a longer search flight when placed to the left (*L*) than to the right (*R*) of the entrance. c) A wasp flying in the vicinity of the burrow also orients to distant points. Search flights last longer when the view of the horizon is blocked by a screen (*A*) than when a window is opened in the screen (*B*) (Modified from [391])

visible to the side of it. Tinbergen then compared the relative effectiveness of various stimulus characteristics (see 2.3.1) by giving the wasps a choice of two different rings. The more three-dimensional ones were preferred. Color and odor had no significant effect. These experiments clearly show that the wasp's return is guided by the relation of the nest entrance to the whole configuration of landmarks. It is even more important than the

Fig. 3.1/9 The digger wasp *Philanthus triangulum* "returns" to the middle of a circle of pine cones that had been girding its burrow entrance when it departed. (Modified from [856])

characteristics of an individual landmark (Fig. 3.1/10). Social bees and wasps also note the position of the hive or nest entrance relative to the surrounding landmark configuration. If the entrance is shifted, a swarm of insects gathers in the air precisely in front of its previous location ([60, 426, 687] cited in [128]).

Different landmark configurations may be used for different sections of an extended path. Jander [401] had ants carry pupae to nests in three different locations in short succession. In area A the nest was to the north; in B, to the south; and in C, to the west. the next day all three nest entrances were moved, but the ants still walked in the direction of the original nest locations. Other observations also indicate that insects use different sets of

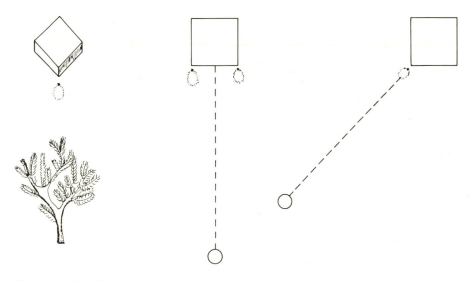

Fig. 3.1/10 The digger wasp *Philanthus triangulum* orients with respect to the relative positions of two landmarks. Left: Originally the nest was located between a small pine tree and one corner of a square. Middle: If the square is turned so that the pine is equidistant from two corners, the wasp digs at both corners. Right: If the pine is then moved so that it is opposite one corner, the wasp digs at that corner. (Modified from [61])

landmarks along an extended route [1022]. It is not yet known exactly why an insect selects some features of its environment and ignores others. Van Iersel's results on *Bembix* suggest that landmarks can have different weightings. Does an insect follow a continuum of landmarks, or does it fly in stages between single ones as suggested by von Frisch's experiments?

Ammophila does not home equally well from all locations. From some it immediately flies off in the home direction, but from others it first makes a few spiraling orientation flights, apparently searching for familiar cues [16]. Other observations indicate that at least in the nest vicinity, wasps are able to return from various directions. No matter from which direction *Philanthus* or *Ammophila* approaches the nest area, knowledge of the position of the nest relative to the landmark configuration guides them right to the entrance [857, 16]. The hover fly *Eristalis* also remembers its position in space relative to visual landmarks in its surroundings [138]. It hovers in midair, leaving its station periodically to chase passing insects. Regardless of the chase direction, it returns to the same home position. The accuracy of its return is highest when there is a nearby object such as a bush. Over an open lawn the home station is less well defined.

The critical factors for the desert ant are the apparent heights of the landmarks and their apparent intervals, i.e., the angular size of the visual landmark. Orientation is disrupted if the distance between two landmarks and the nest entrance is doubled. However, if the landmarks are also doubled in size, the ants can orient correctly. Clearly, ants do not rely on the concept "the nest is positioned between two identical markers," but try to match the current image with a memorized panoramic image [1022].

Landmark orientation is often part of a multimodal system. Beach-dwelling hermit and fiddler crabs [873, 874, 4, 3, 332] orient to conspicuous landmarks on the horizon (or nearby path markers) and to the sun. Hermit crabs can also orient to wind and probably to the slope of the terrain [873, 874]. Ants [404, 721] and bees [235] can even use sun and landmarks simultaneously.

Competition between landmark and sun compass orientation again raises the question of weighting. Von Frisch trained bees to find food in the south next to the edge of a forest that ran north-south (Fig. 3.1/11a). When their hive was moved to a location adjacent to a similar forest that ran east-west, most of the bees flew west. Very few found the food source to the south. When the experiment was repeated about 200 m from the forest edge (Fig. 3.1/11b), most of the bees flew south, i.e., they oriented to the sun. Experiments near shorelines or paths provide similar results. Individual landmarks, such as single trees, are, however, no competition for sun compass orientation in spite of their conspicuousness in an otherwise featureless landscape.

The precise weighting rules for such multimodal systems are as yet un-

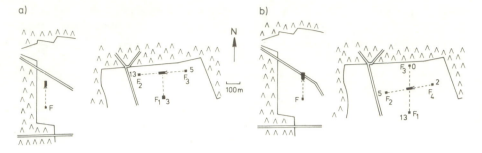

Fig. 3.1/11 Landmark orientation in bees. a) Bees trained to a food source (F) about 60 m from the edge of a wood running north-south (left) were presented with three food sources (F_1–F_3) near a wood running east-west (right). Most of the bees (numbers) were recovered at F_2, the food source with the same position relative to the east-west wood as F to the north-south one. b) When the bees were trained in the same meadow but 210 m from the wood (left), most of the bees flew south (right), i.e., they oriented to the sun instead of to the edge of the wood. (Modified from [235])

known (compare multimodal systems, 2.7). The above findings clearly indicate that landmark orientaton and sun compass orientation are different mechanisms. Two further arguments for this are: (1) Only sun compass orientation is coupled to a time mechanism (compare 2.8.1), and (2) a bee cannot pass on landmark information to other bees as it does sun compass values in the waggle dance [235].

The cockchafer, *Melolontha vulgaris*, uses an unusual combination of landmark and compass orientation [705]. The female must fly over great distances three times in its adult life: (1) after hatching, to find a feeding site, (2) when it is ready to lay eggs, and (3) after egg laying, to return to its feeding site (Fig. 3.1/12). An apparently inborn preference guides its first flight toward the highest contour on the horizon. If a distant mountain range is seen under the same visual angle as a nearby hill, an equal number of beetles fly to both contours. The maximum range for this orientation is about 3,000 m and is probably determined by the sharpness of the contours. The cockchafer cannot distinguish more distant contours from their background [759, 760]. (Schneider uses the term hypsotaxis for orientation to

Fig. 3.1/12 Orientation behavior of cockchafer females. Left: Normal behavior. Right: Second and third flight after displacement to the right of the forest. (Modified from [705])

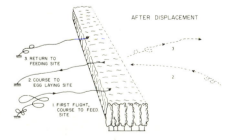

high segments of the horizon.) If the target turns out to be unsuitable because the hill is not wooded or the trees are not food trees, the beetle makes orientation flights to seek out a new target and heads for it. After a few weeks the female beetles fly to egg-laying sites. Displacement experiments show that they fly in the opposite direction of their first flight [705]. It is not completely clear what references they use to determine this direction. Horizon landmarks appear to be unimportant [705], and polarized skylight can be excluded since orientation is possible even under cloudy skies. Schneider concludes from experiments on the resting positions of newly hatched beetles that they orient to the magnetic field or another "ultra-optical" reference [761, 762]. After it has laid its eggs, the female flies back to its original feeding site. This time, however, it is not guided by landmarks [705].

3.1.6 Optokinetic Orientation

When an animal moves in space, its eyes register a shift of its visual environment in the opposite direction. Many animals orient their locomotion to such "optokinetic" stimuli. For instance, the shift of the ground pattern indicates to a flying bee its flight direction relative to the earth. This is an integral process of any course orientation during flight (3.8).

If the visual field of an animal is turned around it, the animal turns with it, i.e., it shows an "optomotor" response. Cybernetic analysis of the optomotor response was initiated by Hassenstein on the beetle *Chlorophanus viridis* [308, 313, 310, 311]. Reichardt and his colleagues have since used systems analysis to develop a "phenomenological theory" describing the observed input-output relationships of the visual orientation behavior of the fly [692, 693, 672]. Experimental flies, which are fixed by their backs so that their wings are free for flying, are suspended in the middle of a patterned cylinder. Free-flight conditions can be simulated by coupling cylinder movement to the torque generated by the wings via a torque compensator (closed-loop system). Instead of the fly turning toward a vertical stripe (on the cylinder), the stripe is moved into the fly's flight direction. For the fly these two stimulus situations are equivalent. Height orientation can be investigated in a similar set-up by relating the lift produced by the wings to the vertical displacement of a horizontal stripe (Fig. 3.1/13b).

When the torque compensator is uncoupled, the fly can no longer influence the stripe movement (open-loop system). The turning tendency of the fly is maintained, and the dependence of torque on various optokinetic parameters can be measured. Figure 3.1/13c shows that the angular distance (ψ_{tr} = error angle) between the fly and a stripe it is tracking is proportional to stripe velocity (α_p, see Eq. 1). The lag is greater when the stripe is moved

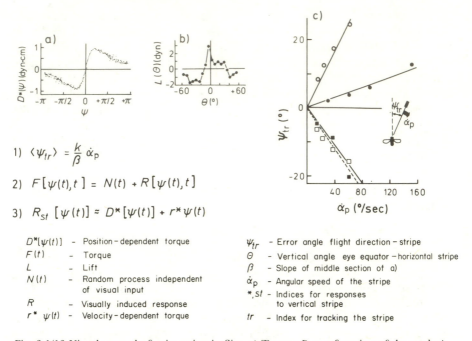

1) $\langle \psi_{tr} \rangle = \dfrac{k}{\beta} \dot{\alpha}_p$

2) $F[\psi(t),t] = N(t) + R[\psi(t),t]$

3) $R_{st}[\psi(t)] = D^*[\psi(t)] + r^* \psi(t)$

$D^*[\psi(t)]$	Position-dependent torque	ψ_{tr}	Error angle flight direction-stripe
$F(t)$	Torque	θ	Vertical angle eye equator-horizontal stripe
L	Lift	β	Slope of middle section of a)
$N(t)$	Random process independent of visual input	$\dot{\alpha}_p$	Angular speed of the stripe
		$*,st$	Indices for responses to vertical stripe
R	Visually induced response		
$r^* \psi(t)$	Velocity-dependent torque	tr	Index for tracking the stripe

Fig. 3.1/13 Visual control of orientation in flies. a) Torque D as a function of the angle ψ between the fly and a black vertical stripe, subtending 5°. b) Lift L as a function of angle θ. c) Error angle ψ_{tr} as a function of stripe velocity α_p. When the stripe is moved in front of a randomly patterned background, the fly tracks with a large lag ($+ \psi_{tr}$, open circles). When the background is white, the fly tracks the stripe more closely (closed circles). If a patterned background is moved in the same direction as the stripe, but faster, the error angle during tracking becomes a lead ($- \psi_{tr}$, closed squares). The open squares are the values predicted from the circle values by Equation 1. (Modified from [692])

relative to a background of random dots (open circles) than when the background is uniformly white (closed circles). Moving the background in the same direction as the fly's attempted turn signals to the fly that its flight velocity is too slow, so it speeds up. Instead of following the stripe, the fly leads it (closed squares). The "attractiveness" of a stripe can be measured as the slope β of the linear part of the torque curve (Fig. 3.1/13a). It depends on the stripe's dimensions and how much the stripe stands out from the background.

Equation 2 of Fig. 3.1/13 defines the fly's torque as the sum of two components: (1) a stationary Gaussian random process (= noise), which is independent of visual input and (2) a visually induced response consisting of two basic operations (Eq. 3). One converts pattern position (error angle) into torque; the other, pattern velocity into torque. Position and movement input via many parallel channels (the photoreceptor array of the compound eye) and are transformed into the torque. This multiple-input, single-output system can be modeled using a Volterra-like formalism, which agrees well with experimental findings on the anatomy and functional interactions of the CNS [672, 692].

This theory does not specify the origin of the noise component in Eq. 2, which includes the possibility of "spontaneous" behavior changes (changes of mood). Recent analyses [319a, 1028] show that the spontaneous turns (= changes of controlling variable) of a flying *Drosophila* are not randomly distributed but are a function of simultaneous light (e.g., general illumination) and optokinetic stimulation. Spontaneous actions appear to play a far greater role in the orientation behavior of flies than "simple" optomotor responses (compare 2.4.1).

3.1.7 Target Orientation

Many predatory animals orient visually to their prey. The prey-catching movement is usually a rapid open-loop process requiring no sensory feedback (Fig. 3.1/14). The prey is fixated; its direction and distance are measured; and the strike is carried out accordingly. Fixation may also be an open-loop process (3.1.8.3). The appearance of prey in the visual field elicits a motor response that brings the prey image into the fixation region, or fovea, of the retina. The fovea is an area with high resolution due to high receptor density or small angular distance between the optical axes of the single eyes. Vertebrates as well as predatory insects such as dragonflies, dragonfly larvae, tiger beetles, robber flies, digger wasps, and mantises possess foveas [446]. The praying mantis moves its head to keep the prey image centered on its fovea [500]. Experiments in which the mantis's eye was blinded area by area show that its fovea is horseshoe-shaped [550, 549, 27].

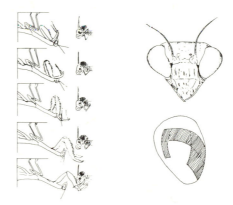

Fig. 3.1/14 Left: Film sequence of a praying mantis strike (240 frames/sec) with every other frame (i.e., 1/120th sec between each frame). During the strike the mantis moves its body forward. Upper right: Frontal view of head. Lower right: The right eye with the fixation area (fovea). (Left, modified from [550]; upper right, [549]; lower right, [27])

In arthropods with simple lenticular eyes, two are usually specialized for fixation. For example, although *Acilius* larvae use all 12 stemmata for prey capture, the no. 3 pair is sufficient to guide a normal strike (Fig. 3.1/15). The other eyes detect the prey at a distance of 4–6 cm and elicit tracking.

As a rule binocular vision is necessary for accurate distance estimation. In the mantis loss of one eye reduces the range of strike accuracy from about ⅔ to ⅓ the length of the striking leg [551].

The archer fish, *Toxotes jaculatrix*, presents an extraordinary example of target orientation. This fish uses its mouth like a water pistol to squirt at insects in the air (Fig. 3.1/16). The tongue is placed against the upper palate forming a tight seal on both sides and leaving a narrow channel in the middle. When the gill covers are snapped shut, a jet of water is forced through this channel and out the mouth. The fish tracks flying insects from just beneath the water's surface. When an insect lands within spouting range (up to 50 cm for a 10 cm long fish), the archer fish swims toward it, raises itself into a more vertical positon, and fires. The volley usually knocks the

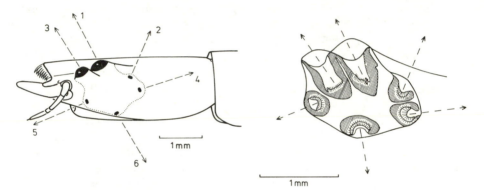

Fig. 3.1/15 Left: The head of the water beetle larva *Acilius sulcatus* with the six stemmata and their primary optical axes. Right: Section through the medial plane of eyes 1 and 3; the lenses of the other eyes are out of the plane of the section. Note that the retinas are composed of many receptor cells. (Modified from [770])

Fig. 3.1/16 The archer fish, *Toxotes jacula-trix.* a) Seven phases of a spout from a slow-motion film (500 frames/sec). The numbers indicate the frame number. Just before firing, the fish pivots into a vertical position, which becomes slightly more vertical during spouting (frames 8 and 12), thus bending the water jet upward. The later frames (from frame 20) show the spout dispersion following frame 8. b) Archer fish can also leap out of the water to snatch prey. (Modified from [316])

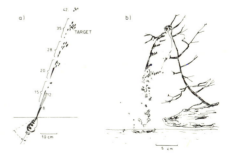

insect off its perch into the water. Insects that are close enough can also be seized in a leap. Target distance is probably determined binocularly since fish with only one good eye have very poor aim. The refraction of light as it enters the water must be accounted for in the aiming process.

3.1.8 Neurophysiology

At present the best known visual systems are those of insects and vertebrates. We shall look briefly at insects and then deal with vertebrates in greater detail. A wealth of material on the anatomy and fine structure of the fly's brain has been compiled by Strausfeld in *Atlas of an Insect Brain*. This standard work provides an insight into the incredible complexity of insect integrative centers [837]. For a survey of vertebrate visual systems see the *Handbook of Sensory Physiology* [836] and [378, 665].

3.1.8.1. Insect Visual System

The insect visual system can be divided anatomically into four parts, corresponding to four levels of information processing: retina, lamina, medulla, and lobula (Fig. 3.1/17). In Diptera the latter is subdivided into two sections.

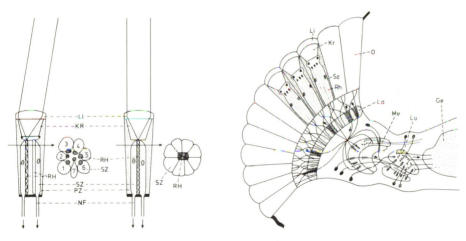

Fig. 3.1/17 The insect eye. Left: Longitudinal and cross sections of ommatidia with separate rhabdomeres as in flies (left) and with fused rhabdomeres as in bees (right). *LI* = lens, *KR* = crystalline cone, *SZ* = visual cell, *PZ* = pigment cell, *RH* = rhabdomere (cross sections show microvilli orientation), *NF* = visual cell axon. Right: Horizontal section through a fly's eye and visual centers. *O* = ommatidium, *La* = lamina, *Me* = medulla, *Lo* = lobular complex, *Ge* = brain. Most of the visual cell axons terminate in the lamina, but some go directly to the medulla. There are two chiasmata, one between the lamina and the medulla and one between the medulla and the lobular complex. (From [449])

The retina is composed of many ommatidia, each containing several elongated retinula cells. The retinula cells are arranged radially around the longitudinal axis of the ommatidium with their light-sensitive rhabdomeres toward the center [449]. In some insects (flies) the rhabdomeres are separate (open rhabdom); in others they are fused to form a common light guide (fused rhabdom) (Fig. 3.1/17).

Different retinula cells appear to be associated with diverse functional systems (3.1.2, [902]). Of the bee's nine retinula cells (Fig. 3.1/18) three are maximally sensitive to ultraviolet (350 nm); two to blue (440 nm); and four to green (530 nm). The UV-sensitive cells are also involved in perception of polarized light. The rhabdomeres are transverse stacks of parallel, densely packed microvilli, which carry the photopigment. Maximum absorption of polarized light occurs when the axis of polarization coincides with the microvillar axis. Cells 1–8 are twisted like the strands of a rope by 180°. Since the alignment of their microvilli changes along the length of the ommatidium, they are unable to detect a particular direction of polarization. Cell 9, however, is short and confined to the base of the ommatidium. It is twisted only about 40° and thus retains sensitivity to polarized light. The dorsal edge of the bee's eye is especially well adapted for the analysis

Fig. 3.1/18 Longitudinal (right) and cross (left) sections of a honeybee ommatidium. *LI* = lens, *KR* = crystalline cone, *RH* = rhabdom, *SZ* = visual cell. Of the nine visual cells, nos. 1–8 are elongated and no. 9 is short and confined to the base of the ommatidium beneath no. 5. Serial cross sections demonstrate that the retinula cells and the rhabdom twist by 180°. The arrows indicate the change in no. 5's position from one section to the next. (Modified from [902])

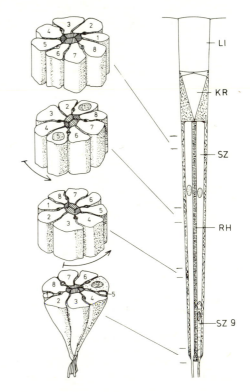

of polarization direction. The cells of the ommatidia in this region do not twist and are the same length [999]. Adjacent ommatidia are slightly turned relative to each other, so that the entire dorsal region forms a fan-shaped array [1023].

3.1.8.2 Vertebrate Visual System

The primary visual pathway of vertebrates begins with the receptor cells in the retina, the rods and cones. These synapse with a set of more anterior cells, the bipolar cells, which lead farther forward in the retina to the ganglion cells (Fig. 3.1/19). The fibers of the ganglion cells run along the inner surface of the eye, exiting at a point called the blind spot to form the optic nerve. The optic nerves from the two eyes meet at the optic chiasma, where half of the fibers from each nerve cross over to the opposite brain hemisphere, forming two tracts, each containing fibers from both eyes (Fig. 3.1/20). These tracts proceed to the optic thalamus, where they terminate in the lateral geniculate bodies. From here new fibers go to areas 17, 18, and 19 of the visual cortex (Fig. 3.10/28).

The receptor cells are interconnected via the cells in subsequent levels of the pathway. Those areas of the retina that feed into a single cell at any level comprise its receptive field (Fig. 3.1/19, 3.1/21). It can be determined

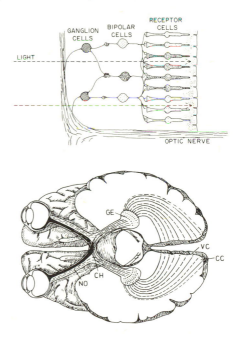

Fig. 3.1/19 The structure of the vertebrate retina is depicted schematically with the eye looking to the left. Several receptor cells transmit messages via the bipolar cells to a single ganglion cell, making up its receptive field. (From [378])

Fig. 3.1/20 The visual pathway of the human brain as viewed from below with the lower part of the cerebrum removed. The optic nerve (NO) leads from the retina to the optic chiasma (CH), where half of the fibers cross over into the opposite hemisphere, the other fibers remaining on the same side. Thus, the left visual field of each eye is represented on the left side of the brain; and the right field, on the right side. In the lateral geniculate bodies (GE) the ganglion cells synapse with cells that run through the brain to synapse with cortical cells (CC) in the visual cortex (VC). (Modified from [665])

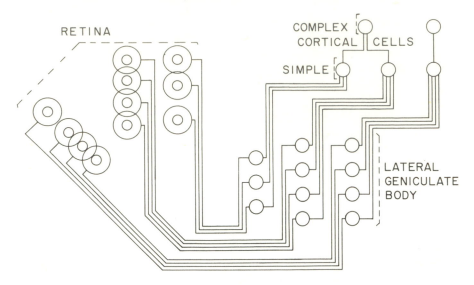

Fig. 3.1/21 Processing of visual information. Excitations from the receptive fields (concentric circles) of the ganglion cells are transmitted by cells of the lateral geniculate bodies to the cortex for further processing. A simple cortical cell responds strongly to stimuli striking rows of (ganglion cell) receptive fields having a particular orientation. A complex cortical cell receives input from several simple cells, bringing together information about lines with the same orientation in different sectors of the visual field. (Modified from [378])

by recording from a cell while systematically stimulating the retina with small points of light.

In general the receptive field of a ganglion cell is organized as a small circular area (field center) surrounded by a concentric ring. If stimulation of the field center elements excites the ganglion cell ("on" elements), stimulation of the ring elements inhibits it ("off" elements) and vice versa. A ganglion cell converts the stimulation of its field elements into a single signal by summation. When all receptive field elements are stimulated, excitation and inhibition cancel out, and the ganglion cell does not respond. However, if a bar-shaped stimulus falls on a field, the "on" elements predominate, and the firing rate of the ganglion cell increases. The number of individual receptors in the field center of a ganglion cell varies from a single cone in the fovea to hundreds of receptors, mostly rods, in the retinal periphery. This accounts for the higher acuity of foveal versus peripheral vision. Since a ganglion cell summates the excitation of its elements, cells with large field centers are more light sensitive. We can thus see better in dim light if we use our peripheral vision.

The receptive fields of cells in the lateral geniculate are also concentrically organized. In comparison to ganglion cells, the ring elements of geniculate cells have an enhanced capacity to neutralize the effect of the center.

Cortical cells can be classified by function into three groups: simple, complex, and hypercomplex (Fig. 3.1/21). The receptive field of a simple cell is a slit-shaped region flanked by an antagonistic region or regions because it combines the lined up fields of several ganglion cells. Each simple cell responds best to line stumuli with a particular orientation, which is termed its receptive field orientation. This optimum can be vertical, horizontal, or oblique, depending on the cells' connections with fibers from the lateral geniculate [379]. Several simple cells with the same field orientation converge on a single complex cell, so that pattern recognition is independent of position in the visual field. Hypercomplex cells bring together simple cells with different receptive field orientations, making analysis of complicated figures possible. Complex and hypercomplex cells are located in areas 18 and 19 (Fig. 3.10/28). Area 17 contains only simple cells.

The cells of the cortex are arranged in columns extending inward perpendicular to the brain's surface [380]. The receptive field orientation is the same for all the cells in one column but differs from column to column (Fig. 3.1/22). Furthermore, the whole visual cortex is retinotopically organized [1015, 1016, 1017].

Although the lateral geniculate-cortex pathway is the primary visual pathway in higher vertebrates, optic nerve fibers also project topographically to the tectum (= superior colliculus) of the midbrain ([478], Fig. 3.9/9). In lower vertebrates like the frog, which have no cerebral cortex or lateral geniculate body, the tectum is the main visual projection area (Fig. 3.1/23). In the deeper layers of the tectum somatosensory and auditory maps of space are integrated with the visual field map insofar as they overlap (see 3.6, 3.9). This region may constitute a representation of the environment based on spatial information from all pertinent sensory input.

The tectum is thought to be important for the orientation of directed movements. Localized electrical stimulation can release directed movements of the eye (fish [2], cat [8, 1009]), head (cat [337, 1009]), ear (rabbit [739]), and body (toad [206]). In each case the movement is directed toward the locus of the visual field whose tectal projection is excited. Recordings from cells in the tectum during eye movements reveal that they are active

Fig. 3.1/22 Three-dimensional view of the visual cortex, illustrating its columnar organization. Each column consists of thousands of cells. The hatched lines indicate two microelectrode penetrations, one ending in an electrolytic lesion that is used as a marker for histological analysis. Each hatch mark represents one recording site, and its orientation gives the receptive field orientation at that level. The receptive field orientations are the same within a single column, but differ from column to column. (From [378])

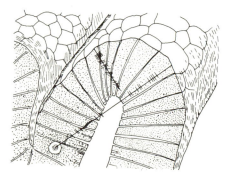

a)

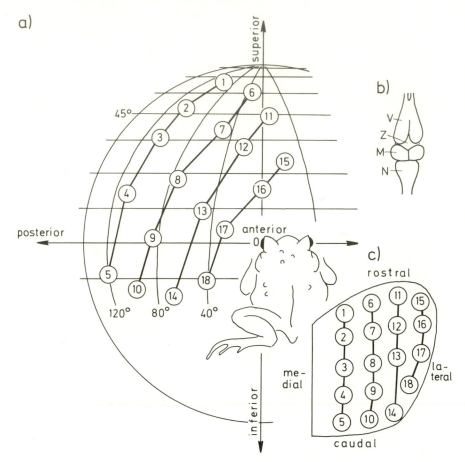

Fig. 3.1/23 The visual field—hemisphere shown in a), with latitude and longitude given in degrees—of a toad's left eye projects on a point-to-point basis (corresponding numbers) to the dorsal surface of the right tectum, c). b) Dorsal view of a toad's brain. V = forebrain, Z = thalamus, M = optic tectum, N = hindbrain. (Modified from [205a])

just prior to the movement [744]. Apparently, directed movements are based on a fixed motor program that is released at the corresponding site of the tectum. The eye movement resulting from simultaneous stimulation of two loci of the superior colliculus corresponds to the vector resultant of the two fixation directions and stimulus intensities ([706], 2.6.2).

3.1.8.3 Identification and Localization

We perceive the wealth of visual stimuli striking our retinas, not as a chaos of points and lines, but as images that we can identify. We register not only what we see but also where it is. Different central structures underlie these two processes of identification and localization (see 2.1.1 and 2.3.1).

As we have just seen, localization in vertebrates is directly associated with the tectum. The visual cortex is essential for identification [763, 1002]. After ablation of their visual cortex, hamsters can no longer distinguish between vertical and horizontal striping but can still turn toward moving objects. Hamsters without a tectum cannot localize but can still distinguish between the stripings [763].

Cat tectal cells are less sensitive than cortical ones to changes in stimulus shape. Both respond to stimulus movement [204]. Monkeys without a visual cortex behave as if they were blind with respect to shape discrimination and object identification, but can still visually track and reach for moving objects [151, 389, 388]. There are indications that people who are blind as a result of visual cortex damage can still perceive movement and can even localize objects with eye movements [497]. These processes, which are thought to be controlled by the superior colliculus [678, 862], are difficult to investigate since they are not conscious.

The tectum is important for vision in the periphery of our visual field where we perceive movements (= ambient vision) but not shapes or stationary objects. The fovea is indispensable for focused vision and for form recognition and differentiation. An ambient mechanism mediates perception of the whole space encompassed by the visual field. It can selectively direct the attention to a particular object, which is then inspected more closely by a focal mechanism. This is accomplished by fixating eye movements, which bring the object's image onto the fovea, linking localization with identification [862, 816].

3.2 ORIENTATION TO HEAT

Heat is a form of energy associated with the motion of molecules; the greater the motion, the greater the energy. Depending on the medium, heat can be transmitted via infrared radiation (Fig. 3.1/1), conduction, or convection. We shall consider two orientations with respect to heat, preferred temperature and prey location.

3.2.1 Orientation to Preferred Temperatures

Many animals prefer and seek out locations having a particular temperature. When placed in a temperature gradient, they aggregate around a temperature optimum (Fig. 3.2/1). It is not known precisely what mechanism they use for this orientation. Presumably it is a kind of kinesis, analogous to the orientation of the sowbug to humidity (Fig. 2.5/1).

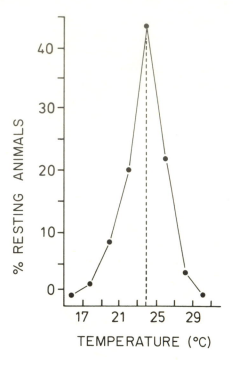

Fig. 3.2/1 Heat orientation of the beetle *Carabus granulatus*. When placed in a temperature gradient most of the beetles aggregate in the 24° region [334].

3.2.2 Prey Orientation

Boas (family Boidae) and pit vipers (Crotalidae, rattlesnakes also belong to this family) have specialized pit organs for sensing radiant heat [636, 111]. These organs enable a snake to detect infrared radiation from objects warmer than their surroundings, e.g., warm-blooded prey. In the boas the labial pit organs are located under scales on the upper and lower lips. In the crotalids the facial pit organs are midway between the eyes and the nostrils (Fig. 3.2/2). The labial pits of pythons and the supranasal sacs of puff adders may have the same function. A pit organ is a cavity with an external opening and a false bottom consisting of a sensory membrane separated from the true floor by an air space. The membrane is only 15 μm thick and densely innervated and vascularized [927, 636, 113].

The prey-locating function of these organs has been demonstrated experimentally on *Boa hortulana* and on the pit vipers, *Agkistrodon mokasen* and *Crotalus adamanteus*. Even with eyes taped shut and nostrils plugged, a snake can detect a swinging light bulb (25 watt, wrapped in cloth) at a distance of 40–50 cm and strike it from 30–35 cm. If the pit on one side is filled with gel, the snake strikes as soon as the light bulb swings over to the unblocked side. If both pits are blocked, it cannot detect the heat source

a)

b)

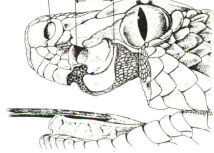

Fig. 3.2/2 a) The pit viper *Crotalus viridis* uses facial pit organs to sense out warm-blooded prey. b) The receptive cone of the facial pits. c) The head of a pit viper with an exposed facial pit. The sensory membrane lies behind the opening and in front of an air chamber. (Modified from [112])

but regains its ability to do so after the gel is removed [636]. Similar results have been obtained on pit vipers using freshly killed, still warm rats.

The neurophysiology of the receptors has been investigated by Bullock and Diecke [112]. The primary excitation process is fundamentally different from that of visual receptors, where radiant energy is first absorbed by pigments whose conformation changes initiate neural excitation. The receptors of the pit organ are stimulated directly by infrared radiation. They are remarkably sensitive to differences in temperature, responding to differences of three- to five-thousandths of a degree.

How these organs function in prey localization has not yet been investigated in detail. Since the pit opening is about 35%–50% smaller than the sensory membrane, the organ works like a pinhole camera. A heat source forms an image on the membrane providing directional information. There is a narrow region of overlap in front of the receptive cones of the two organs (Fig. 3.2/2b).

The organization of the central projections provides some insight into the localization mechanism [266, 849]. Recordings were made from the tectum during light and infrared stimulation. As in other vertebrates, the pit viper's visual field projects topographically onto the surface of the contralateral tectum (see 3.1.8.2). The receptive cone of the pit organ projects onto deeper layers of the contralateral tectum. The receptors are organized into receptive fields, which are larger than the visual ones, but have a similar topographical arrangement (Fig. 3.2/3). This points to an arraylike organization of the sensory membrane. Bimodal neurons that respond to both visual and infrared stimuli have been found in the tectum of the rattlesnake [1005].

Neurons have also been found in the tectum that respond to stimulation not only of the contralateral, but also of the ipsilateral, organ [266]. These units are excited by stimuli in the overlap region. Since a stimulus in this region hits both organs, it activates the overlap units in the tectum more strongly than a stimulus outside of this region (summation). This provides a basis for three-dimensional perception of the prey.

Prey localization and capture probably proceed as follows: When a mouse

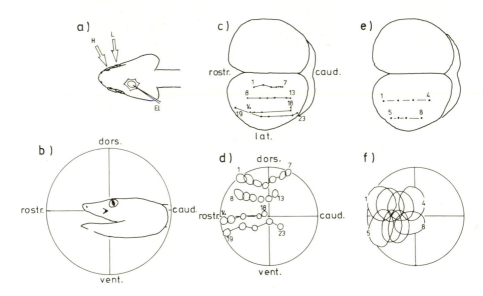

Fig. 3.2/3 Tectal projections of the visual field and the receptive cone of the pit organ in the pit vipers, *Agkistrodon brevicaudatus* and *A. caliginosus.* a) Dorsal view of the head illustrating stimulation of the right organs with heat (*H*) and light (*L*) while recording (*El*) from the left tectum. b) Labeling of the stimulus field. c) Recording sites in the tectum. The numbers correspond to the areas of the visual field shown in d), which were stimulated to elicit tectal activity. e) Recording sites deeper in the tectum, corresponding to areas of the receptive cone of the pit organ, shown in f). (Modified from [266, 849])

comes within range of a pit organ, its heat radiation enters the pit opening and excites receptors, causing the snake to turn toward it. This fixation movement brings the mouse's "image" into the overlap region. The turn may correspond to the angular distance of the stimulated site from the medial plane of the snake (open loop). Since the receptive cones are comparatively large, fixation does not always succeed on the first try. This leads to side-to-side head movements, as have been observed in pit vipers [266], and eventually to fixation of the mouse. Fixation activates the overlap units in the tectum, releasing the directed strike. Distance estimation may be based on a triangulation process (see 2.3.4).

3.3 ORIENTATION TO ELECTRIC FIELDS

The ability of fish like the electric eel and the electric ray to give an electric shock has long been a focus of curiosity and research. However, it has been barely 30 years since Lissman discovered that weakly electric fish not only generate an electric field but also sense it and use it for orientation [513, 514, 515]. An electric sense has since been found in other species of fish—not all of which have electric organs [516]. The current state of knowledge in this field has been compiled in several comprehensive reviews [49, 50, 110, 742, 844, 846, 618, 845, 318].

There are two modes of electrical stimulation, active and passive. Stimulation is said to be active when it results directly from the animal's own activity and passive when the stimuli are imposed by an extrinsic source. The signals are used in two classes of behavior, spatial orientation and social communication. Orientation can be subdivided into target orientation, i.e., to single objects, and positional orientation, i.e., the animal's position relative to its surroundings as a whole.

3.3.1 Electric Fields

The source of a biologically effective electric field can be inanimate or animate (bioelectric). An inanimate field may arise via induction when a fish either moves itself (active) or is carried along by current flow (passive) through the earth's magnetic field. Although this stimulates the electroreceptors, the orientation is with respect to the magnetic field and is therefore treated in the section on magnetic field orientation (3.4).

Bioelectric fields may be generated by electric organs or by other electrochemical processes. Fields of the latter kind have been found in many aquatic animals [419]. Their origin is based on the physical phenomenon that ions migrate between two chemically different solutions producing a potential difference across their interface and thus an electromotive force. In aquatic animals such processes are especially important at those surfaces of the body where ion permeability is high, such as the mucous membranes and the gill epithelia. These *dc* fields are about ten times stronger around the anterior body openings (mouth and gill regions) than at other places on the body [419]. They are modulated by rhythmic movements such as breathing. Additional nonelectric-organ fields may originate from action potentials of muscles like those of the operculum and heart.

It is well known that the strongly electric fish (electric eel, electric ray, electric catfish) possess specialized organs for generating brief, but powerful, electric fields. These high-voltage pulses serve to paralyze prey or frighten off enemies. Like the weakly electric fish they are also capable of giving off a series of weak discharges for orientation and social communication.

The electric organs of fish (Fig. 3.3/2) develop from striate muscle. They are organized in columns of electroplates, which are the modified muscle cells. The columns are parallel to the dorsoventral body axis in rays, and to the longitudinal axis in the electric eel (Fig. 3.3/1) and the weakly electric fish. Each electroplate (Fig. 3.3/1) is embedded in a jellylike mass and tightly surrounded by insulating connective tissue. In the electric eel the rostral surface of a plate is covered with many papillae, and the caudal surface is innervated. The resting potential across the plate membrane is about +84 mV with the inside negative to the outside. Nerve stimulation changes the membrane conductance only of the innervated surface, reversing the potential across this membrane to −67 mV, so that the potential difference across the cell is 84 + 67 = 151 mV. The electroplates are stacked in columns with like surfaces facing the same direction, and they function

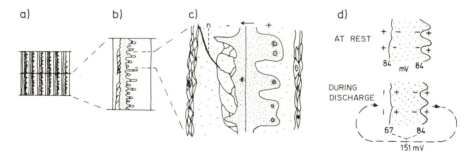

Fig. 3.3/1 Electric organ of the electric eel *Electrophorus electricus* (caudal, left; rostral, right). a) Section of two columns. b) An electroplate. c) Section of an electroplate flanked by connective tissue septa; *n* = nerve. d) Functional scheme. Nerve impulses reverse the potential across the caudal membrane from +84 mV (outside relative to inside of electroplate) to −67 mV. This results in a potential difference across the cell of approximately 150 mV. (a and b, modified from [140]; c, from [834])

like tiny batteries connected in series. The greater the number of plates, the higher the voltage of a column. The columns are connected in parallel, thus, the more columns, the greater the amperage of the organ. From the above figures we can calculate for the electric eel that simultaneous excitation of all 6,000 electroplates in one column would produce about 900 V. This has the same order of magnitude as the 600 V which have been measured. The organ of a weakly electric fish such as a mormyrid produces only about 6–17 V with its 150 to 200 plates. The electric organ of an eel has about 70 columns, so a discharge lasting 2.5 ms may produce a current of about 0.6 amps or about 600 watts. Electric rays can produce 1,000 to 6,000 watts depending on their size. An electric organ discharge can be released by vibration, touch, or prey.

During each discharge, the tail end of the organ becomes momentarily negative relative to the head end. The lines of potentials from head to tail form an electric field resembling a dipole field (Fig. 3.3/2). Objects with a different electric conductivity than water distort the configuration of this field. Field lines converge on objects with higher conductivity and diverge from ones with lower conductivity. The voltage falls along the field lines from the anterior to the posterior pole. The shorter the line, the steeper the voltage gradient. For field lines that swing far out, e.g., those which enter at the head, the voltage decrease per unit line (segment) is relatively small.

3.3.2 Electroreceptors

The electroreceptive organs are derived from the lateral line organs. Two classes can be distinguished on the basis of structure and function, am-

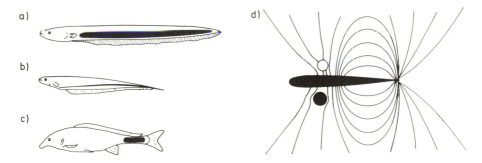

Fig. 3.3/2 Electric organ distribution in a) *Electrophorus electricus*, b) *Gymnotus*, and c) *Mormyrus*. d) Electric organ discharge produces a field that is distorted by objects according to their conductivity. Field lines converge on a good conductor (open circle) and diverge from a poor conductor (filled circle). (a, modified from [49]; b and c, [842]; d, [845])

pullary and tuberous. Ampullary organs are found in sharks and rays (elasmobranchs), catfish (Siluridae), and in electric fish (Gymnotidae, Mormyridae, Gymnarchidae). Some histological reports also place them in certain dipnoan and brachopterygian fish and in gymnophionan amphibians [110, 844]. Tuberous organs (*Knollenorgane*) are found only in teleosts with electric organs (Gymnotidae, Mormyridae, Gymnarchidae, Malapteruridae) and one marine family, Uranoscopidae. They respond to self-generated electric fields (active stimulation).

Ampullary organs. The ampullary organs are blind jelly-filled canals whose openings are visible as small pores in the skin (Fig. 3.3/3). The blind end is enlarged and lined with sensory cells embedded in a layer of supporting tissue. Only a relatively small surface of the sensory cell membrane contacts the jelly (mucopolysaccharides). The canals of marine fish, i.e., the ampullae of Lorenzini in sharks and rays, are quite long. In a 40 cm long ray they can be up to 16 cm long with a diameter of only 2 mm. They run in bundles under the skin from the external opening to the sensory cell clusters, which are often surrounded by a capsule (Fig. 3.3/4). In fresh-water teleosts the canals are short, often microscopic (microampullae). The difference in canal length corresponds to the different environmental pressures faced by marine elasmobranchs and teleosts (Fig. 3.3/5). In a voltage gradient the inside of a fresh-water teleost is equipotential due to its high-resistance skin and conductive body fluids. The greatest voltage differences occur across the skin. In contrast, a voltage gradient extends throughout the body

Fig. 3.3/3 Ampullary organs a) and b) and tuberous organs c) and d) of weakly electric fish with the external surface up. The drawings on the right are simplified renditions of the ones on the left. Inserts show cross sections through the canals. *BM* = basal membrane, *J* = jellylike substance, *SC* = sensory cell. (Modified from [842])

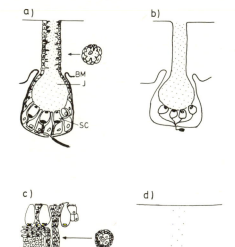

Fig. 3.3/4 Distribution of the ampullae of Lorenzini in the head of a dogfish, *Scyliorhinus canicula*. Dots and circles indicate pores in the skin that are connected by long canals (broken lines) to clusters (stippled areas) of sensory cells. Four clusters are situated on each side of the nose and five under each eye. Ventral pores are not shown. Arrows indicate the main direction of the canal bundles. N = nostril, K = first gill slit, SP = spiracle. (Modified from [172])

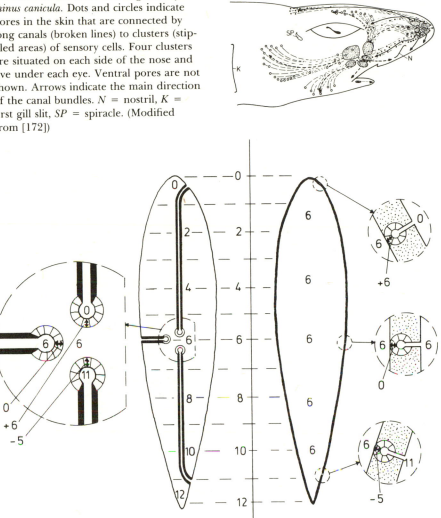

Fig. 3.3/5 Stimulus voltage (in arbitrary units) at the electroreceptors of a marine elasmobranch (left) and a teleost (right) in a voltage gradient. Broken lines indicate equipotential lines; heavy outlines, high-resistance structures. The voltage gradient extends throughout the body of the elasmobranch because of its low-resistance skin. In contrast, the inside of a teleost remains equipotential due to its high-resistance skin. The long insulated canals of the ampullae of Lorenzini enable elasmobranchs to make voltage comparisons in a gradient. Short canals suffice for the teleosts. The inserts are enlargements of the sites across which (double-headed arrows) the stimulus voltage (no. = potential difference) is measured. (Modified from [618])

of a marine elasmobranch due to its relatively permeable skin. The greatest potential differences occur across the high-resistance ampulla wall. The long canals allow marine elasmobranchs to make voltage comparisons in a gradient, whereas short canals suffice for the teleosts.

Ampullary receptors function like voltage meters, measuring the difference between inside and outside. They give a primarily tonic response to slow changes in field potential (= low frequency) and are not excited by the high-frequency fields of electroorgans.

Tuberous organs. The tuberous organs contain a number of sensory cells within an epidermal capsule. In general these cells have no direct connection to the outer medium. Access to the body's surface is blocked by specialized tissue that has the same electrical permeability as the surrounding skin. In contrast to ampullary receptor cells, most of the receptor cell surface is exposed to the perisensory cavity. These large surface areas are thought to function like capacitances [50, 844, 845], giving the phasic receptors high pass filter properties. They are relatively unresponsive to low-frequency voltage changes.

3.3.3 Signal Coding and Central Processing

Each electroreceptive organ encodes some stimulus parameter into neural excitation, first of all its intensity and eventually its duration and variations in time. Five categories of coding units can be distinguished according to the major parameter coded [109, 742]. They are: (1) burst duration coders (*B*) for duration of impulse trains and impulse number, (2) burst dispersion coders (*D*) for latency and the temporal distribution of impulses within a burst, (3) probability coders (*P*) for probability of impulses, (4) phase coders (*T*) for the phase relationship to a self-generated stimulus, and (5) frequency coders (*F*) for impulse frequency.

The ampullary organs, which respond to single electric pulses (= pulse detectors) in a frequency range of about 0–20 Hz, are characterized by a regular resting discharge. They encode according to category (5). The tuberous organs, or wave detectors, with a frequency range of 60–2,000 Hz, encode according to categories (1)–(4).

The above coding parameters are quantitative. The sensor-site label, which is a qualitative parameter, must also be considered. Not only the receptor characteristics of the individual organs but also their arrangement on the body are important for orientation. In electric fish the tuberous and ampullary organs are distributed all over the body, but not uniformly (Fig. 3.3/6). They are particularly numerous on the head, especially around the mouth. The ampullary organs of sharks and rays are limited to the head.

As in the visual system, a receptive field can be assigned to each receptor.

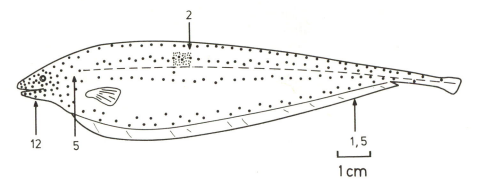

Fig. 3.3/6 Distribution of electroreceptors in the electric fish *Sternarchus*. Large dots = ampullary organs; the numbered arrows indicate the density of tuberous organs/mm². The
area at arrow 2 shows the density of tuberous organs (small dots). (Modified from [842])

For the organs of the weakly electric fish, which respond to a self-generated
field, "the receptive field of an electroreceptor is that sector of the outer
world which projects onto the receptor via the effective vector of the electric
organ discharge" [742].

Signals from the electroreceptors are processed in the brainstem, midbrain, and cerebellum. Their afferent fibers proceed via the lateral line
nerves to the brainstem, where they terminate in the lateral lobes. The
lateral lobe cells are direction-sensitive. Their firing rate depends on the
position of the stimulus in the receptive field. Fibers originating in the
lateral lobes lead to the torus semicircularis, a structure in the midbrain
underneath the optic tectum. Recordings show that torus units differentiate
stationary from moving objects and respond to the direction of movement.
The electroreceptive surface of each side of the body is topologically mapped
onto the contralateral torus [742].

3.3.4 Orientation

3.3.4.1 Orientation in Self-generated Fields

The electric sense of the weakly electric fish is "a true picturing sense where
spatial parameters of the outer world project on the animal's body surface"
[742]. The receptors comprise an array (2.3.3.1) that registers where field
lines enter the body of the fish (Fig. 3.3/2). Distortion caused by objects
whose conductivity differs from that of the surrounding water alters this
configuration. The objects "cast a self-image."

Lissman showed that fish can distinguish between externally identical
objects that cause a different degree of distortion of the electric field [514,

515]. The fish *Gymnarchus niloticus* was trained to accept food when a porous clay pot next to it was empty and to reject it when there was a glass rod in the pot. The electric sense of these fish is so sensitive that they can detect a glass rod only 2 mm in diameter. The range for this differentiation and orientation has been shown in the mormyrid species *Gnathonemus petersii* to be only 4 cm [45].

The electric sense permits a behavior analogous to optokinetic orientation [317]. When blinded *Eigenmannia* are presented with three vertical Plexiglas strips that are swung back and forth, the fish follow the movement. This electrokinetic tracking depends on the frequency and amplitude of the stimulus oscillation. Tracking is optimal at about 0.05–0.1 Hz and 40 mm amplitude. Under these conditions the fish follow synchronously, i.e., without any phase shift, and with approximately the same amplitude, i.e., gain = 1.

Orientation to "electric landmarks" has been investigated in the gymnotids, *Eigenmannia, Gymnotus, Hypopomus,* and *Sternopygus*. Fish given a shuttle box avoidance task in a tank containing electrically connected carbon rods find the open door sooner when the pattern of connections is one they are familiar with [109]. Electric fish, *Gymnotus carapo* and *Apteronotus albifrons*, which are accustomed to swimming through one of two doors, ignore it when it is covered by a polyethylene sheet (electrically insulating) and try persistently to swim through the other door, which is blocked by a layer of agar (electrically transparent) [419].

3.3.4.2 Orientation to Extrinsic Fields

Electric fish can localize prey from the low-frequency electric fields that arise in the region of the prey's body openings ([419], 3.3.1). They snap at goldfish behind an agar plate even when a silver mesh is embedded in the agar that shields their own high-frequency fields but passes the low-frequency fields of goldfish. Electric fish also attack agar-coated electrodes that simulate the field of the prey.

The electric eel can also locate the extrinsic field produced by the high-frequency, low-voltage discharge of another electric eel [742]. When two eels are in separate tanks connected by wires, an increase in the discharge rate of one attracts the other over a range of at least 5 m. An electric eel is also attracted to a field simulating a conspecific.

Orientation to extrinsic fields is also important for fish lacking electro-organs, such as sharks, rays, and some catfish. The catfish *Ictalurus* attacks live goldfish protected by an agar plate but ignores them when a polyethylene film is added to the agar. They also attack electrodes behind the agar that simulate the field of the goldfish (Kalmijn and Adelman, cited in [419]).

Catfish can learn to distinguish hiding places according to the presence or absence of an electric field [722, 723, 724]. The ability of catfish to orient to a particular hiding place in a uniform electric field indicates that they can hold a compass course to an electric field [422, 423]. The dogfish *Scyliorhinus canicula* is also capable of compass orientation in an electric field by using the local geo-electric fields that occur along the sea bottom as topographical features [1006].

Dijkgraaf and Kalmijn [172, 173] found that the dogfish and the ray *Raja clavata* respond to weak electric fields with reflexes of the eyelids (shark) or spiracles (ray). Denervation and recording experiments showed that the ampullae of Lorenzini are responsible for this sensitivity. When the rate of heartbeat is used as the sensitivity indicator, it can be demonstrated that the system is very sensitive indeed. A stimulus of only 0.01 μV decelerates the heartbeat. It is also slowed down when the field of a flatfish in a separate tank is picked up and reproduced 10 cm from the ray.

The electric sense is used to detect hidden prey (Fig. 3.3/7). Sharks dig in the sand where they detect the field of a prey animal or where electrodes simulating the prey are buried.

In field studies, sharks (*Mustelus*) were lured by fish extract fed into the water via a tube (Fig. 3.3/8). They approached the tube, swaying from side to side, but then veered sharply to the side and attacked electrodes on the sea bottom that emitted electric fields simulating prey. One shark even managed to rip away the electrodes [420].

A behavior of catfish that may be associated with its electric sense has been found to be an earthquake predictor. The catfish *Parasilurus asotus* displayed hypersensitive fright reactions to mechanical vibrations some hours before an earthquake [314, 315]. The hypersensitivity disappeared when the water flow from a nearby stream was cut off. The increase in sensitivity may be related to the characteristic earth potentials that precede an earthquake. Artificial electric fields also produce an increase in sensitivity [463].

3.4 ORIENTATION TO MAGNETIC FIELDS

The earth's magnetic field is like the dipolar field of a gigantic bar magnet that is tilted 20° from the earth's rotational axis. Lines of magnetic force run between the magnetic north pole at 70°40′N, 96°5′W and the magnetic south pole at 72°S, 155°E (Fig. 3.4/1). The closer to the poles these lines enter the earth, the more perpendicular they are to the earth's surface. At the magnetic equator they are parallel to the surface. The angle between the geomagnetic field and the horizontal plane at any specific location is called the magnetic inclination or dip. The inclination is 0° at the equator and 90° at the poles. Magnetic intensity is measured in Oersteds (1 Oe =

a)

b)

c)

d)

e)

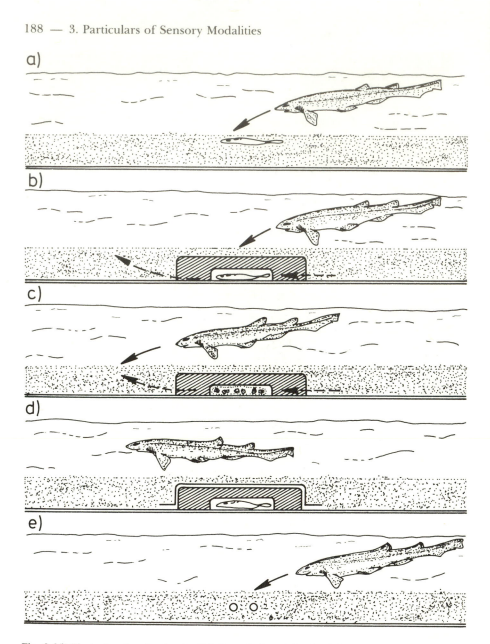

Fig. 3.3/7 Electrolocation by the dogfish *S. canicula.* a) The dogfish digs in the sand for the buried flatfish. b) It digs for the flatfish in an agar chamber. (Agar is electrically permeable, but prevents diffusion of chemical substances.) c) It ignores pieces of fish in an agar chamber and searches where the current carrying the fish odor leaves the chamber. d) When the chamber is shielded electrically by a polyethylene film, it no longer responds to the flatfish. e) It digs in the sand for buried electrodes that simulate the electric field of the flatfish. (Modified from [420])

Fig. 3.3/8 Field experiment on electrolocation of the shark *Mustelus canis*. Dipole electrodes that simulate the field of a prey animal are attached to each end of the crossbar of an H-shaped frame. Sharks are attracted by fish extract fed into the water via a tube whose mouth is attached to the middle of the crossbar. When a shark nears the odor source, it veers sharply toward the right electrode and attacks it. (Drawing by M. A. Müller, modified from [420])

1 gauss = 10^{-8} voltsec/cm²). Geomagnetic field strength is about 0.7 Oe near the poles and 0.3 Oe at the equator.

3.4.1 Orientation to the Earth's Magnetic Field

The influence of magnetic fields on positional and locomotory orientation has been investigated in a large number of organisms. Magnetic fields affect the oriented movements of *Paramecium* [460, 647] and the turning direction and frequency of *Volvox* [648]. Light orientation of the planarian *Dugesia* and the snail *Nassarius* is influenced by magnetic fields in a circadian rhythm [94, 26].

Insects (termites, beetles, flies, grasshoppers, crickets, cockroaches, wasps) prefer a north-south or east-west resting position in both natural and artificial magnetic fields. The course of *Drosophila* walking on an inclined

Fig. 3.4/1 The earth's magnetic field.

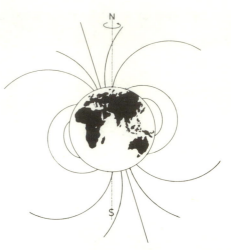

surface can be altered by magnetic fields [904]. The geomagnetic field may also be involved in the "ultra-optical" orientation of resting position in the cockchafer [761, 762] and in the course set by beetles walking on a horizontal surface [602].

Objects can also be oriented with respect to magnetic fields (2.2.1). Experiments with artificial fields have shown that termites orient their tunnels to the geomagnetic field [38]. Likewise, honeybees build their combs in a defined direction relative to the earth's magnetic field [565]. If the magnetic field is rotated 40°, the bees change the direction of their combs by 40°.

The slight discrepancies in the waggle dance of the honeybee between the actual direction of a food source and the direction indicated by the bee [236, 235] are due to the influence of the earth's magnetic field [507, 565]. These "misdirections" show a diurnal periodicity and vanish when the geomagnetic field is compensated by an artificial field (Fig. 3.4/2).

The biological significance is not known for the above magnetic field effects, but is clearer for the following examples. Birds that must fly over long distances orient the direction of their flight to the geomagnetic field [752]. Mice and men appear to be able to home using the magnetic field [984, 1001]. Young salmon can maintain a particular course relative to the magnetic field [1007]. Magnetic field orientation is best understood for bacteria and birds.

Magnetic bacteria such as *Aquaspirillum magnetotacticum* have a specialized organelle, the magnetosome, consisting of a chain of magnetite particles that functions like a bar magnet. In a magnetic field these bacteria swim north (magnetotaxis) [986], and even dead bacteria are swung around to face the magnetic north. The influence of O_2 concentration on the behavior

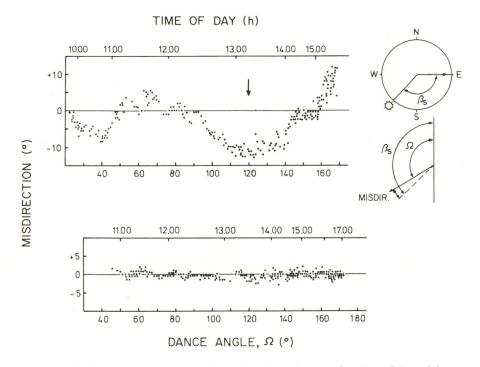

Fig. 3.4/2 Misdirection in the waggle dance of the honeybee as a function of time of day and dance angle with a normal geomagnetic field (upper diagram) and when the geomagnetic field is compensated by placing the hive in the center of a Helmholtz coil (lower diagram). The insets illustrate the situation indicated by the arrow. The misdirection is the difference between the sun compass angle (β_s) and the angle (Ω) danced by the bee on the comb (Modified from [507])

of the bacteria indicates that magnetotaxis is not purely automatic, but is an active process. The preferred habitat of magnetic bacteria is mud with a low oxygen content. Magnetotaxis probably occurs only when they encounter unfavorable conditions such as oxygenated water. The bacteria then follow the magnetic field lines downward (inclination!) into the muddier regions.

Homing pigeons use magnetic field orientation when the sun is obscured by clouds. This was shown by attaching small bar magnets to the backs of experimental pigeons and brass bars to the controls [429]. Homing was equally good in both groups under sunny skies (Fig. 3.4/3a). However, under overcast skies only the control pigeons showed good homing (Fig. 3.4/3b). Magnets disrupt the homing of inexperienced pigeons even under clear skies (Fig. 3.4/3c). Apparently, pigeons must first learn to discriminate

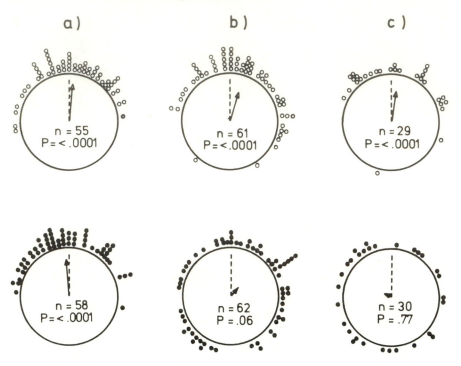

Fig. 3.4/3 Homing of pigeons carrying a brass bar (upper row) or a bar magnet (lower row) a) under clear skies, b) under cloudy skies, and c) first-flight juveniles under clear skies. Each data point is the vanishing bearing of one pigeon released 27–50 km away from the home loft. The arrows give the mean vector of all points, the dashed line, the home direction. (Modified from [429])

between the two orientation systems and to use the sun as their main reference cue.

Artificial magnetic fields generated by Helmholtz coils around the heads of pigeons have also been shown to impair their homing [889].

Magnetic field orientation in migratory birds was suggested by earlier findings that migratory restlessness (2.8) showed particular directional tendencies even when the birds could not see the sky [238, 580, 581]. This has since been confirmed for the European robin, whitethroat warbler, garden warbler, subalpine warbler [948], and the indigo bunting (Emlen et al., cited in [948]). Figure 3.4/4 shows the effect of changes in the magnetic field on the direction of migratory restlessness [945].

Magnetic field orientation is set to a particular field intensity. Birds became disoriented when exposed to a stronger (0.68 Oe) or weaker (0.34 Oe) field intensity than usual (0.46 Oe) [947]. However, after three days in a field of only 0.16 Oe, birds can regain their ability to orient. This

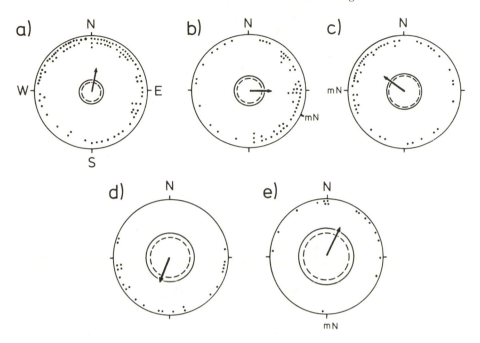

Fig. 3.4/4 The effect of magnetic fields on migratory restlessness of European robins in the spring a)–c) and of garden warblers in the fall d), e) *mN* indicates the magnetic north of the artificial fields. Each point is the mean direction of migratory restlessness of a single bird in a night. The arrows give the mean vector of all points; the broken circles, the 5% significance limits; and the solid circles, the 1% limits according to the Raleigh test. (a–c, from [944]; d and e, from [945])

capacity to accommodate to new field intensities is especially important for birds that migrate from polar regions with high field intensities (about 0.6 Oe) across the equator (about 0.3 Oe).

The horizontal component, i.e., the north-south alignment of the earth's magnetic field is critical for the above processes. Alignment with respect to this component can, however, be in either of two directions separated by 180° (Fig. 3.4/5). Animals may be able to use the inclination to differentiate between these [947]. When the inclination is experimentally reversed from 66°N to 66°S, European robins fly in the opposite direction. They appear to adjust their flight so that the field lines transect their bodies from dorso-posterior to ventro-anterior end (Fig. 3.4/5c).

The findings on inexperienced homing pigeons indicate that magnetic field orientation is of primary importance in birds. This is further substantiated by evidence from garden warblers that the magnetic mechanism is genetically fixed. The direction of migratory restlessness is species specific even for young birds that have never seen the sky [946, 1027]. Experiments

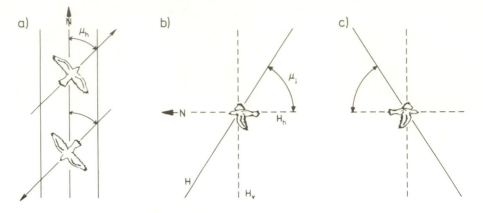

Fig. 3.4/5 Orientation of a bird to magnetic fields. a) The horizontal component of the geomagnetic field transects the bird's body at the same angle (μ_h) whether it is flying northeast or southwest. b) The bird flies in a direction so that the inclination is equal to μ_i. H is the magnetic field direction, H_v is the vertical, and H_h, the horizontal component of the field. c) When the inclination direction is experimentally reversed, the bird orients in the opposite direction. (Modified from [944])

on warblers and European robins show that they learn to associate star compass directions with magnetic field directions (2.8.1.2).

The nature of the receptive mechanism is still obscure. Small deposits of magnetite, which have recently been found in the heads of pigeons, may be involved [1018]. According to one hypothesis [895], a magnetic field is sampled from different flight directions using a direction-sensitive probe. This process would be analogous to scanning an auditory field with one ear to pinpoint a sound source.

3.4.2 Orientation to Induced Electric Fields

Movement of an electric charge through a magnetic field induces an electric field that is perpendicular to the magnetic field and to the direction of movement (Fig. 3.4/6). The inductive effect is maximal when the movement is at right angles to the magnetic field. Induction may result from either passive transport of an animal by a current moving relative to the vertical component of the geomagnetic field or from the active movement of an animal relative to the horizontal component [419].

An example of the first case would be a shark that is carried along headfirst in an ocean stream (Fig. 3.4/6a). The induced electric field passes through the shark from left to right. If it turns to the right, the field will transect the shark from tail to head. With sensors that respond to such

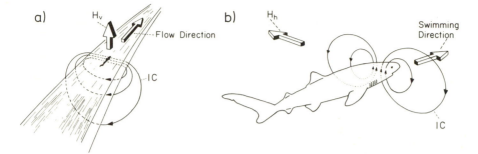

Fig. 3.4/6 Movement in the geomagnetic field induces an electric field. The electric and magnetic fields are perpendicular to each other and to the direction of movement. a) A fish that is carried along by an ocean stream is in an induced electric current (*IC*) generated by the flow of water relative to the vertical component (H_v) of the geomagnetic field. Note that the induced current arises independently of the fish. b) Active locomotion of a shark relative to the horizontal component (H_h) of the geomagnetic field induces an electric current. (From [419])

changes a shark could tell how it was oriented relative to the direction of flow. However, since the electric field direction is related only to the flow direction, the fish cannot determine the orientation of the stream in space without additional information. If, for example, the shark "knows" in which of the great ocean streams it is swimming, it may relate its position within the stream to the earth's coordinates. The conditions for such a mechanism are particularly favorable in the polar regions where the vertical component of the geomagnetic field is especially pronounced (see Fig. 3.4/1). Although this kind of orientation has not yet been demonstrated in marine animals, sharks and rays do possess the necessary sensory equipment in the ampullae of Lorenzini (see 3.3.2).

A shark's active movement relative to the horizontal component of the geomagnetic field induces an electric field passing from its dorsal to its ventral surface (Fig. 3.4/6b). Electroreceptors such as the dorsoventrally aligned ampullae of Lorenzini register stimulus voltage that is a function of electric field intensity. Since the intensity depends on the angle between the direction of locomotion and the magnetic north, being maximal when the shark is swimming at right angles to the magnetic field, the shark could determine the magnetic north by taking several readings over time (successive sampling with direction-sensitive sensor, 2.3.3).

Preliminary evidence of orientation to the horizontal component of the geomagnetic field has been reported for the shark *Triakis semifasciata* and the ray *Urolophus halleri* [421]. The orientation of the normal behavior of sharks can be affected by artificial magnetic fields. In one experiment rays were presented with several hiding places in a circular tank and trained to go to the one facing in a particular direction relative to a magnetic field. Reversing the field polarity resulted in the rays seeking out a hiding place facing in the opposite direction.

3.5 CHEMOSENSORY ORIENTATION

Chemosensory orientation is usually goal orientation and only rarely positional orientation. As a rule it involves finding an odor source such as food, a social partner, or home quarters. The marking of territory with scent (ants [355], mice [542a], rabbits [621a], wolves [664a]) only indirectly concerns orientation. Although foxes mark their territorial boundaries with urine, they recognize these boundaries even without the marks (Mac-Donald, 1978, personal communication). Apparently, the main function of marking is to make the boundaries of an animal's territory known to others. It remains to be seen whether animals use scent marks to orient within their own territory.

Stimulus propagation. Odors propagate by diffusion. In a still medium, diffusion produces a radially symmetrical gradient around the odor source. In moving air or water, however, odors are carried along in the direction of the current. Scent marks that occur in a row or continuous band make up a trail.

As far as is presently known chemosensory organs are only intensity-sensitive. Organs that discriminate the incident directions of an odor have not been found. As intensity-sensitive sensors, they are suitable for orientation in gradients. Chemical orientation is, as a rule, gradient orientation. In addition, chemical stimuli can release an orientation to a current.

3.5.1 Orientation in Gradients

Orientation in an odor gradient may consist of gradient sampling reactions that refer directly to the stimulus. In this process the odor samples at different loci are compared. Gradient orientation may also arise indirectly (kinesis reactions). Time interval measurements have been reported for humans [42, 43]. Since the concepts and mechanisms of direct and indirect gradient orientation were covered in 2.3.3 and 2.5.4.2, we shall only treat them briefly here.

The shark *Mustelus* orients in odor gradients by moving the front part of its body from side to side (= successive sampling with one sensor). Even with one nostril plugged a shark can sniff out pieces of food. It still turns toward both sides, but more frequently to the unplugged side [301].

Depending on the steepness of the odor gradient, walking bees orient using simultaneous sampling with both antennae (bisensor process) or successive sampling (unisensor process).

Insects also use successive sampling when they have only one antenna. Bees move their antenna from side to side, turning toward the higher odor concentration [563]. Wasps and dung beetles with only one antenna can follow an odor gradient upward [619, 646].

Von Békésy [43] has investigated the localization of odor sources in humans. The precision of localization that he found is amazing. Within an area 65° from the median plane, experimental subjects could localize an odor source to within 7°–10°. The odor sources were perforated plastic balls that released an odor mixture. Von Békésy describes two processes that might be involved, a simultaneous process with two sensors and a time interval measurement. For simultaneous measurement a concentration difference of 5%–10% was enough to localize the odor to the side of the nostril that received the higher concentration. In the time interval process very slight differences (0.3 ms) in the arrival time of the odor at the right and left nostrils were enough to determine which side the odor came from.

3.5.2 Trail Orientation

A trail consists of a row of discrete odor sources or a continuous band of odor. The trail follower scans the diffusion gradients that spread out from these stimulus sources [943, 72].

Trails may originate from conspecifics, prey, or objects, A poisonous snake finds a mouse it has bitten by crawling along the mouse's trail (Fig. 3.5/1). The snake can tell the difference between a trail made by its injured quarry and one made by dragging a dead mouse along the ground [32]. Newts follow the trail of earthworms [247] or their own tracks back to their burrows [144] as do land snails [1008]. Many tidal zone snails orient to the slime trails of conspecifics [864]. Firefly larvae find snails (their prey) by following their slime trails [797]. A dog keeps to its master's trail even when it is crossed by other tracks [746] and can also differentiate the trail of one horse from another.

When the odor sources comprising a trail are widely spaced, an animal must orient from one source to another. This kind of trail orientation plays an important role in the foraging behavior of a stingless bee (Meliponini [506]). Every 2–4 m on its way back to the hive from a new food source, the forager marks blades of grass, pebbles, clumps of earth, and so on, with a secretion from its mandibular glands (Fig. 3.5/2). When it nears its hive, it flies in zigzags to alert other bees, which then search for the scent markers and follow them back to the food source.

A trail may also consist of a continuous band of odor. Orientation to

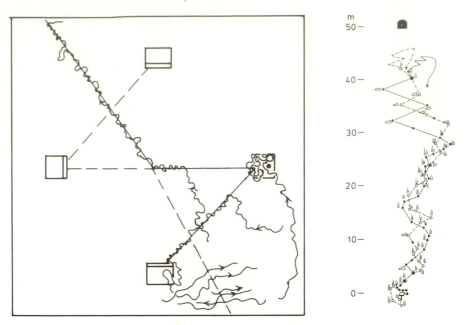

Fig. 3.5/1 (*left*) The search of the viper, *Vipera aspis*, for prey. The lines indicate the path of the head of a viper as it follows a trail (solid straight lines) along which a mouse, which has died as a result of being bitten by the viper, has been dragged. The viper ignores the trail (dashed lines) of a live mouse. The squares indicate small boxes in which the mouse can be hidden. A dot represents a hidden mouse. The experimental terrarium is 1 m on each side. (Modified from [32])

Fig. 3.5/2 (*right*) Odor orientation of the bee *Trigona rufricus*. On its way home from the food source, the forager makes intermittent landings to lay scent marks with its mandibles (the closed circles represent the first marking flight; the open circles, the second of the same bee). Fellow hive members follow this trail of scent markers to the food source. (Modified from [506])

such trails has been best studied in ants. In extensive field studies Brun [96] found that the trail substances are effective over hours and even leave their traces on objects placed on the trail. He also found that ants can simultaneously follow scent trails and orient to the sun (2.7.2).

When a new food source is discovered, foragers are recruited. Both short-range and long-range recruitment has been found in the ant *Novomessor* [354]. In recruitment over shorter distances, the recruiter emits a scent from the tip of its abdomen that is carried to its nestmates by the wind. These flock to the recruiter, orienting against the wind (see below). If nestmates must be recruited over a greater distance, the recruiter lays a trail on the ground.

The simplest way to indicate the path to be taken is by leading with direct body contact (tandem running). It should be noted that in tandem running the recruit follows only if aroused by special recruiting signals. Following must be "released" by the recruiting signals (see 2.1.1). In *Bothroponera tesserinoda*, nestmates are alerted and induced to follow by secretions from the poison gland. When touched by the new recruit, the recruiter turns around and heads back to the food source. The recruit follows it by maintaining antennal contact [565a, 604]. Tandem running has also been observed in *Camponotus sericeus* [352, 353]. In this species the recruiter makes forward thrusts with its body to induce the other ant to follow it (Fig. 3.5/3).

Chemical stimuli play a decisive role in tandem running. The recruit follows only when the leader (a dummy in experiments) smells right [565a]. This raises a question of classification. To what extent is this a tactile orientation (compare 3.9)? Should the leader be regarded merely as a moving odor source to be followed? Instead of following a continuous band of stimulus on the ground, the recruit follows a stimulus source on a moving substrate. In any case both olfactory and tactile stimuli appear to be important [995]. Trail orientation and tandem running thus seem to be closely related.

In *Camponotus socius*, recruits are alerted by abrupt sideways movements of the head [348]. They then follow the trail that the recruiter lays by pressing its abdominal tip to the ground and releasing a mixture of rectal pouch contents and poison gland secretion. *Formica fusca* recruits nestmates and leads them to a food source in the same way [603]. Figure 3.5/4b demonstrates that the recruits actually follow the trail. When an artificial trail leading in the "wrong" direction was laid using the contents of several

Fig. 3.5/3 Tandem orientation of the ant *Camponotus sericeus*. The recruiter (dark) meets a nestmate, thrusts its body back and forth (upper), turns around (middle), and is followed by the other ant, which keeps its antennae on the recruiter's abdomen (lower). (Modified from [353])

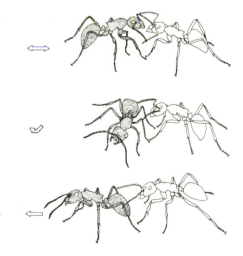

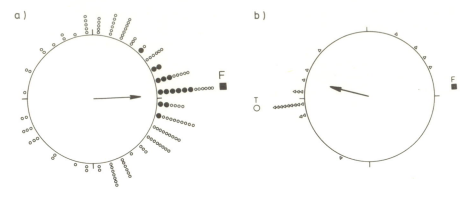

Fig. 3.5/4 Trail orientation of the ant *Formica fusca*. The ants enter the arena through a hole in the middle of the floor. F = food source; arrow = mean vector of walking directions. a) The open circles indicate the directions of individual ants; the closed circles, of groups of 10. b) The floor of the arena was replaced, and a trail was drawn from its middle to T with the contents of rectal pouches. (Modified from [603])

rectal pouches, the recruits followed this trail. In fire ants the trail substance comes from the Dufour glands [940]. The dosage of the secretion and its effectiveness can be controlled.

The richer the food source, the better marked the trail. Thus, the trail also holds information about the quality of the source [299]. How long an ant trail lasts can vary. Long-lasting trails are found leading to abundant food sources that are used over a longer time. In contrast, trails to poorer sources are composed of "short-lived" volatile substances (Fig. 3.5/5) [351, 352].

The mechanism of trail following. A snake sways from side to side flicking the trail with its tongue, registering stimulus intensities successively at different loci along the trail. After it has touched the ground, the tip of the tongue is brought into the Jacobson's organ, an olfactory organ in the palate, where the absorbed odor particles are analyzed. Carnivores and even newts "sniff," i.e., they take a rapid sequence of odor samples into their nasal passages. In this way they scan both cross gradients of the trail successively with one sensor and determine the line of highest concentration. Males of the moth *Trichoplusia* follow a wavy trail of female pheromone that has been drawn on the ground by an experimenter [810].

Hangartner has more closely investigated the trail following of ants (Fig. 3.5/6). An ant walks in a slightly wavy line, so that the area of maximal odor concentration is kept between the tips of its antennae. When two parallel trails are laid, separated by the distance between the antennae, an ant walks in a straight line with the tip of one antenna on each trail. Apparently it compares the excitations of the two antennae. Animals with

Fig. 3.5/5 Persistance of an odor trail of the fire ant *Solenopsis sevissima*. The trail was laid from the food source to the nest. The wormlike band indicates the threshold odor concentration for an ant to follow the recruiter. *t* = sec after the trail is laid. After about 100 sec the trail has disappeared. (Modified from [72])

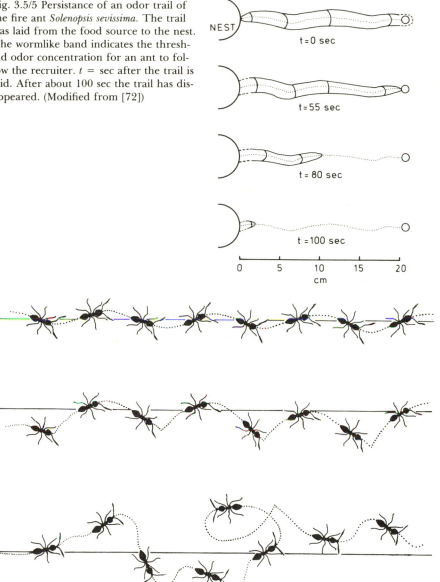

Fig. 3.5/6 Trail orientation of the ant *Lasius fuliginosus*. Upper row: The normal wavy path of an ant following an odor trail. Middle row: An ant missing its left antenna can follow the trail by making a sharp left turn whenever it goes "too far" to the right. Lower row: Even an ant with crossed antennae can follow a trail. When it starts to lose the trail, it makes a "correct" turn even though left and right signals are exchanged. (Modified from [299])

only one antenna can also follow a trail. Trail following is even possible when the antennae have been crossed over experimentally, although there are many "wrong" turns and loops. An animal with one antenna always makes a sharp turn when the antenna side happens out of the odor zone. This turn is directed to the side without the antenna (= unisensor successive process). This is contrary to the way a (bisensor) simultaneous mechanism works. In a simultaneous system the turn is always to the more strongly stimulated side, i.e., the side with the antenna. The fact that the animals turn to the side without an antenna suggests that the simultaneous mechanism is turned off. This is, however, contradicted by the behavior of ants with one antenna in a homogeneous odor field [298]. They walk in curves toward the antenna side, which can only be explained by a simultaneous mechanism (bisensor system). It would thus seem that both simultaneous and successive mechanisms are at work. This is supported by the orientation of the animals with crossed antennae (Fig. 3.5/6). The successive mechanism makes it possible for them to stay on the trail, whereas the simultaneous mechanism causes them to repeatedly make wrong turns.

As regards the polarity of a trail Brun [96] found that when ants were placed in the middle of a trail, they were not immediately able to tell which direction was "coming" and which was "going." However, after they had walked a short distance in the wrong direction they occasionally turned around. Brun attributed this to variations in the odor components of the trail that depend on the distance from the nest. (As can be seen in Fig. 3.5/5, the odor fades as a function of time.) An ant can only recognize such a gradient by following the trail for a while.

3.5.3 Olfactory Orientation in a Flowing Medium

When wind passes over a small odor source, the cloud of odor takes on the shape of a plume. The length of the odor plume decreases with increasing wind velocity (Fig. 3.5/7). This is just the opposite of what one would expect and is a result of the greater turbulence caused by increased wind velocity. Odor distribution is not uniform within an odor cloud. Turbulence gives rise to bursts of concentration [1004].

Olfactory orientation in a flowing medium combines the response to an odor with the response to current flow. For orientation to a current we have to distinguish between animals on a substrate and animals freely suspended in a medium. The former can orient to the mechanical stimuli of the current, but the latter cannot. The orientation of a flying or swimming animal in a flowing medium is a visual orientation (compare 3.8).

Orientation on a substrate. Land snails crawl against the wind toward their

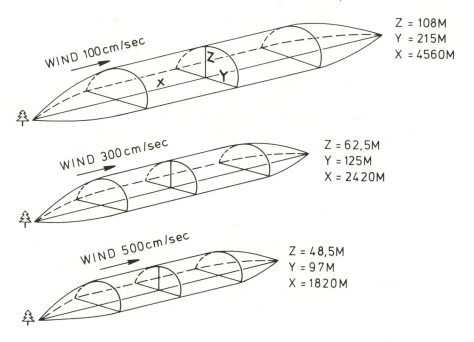

WIND 100cm/sec

Z = 108M
Y = 215M
X = 4560M

WIND 300cm/sec

Z = 62,5M
Y = 125M
X = 2420M

WIND 500cm/sec

Z = 48,5M
Y = 97M
X = 1820M

Fig. 3.5/7 Odor plumes produced by wind. In a wind the sex pheromone of a female moth forms an odor plume that is bounded by the threshold concentration for releasing the approach flight of the male moth. The odor plumes were calculated from wind parameters and the rate of pheromone release. (Modified from [943])

shelters [1008]. The marine snails *Aeolidia papillosa* and *Trinchesa aurantiaca* start to crawl upstream when nutritive juices are added to the water [880]. Locusts and potato beetles walk upwind toward the source of food odors [305, 938]. The short-range recruiting of the ant *Novomessor* also belongs to this category. The recruiter emits a secretion from the poison gland on its upstretched abdomen. Nestmates as far away as 2 m are alerted and start to walk upwind [354] (see 3.5.2).

Strictly speaking these are orientations, not to odor, but to current flow. The chemical stimulus functions as a releaser, which makes the animal move against the current flow. The odor gates the anemotactic behavior. As is shown later for "flyers," chemical, idiothetic, visual, and current flow signals are often complexly intertwined.

Male silk moths walk a slightly wavy path into wind containing the female pheromone, bombykol [805]. As Kramer [469] found, they hold a certain course angle relative to the wind. When they enter an area of lower pheromone concentration at the edge of an odor plume, the silk moths make a sharp turn so that they are still oriented in the same angle relative to the wind but to the other side (= zigzag path).

Walking bees find an odor source by following a particular odor concentration upwind in a zigzag line [468]. The concentration depends on how full their honey sacs are.

Orientation freely suspended in a medium. Drosophila flies straight into wind carrying the scent of bananas [966]. Carrion beetles (*Necrophorus, Silpha noveboracensis, Silpha americana*) steer a zigzag course into wind carrying the odor of rotting meat [152]. They can do this missing one antenna but not missing both (although they can still fly). The fish *Diplodus sargus* faces upstream when an attractant is added to the water [451, 452]. Salmon returning to their spawning grounds recognize their home river by the characteristic combination of chemicals in the water [306, 307, 997]. The salmon become "imprinted" to this odor mixture when they are young.

A zigzag path is characteristic of the locomotion of many animals following an odor trail in water or air [440]. Kennedy and his colleagues [444, 562] have investigated the mechanism of such orientation in the male of the Indian meal moth, *Plodia interpunctella*. As soon as the female pheromone is added to the air current, the male moths head upwind at an angle

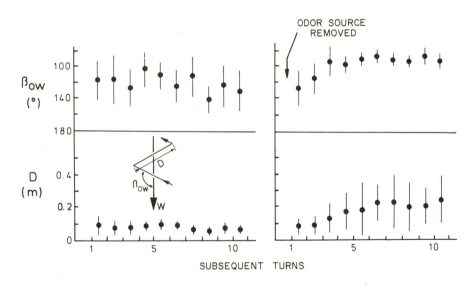

Fig. 3.5/8 The flight path of the male moth *Plodia interpunctella* in an airstream containing the female sex pheromone (left) and after removal of pheromone (right). The airstream direction is indicated as W in the inset. The angle of the path (β_{ow}) and the distance flown between turns (D) are shown as a function of the sequence of turns. When the odor source is removed, the path angle decreases to approx. 90° (= the moth does not advance) and the distance (D) between turns increases. Each point gives the mean with standard deviation for 5–10 moths. (Modified from [562])

of $\beta_{OW} = 100 - 140°$ (Fig. 3.5/8). The moth holds the path angle and velocity constant during fluctuations in wind velocity by adjusting its own velocity and the drift angle (see 3.8). Path velocity decreases as the moth nears the source, i.e., as odor concentration increases, but the path angle is maintained. When the pheromone is removed, the path angle decreases to $\beta_{OW} = $ approx. 90°, and the moth flies ever-lengthening forays back and forth at approximate right angles to the wind.

Whether the course changes that make up a zigzag path are released by the odor stimulus, e.g., by a decrease in concentration, or whether they are idiothetically oriented (3.11) has to be determined for each individual case.

Olfactory orientation with "current flow" probe. Brock [89] describes an olfactory orientation in hermit crabs in which the animal creates a side current that swirls back on itself. The stream of water flowing forward from the gill chambers can be guided in different directions by the beating of the maxillipeds. The antennules bearing the odor receptors are held out in the opposite direction monitoring the "back" current. The crab can thus sample water from different directions and then go directly toward the strongest odor stimulus (Fig. 3.5/9). Eddy formation depends on the structure of the surroundings. The system can only work if there are structures in the surroundings that form a locally bounded space, so that water is forced back toward the crab.

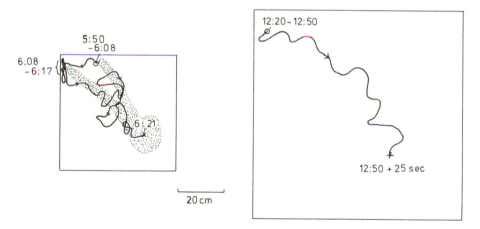

Fig. 3.5/9 The food search of the hermit crab *Pagurus arrosor* by means of a current probe. Left: At 5:50 a piece of food (cross) was introduced into the tank with some eosin dye, which spread from the food toward the crab as shown by the stippling. At 6:08 the crab moved a short distance to the left, and a second band of color grew toward the crab's new position. The crab then proceeded to inspect the "chemical sector," finding the food after 4 min. Right: The crab sat still for 30 min after food was placed in its tank, then walked to the food in 25 sec over a slightly curved path (current band not shown). (From [89])

3.6 ORIENTATION TO SOUND

Hearing is often particularly well developed where vision cannot be used. A barn owl catches mice in total darkness. It can determine the location of a rustling mouse to the centimeter and pounce on it (Fig. 3.6/7). Many birds that nest in deep caves orient acoustically by echolocation.

Bats have developed a highly differentiated system of echolocation, which furnishes information not only about the direction and distance of the target but also about its structure. It is a peculiarity of echolocation that it is independent of the external productions of stimuli. The orientation sounds are produced by the orienting animal, not by its target.

Acoustic orientation is such an extensive topic that we can only single out a few examples. We shall limit our discussion to the sound localization of humans; the prey orientation of owls; the echolocation of bats and dolphins; the sound location of frogs; the acoustic orientation of crickets, grasshoppers, and moths; and, as a special case, the ability of mosquitoes to localize a sound source.

Likewise, it is possible to cite only a fraction of the abundant literature. The anatomy and physiology of hearing is treated comprehensively in the articles of the *Handbook of Sensory Physiology* (vol. V/1, compare [809]). A comparative overview of more recent findings on sound localization can be found in Erulkar [198]; and a review of directional hearing of humans, in Keidel [431].

3.6.1 Physics and Stimulus Process

The vibrations of a sound source, such as the vocal cords, cause the molecules of the medium to oscillate back and forth in the propagation direction (= longitudinal). These molecules hit neighboring ones, setting them in oscillation. A spatial-temporal sequence of vibrating molecules arises, a sound wave. Sound travels as a longitudinal wave with a velocity of 330 m/sec in air, 1,047 m/sec in water, and 5,100 m/sec in iron.

As adjacent particles in the longitudinal wave get closer and farther apart, there are periodic changes in the density of the medium and, therefore, pressure fluctuations. The pressure maximum depends on the amplitude of the particle movement. The greater the amplitude, the closer the molecules and the higher the sound pressure. Sound pressure is perceived as loudness. It can be measured in microbars ($1\mu b = 1/10$ N/m^2), a unit of pressure, in decibels (db), or in phons. The decibel expresses the relative difference in power between the sound pressure and a reference pressure, $\Delta p_2 = 2 \times 10^{-5}$ N/m^2, according to the equation $D = 20 \log \Delta p_1/\Delta p_2$. The phon is also a relative measure for sound intensity. The reference value

$b_{min} = 2 \times 10^{-12}$ watt/m² is approximately the auditory threshold of the human ear. The phon is the logarithmic expression of this unit, $L = 10$ log b/b_{min}. The ticking of a watch is about 10 phon; normal conversation, about 50; a running motorcyle, about 90; and ten motorcycles, about 100. Because of the logarithmic progression, a tenfold increase in sound intensity is reflected by a numerical increase of only 10 (90 + 10 = 100). Thus, an increase in the noise level from 50 to 60 phon means a tenfold increase in loudness, not a mere increase of one-fifth.

Since the sound pressure at any locus is independent of the direction of the sound wave that is generating it, it is defined only as a scalar quantity, and not by a direction. At the receptor, however, the pressure might become a function of direction. For example, when the receptor is shielded by sound-damping structures, the receptor is in a "sound shadow." The shadow effect depends on the size of the obstacle relative to the wavelength. The obstacle must be larger than the wavelength. For the human head with an approximate diameter of 20 cm, a wavelength of about 35 cm (= about 900 Hz) is the upper limit. Higher tones are attenuated by the head so that they reach the ear on the far side with less intensity than lower tones (Fig. 3.6/1).

Pitch is determined by the number of oscillations per unit time (oscillations/sec = Hertz or Hz). The frequency range for the human ear extends

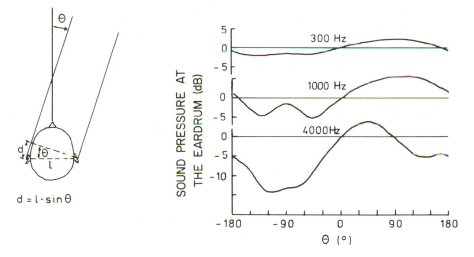

Fig. 3.6/1 The effect of sound on the human ear. Left: The difference (d) in the length of the sound paths to the two ears as a function of the angle of incidence (θ) and the distance between the ears (L). Right: Pressure at the eardrum as a function of θ for three different frequencies. Note that for 300 Hz there is little difference between +90° (= side of the measured eardrum) and −90° (= opposite side). (Left, modified from [431]; right, from [809])

from about 20 Hz to about 20,000 Hz. Low frequencies are perceived as deep; high frequencies, as high tones.

Some sound receptors register the actual displacement of molecules, i.e., the vibration along the path of the sound. Since this displacement has a constant direction, it can be expressed as a vector. Other sound receptors respond to the pressure decrease at a membrane, such as the eardrum, obstructing the path of the sound (pressure gradient receptor). The outside pressure at the eardrum rises and falls in the rhythm of the oncoming sound waves. "Inside," on the other side of the eardrum, this does not occur. The fluctuating difference in pressure between the outside and the inside causes the eardrum to bulge inward and outward so that it too oscillates.

In some cases sound can also reach the inside of the eardrum, as in birds [502], frogs, and insects (see below) that have structures that conduct sound through the body. When the waves arrive at the inner and outer surfaces in phase, i.e., when the difference is one wavelength or a multiple thereof, the pressure is the same on both sides and the eardrum remains stationary. The effect is maximal when a pressure maximum on one side coincides with a pressure minimum on the other side (phase difference = 180°). The phase difference depends on the difference in length of the internal and external pathways and thus on the sound direction.

3.6.2 Localization by Humans and Other Mammals

3.6.2.1 Stimulus Parameters

When the sound source is to one side, the sound on the other side is less intense (for frequencies over 900 Hz), and the sound waves arrive later since they have farther to go.

The difference in arrival time results from the difference in the length of the pathways, which is a function of the sine of the angle between the incident sound direction and the medial plane (θ, Fig. 3.6/1). For $\theta = 30°$ the length difference is about 10.5 cm (21 cm × sin 30°). At a velocity of 330 m/sec, sound takes 0.0003 sec to cover this distance. Sound direction can be calculated from arrival differences of tenths of milliseconds.

Differences in intensity and arrival time are both important for direction localization. This was shown in experiments in which left and right ears were played off against each other using separate stimulation [371, 431]. Holding one of the parameters constant while changing the other imparts a sensation of direction. As von Békésy [41] discovered, they are interchangeable (trading function). For instance, a difference in arrival time can be canceled by a difference in intensity in the opposite direction, so that the sound is perceived in the middle. For frequencies over 900 Hz the determining factor is the intensity difference; and for lower frequencies, the arrival time difference.

A further binaural cue that plays a role in localization is the frequency dependence of the sound shadow (Fig. 3.6/1, [455]). Since the higher frequencies are attenuated at the ear on the shadow side, the tonal quality of the sound is deeper on the far side than on the near side. Such differences also provide directional information.

Directional hearing is also possible with only one ear. People who are deaf in one ear can localize sounds almost as well as people with normal hearing [7, 30]. The pinnae appear to play a decisive role in both monaural and binaural directional hearing [411]. Batteau [30, 31] used models to investigate how the human auricle works. His conclusions apply also to the pinnae of animals (Fig. 3.6/2). The upward and rearward foldings diffract and reflect the diverse frequencies of a sound in different ways depending on the incident direction. This brings about changes in the transmission of the sound to the eardrum that modify the frequency mixture in a way that is specific for the incident direction. This effect plays a major role in direction analysis in the horizontal plane and is presumably decisive for localization in the vertical plane.

Experiments in which the subjects had to estimate the distance of a loud noise showed that distance estimation is based on the composition of the frequency spectrum [431]. The lower frequencies were gradually filtered out. The higher the remaining frequencies, the farther away the sound seemed to be.

3.6.2.2 Sensory Physiology and Neurophysiology

Sound vibrations are conducted from tympanic membrane (eardrum) over the ossicles (hammer, anvil, and stirrup), through the tympanic cavity, to the oval window (Fig. 3.6/3), and from here to the fluid of the scala vestibuli (= the part of the cochlea above the basilar membrane). At the apical end of the cochlea the scala vestibuli is connected to the scala tympani, the canal

Fig. 3.6/2 The outer ear as a frequency analyzer. Upper left: The human pinna or auricle. Lower left: Cross section at plane indicated by arrows. Middle and right: Technical system of bow-shaped slats that diffract sound waves according to altitude and azimuth; paired slats can provide distance information. (Left, modified from [809]; middle and right, from [30])

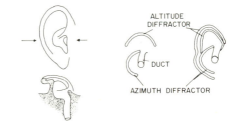

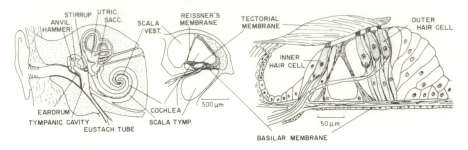

Fig. 3.6/3 The human ear. Left: Auditory and vestibular organs. Middle: Cross section of the cochlea. Right: The organ of Corti. (Modified from [145])

that leads back beneath the basilar membrane to the round window, facing the tympanic cavity. The sense organ, the organ of Corti, lies between the basilar and tectorial membranes. Vibration of the fluid in the scala tympani causes the basilar membrane to move relative to the tectorial membrane, exerting a shear force on the cilia of the hair cells. In contrast to the cells of the semicircular canals and statolith maculae, the sense cells of the cochlea have only stereocilia and no kinocilia.

Since the basilar membrane widens toward the apex of the cochlea, various parts of it resonate best to particular frequencies of sound. The pitch of a tone can thus be represented by a particular locus on the organ of Corti and the loudness, by the intensity of excitation at this locus.

Afferent fibers lead from the cochlea via the acoustic nerve to enter the pons at its junction with the medulla and connect with the cochlear nuclei (Fig. 3.6/4). From here the central acoustic pathway proceeds to the auditory cortex via relays in the trapezoid bodies, the superior olivary nuclei, the inferior colliculus, and the deeper layers of the superior colliculus (compare Fig. 3.10/28).

The processing of binaural excitations probably takes place in the brainstem, perhaps in the trapezoid bodies or the cochlear nuclei [431].

The trapezoid bodies and the olivary nuclei are thought to process directional information [198]. Many of their neurons receive afferents from both ears. The next higher station, the inferior colliculus, may also participate in this processing. The right-left difference is assumed to already be available as directional information at this level [262, 720].

Excitations from the two sides may arrive centrally at different times not only because the sound must travel farther to one ear than the other but also because the sensory response has a latency that is dependent on intensity. Loud noises excite sooner than soft ones. Thus, a right-left difference in intensity augments the time difference due to different pathway lengths.

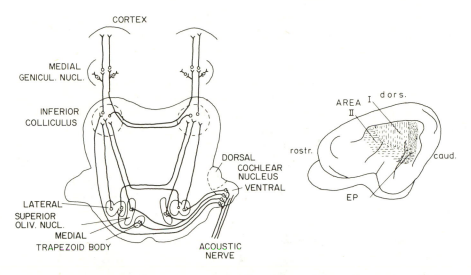

Fig. 3.6/4 Mammalian auditory centers. Left: The pathway of the auditory system. Right: The three auditory areas of the cat cortex. (Modified from [303])

A number of mechanisms have been suggested for transforming binaural differences into direction signals. According to a model proposed by Jeffress [406] the afferent neurons of each side give off a set of branches with different lengths and diameters. Each branch from one side converges with a branch of reciprocal length from the other side at one of a set of processing stations (Fig. 3.6/5). Since the length and diameter of a branch

Fig. 3.6/5 Model for converting the time differences between excitation of the left (L) and right (R) ears into directions. Reciprocal conduction time delays from each side lead to a set of processing stations (numbered). For each time difference, excitations from L and R arrive simultaneously at only one processing station, summate, and cross threshold. (Modified according to [406] from [198])

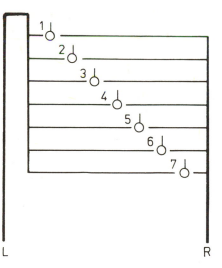

determine its conduction time, this establishes a set of delays between afferent excitation and the arrival of the signal at the processing station, which are reciprocal for the two sides. Excitations from the right and left side arrive simultaneously at only one of the processing stations. For example, when the sound comes from the right, the right afferent will be excited sooner than the left. This time difference is compensated by the delay in the branches at processing station 6 (or 7). Only here do the excitations from both sides summate and reach threshold.

The directions of the auditory field are topographically represented in the deeper layers of the superior colliculus. This map is in register with those of the visual and somatosensory fields, which also reside in the superior colliculus (Fig. 3.6/6; cat [264], mouse [179, 180], hamster [127]). Orientation movements can be triggered by electrical stimulation of this important orientation center (see 3.1).

The cortical representation of auditory stimuli is not necessary for simple orientation processes. Monkeys, cats, and opossums with lesions of the auditory cortex can still perform behaviors that require the ability to distinguish between sound from the right and from the left [928, 929].

3.6.3 Prey Orientation of Owls

The barn owl, *Tyto alba*, can locate and capture its prey in complete darkness [658, 659, 465]. Figure 3.6/7 illustrates that it is the noise that directs the approach flight of the owl and not olfactory or heat stimuli emitted by the mouse. Instead of pouncing on the mouse, the owl pounces on a piece of rustling paper pulled along by the mouse. The owl is able to correct for changes in the position of its target even after it has started its strike.

For a flying animal, locating an object in the horizontal plane is not

Fig. 3.6/6 Coincidence of the representations of the auditory and visual fields in the deeper layers of the cat's superior colliculus. The diagram shows the receptive field borders (in angular distance to vertical meridian of visual field) of cells in the superior colliculus that responded maximally to both light and sound (closed circles) and to sound only (open circles). The values are clustered around a diagonal. This means that light and sound stimuli from the same spatial meridian of the cat's environment project to a single cell in the colliculus. (Modified from [264])

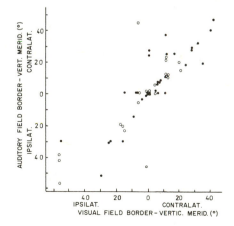

Fig. 3.6/7 In total darkness a barn owl pounces on a piece of rustling paper pulled along by a mouse. (Drawn from photographs, taken at 5 frames/sec with an infrared flash, in [465])

sufficient; it must be able to locate objects three-dimensionally. Indications for such locating mechanisms have been found in barn owls. One-eared owls can determine the direction of their prey but not how far away it is [675]. The owl's facial ruff (Fig. 3.6/8) appears to play a special role, focusing the sound like a parabolic antenna [465]. Removal of the ruff feathers impairs an owl's ability to localize a sound. The special shape of the ruff may also serve by diffraction and reflection to direct the sound waves along diverse paths to the eardrum. This would create direction-dependent differences in timbre (frequency spectrum) and intensity, which could be used for localization [803]. One theory proposes that the sound localization of the owl according to elevation and azimuth is based mainly on binaural differences in time and frequency spectrum [998]. Localization according to elevation is also attributed to the difference in shape of an owl's outer ears (Fig. 3.6/8). The consequent asymmetries in the directional fields of the two ears can be used for localization according to elevation (Fig. 3.6/9, [998]).

3.6.4 Sound Orientation of Frogs and Toads

A frog can only hear well with its mouth shut. Its auditory threshold increases when its mouth is open [124, 522, 666, 131]. The eardrums are connected via the Eustachian tubes and oral sinuses. The amplitude of

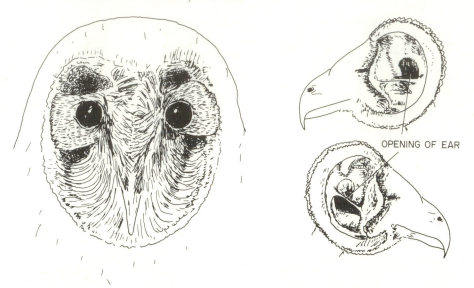

OPENING OF EAR

Fig. 3.6/8 Asymmetry in the position of the outer ears of the owl. Left: The feathers of the facial ruff of a barn owl have been removed to expose its ears. Note that the flap of skin in front of the auditory canal is lower on the right than on the left. Right: The ear opening of the long-eared owl is lower on the right (below) than on the left (above). (Left, modified from photos in [465]; right, from [802])

eardrum deflection decreases noticeably when the frog's mouth is opened and also depends on the direction of the sound source [131]. The stimulus process appears to be based on the same principle as is described later for crickets (3.6.6). The eardrum responds to pressure gradients generated by the phase difference in the sound waves of the external and the internal pathways. This phase difference is a result of the different length of the pathways [992]. The internal pathway leads over the opposite eardrum, the Eustachian tubes, and the oral sinuses (see Fig. 3.6/16). The direction of the sound source can be calculated from the difference in stimulation of the right and left tympana (bisensor mechanism).

A tree frog approaches a sound source in a zigzag course of leaps and bounds [696, 697]. Between leaps it moves its head from side to side, apparently getting a bearing on the direction of the sound. The subsequent leap is reaimed at the sound source, and once initiated, cannot be corrected, i.e., it is an open-loop process (compare 3.6.6).

Female toads and frogs are attracted by a loudspeaker emitting the calls of males of their species [124, 696]. (The croak of a frog is made up of a series of pulses.) When tree frogs are offered a choice between two croaks differing in frequency spectrum, pulse pattern, and other parameters, they choose the one that most resembles the call of their species, placing special emphasis on certain frequency combinations and pulse rates [246].

Fig. 3.6/9 Head orientations of the barn owl to a single noise target (= center). Effect of plugging the left (closed circles) and the right (triangles) ear. Occlusion of left ear causes misses above, and to the right of, the target; of the right ear, below and to the left. (Modified from [998])

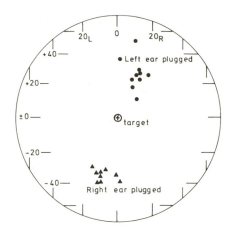

3.6.5 Echo Orientation

Bats. "They see with their ears," wrote Spallanzani in 1794 about the amazing ability of blinded bats to find their way flying about a room [818]. Lazzaro Spallanzani, one of the first "modern" physiologists, discovered and investigated the ability of bats to orient with their sense of hearing. He even postulated the use of echoes: "The sounds of the wing beats might be heard when they are reflected by obstacles." We owe the rediscovery of his careful and insightful experiments to Dijkgraaf [162, 169].

Physiologists started to become interested in "inaudible" sound, i.e., sound beyond the limits of human hearing, in the forties, when physicists were developing the field of ultrasonics. Ultrasound production and echolocation by bats was then discovered independently by Griffin [668, 241, 242] in America and by Dijkgraaf [159, 160] in Holland. Because of the war, each remained unknown to the other. After the war it was Griffin who provided the major experimental impetus and to whom we owe our basic understanding of this field. His book, *Listening in the Dark* [278], gives a thorough account of the works and insights of these early years, including historical background, discussion of the biological relationships, and description of the mechanisms. The efforts of the pioneers of the fifties (Dijkgraaf, Grinnell, Hartridge, Möhres, Novick, and many others) are given due credit. A summary of the results of more recent research can be found in Schnitzler [765] and a brief review in Neuweiler [633].

Orientation behavior. A bat uses echolocation to assess the physical properties and spatial coordinates of an object. The object is identified and localized. A bat can extract information about the size, form, and substance of an object from its echo. The little brown bat can pick out a mealworm that is tossed into the air with rubber discs of the same size (Fig. 3.6/10). It uses the intensity relationships of the echo frequencies to distinguish different materials.

Fig. 3.6/10 A bat picks out a mealworm thrown into the air along with two other objects. Numbers refer to frames of a film sequence. (Modified from [633] according to Webster, Durlach)

Echo orientation serves two purposes, target orientation to prey (usually flying) and becoming acquainted with the surroundings. Bats get to know an unfamiliar environment relatively quickly. They form a "sound picture" of their surroundings by systematic scanning movements of the head and ears (for rhinolophids only). As they fly around in an unfamiliar space, they explore the echo behavior of their surroundings, get to know its dimensions and its shape. The pattern of the attendant movements is idiothetically learned (3.11). Later the bats "automatically" avoid obstacles, i.e., without any acoustic control. Whether flying through the opening in a cage or landing on a perch, everything is idiothetically oriented. This can be clearly demonstrated by placing an obstacle in a space that the bat is familiar with. The bat flies right into it, something the bat never does in an unfamiliar environment.

In flight the ears of the vespertilionids face forward, whereas those of the rhinolophids flick rapidly back and forth. (Most of the bats found in the United States and Canada belong to the family Vespertilionidae. The rhinolophids, or horseshoe bats, so-called because of the shape of their nose, are Old World species.)

The horseshoe bat moves its ears back and forth in the rhythm of its echolocating calls. This successive sampling of the echo field appears to be especially important for localization in the vertical plane. Immobilizing both ears seriously impairs the ability of horseshoe bats to avoid horizontal wires; immobilizing only one ear has no effect. Normal animals can avoid horizontal wires almost as well as vertical ones. As a bat flies in a curve, its head anticipates the turn. The bat scouts out its path and takes the bearings of objects lying to the side of the path by facing them and flicking its ears back and forth.

The hunting behavior of an insectivorous bat can be divided into three phases: the search, the approach, and the terminal phase. During the search phase the bat sweeps the area with regular pulses. When it detects prey, the approach phase begins and the pulse frequency speeds up. During the terminal phase, pulses are emitted in very rapid series (Fig. 3.6/14).

Bats perform astonishing feats of localization. The little brown bat *Myotis* avoids wires as fine as 0.19 mm in diameter; horseshoe bats, as fine as 0.05 mm. As evidenced by the rise in the pulse emission rate, obstacles with a diameter of 1 mm are detected from as far away as 2 m (Fig. 3.6/11). Prey as small as fruitflies can be detected and caught in rapid succession. Since a hunting sequence lasts 0.5 sec, a bat can catch on the average one *Drosophila* every 4 sec.

Some bats also catch fish [278, 841, 814]. They echolocate parts of a fish that might protrude above the water, such as the dorsal fins, or even surface ripples caused by the fish underwater (Fig. 3.6/12).

Orientation mechanisms. The echolocating calls are generated in the larynx and arise in the rhythm of breathing. Vespertilionid bats emit their cries through the open mouth, but rhinolophids emit their cries through the nose. The nose leaf is thought to function like a megaphone, directing the sound forward. A bat is able to call and swallow simultaneously because of the tubelike extension of the larynx that leads to an opening in the palate (Fig. 3.6/13). The esophagus pouches out to each side of this tube, so that food can slide around it and be swallowed.

The vespertilionid and rhinolophid calls differ in their frequency structures. The cry of the vespertilionids consists of a series of brief (2 msec duration) pulses emitted at a rate of 5–10 Hz in the search phase and increasing to 50 Hz in the approach phase (Fig. 3.6/11). Each pulse is

Fig. 3.6/11 The time interval between pulses emitted by the little brown bat as a function of the distance to wires of different diameters (0.28 and 1.06 mm). The increase in pulse rate at about 2 m for the 1.06 mm wire demonstrates that the bat has detected the wire. (Modified from [279])

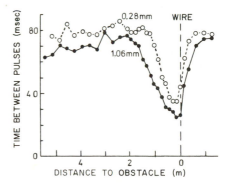

Fig. 3.6/12 A fish-eating bat, *Noctilio leporinus*, was trained to trawl for food marked by little sticks protruding above the water's surface. It learned to distinguish between sticks slanted in different directions. The bat is about to trail its hooklike claws through the water to gaff a fish. (Drawn from a photograph in [841])

Fig. 3.6/13 Schematic longitudinal section through the head of a horseshoe bat with arrows indicating the path of the air and of emitted cries. (Modified from [605])

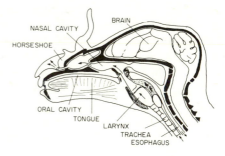

frequency modulated, falling from about 70 kHz to 30 kHz. In contrast, horseshoe bats emit a long (about 65 msec) pulse at a constant sound frequency of about 80 kHz. Pulse duration and interpulse interval shorten in the approach phase (Fig. 3.6/14).

The pinnae are important for receiving the echo. They gather the sound waves, focusing them onto the auditory canal. Presumably, their strangely convoluted structure plays an important role and is responsible for changes in arrival times and for diffraction processes that lead to a direction-specific modulation of an echo parameter. Binaural intensity differences may also aid in the determination of direction. In addition to this bisensor method, horseshoe bats employ a successive sampling process that enables them to localize with only one ear.

Compared with the intense cries, the echoes are faint. To enable the echo to be heard at all, the pulses are timed so that the echoes arrive during the intervals between pulses. Sensitivity is maintained by "closing" the ears during the emitted pulse. The bat contracts the muscles of its middle ear to shield the receptors against the high intensity of the cries. A neurophysiological mechanism functions in a similar way. Neurons have been found that are sensitive only to weak sound pressures.

A physical phenomenon comes into play in echolocation that is based on the convergence of transmitter and receiver, the Doppler effect. As an observer approaches a sound source, the number of vibrations received per unit time increases, causing the pitch of the sound to increase. Horseshoe bats compensate for the shift in echo frequency (Fig. 3.6/14) by varying the sound frequency of the cries, so that the sound frequency of the echoes remains constant. This is probably accomplished by a feedback control mech-

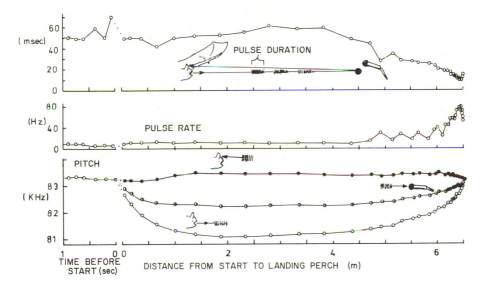

Fig. 3.6/14 Doppler compensation by the horseshoe bat, *Rhinolophus ferrum equinum*. Pulse duration (upper diagram), pulse rate (middle diagram), and sound frequency of the pulse (= pitch) (lower diagram) were recorded by a microphone in the landing perch just before and during a 6.5 m flight to it. The pitch recorded by this method (lower diagram, middle curve) and the flying velocity of the bat were used to calculate the echo frequency heard by the bat (lower diagram, top curve) and the frequency of the cry emitted by the bat (lower diagram, bottom curve). The bat decreases the sound frequency of the emitted pulse to keep the echo frequency constant. Pulse duration decreases and rate increases as the bat approaches the goal. (Modified from [764])

anism that compares the echo frequency with a reference value and changes the cry frequency to correct for any error. If the echoes coming from straight ahead have a constant sound frequency, they can be easily distinguished from echoes coming from the sides. The bat can tell whether an object is not in its path and whether the object is moving, since both instances would perturb the Doppler compensation.

Experiments on the big brown bat *Eptesicus fuscus* [812] illustrate the precision with which bats measure distance. Bats that were trained to fly to the closer of two adjacent platforms could discriminate between platforms that differed by only 1 cm from 30 cm away. The time between emission of the cry and reception of the echo seems to be the critical factor in distance estimation.

Birds. A more primitive echo orientation has been found in birds that nest in dark caves [278, 802]. The swiftlet *Collocalia brevirostris unicolor* emits rattling calls of about 4–5 kHz when it flies into its cave or when it is forced to fly in a dark room or with its eyes blindfolded. It is able to avoid flying into walls unless its ears are plugged, whereupon it becomes disoriented. The oilbird *Steatornis caripensis* nests in the rocky ledges of caves that are several hundred meters deep and emits calls (7.3 kHz) to help it find its way about in the darkness.

Porpoises and whales. Toothed whales use sonic pulses not only for finding their food, but also for making distinctions between food items (for reviews, see [445, 198]). Porpoises possess a highly sophisticated ultrasonic localization system, which is easily studied thanks to the intelligence of these animals. In murky water or wearing opaque eye caps, porpoises are able to find holes in nets, swim a slalom through a forest of poles, or differentiate small from large fish. The bottle-nosed dolphin *Tursiops gilli* emits orientation clicks only in muddy water.

In 1947 Arthur McBride, Curator of the Marine Studios in Florida, discovered that bottle-nosed dolphins were able to evade nets even when they were unable to see them [743]. He suggested that they were using an echolocation system similar to that of bats. Four years later Kellogg and his colleagues [433, 434] provided the first experimental support for this theory. The capabilities of cetacean sonar are no less amazing than those of the bat system. A dolphin can detect a 3 mm ball from a distance of 3 m and a 6 cm air-filled cylinder from 400 m. It avoids nylon threads as thin as 1 mm.

Exactly how porpoises and whales generate sounds is not yet known. Vocal cords are either rudimentary or nonexistent. Apparently, the echolocation clicks are produced by rapid movement of air from one nasal air sac to another through special valves. The sound waves generated in the nasal passages are then focused and projected forward by a lens-shaped fatty structure on the forehead called the melon (Fig. 3.6/15).

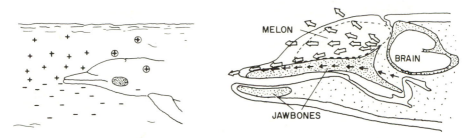

Fig. 3.6/15 Echo orientation of the bottle-nosed dolphin *Tursiops truncatus*. Left: A dolphin wearing opaque eye caps can still detect and eat pieces of food (indicated by plus signs). It may even return to pick up pieces it has passed (plus signs in circles). Undetected pieces are indicated by minus signs. Right: Proposed pathways of sound projection. White arrows illustrate the focusing of the sound beam by the melon (Evans hypothesis). Black arrows show sound conduction by the bones of the upper jaw (Purves hypothesis). (Left, modified from [638]; right, from [200])

The frequencies of the sounds may be as high as 100 kHz. The clicks are brief (0.01 sec), and when emitted in rapid succession sound like the creak of a door that needs oiling. As with bats, the pulse rate increases as the target is neared.

The localization mechanism is thought to be based on a binaural intensity comparison [114]. Dolphins sweep the target with their sonar beam using side-to-side movements (about 10°–30°) of their heads.

Humans. Blind people sometimes report that they can "feel" obstacles with their faces. This "facial vision" is based on a kind of echolocation [139, 278] for which the ears are necessary. The sensory information is provided by sound reverberations, perhaps from the blind person's own footsteps. These reverberations are a function of the shape and composition of the surrounding space. Frequencies above 10 kHz appear to be most important. Changes in pitch due to the Doppler effect may also contribute to facial vision.

3.6.6 Acoustic Orientation of Crickets and Grasshoppers

Grasshoppers (Acrididae), crickets (Gryllidae), and katydids (Tettigoniidae) belong to the insect order Orthoptera, which is characterized by the ability of its members to communicate acoustically with their own species. The chirping of the house cricket, *Acheta domesticus*, is the male's way of attracting a mate and guiding her to him. These insects hear and localize the song with their tympanal organs. The term "phonotaxis" has become popularized for this orientation behavior.

The male produces sound by rubbing one part of its body (the file) against another part (the scraper). The file has ridges that strike the scraper and set up vibrations. The scraper is always on the wing, but the file may be on the hind leg, as in grasshoppers, or on the opposite wing, as in crickets.

3.6.6.1 Sound Reception and Orientation Behavior

The tympanal organs of crickets and katydids are located on the forelegs (Fig. 3.6/16), and those of grasshoppers, on the sides of the first abdominal segment.

The orientation behavior. Seventy years ago Regen [690] first demonstrated that the female cricket uses acoustic signals to find a male. The female cricket walked to a loudspeaker that was broadcasting the song of a male. This experiment proved that the signals were conducted by the air and not by vibrations in the substrate.

When the female cricket is aroused by a species-specific song, she emerges from her hiding place and scans the auditory field, turning from side to side on her "hindquarters" and taking successive directional readings (Phase

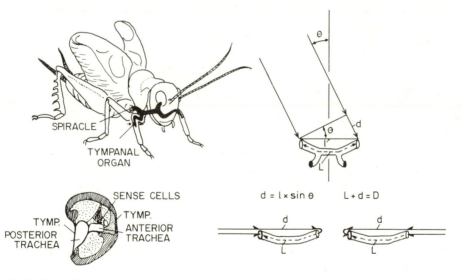

Fig. 3.6/16 Cricket. Upper left: Tympanal organs with connecting tracheal system. Lower left: Section through the tibia at the level of the tympanal organ (arrow in upper picture). Only the large, posterior tympanal membrane appears to participate in sound reception. Right: The relationships between sound direction (θ) and pathways. "Internal" pathways (L = dashed line). The lower drawings illustrate for the left tympanum the difference (D) between "external" and "internal" pathways ($D = L + d$) for sound from the left (= ipsi-lateral) and from the right (= contralateral). The difference in the length of the pathway determines the difference in the sound pressure on each side of the tympanum and thus the excitation. (Left, modified from [489])

I). She then starts walking, usually in the direction of the chirping male (Phase II, Fig. 3.6/17). The female's walk is interrupted by pauses, which are often followed by a course correction. The direction signals are usually acquired during a pause [17, 617, 979, 1021] but may also be used for orientation during the walk [1021, 1026]. As she nears the source of the song, the female cricket walks faster and faster [146].

These experiments bring out the distinction between identification and localization. During Phase I it is the physical properties of the song that are critical. Only after the sounds have been identified as species specific does the female begin Phase II [979]. Now localization comes to the fore. The species specificity is no longer as important, and the female will continue walking toward the sound even after the song is changed to one that would have been ineffective during Phase I [979, 1021].

What are the physical properties that release the orientation? The cricket song is composed of a series of chirps that are themselves subdivided into pulses. Parameters that are important for identification are pulse rate, chirp duration [698], and frequency [339, 677, 606]. The following experiments illustrate the importance of frequency. Flying crickets turn away from a sound source that is emitting high-frequency signals (30–70 kHz) [677, 606] but turn toward one emitting signals in the frequency of the species song (3–9 kHz) [606]. Female mole crickets also fly toward sound sources

Fig. 3.6/17 Orientation behavior of a female cricket, *Scapsipedus marginatus*, to a source of male song. The cricket walks for about 0.4 sec (represented by one arrow), stops, makes a course correction, and resumes walking (shown by next arrow). The dots next to the arrows indicate when the male call was broadcast (about every 1.6 sec). At the beginning of the cricket's walk the points are close together, but become more spread out as the cricket approaches the loudspeaker. This indicates that the cricket increases its speed as it nears its goal. (Modified from [617])

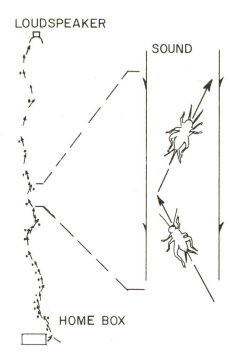

LOUDSPEAKER

SOUND

HOME BOX

that broadcast the species song [869, 870]. The turning away can be interpreted as escape behavior from echolocating bats. There are isolated reports that flying crickets plummet to the ground when bats are hunting nearby [675]. The fact that the behavior consists of merely falling out of the sky suggests that it is released, but not directed, by the sound signals. Similarly, when a cricket sitting near a light is bombarded with high-frequency sound, it turns away from the light [811]. In both cases the sound only triggers the responses, which are then oriented with respect to light or gravity.

The neurophysiological bases for these phenomena are still obscure, but the identification probably depends on a complex neural network and not on single detector neurons [544, 804].

Receptors and directional characteristics. The sound receptors are the tympanal organs (Fig. 3.6/16). The tympanic membranes or eardrums are thin, double-layered membranes that separate the external space from the air space in the leg tracheae (in crickets). The outer layer arises from the leg wall; the inner, from the tracheal wall. This tracheal branch is specialized for hearing and serves practically no function in breathing. It runs through the leg into the ipsilateral thorax, where it bends caudally and opens to the outside via a tracheal opening (spiracle). The opening is shut by a movable valve. At the bend the trachea bifurcates, sending a thick branch toward the medial plane where it joins its counterpart from the other side of the body. Thus, the tracheal system of the cricket is roughly H-shaped. In the tettigonids the tracheae get wider toward the spiracle, taking on the form of a trumpet.

Various theories are under discussion concerning the nature of stimulus conduction and transduction. A number of parameters are involved, such as the resonance in the "tube of the trumpet" or in the bilateral tracheal system, the decrease in intensity due to damping, and the temporal differences between the inner and outer sound pathways [981, 13, 14, 637, 501, 340, 489, 582, 808]. The following presents a somewhat simplified picture for the cricket.

Sound reaches the tympanum via two pathways, directly from the outside and through the tracheae from the inside (Fig. 3.6/16). There is no consensus on whether the main internal pathway is across the ear on the contralateral side or through the spiracle. In any case it is the difference in length (D, Fig. 3.6/16) between the internal and external pathways that is decisive. When the sound comes from the side of the receiving ear, the internal pathway is longer, so a sound wave arrives later on the inside than on the outside. When the difference (D) is equal to ½ the wavelength (= phase shift of 180°), the difference in pressure between the inside and the outside is maximal. Consequently, the movement of the tympanic membrane will be maximal. In comparison, when the sound source is on the

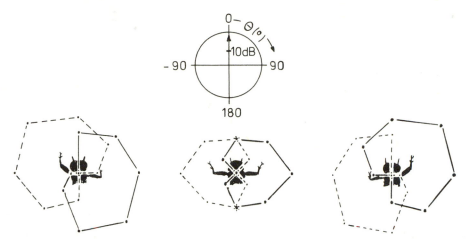

Fig. 3.6/18 Directional characteristics of both ears of the cricket *Teleogryllus commodus* for three different leg positions. The coordinate system is shown in the top figure with the 0°–180° line coinciding with the midline of the cricket; calibration is threshold stimulus intensity (in dB) needed for receptor excitation. (Modified from [340])

opposite side of the receiving ear, the internal and external pathways are about equal. The pressure difference will be slight, so the tympanic membrane will not be stimulated. The tympanic membrane responds to the pressure difference between inside and outside; it is a pressure gradient sensor. The relationship between the direction of the sound and the level of excitation is presented graphically as a directional characteristic (e.g., Figs. 3.6/18, 3.6/19).

Directional characteristics and orientation. If the sound pathways in the legs are critical for receptor stimulation, a change in the position of the legs must alter the directional characteristics [340, 489, 808]. Figure 3.6/18 illustrates this effect. Is the orientation also affected? When a cricket pauses (and supposedly listens), its forelegs are not always symmetrical to its body. Observations on *Teleogryllus oceanicus* suggest that the angle of course correction is greater when the foreleg points toward the sound source than when it is perpendicular to the sound direction [17]. This may be a source of orientation errors. Figure 3.6/20 shows that the oriented turns are quite variable. It could, however, be that idiothetic signals concerning the position of the legs (sensor-carrying appendages) are taken into account (see 2.4.4).

The two ears are two direction-sensitive sensors. We can assume that, as in other bisensor systems, the difference in excitation between them is converted into a direction signal [617, 637]. The relationships are illustrated in Fig. 3.6/20a. Details will be discussed within the framework of neurophysiological findings (see 3.6.6.2).

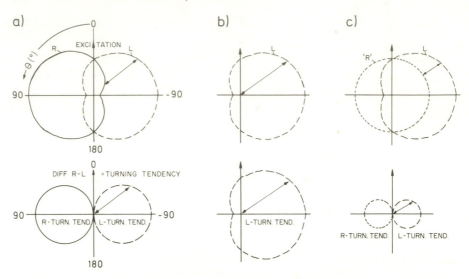

Fig. 3.6/19 The effect of the loss of one sensor of a bisensor system on the relationship between excitation and incident direction and on difference formation (hypothetical). Upper row: The excitation on the right (R) and left (L) as a function of the angle of stimulus incidence (θ). Lower row: The difference between the excitations shown in the upper diagrams, which is assumed to determine the turning tendency. a) Normal system (= two intact organs). b) Right organ eliminated. c) Compensation for the loss by a central "compensation excitation" ('R'). Note that after compensation the differences (turning tendencies) are smaller than for the normal system, a).

As for any bisensor system the loss of one organ must perturb this system considerably (see 2.11.3). Crickets with only one tympanal organ walk in circles toward the intact side [617]. There are some indications, however, that crickets are capable of compensating for this loss [690]. Although the definitive experiments have not yet been performed, it is reasonable to expect that compensation proceeds here as in other systems (Fig. 2.11/4, 2.11.3.2), namely that the cricket eventually stops circling and walks in a straight line toward the sound. This could be based on a central compensation excitation (Fig. 3.6/19c). If this excitation is dependent on stimulus intensity, then the orientation of a one-eared cricket that has already compensated for its loss would again be perturbed by changes in sound intensity.

3.6.6.2 Neurophysiology

The central nervous system of orthopterans consists of a chain of ganglia that starts in the head above the esophagus, reaches around the esophagus with two connectives, and proceeds caudally as the ventral nerve cord. Anterior to the esophagus is the supraesophageal ganglion, which, as the

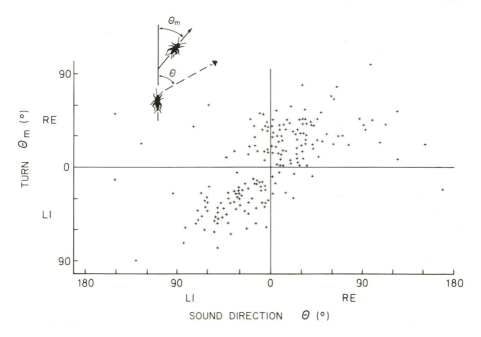

Fig. 3.6/20 Sound orientation of the cricket. Angle of turn (θ_m) as a function of sound direction (θ). (Modified from [617])

"brain," fills most of the head capsule and receives the antennal and optic nerves. Still in the head, but posterior to the esophagus, is the subesophageal ganglion. It innervates the mouthparts and is attached to the three thoracic ganglia, the pro-, meso-, and metathoracic ganglion.

At present the best understood orthopteran central nervous systems are those of the gryllids and the acridids [387, 192]. The first brain stimulation experiments on insects were performed on crickets to study the role played in certain behaviors by the various supraesophageal nuclei and the central bodies [385, 386].

The tympanal nerve of the locust enters the third thoracic ganglion (Fig. 3.6/21). As its fiber tract continues up to the prothoracic ganglion, it synapses with interneurons in the neuropil of each thoracic ganglion. The interneurons can be divided into three groups. The fibers of one group can be traced as far as the supraesophageal ganglion, where they terminate in a lateral region. They do not, however, come into direct contact with the mushroom bodies (corpora pedunculata), which are thought to be important associative centers. The fibers of a second group bifurcate forming a T, with one branch running caudally and the other rostrally to the supraesophageal ganglion. The third group is restricted to the thoracic ganglia.

Directional sensitivity and the direction signal. Stimulus intensity can affect

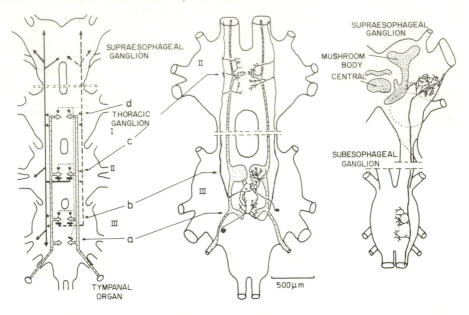

Fig. 3.6/21 The acoustic CNS of the migratory locust. *a–d* indicate the locations of the four acoustic neuropils of the thoracic ganglia. Left: Schematic representation of neurons. The stippled band is the tympanal tract; the solid line, a *T* neuron; the dashed line, an ascending neuron; the dotted line, an interthoracic neuron. Middle: Tympanal fibers and two ascending neurons in the mesothoracic and metathoracic ganglia. Right: An ascending neuron in the subesophageal and supraesophageal ganglia. The drawings in the middle and on the right are from preparations in which the axons have been selectively stained by cobalt iontophoresis. (Modified from [691])

the excitation difference between the right and the left side in two ways, directly via the degree of excitation or indirectly via its latency. The latency, i.e., the time from stimulus onset to the beginning of the response, is shorter the stronger the stimulus. This can lead to temporal differences in binaural excitation (up to 6 msec) [15, 802, 803, 608], which may play a role in the formation of a direction signal in the CNS.

The discharge rate of the receptor neuron as a function of the sound direction results in a cardioid figure when plotted in polar coordinates (Fig. 3.6/19, Fig. 3.6/22a). This indicates a sinusoidal relationship between incident sound direction and excitation (Fig. 2.3/5). Some interneurons also exhibit this sort of receptor-specific directional characteristic. It characterizes the input of only one ear and is completely unaffected by the loss of the other ear [695]. Other interneurons, however, are influenced by both ears. This effect has been described as mutual excitation or inhibition. It shifts the directional characteristic toward one side, i.e., the directional sensitivity becomes more sharply focused. This effect can be demonstrated

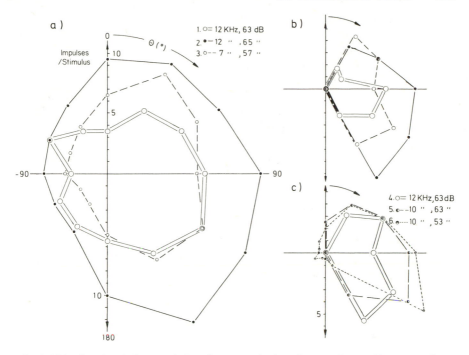

Fig. 3.6/22 Directional characteristics of neurons in the migratory locust. Shown are the impulses per stimulus as a function of sound direction (θ) (stimulus duration = 20 msec, stimulus rate = 2/sec). a) Responses of receptor neurons. b) "Difference" curves. Each curve was calculated from the curve shown in a) and its mirror image (compare Fig. 3.6/19). c) Responses of "difference" neurons. Curves 1 and 4 are from one *F* neuron; 2 and 3, from one *C* neuron; and 5 and 6, from another *F* neuron. (a and c, modified from [425])

up to the supraesophageal ganglion [698] and might be thought of in terms of building up a difference between right and left (Fig. 3.6/19 lower). Since a single "difference" neuron controls the turning tendencies for only one side, it shows only one circle of the double circle difference characteristic. The *F* neurons appear to be typical "difference" neurons [424]. Curve 4 of Fig. 3.6/22c gives the directional characteristic of an *F* neuron when both ears are intact (= difference curve). Loss of the contralateral ear results in curve 1 in a), which resembles a receptor curve. In b) the difference curve is calculated from curve 1 in a) and its mirror image. (Contralateral and ipsilateral refer to the CNS side of the *F* neuron.) Let us review the features that in theory distinguish the receptor-specific directional characteristic from the difference curve (compare Fig. 3.6/19). The directional characteristic of an organ is a cardioid curve. It extends far over to the contralateral side or intersects the 0°–180° line at widely separated points. Each circle of the difference curve lies completely, or almost completely, on the ipsilateral side and ideally intersects the 0°–180° line at only one point. This means that a difference neuron remains silent when sound comes from the contralateral side.

Since F neurons are relatively independent of intensity over a wide range (about 10–14 kHz) (Fig. 3.6/23), they furnish "pure" direction signals. The firing rate varies only between 2 and 6 impulses/sec with input from both ears and when the sound comes from the ipsilateral side (contralateral sound being ineffective). Elimination of an organ changes the situation radically. The excitation of the neuron increases steeply with intensity (for sound from ipsilateral, as well as contralateral, directions). A buildup of binaural difference can also be seen. Subtraction of the contralateral curve from the ipsilateral curve from the experiment with only one ear gives practically the same curve as the experiment with both ears.

A circuit diagram that is compatible with this computation is shown in Fig. 3.6/24. The two outputs represent F neurons, each of which supplies the result of a subtraction (performed by inhibitory and excitatory synapses) of input from the right and the left.

3.6.7 Escape Response of Moths

The escape response to the cries of a bat is widely distributed among moths [709, 712, 713, 714, 715]. Roeder used an ingeniously simple method to first document this behavior. He took a tape recorder and a camera with a quickly recharging flash attachment into his garden in the evening. As soon as he sighted a moth, the call of a bat was broadcast, the aperture of the camera opened, and the flash set off. The moths showed up in the photographs as streaks of light that abruptly changed their directions.

Not all moths respond in the same way. Some make irregular loops and zigzags directed downward, while others fly more or less away from the sound source. Behavioral experiments on tethered flying animals (e.g.,

Fig. 3.6/23 Excitation of an F neuron of the migrating locust as a function of sound intensity. Elimination of the contralateral tympanal organ makes the F neuron strongly intensity dependent for both ipsilateral and contralateral sound (open circles). Subtracting the contralateral from the ipsilateral sound curves for only one intact ear gives a curve (dotted line) that is similar to the one for ipsilateral sound with both ears intact (solid line, closed circles). (Modified from [424])

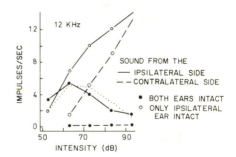

Fig. 3.6/24 Circuit diagram for F neurons. The excitations of the right and left tympanal organs inhibit (input triangles) or excite (input arrowheads) processing interneurons. The outputs (F neurons) carry the result of this subtraction between right and left. (Simplified from [424])

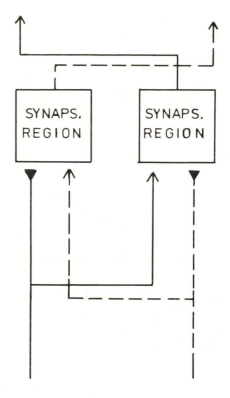

Feltia subgothica) show that they turn away from ultrasonic stimuli (20–60 kHz) [712]. Electrophysiological recordings from the tympanal nerve (the tympanal organs are located on each side of the metathorax) show that the tympanal organs have a directional characteristic (e.g., *Lucania, Graphiphora, Acronycta* [715]).

The auditory organs of some moths (Choerocampinae) have a completely different construction. The enlarged labial palps of *Celerio lineata* permit sound detection but do not furnish any direction information [716, 717]. These animals probably just let themselves fall when they hear the cry of a bat. The response is triggered by the sound stimulus but is oriented (passively) to gravity.

3.6.8 Sound Orientation of Mosquitoes

"He only has ears for the girls," might be said of the male mosquito, which detects and locates female mosquitoes from the sound of their wings [859, 802, 803]. The localization mechanism is based on a different principle than the ones we have discussed up to now. The mechanism presumably operates as an array process instead of a bisensor one (compare 2.3.3). Correspondingly, a male with only one antenna can still find a female.

The receptive mechanism is based on the response of the antenna to displacement instead of to sound pressure. The flagellum of the antenna with its numerous bristles is displaced by the sound oscillations. It is built so that it resonates to the fundamental frequency of the female wing tone (300–400 Hz). The movement of the antenna is transmitted via the base plate to the receptor (Fig. 3.6/25), which is a giant Johnston's organ in the very large, balloonlike base of the antenna, the pedicel. The Johnston's organ is composed of several 10,000 scolopidial receptors, which are grouped in two rings around the base plate [704]. One ring is aligned with the

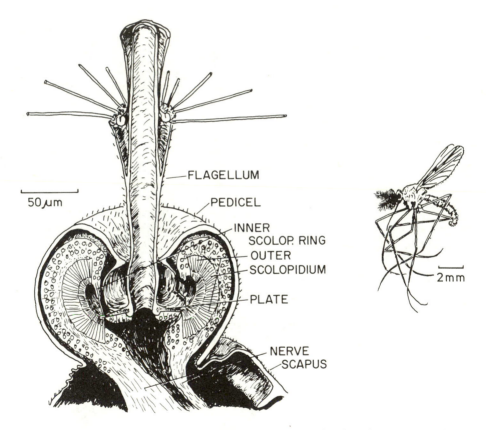

Fig. 3.6/25 The auditory organ of the mosquito *Anopheles*. Left: The Johnston's organ in the pedicel of the male has about 30,000 scolopidia. The scolopidial rings are surrounded by a layer of sense cells (whose nuclei are represented by circles). Right: An *Anopheles* mosquito. (Left modified from [704]; right, from [838])

horizontal plane of the pedicel, and the other inserts from above like an upside-down cone. The two rings thus encompass all spatial directions. Since the scolopidial rings are connected to the brain by many nerve fibers, it is probable that every antennal displacement is transmitted to the brain as a particular value for direction via a separate connection. The whole organ represents a three-dimensional array onto which the sound directions are mapped.

Not only the resonance of the antennal flagellum, but also the receptors are tuned to the female wing tone. They show very little response to the higher tone of the male wingbeat (510 Hz) [802, 803], so the male mosquito can hear neither himself nor other males. As we said in the beginning, he only has ears for the girls.

3.7 ORIENTATION TO VIBRATION

There is no sharp boundary between vibration and sound. In general the term vibration refers to oscillations of ground, water, or air that are registered by mechanoreceptors mostly at interfaces of the media [233, 13, 14]. In contrast, sound refers to the oscillations of the medium that are sensed by ears.

The ability of cockroaches and spiders to sense things at a distance is attributable to a vibratory sense. A cockroach can evade a rapidly approaching hand by detecting the air movement with sensory hairs on its cerci [988]. The spider *Agelena labyrinthica* can capture prey that is buzzing around near it. Ablation and stimulation experiments suggest that the receptors for this behavior are the trichobothria, sense hairs on the legs [272]. Walcott [888] ascribes the orientation of the spider *Achaearanea tepidariorum* to buzzing insects to the lyriform sense organs on its legs.

Many aquatic animals locate prey or obstacles from surface waves. The movement of particles in a surface wave describes a circle. Some animals are able to sense surface waves from underwater. The lateral line receptors of the frog *Xenopus* respond to the horizontal component of the circling movement [271].

3.7.1 Localization by Aquatic Insects

The whirligig beetles (Gyrinidae) rush about in circles or zigzags across the surfaces of pools and ponds. They orient to surface waves spreading out from obstacles. The waves are produced by other objects or are reflections of the beetles' own movements. The receptor organs are the Johnston's organs in the pedicel, the second antennal segment (Fig. 3.7/1). The flat-

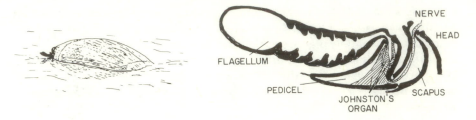

Fig. 3.7/1 A whirligig beetle. Left: A swimming beetle, *Gyrinus substriatus*, with the club-shaped flagellum of its antenna above the water and the pedicel resting on the surface. Right: Longitudinal section through the antenna of *Gyrinus marinus*. (Modified from [725])

tened ventral surface of the pedicel floats on the water surface, and the clublike flagellum sticks up into the air. When a wave tilts the pedicel against the inert mass of the flagellum, the Johnston's organ is stimulated [725].

Whirligig beetles that could only turn in place were presented with vibrations from various directions in open-loop experiments, i.e., the stimulation ended before the response started [694]. The beetles rotated up to 135°. Alignments were more reliable (= less variable) for small angles than for large ones. Vibrations originating from in back of the beetle (= 180°) were either ignored or elicited undirected responses. Beetles with rigidly fixed left antennae turned to the right. The orientation is thought to be based on the difference in arrival times of vibrations at the right and left antennae.

Two water bugs, the back swimmer and the water strider, locate their prey from surface waves when their legs are in contact with the surface. The oriented turn of the back swimmer, *Notonecta*, is a highly accurate open-loop process (Fig. 3.7/2). It preys on insects that flitter about on the water surface, making waves whose frequency spectrum has a maximum

Fig. 3.7/2 Prey orientation to vibrations in the back swimmer, *Notonecta*. Turning angle (θ_m) as a function of the angle (θ) at which the target (source of vibrations) is presented. Values from three animals are shown by different symbols. (Modified from [616])

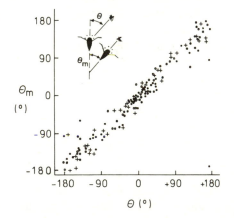

of about 50 Hz [933]. In this range the threshold for experimental release of turns is lowest.

The vibration receptors are located in the tarsus-tibia and the tibia-femur joints of the legs [933, 616]. Locking the tarsus-tibia joints on one side of the body does not significantly impair localization, whereas the same operation on the tibia-femur joints leads to circle movements [616]. This does not, however, exclude the participation of the tarsus-tibia receptors in the intact animal [559]. The importance of these joints has been shown in experiments in which the natural wave was simulated by magnetically generated forces [934]. The tarsal claws were coated with iron filings, and the animal was positioned under a group of magnets. A switching program was used to present the phase relationships of the magnetic fields corresponding to particular wave directions. The insects oriented to the simulated wave direction when the forelegs or the midlegs or both pairs of legs were stimulated. Since the stimulus amplitudes were all the same, analysis must be based on phase differences (= temporal difference measurement) rather than amplitude differences. Apparently, the temporal pattern of stimulation of all receptors is analyzed [934]. This might include signals from receptors on the tip of the abdomen, which are also thought to play a role in localization [616]. The whole can be characterized as an array process based on the temporal relationships of excitations. The sensor-direction value of the receptors that are stimulated first would be decisive. Also compatible with this model is a concept concerning the central mechanism of the localization system of *Notonecta* [615]: The receptor that is excited first reduces the effect of receptors that are stimulated later via lateral inhibition, so that the turning command of the first excited receptor gets to the muscles.

While *Notonecta* hangs beneath the water surface, the water strider *Gerris* stands on top of it. Vibrations elicit a single oriented turn of up to 160° [614]. The accuracy is high: for small angles there is some overshoot; for large angles, an undershoot. Ablation experiments indicate that the receptors for this prey orientation are probably in the tarsus-tibia joint [613]. If the leg receptors are ablated on one side, the water strider can still localize vibrations as long as they come from the intact side. Insects with only one leg are still able to differentiate between stimulus directions. These results show that the receptors of the six legs function as an array like in *Notonecta*. The leg whose receptors are excited first (or most strongly?) determines the turn.

Even with its eyes covered, the larva of the water beetle *Dytiscus marginalis* turns toward moving prey that is 2–5 cm away, and at distances of 1 cm the larva's strike is highly accurate. Cutting off the antennae abolishes this capability [780].

Arrow worms (Chaetognatha) also orient to vibrations produced by their prey. When nearby vibrations stimulate their sensory bristles, the worms turn and snap at the source of the vibrations with their mouthparts [375].

3.7.2 Localization by Aquatic Vertebrates

Fish and aquatic amphibia have lateral line systems, which they use to localize objects and to orient themselves to their surroundings. [161, 170].

The sense organs of the lateral line system are closely related to the receptors of the labyrinth (see 3.10). They lie either exposed on the surface (neuromasts) or embedded in the epidermis and enclosed in canals. The neuromasts can be displaced by the particle movement of a wave. The canal organs are stimulated by the pressure of waves that is transmitted to the canal fluid by elastic portions of the canal wall. The canals are often distributed in a complex pattern.

The blind cave-dwelling fish *Anoptichthys* avoids obstacles by registering the reflections of waves created by its own swimming (echolocation) [296]. The fish *Pantodon* and *Aplocheilus lineatus* maintain direct contact with the surface of the water [798, 799, 800] and prey on insects floundering in it. The accuracy with which a fish can hurl itself at its prey is astonishing. Figure 3.7/3 shows that if the object is 10 cm in front of the fish, its direction estimation is 100% accurate, and its distance estimation is 70% accurate. Even as far away as 30 cm, it judges the direction correctly 90% of the time.

The sense organs are the lateral lines arranged in regular patterns on the flat dorsal surface of the head. *Aplocheilus* has three groups of free-standing neuromasts in furrows in between bulges on each side of its head (Fig. 3.7/4). Each group consists of three single organs whose cupulae each have a different orientation and hence a different directional characteristic. Together the organs comprise an array on which the waves produce a

Fig. 3.7/3 Prey orientation to vibrations in the African butterfly fish, *Pantodon buch-holtzi*. The numbers indicate the percentage of hits within 0.5 cm of the target. Left semicircle: Hits scored according to direction. Right semicircle: Hits scored according to distance. E = distance to target. (Modified from [800])

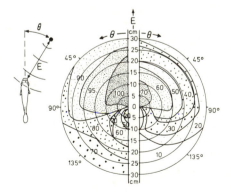

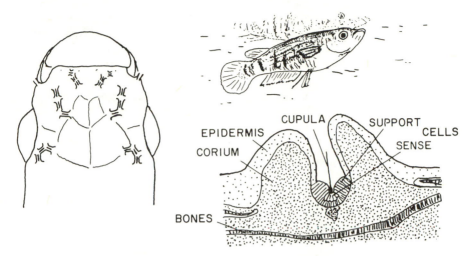

Fig. 3.7/4 Vibration sense organs of the fish *Aplocheilus lineatus*. Left: Dorsal view of head with three triads of neuromasts on each side. Upper right: The typical posture of a fish lurking just beneath the surface of the water. Lower right: Cross section through a sense organ. (Modified from [798])

particular spatial (or spatiotemporal?) stimulus pattern from which the direction and distance of the wave source can be derived. Schwartz's results suggest that it is the curvature of the wave front that is analyzed [798, 800].

The clawed frog, *Xenopus laevis*, has a highly sensitive system that can detect surface waves as small as 0.15–0.25 μm [470, 161, 268, 271]. As yet nothing definite is known about the localization process. Presumably both the lateral line system and the labyrinth are involved [271]. The lateral lines may operate as an array organ like those of the surface-feeding fish.

The lateral lines may also participate in the vibratory sense of the shark [631]. Sharks orient very well to signals produced by slapping the surface of the water.

3.7.3 Localization of Substrate "Sound" Sources

Tapping attracts the ant *Camponotus* [560]. Their usually zigzag approach is suggestive of a successive sampling process. The parasol ant, *Atta*, is attracted to places beneath which buried conspecifics are stridulating [555, 556]. Their orientation movements are more or less goal directed, probably based on a left-right comparison of stimulus intensities (bisensor process).

A stonefly (Plecoptera) finds its mate from the vibrations it produces. These insects may be found on leaves near flowing water. It beats its abdomen against a leaf at a frequency of 50–100 Hz, and the waves propagate through the plant at a speed of 555 m/sec. The vibrations are detected by receptors on the legs. Stimulation of single legs elicits a direction-specific turn. Stimulation of a foreleg favors turning toward the front; of a midleg, toward latero-anterior directions; and of a hind leg toward latero-posterior directions (Fig. 3.7/5). The six legs form an array that registers the distribution of stimuli. Whether the orientation is based on a difference in intensity or time or both is still unresolved. The difference in traveling time to the foreleg and hind leg is theoretically just sufficient to permit a measurement based on temporal differences. Vibration amplitude may also be registered by each of the six legs, so that the amplitude gradient extending from the stimulus source can be read (= gradient sampling with array sensors).

3.8 ORIENTATION TO AND IN CURRENTS

The movement of a medium such as water or air with respect to a system of reference is called a current. Currents may arise in various ways. For instance, when a bird flies through air or a fish swims through water, the medium flows along the animal's body, and the "current" is produced by the animal's own movement. On the other hand, when the wind blows past an animal standing on the ground or when water flows past an animal on the bed of a stream, the medium moves with respect to a stationary reference system. When an animal is moving freely in a medium that is itself

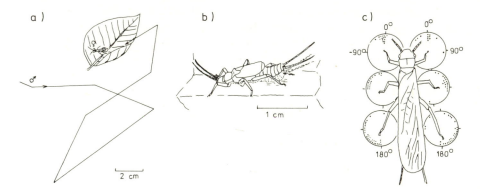

Fig. 3.7/5 Orientation to vibrations in the stonefly (Plecoptera). a) The zigzag approach of a male to a "calling" female. b) A male *Dinocras cephalotes* beats its abdomen on the substrate. c) Orientation turns of *Perla marginata* males. The legs were coated with iron filings and stimulated one at a time with an alternating magnetic field. The animal turned and moved in a particular direction. Each point gives the result of one experiment. (Modified from [727])

flowing with respect to the ground, these two processes occur simultaneously.

3.8.1 Currents due to Movement of the Animal

When an animal moves relative to the medium, the medium flows along its body. The animal can register this current with specialized receptors and gain information about the direction and velocity of its own movement with respect to the medium. In some insects this is performed by the Johnston's organs in the pedicel at the base of the antennae (Fig. 3.8/1, see also Fig. 3.6/25). Locusts have fields of sense hairs on their foreheads that register air currents and are part of the flight control circuit [906, 907, 251, 253]. The hair fields and the antennae regulate the animal's velocity [255]. The former also ensure that the locust flies foward, i.e., that air comes from the front [254]. In birds the breast feathers appear to play a role in the control of flight velocity [256].

All such receptors measure the movement of a flying or swimming animal relative to the medium. They have little to do with the orientation to wind or to water currents, as will be shown in 3.8.3.

3.8.2 Currents due to Movement of the Medium

The movement of a medium with respect to a stationary reference system such as the flow of a river in its bed or the flow of air relative to the earth (wind) is independent of the animal. Only when an animal is connected in some way to the reference system can it register this movement. An animal standing on the bottom of a river is in direct contact with the reference system and can register the direction of the current as it flows past.

Laverack [491, 492] found that lobsters have peg organs that respond to steady current and fan organs that respond to oscillating current, i.e., vibrations. Both are direction-sensitive. A current flowing dorsoventrally

Fig. 3.8/1 Air current receptors on the head of the migratory locust. The numbers 1–5 show the locations of current-sensitive hair fields. Airflow deflects the antennal flagella to the sides, and the rotation in the pedicel joint stimulates the Johnston's organs in the pedicel. (Modified from [254])

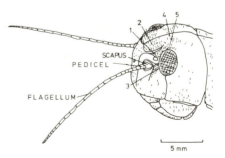

SCAPUS
PEDICEL
FLAGELLUM
5 mm

has almost no effect whereas one flowing from the tail to the head is excitatory.

Proprioceptors in the legs could measure current from the tug or thrust it exerts on the body. Very little is known about this, but it may play a role in the following cases.

Spiny lobsters can orient to currents and to wave direction [896]. Arthropods walking on land can orient to wind (hermit crabs [873]) and hold a compass course with respect to wind direction (beetles, scorpions [510, 511]). In insects the deflection of the antennae gives the wind direction. The sensors are probably the Johnston's organs, which operate as a receptor array in which the direction of deflection is signaled as a body-direction label (see 2.3.3). Since insects can hold a course even after removal of one antenna [511], no left-right comparison occurs.

When the cypris larva of the barnacle attaches itself to a substrate, it orients according to the direction of prevailing current [141]. A few species of caddis fly larvae orient foreign objects to a current. They build funnel-shaped traps so that the current flows into the mouth of the funnel [88].

3.8.3 Free Locomotion in a Moving Medium

Wind flows past a kite that is connected to the ground by its string. A sea gull is in a comparable situation when it rides an updraft over the dunes. It stays in place by maintaining eye contact with the ground.

What is wind? Imagine a mass of still air as it shifts relative to the ground. The air moves, i.e., the wind blows, only with respect to the ground. An animal with no ties to the ground is incapable of perceiving the movement of the air. Usually the connection is visual, as in the case of the sea gull. Fish maintain optokinetic contact with their environment. Blind fish drift helplessly downstream [296]. Flying animals also orient in a current using optokinetic cues [435, 438, 441, 966, 210].

A flying animal moves in a medium that is itself moving through space (Fig. 3.8/2). Its movement relative to the ground, i.e., its track (R) is the vector sum of its own movement relative to the medium (F) and the movement of the medium relative to the ground (W). Unfortunately, the terminology is not consistent for these concepts. Von Frisch [235] spoke of the flight track (*Flugbahn*) of bees. The expression "course over ground" is also in use (e.g., for sailboats). However, since "course" is used in aviation for the direction of an aircraft relative to the medium (see 1.3.4.), we prefer to call an animal's movement over ground its track (Fig. 3.8/4).

A bee or a bird flies with its body axis aligned with its track when there is no wind or when there is a head or tail wind. However, wind from other directions carries them sideways, so that their bodies are no longer aligned

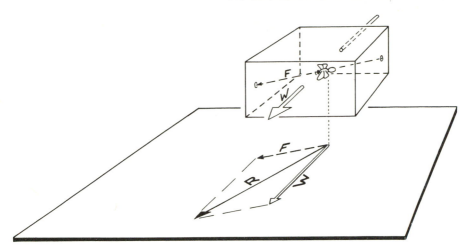

Fig. 3.8/2 The locomotion of an animal in a moving medium. The flight course (*F*) is shown inside a box of air that is itself moving in the direction *W* (= wind). The self-motion (*F*) of the animal within the medium and the movement of the medium (*W*) relative to the ground sum to give the track (*R*), the resultant locomotion of the animal with respect to the ground.

with their tracks. Both birds [195] and bees [504] can counter this drift by altering their flight direction. Bees can compensate in this way for considerable winds (Fig. 3.8/3). Drift angles of up to 30° have been measured [235].

Even though a bird must fly with its body at an angle to its track to compensate for drift, this does not mean that it is flying at an angle relative to the airflow. The air does not flow toward the bird from the side, but from the front along its longitudinal body axis.

As earthbound creatures it is difficult for us to conceptualize and understand these processes. An airborne animal does not perceive the movement of the air as wind the way we on the ground do. It registers no wind (except for turbulence, see below) but is transported along through space as if it were in a giant box of air. Passengers in a hot-air balloon are in a comparable situation and also feel no wind. Although the balloon may be racing along, they do not have the sensation of moving until they look down and see the earth slipping along beneath them. Then they can tell that they are moving in the opposite direction of the observed ground motion and can estimate how fast they are moving. As long as there are no identifiable structures in the ground-flow pattern, it is just an optokinetic pattern and provides no information about where the balloon is going. It is, of course, quite a different situation when there are landmarks or other references such as the sun. The balloon riders will notice when they are

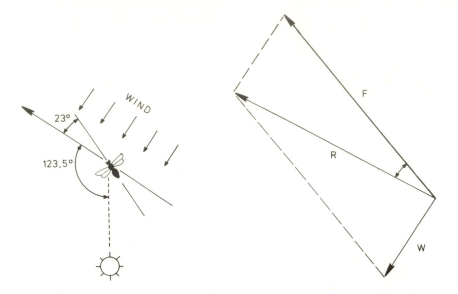

Fig. 3.8/3 The flight adjustment of a bee in a sidewind (W) with a speed of 3.45 m/sec. The air speed (F) of the bee is 8.88 m/sec, and the velocity with which it moves along the track (R) is 8.4 m/sec. Accordingly, the bee flies at a drift angle of 23° and an angle between sun and track of 123.5°. The body axis–sun angle is 146.5°. (Modified from [235])

no longer traveling parallel to the river, and when the sun is now behind, instead of to the side of, them.

The case for active locomotion is in principle the same as for passive transport, but with additional effects. Wind can still only be registered visually. As we have already mentioned, active motion of the animal and passive transport by the wind sum to give the track. The ground pattern flow is identical to the track with respect to velocity and alignment but has the opposite sign, i.e., it flows backward when the animal flies forward. (For the sake of simplicity this is not always explicitly stated in the following.) The angle β_o between the track (R) and the direction of active locomotion (F) is called the drift angle (β_o), since it depends on the drifting effect of the wind. The angle β_{ow} between the track (R) and the wind (W) is the track angle; and the angle κ between the F and W is the course angle (see Fig. 3.8/4).

The importance of the ground pattern for flight orientation has been elegantly demonstrated for bees [330]. The bees had to fly over a body of water to reach a food source. A wind could blow them off course when there was only water below them, but not after a "fixed" pattern in the form of a slatted bridge was placed over the water (Fig. 3.8/7).

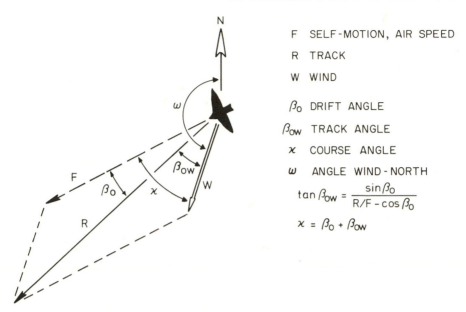

F SELF-MOTION, AIR SPEED

R TRACK

W WIND

β_0 DRIFT ANGLE

β_{OW} TRACK ANGLE

$\varkappa$ COURSE ANGLE

ω ANGLE WIND - NORTH

$$\tan \beta_{OW} = \frac{\sin \beta_0}{R/F - \cos \beta_0}$$

$$\varkappa = \beta_0 + \beta_{OW}$$

Fig. 3.8/4 Track orientation in a flowing medium. The track is recorded by registering the pattern flow. The track angle (β_{ow}, between track and wind) cannot be measured directly and must be computed from β_o, F, and R. The equation for this is derived from $R/\sin (\beta_o + \beta_{ow}) = F/\sin \beta_{ow}$.

3.8.3.1 Orientation to Wind

The orientation to wind by an airborne animal means orientation to pattern flow. An animal can directly measure its own speed (air speed, F), the speed of the pattern flow (ground speed, R), and the drift angle β_o. The first parameter is measured with current-sensitive receptors like those already mentioned; the other two are measured with the eyes (they are optokinetic quantities, see Fig. 3.8/4). The track angle β_{ow} can be calculated from these three variables; and the course angle $\varkappa$, from β_o and β_{ow}.

A flight maneuver can change the velocity (F) and the direction of locomotion within the air mass (course angle $\varkappa$). Drift angle β_o, track angle β_{ow}, and ground speed R are all affected by changes in $\varkappa$.

To head into the wind, an animal lines up its flight so that the ground pattern flows beneath it along its longitudinal body axis ($\beta_o = 0$). The situation is somewhat more complicated for an animal flying at a set angle with respect to the wind. Male moths, such as *Plodia interpunctella*, fly upwind in a zigzag path when they are stimulated by female pheromone. Experiments with different wind intensities (W) have shown that they maintain a constant track angle β_{ow} of about 95° relative to the wind and a constant ground speed (R) but alter the drift angle (β_o) and air speed (F) (Fig. 3.8/ 5, [562]). This process requires an internal computation of the track angle β_{ow}. The vector triangle is defined by the drift angle (β_o), the air speed (F), and the ground speed (R).

The relative ground displacement as it is visually registered by a flying (or swimming) animal is a complex event (Fig. 3.8/9). Due to changes in perspective, the elements of a pattern as seen by an animal appear to get farther apart as it moves toward them and to run together again after it passes them. Pattern flow seems fastest to the animal directly below and abreast of it.

The apparent pattern velocity depends not only on the animal's ground speed but also on how far it is from the ground. The greater its flight altitude, the slower the pattern flow. Flies maintain a particular flight level relative to a horizontal stripe (their horizon) so that they see the stripe just beneath their head horizon [905]. Dung beetles fly faster at higher than at lower altitudes [831]. This may be because the pattern flow appears slower at greater elevations, indicating headwinds to the animal. The flight control mechanism compensates by increasing air speed.

3.8.3.2 Orientation in a Predetermined Direction

Orientation in a predetermined direction is not possible using only the ground pattern flow as a reference. An animal can no more orient to an anonymous ground pattern flow than the passenger of a hot-air balloon. Identifiable reference cues are required for laying a particular track in space.

Let us first consider how to adjust the track (= pattern flow) to a particular compass angle relative to the sun [408, 440]. Figure 3.8/6 shows how changes in wind direction or velocity that perturb the setting might be dealt with in theory. As was mentioned above, insects can compensate for wind perturbations by changing their flight speed and drift angle (Fig. 3.8/5). Bees alter their flight direction as a function of the wind (Fig. 3.8/3) and adjust their speed to fit the wind conditions [235].

Figure 3.8/8 presents a hypothetical and somewhat simplified flow diagram, which does not include all complications due to wind. There are two inputs into the feedback loop: β_o, the angle between pattern flow and body axis, and β_s, the angle between sun and body axis. Their signals, β_{oi} and

Fig. 3.8/5 (opposite) Flight control by the moth *Plodia interpunctella* for three wind speeds (W). Above: Percentage of animals as a function of track angle β_{ow} and drift angle β_o. Below: Percentage of animals as a function of track velocity (R) and air speed (F). Drift angle and air speed change as wind speed changes in such a way that track angle and track velocity are kept constant (see also vector diagrams in top row). (Modified from [562])

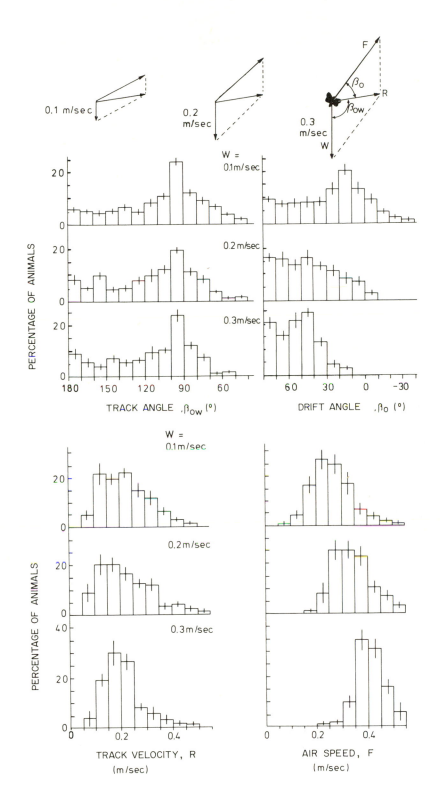

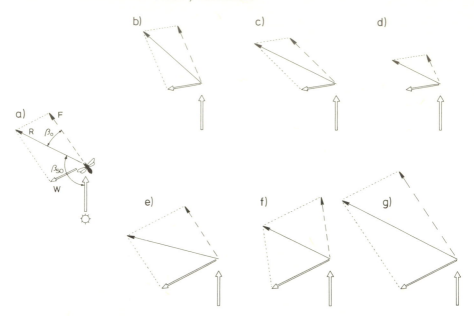

Fig. 3.8/6 The correction of perturbations of flight direction due to changes in wind direction b)–d) or wind speed e)–g). The animal tries to keep β_{so}, the direction of the optomotor pattern flow relative to the sun (= compass direction) constant. a) The starting position. b) An increase in β_{so} due to a change in wind direction is corrected by c) a change in β_o or d) in air speed F. e) A decrease in β_{so} due to a change in wind speed is corrected by f) a change in β_o or g) in air speed F.

β_{si}, are combined to give β_{soi}, which signals the angle between pattern flow (track) and sun. This is the orientation parameter to be set and held. Bees apparently use this parameter since they dance the angle track–sun (β_{so}) and not the angle body–sun (β_s). In our circuit diagram β_{soi} is used to control the flight direction within the air mass (course angle κ). The output κ directly affects the pattern flow β_o, which is also under the influence of wind speed W and the animal's air speed F. (The vectorial transformation of κ, W, and F into β_o is an external physical event.) The adjustment of κ also affects the sun compass angle β_s. Wind direction ω also has an effect on β_s, adding to κ and affecting β_{soi} via β_s. The consequent error (β_{sor} − β_{soi}) leads to a turning command that changes κ, so that the sum of the new β_o and the new β_s equals the old value of β_{so}, corresponding to the reference value (β_{sor}) for the track with respect to the sun.

3.8.3.3 Orientation with the Wind as a Reference

Theoretically, there are ways in which the wind direction could be directly registered. The flow of air past objects and irregularities on the ground

Fig. 3.8/7 The track of a bee over water.
Left: The wind (arrows) blows the bee off
course. Right: A slatted bridge furnishes a
fixed ground pattern enabling the bee to
hold its course. (Modified from [330] and
[235])

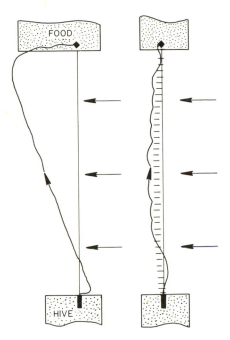

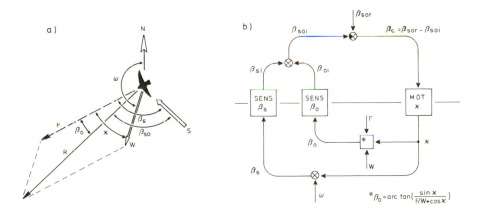

Fig. 3.8/8 Using the ground pattern flow to hold a track to the sun in a crosswind. a) Vector diagram illustrating the various parameters. b) Flow diagram. The input β_s is measured as the angle between sun and animal; and β_o, as the angle between pattern flow and animal. The angle β_{so} of the track to the sun cannot be measured, but its signal β_{soi} is computed from the input signals β_{si} and β_{oi}. The error (difference between reference value β_{sor} and β_{soi}) affects the motor output κ. The angle κ together with F and W affects β_o and with ω affects β_s, thus controlling β_{soi}.

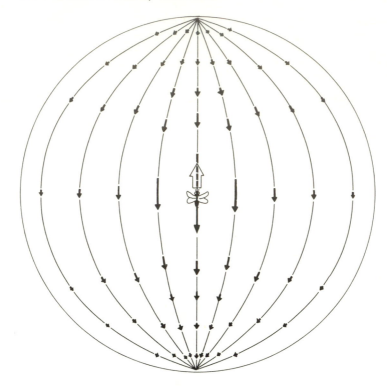

Fig. 3.8/9 The panoramic view of ground pattern flow for an animal flying at an altitude of 20 m and a speed of 0.8 m/sec. The distance between the animal and the front and back vanishing points is 120 m. The length of the arrows approximates the apparent ground movement/min.

creates turbulence. Even at higher altitudes, airflow is not laminar due to thermal currents, drafts, and differences in speed between adjacent air streams. Convection currents arise when the sea is warmer than the air. The direction in which the air circulates depends on wind direction [634].

Can a flying animal determine the direction of the prevailing winds from such processes? This question has received considerable attention [280, 195, 430]. Birds may use this kind of information to orient directly to wind [47, 1000]. Gusts of wind produce linear accelerations of a bird's body that could be registered by its labyrinths (statoliths) to provide signals about wind direction.

Another possibility that has been scarcely considered is that certain cloud formations have a particular relationship to wind direction [280]. Migratory birds may also be able to use this kind of information.

Migratory birds are known to take the wind into account. Many species migrate preferentially when the wind direction is favorable, i.e., when it coincides with the migration direction. Some seek out an altitude with the appropriate wind direction; others even migrate against a headwind [47]. Emlen [196] suggests that migratory birds adjust their migratory behavior according to information extracted from weather conditions. For example, changes in temperature, atmospheric pressure, and/or humidity may indicate weather fronts associated with certain wind directions.

To conclude this section let us emphasize again that a flying animal always flies "forward," that is, airflow hits it head-on. Normal flight is designed in nature and in technology so that air flows onto the wings from the front (= flying forward). Other directions of flight, which might be visually guided according to landmarks or pattern flow, would have an unfavorable effect on the aerodynamics. The resulting increase in resistance and reduction in lift would expend more energy, so such flight behavior is not very common. Birds, for instance, tolerate a sidewind when they are gliding toward a stationary target on the ground (= sideways glide). Aircraft are often subjected to some sidewind during landing, since the wind does not always blow in the direction of the runway.

3.9 ORIENTATION BY TOUCH AND FEEL

Probably the most primitive way to determine the position of an object is by feel. All animals have receptors that respond to tactile stimuli. Touch-sensitive receptors are distributed over the entire body surface (for a review of vertebrates, see [117]). The sensor-site label of the stimulated receptors is often very precise. A frog scratches the exact spot on its back that was tickled [231].

3.9.1. Touching and Feeling

Whereas the word touch may refer only to the contact between a sensitive part of the body and an object, the word feel includes the possibility of using movable body appendages to determine the location of an object. Tactile bristles, tentacles, palps, and antennae are only a few of the specialized appendages with which animals feel out their environment. The hands and feet are also used to explore the surroundings and to "grasp" the three-dimensionality of an object. This is also called the "haptic" sense [258]. A review of the receptors involved in these processes in mammals is given by Skoglund [817].

The octopus is undisputed master in the tactile identification of objects. When it wraps its long flexible arms with their richly innervated suckers around various objects, it can distinguish differences in their shape and surface structure like the spacing of grooves [911, 912].

When an animal touches an object with one of its appendages, two processes are taking place: (1) Contact receptors are stimulated, and (2) the position of the appendage relative to the rest of the body conveys information about the position of the object, and sometimes about its form.

3.9.2 Tactile Orientation

An animal can orient itself to an object when it knows the position of the object relative to its body. It can also direct parts of its body toward the object. The nymph of the damsel fly *Calopteryx splendens* spans its prey with the tips of its antennae before it snaps it up with its "mask," a pincer-tipped specialization of the labium (lower lip) (Fig. 3.9/1, [97]).

An animal can orient in space by touch, for example, by feeling its way along a wall. Such orientation is called thigmotaxis. The tandem running of ants may also be included in this category (see 3.5.2). The recruit maintains antennal contact with the recruiter, which is running in front of it. Both tactile and chemical cues are important for this behavior.

Tactile information can elicit a sensation of apparent motion similar to the circular vection that was discussed in 2.9.2 for visual phenomena. When a drum is turned around an experimental subject whose outstretched hand is touching the drum and being moved along with it in a motion similar to nystagmus, the subject soon has the sensation of rotating inside a stationary drum (Fig. 3.9/2, [81]). Nystagmic eye movements also occur. The name arthrokinetic circular vection has been proposed for this phenomenon.

Another phenomenon reminiscent of circular vection arises during the "stepping around test" [987]. The subject holding on to a stationary bar walks in place on a revolving disc. The legs step in a circle, but the body stays in place. The somaesthetic signals of the stepping movements create a sensation of being turned (= circular vection).

Substrate orientation. The ground on which an animal is standing or moving is naturally an important spatial reference for the orientation of its body position and movement. The ground has a special importance for

Fig. 3.9/1 Tactile prey orientation of a nymph of the damsel fly *Calopteryx splendens*. From left to right: The nymph approaches, spans the prey with its antennae, and strikes with its mask. (Modified from [97])

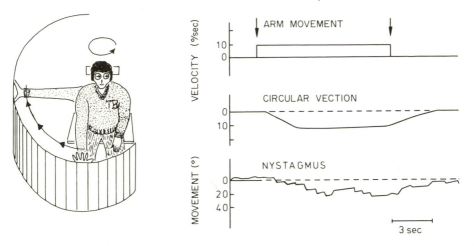

Fig. 3.9/2 Allowing the arm to be carried along by a rotating drum (left and upper right) elicits circular vection (shown by arrow over experimental subject). The subject sets a dial to the speed of this apparent rotation (middle right). The eyes show nystagmus (lower right). (Modified from [81])

the orientation of balance. The contact of the feet (or of the parts of the body touching the ground) supplies information via two somatosensory systems that are hard to separate. One is stimulated by the effect of gravity pulling the body against the ground; the other registers haptically the position of the body with respect to the substrate.

Signals from touch and pressure receptors, joint position receptors, and stretch receptors in muscles and tendons work together with statolith organ signals to keep the body's center of gravity over its base, i.e., balanced. People with defective labyrinths depend mainly on the somatosensory system especially when there are no visual spatial references. The gravity-dependent tactile somatoreceptive influence on spatial orientation of humans is treated in 2.9.1.1.

Orientation of preference position with respect to the substrate is not the same as the reflexive maintenance of balance. Usually an animal turns its ventral side toward the substrate. Some animals (for instance, insects or crustaceans) walk in this preference position not only on horizontal surfaces but also on tilted and vertical surfaces.

It has been known for some time that crustaceans use the substrate as a reference cue (crayfish [479], shrimp [5]). A recent series of experiments has quantitatively analyzed this system and its association with gravity orientation [829, 785, 783, 738, 628]. When the position of the ground with respect to its body is altered by tilting a substrate board sideways, the spiny lobster makes compensatory eye movements as well as positional responses.

It throws its antennae to its "uphill" side and pushes against the board with the legs on this side (Fig. 3.9/3).

The position receptors that measure the angle between the legs and the body are located in the proximal leg joints. The effect of these receptors is additive on each body side and may also sum individually across sides. Receptors in the terminal leg segments appear to signal contact with the ground [985].

Since a spiny lobster (or a shrimp) adjusts its body position to conform to the surface it is standing on, it is tilted with respect to gravity when its substrate is tilted. It orients simultaneously to ground contact and gravity [5, 784, 785]. The weighting (see 2.7.3) of the two reference cues depends on (1) the animal's position with respect to gravity (statocyst stimulation) [829] and (2) the number of legs touching the substrate (see Fig. 3.9/4, [784]). The fewer legs on the ground, the stronger the response to a change in position with respect to gravity. This gives rise to the apparent paradox that a single pair of legs exerts a stronger thrust on the substrate than five or even all ten legs.

3.9.3 Central Somatosensory Projections

The organization of somatic zones and their central representation has been extensively studied [23, 244, 965, 964, 919, 920, 921, 922, 923]. Electrophysiological recordings show that tactile stimulation of body loci results in local excitation in somatosensory areas of the cortex (Fig. 3.9/5). The projections are disproportionate, insofar as certain body parts like the feet, hands, and mouth occupy comparatively large areas, while others such as the back are represented by small areas.

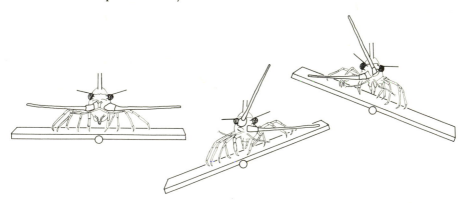

Fig. 3.9/3 The response of a spiny lobster (held in place by a rod attached to its back) to tilting of the board on which it is standing. Its eyes have been covered with a cap and elongated with a bristle. The eyes follow the ground movement. The antennae are thrown to the "uphill" side. (Modified from [785])

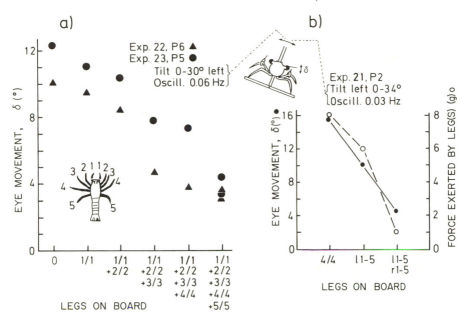

Fig. 3.9/4 Positional orientation to substrate and gravity in the spiny lobster when board and lobster are tilted from side to side. a) Eye movement (δ) as a function of the legs on the board. b) Eye movement and force exerted on the board by the legs as a function of the legs on the board. Note that both eye movement and force are greater, the fewer the legs on the board. (Modified from [784])

The cortical representation of the body surface is subject to a complicated projection process that reflects the organization of the surface into zones called dermatomes. This transformation makes it possible to meaningfully represent the three-dimensional closed surface of an appendage (e.g., a leg) on a two-dimensional map. The central map is organized according to particular sequences of receptive fields called trajectories. For example, one trajectory runs down the posterior outside edge of the leg, loops under the sole of the foot and over the instep, and continues up the anterior outside edge of the leg (Fig. 3.9/6b). The trajectory is composed of three overlapping dermatomes whose afferents enter the dorsal root of the spinal

Fig. 3.9/5 The projection of the body surface onto the two somatosensory areas (SI, SII) of the cortex in the mouse musculus. The acoustic (AUD) and visual (VIS) regions are also indicated. (Modified from [964])

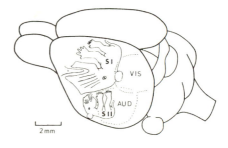

a)   b)   c)

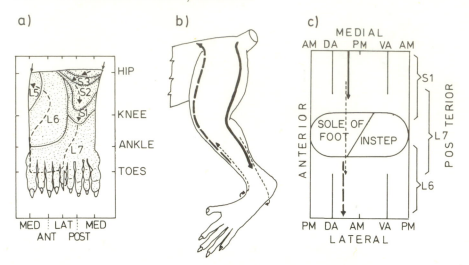

Fig. 3.9/6 Somatosensory projection of the hind-leg surface onto the cortex in the monkey. a) The leg surface has been slit and rolled out to show the organization of the derma-tomes. The arrows on the upper edge mark the line of the cut, which coincides with the ventro-axial line, the natural dividing line between the dermatomes. The dashed line indi-cates the sequence of dermatomes comprising the trajectory. b) The trajectory crosses three dermatomes, running down the posterior outside edge of the leg, under the sole of the foot, up over the instep, and up the anterior outside edge of the leg. c) The central repre-sentation of the trajectory shown in b). The labels on the edge of the map (medial, lateral, anterior, posterior) give its orientation in terms of the cortex; the letters on the upper and lower edges, in terms of the leg. AM = anterior midline; PM = posterior midline; DA = dorso-axial line; VA = ventro-axial line; S1, 2, 3 = sacral dermatomes 1, 2, 3; L7, 6, 5 = lumbar 7, 6, 5. (Modified from [921, 919])

cord (sacral 1 to lumbar 6). The leg trajectories arise from the caudo-rostral sequence of the dermatomes. This sequence can be better understood if the leg surface is cut open along its ventral (= medial) axis and rolled out flat (Fig. 3.9/6a). The trajectory loop is represented as a straight line from the medial to the lateral margin of the somatosensory map (Fig. 3.9/6c). Hence, the central representation is not a linear topological map of the body surface, but a sequential organization of body segments. Anterior and posterior margins of the map represent the same trajectory (Fig. 3.9/6c). The order of the trajectory projections differs for the medial and lateral margins. We can turn this two-dimensional map into a three-dimensional surface and still preserve the order of the trajectories by making a Klein bottle [919, 921]. First the map is rolled up into a cylinder (Fig. 3.9/7); then its lower end is bent, threaded through a hole in the cylinder wall, and pulled up through the inside so that both ends meet. Corresponding tra-jectory ends are now adjacent to each other, and the order along the two margins is the same.

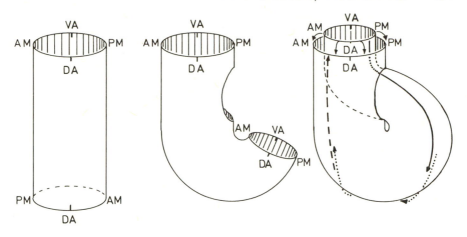

Fig. 3.9/7 Transformation of a two-dimensional map into a closed three-dimensional object, a Klein bottle. The map shown on the right in Fig. 3.9/6 is rolled up into a cylinder (left). The lower end of the cylinder is bent up (middle) and pulled through a hole in the cylinder wall (right). The corresponding margins lie next to each other; the vertical trajectories of the map describe loops going around this "leg."

Werner [919] formulated the hypothesis that this cortical map in its uniform tactile-kinaesthetic representation of the space around an animal forms the basis for the haptic sense.

As in the visual system the tactile-somatosensory system projects to another brain region, the superior colliculus [830]. This map is in register with the map of the visual field [180, 127, 264]. The best-represented somatic fields are those whose body directions fall in the sector of the visual field (Fig. 3.9/8). For example, the somatotopic projections of the snout,

Fig. 3.9/8 Projection of receptive fields of the right body surface onto the left superior colliculus in the cat. The orientation of the superior colliculus is given by the labels rostral, caudal, lateral, and medial; the lines denote the visual field coordinates relative to the body, 0° being either the horizontal (naso-temporal) or the vertical (dorsoventral) meridian (see inset, above). (Modified from [830])

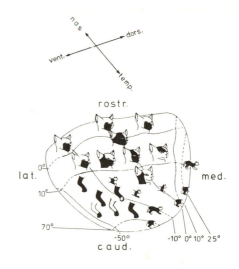

the side of the head, the shoulder, and the side of the body are lined up in a row along the nasal-temporal line of the visual field. In this context it is especially suggestive that the tactile field of a mouse's vibrissae maps into the same subtectal region as do the forepaws and ears (Fig. 3.9/9, [179, 180]).

The subtectal layers might be considered a substrate onto which the spatial values from the various modalities (visual, somatosensory, acoustic)

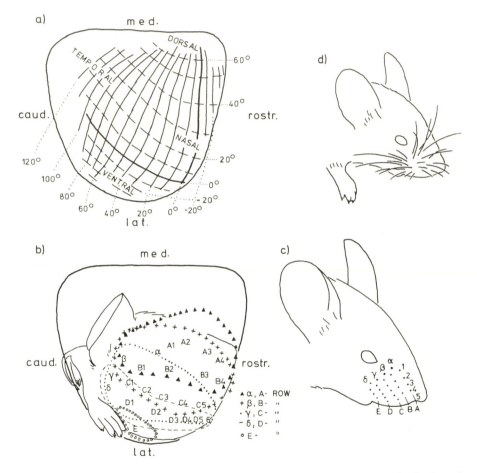

Fig. 3.9/9 Sensory projections of the right superior colliculus in the mouse. a) Projection of the left visual field with coordinates. Regions of the right visual field are mapped to the right of the 0° vertical meridian (compare also Fig. 3.9/8). b) Projection of the left side of the head, including the base of the ear, forepaw, and vibrissae, numbered as shown in c). The somatosensory map overlaps considerably with the visual map. c) Organization and labeling of the vibrissae on the snout. d) The mouse's head with vibrissae and forepaws. The right side of the head is shown in c) and d) to facilitate comparison. (a, b, and c, modified from [180]; d, from [179])

are topologically projected. This region appears to be an important center for the transformation of sensory-spatial information into motor-spatial action (see 3.1, 3.6).

3.10 ORIENTATION TO GRAVITY AND ANGULAR ACCELERATION

The senses of gravity and angular acceleration have a close functional relationship. Changes in position with respect to gravity are also rotational processes that are registered and monitored by rotation sense organs like the semicircular canals. The performance of one system is tuned to that of the other, as is evident in the behavior of frogs with utricles but no semicircular canals [576, 848]. Such frogs can adjust their posture to compensate for slow tilting of the substrate, but when the tilt is over, their heads bob up and down. Locomotion is also accompanied by rhythmic bobbing of the head.

The semicircular canals make the precise execution of a turn and the fine adjustment of its alignment possible. They operate in every plane, whereas the sense of gravity is limited to the vertical. Information on spatial positions in the horizontal plane must be provided by other sensory modalities, such as vision (position with respect to the visual field).

Mayne [573] analyzed the operating principles of the vertebrate vestibular system as if it were an inertial navigation system. In his "systems concept" the basic function that supplies signals for velocity and position is the measurement of acceleration, both linear (statolith organs) and angular (semicircular canals). He compared this mathematical model with other models for the semicircular canals [547, 975] and the statolith organs [972, 970].

Linear accelerations that are not due to gravity, such as a sudden start or stop in forward motion also stimulate the statolith organs. Why don't we perceive a change with respect to gravity during such movements? The statolith organ signals are interpreted as an indication of what caused them, i.e., a change in the velocity of linear movement, and not a change with respect to gravity because the semicircular canals are not stimulated during such movements. Consequently, the statolith organs appear to be more than just gravity sensors (see also 2.9 and 3.1).

Anatomically the two systems often occur as a single complex, such as the statolith organs (vestibular sacs) and the semicircular canals in the vertebrate labyrinth (Fig. 3.10/1). Afferents from both systems terminate together in the vestibular nuclei, where neurons can be found that respond to stimulation of either (see 3.10.3). In crabs [729] and cephalopods [104], gravity and angular acceleration receptors share a common statocyst sac (Figs. 3.10/15, 3.10/22).

Fig. 3.10/1 The labyrinth of a minnow.
K = metencephalon, L = lagena, M =
mesencephalon, S = saccule, V = vagus
nerve, VR = medulla oblongata, U =
utricle. (Modified from [237])

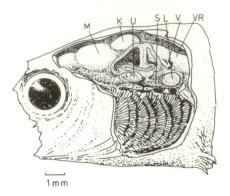

1 mm

These systems perform the functions of maintenance of physical balance; orientation of locomotion; perception of objects within a spatial context; and space constancy, which includes compensatory movements.

Let us first touch on the subject of eye movements. Very generally, eye movements can be classified as compensatory, fixating, or tracking. The last two are not directly monitored by the vestibular organs. Compensatory eye movements contribute to the constancy of the visual field. They occur in response to stimulation of the statolith organs and the semicircular canals. The role of the statolith organs has already been discussed elsewhere (2.9, 2.10). The semicircular canals release eye movements called nystagmus. As the head is turned, the eyes make a countermovement that holds the visual field in place, then jump back to catch up with the movement of the head, and finally begin another slow countermovement.

Fixation responses direct the gaze onto a particular object and try to bring its image into the fovea. Tracking responses keep a moving object in the visual field. When fixation and tracking are accompanied by a head movement, the semicircular canals must participate in the control of the eye movements for a precise tracking to be possible. People with labyrinth defects cannot keep their eyes on an object when they are turning their heads. The direction of their gaze shifts a little relative to the viewed object [11]. This shift is perceived as an unsteadiness of the object in space. This phenomenon can be understood in terms of the mechanisms of space constancy (2.10). Since there is no, or insufficient, information on the movement of the eyes, any shift of the image on the retina is interpreted as a movement of the object.

3.10.1 Orientation to Gravity

The physics of gravity stimulation. Gravity is probably the most important spatial reference cue for an organism. Terrestrial forms in particular have been forced to adapt their behavior to the continuous downward pull of gravity.

Force is the product of mass and acceleration ($D = m \times b$). The force of gravity is determined by the acceleration of a body during free fall. This is 981 cm/sec^2 or one unit of gravity, 1 G.

Other accelerative forces, such as those resulting from centrifugation, have the same physical effect as gravity. They sum vectorially to give the gravito-inertial force that we refer to simply as "gravity." The additional forces change the direction and length of the gravity vector. The directional change alters the relationship of the body to gravity. As Mach [537] emphasized, this is equivalent to a change in position. For this reason the practice of referring to the perception of these changes as illusions, e.g., oculogravic illusion for the change in direction of the visual subjective vertical (2.9), should be avoided.

Increasing the magnitude of gravity, by centrifugation for example, makes things heavier. In gravity organs that respond to shear, an increase in the weight of the statoliths affects the position signals. This effect is occasionally overlooked in the interpretation of results from centrifugation experiments.

A gravity stimulus is always based on the weight of a mass affecting sensory elements. The specific gravity of the mass must differ from that of its surroundings. Usually it is higher, as in the statolith. Typically, statoliths are inclusions of inorganic, usually calcareous, material contained in a fluid-filled vessel. The specific gravity of the vertebrate endolymph is 1.003, and that of calcite, for example, is 2.71 [125]. Since the difference in specific gravities is what determines the weight of the statolith, it is irrelevant whether the animal is in or out of water.

In some cases the specific gravity of the inclusion is lighter than its surroundings. In water bugs small air bubbles impart a buoyancy to the sense hairs (3.10.1.3).

Gravity receptors. The effect of gravity can be detected in various ways, for instance, via specialized gravity organs or via receptors at joints between two body parts. When one part is freely suspended from the other, it works like a statolith. Gravity pulls it down so that it stimulates the sensory elements. These two possibilities are discussed later in more detail. Here we shall touch on two further mechanisms of gravity detection about which little is known and which are turning out to be more important than was at first thought.

The forces that the body exerts against the substrate can stimulate receptors. Putative receptors for direct substrate pressure are pressure-sensitive units in the skin and deeper tissues (3.9). Distortion of the joints by the pull of gravity on the limbs could indirectly stimulate receptors in the tendons and joints. This resembles the above-mentioned gravity reception based on a freely hanging body part. This complex is usually included under the general heading of somatoreception or somaesthesia and plays an important role in human spatial perception (2.9, 3.10.1.1.4).

The pull of the internal organs on their mesenteries can stimulate sensors in the body cavities. Experiments on pigeons point to such a mechanism [815, 861, 62, 150]. Pigeons without vestibular organs or with severed spinal cords show postural reflexes during passive turning. Systematic cutting of the dorsal roots suggests that the receptors are in the intestinal mesenteries. There are indications for similar position receptors in the monkey [398].

The following section is limited to the statolith organs of crustaceans, vertebrates, and cephalopod molluscs and the gravity receptors of insects. A comprehensive review of the physiology of gravity organs in invertebrates is presented by Markl in the *Handbook of Sensory Physiology* [558]. Further articles in this handbook deal with vertebrates, mainly mammals. Additional details can be found in Werner's book, *Das Gehörorgan der Wirbeltiere und des Menschen* [918] and in the book by Vinnikov and his colleagues in Russian, *The Balance Receptor* [880a].

Statolith organs or statocysts are sense organs in which the sense cells are stimulated by a mass called the statolith (also referred to in vertebrates as the statolithic or statoconial membrane). The names otocyst, otolith organs, and otolith derive from *otos*, the Greek root for hearing. They stem from the time when the entire organ complex of the inner ear was thought to be involved in hearing (as were the "auditory" sacs of crustaceans). In his now famous experiments Kreidl [477] demonstrated that the auditory sacs of crustaceans have nothing to do with sound perception but are concerned with the postural response to gravity. He kept shrimp in an aquarium, the bottom of which was covered with iron filings. After their moult the shrimp filled their sacs with iron particles instead of the usual sand. When these shrimp were placed in a magnetic field, they moved with their ventral side facing the magnets. The nomenclature based on *otos* is still widely used, especially in the vertebrate neurophysiological literature. The labels using the root "stato" are, however, more accurate [508] and are recommended in the *Nomina Anatomica* (1966). Stato is derived from the Greek *statos*, meaning "to place," or from the Latin *stare*, meaning "to stand."

The stimulus process and the production of the signal in the statolith organs may follow diverse principles. Kühn [480] developed the well-known statocyst model found in older textbooks. It involves an array process in which a statolith rests on a carpet of sense hairs lining a round cavity. The statolith always lies on and stimulates the sense hairs at the lowest point in the cavity. The sensor-site label of these elements provides the direction signal. This principle was first described by Mach [538]. There are only a few examples in the animal kingdom, e.g., in snails and clams [171, 248, 962, 963].

The gravity sense organs of crustaceans (mysids and decapods) and of vertebrates operate according to a different principle.

3.10.1.1 Crustaceans and Vertebrates

The gravity organs of these two widely disparate taxonomic groups have two features in common. The adequate stimulus is a shearing force and the sensory elements are arranged so that the directions of their maximum sensitivities form a fan-shaped array.

The fine anatomy of the sensory elements. The sensory elements are morphologically and physiologically polarized. The morphological polarization was discovered first in the vertebrates ([532], review [926]). Each sense cell bears a patch of cilia, one of which, the kinocilium, is longer and more differentiated than the others, the stereocilia (Fig. 3.10/2). The kinocilium contains several regularly arranged fibrillae and is "anchored" to the cell by a basal body. Its position at the edge of the group determines the cell's physiological direction of polarization (Fig. 3.10/2a, [925, 531]). The re-

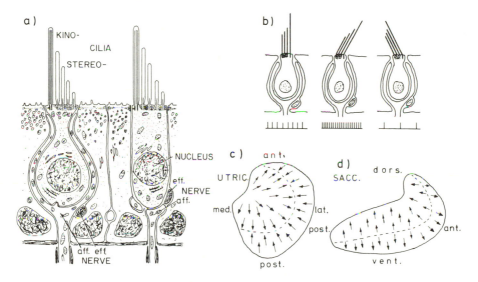

Fig. 3.10/2 Vertebrate statolith system. a) Two types of vestibular hair cells. Type I is embedded in a cup-shaped dendritic process of the afferent nerve. Type II, the phylogenetically older form, is cylindrical. Efferent terminals synapse on the outside of the afferent process of Type I and on the Type II hair cell itself. b) Excitation of the sense cell. The trace beneath the cells represents the discharge pattern. Left: Resting discharge. Middle: Discharge frequency increases when the cilia are bent toward the kinocilium. Right: The discharge decreases when the cilia are bent the other way. c) The right utricular and saccular maculae in humans showing polarization directions of the sensory elements. (a and c, modified from [508]; b, from [925])

ceptor cell is maximally sensitive to shearing force across the stereocilia toward the kinocilium. Bending in the opposite direction leads to a decrease in impulse rate (Fig. 3.10/2b).

The sense hair of the crustacean statocyst works like a lever that translates a bend of the hairshaft into a pull on a threadlike element, the chorda, attached to the sense cells (Fig. 3.10./3, [789]).

3.10.1.1.1 Shear and the Positional Signal

Breuer first proposed the shear theory of statocyst stimulation, which states that the hair cells are stimulated by the tangential force (shear) and not by the pressure exerted by the statoliths [86]. Von Holst confirmed and expanded this theory in centrifugation experiments on fish [366]. Fish orient

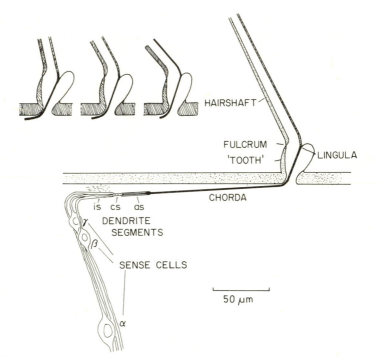

Fig. 3.10/3 Sensory hair of the crayfish statocyst. The hairshaft works like a lever, which turns on a fulcrum formed by an extension of the cyst wall called the tooth. Three degrees of bend are shown on the upper left. Bending the hairshaft toward the tooth side tautens the chorda and stimulates the sense cells connected to it. Most of the hairs are oriented with their tooth side toward the middle of the statocyst. Only in the most posterior transverse row are they the other way around (compare Fig. 3.10/8). as = outer, cs = ciliary, is = inner dendrite segments. The inner segments appear to be attached to the cyst wall by specialized tissue. (Modified from [789])

their position to both light and gravity following the vector resultant (Fig. 2.7/1). When the magnitude of gravity is changed, the shear on the utricle (defined by $G \times \sin \alpha$) is kept constant (2.7.1, Fig. 2.7/2).

The validity of the shear theory is unquestioned today. It has been corroborated by the fine structure of the sensory elements as well as by electrophysiological studies on statolith organs (rays [530], teleosts [794], guinea pigs [260], cats [517], monkeys [216]) and semicircular canal receptors [863]. Recordings from afferent neurons show that the activity changes, as does shear, with the sine of the angle to gravity. Usually there is a resting discharge that is sinusoidally modulated by the statolith stimulus (Fig. 3.10/4, 3.10/9). A number of earlier ideas on how the statolith organs of vertebrates function have been abandoned, such as the push-pull hypothesis [685, 543], the "buoy" hypothesis [848], and others [918, 620].

Crustacean statocysts operate according to the same principle (Fig. 3.10/3). The sense hairs are bent by the shearing force of the statoliths [768]. The findings of electrophysiological studies correspond to this stimulus process (Fig. 3.10/4). The behavioral responses can also be interpreted in terms of the shear on the sense hairs (decapods [768], mysids [624, 625, 626]). When shrimps are rotated around their longitudinal axis, their eye movements are a sinusoidal function of body position with respect to gravity and are greatest at that position in which the statoliths exert maximum shear (Fig. 3.10/5a). Adding the eye movement curve for a shrimp with only a left statolith to that of a shrimp with only a right statolith yields a curve that is identical to that of an intact shrimp (Fig. 3.10/5).

Van der Hoeve and de Kleijn [344] showed that the effects of the right and left organs also sum in vertebrates. The curve of compensatory eye movements for normal rabbits can be reconstructed by adding the curves from animals with only a left and only a right labyrinth. In humans uni-

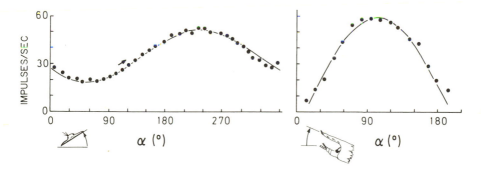

Fig. 3.10/4 Sense cell excitation as a function of position with respect to gravity (directional characteristics). Left: Utricular unit of the thornback ray, *Raja clavata*. Right: Unit from the statocyst nerve of the lobster *Homarus americanus*; average of an upward and downward movement of the rostrum. (Left, modified from [530]; right, from [135])

PALAEMONETES VARIANS (n=21)

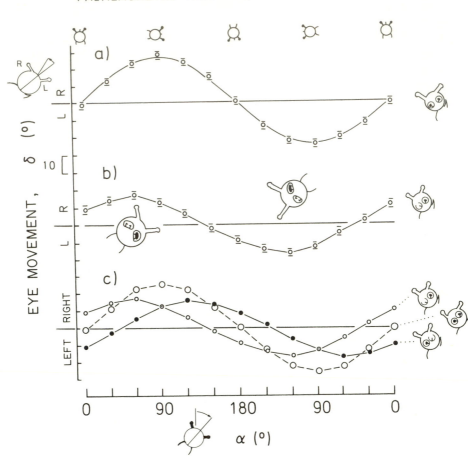

Fig. 3.10/5 Eye position (δ) as a function of position with respect to gravity (α) in the shrimp *Palaemonetes varians*. a) Intact animal. b) Right statoliths removed (statoliths are shown as black dots in the outlines of the body). c) Right (small open circles) and left (closed circles) statoliths removed. Addition of these two curves gives a curve (large open circles) that is the same as the curve for intact animals. Note that the change of eye position is proportional to statolith shear (sinusoidal). (Modified from [768])

lateral labyrinth ablation decreases ocular countertorsion by half [632]. Fish with only one utricular statolith act as if the intensity of gravity has been halved (Fig. 3.10/6).

The right-left interaction is straightforward when only the statolith is removed but the sensory epithelium (and hence the resting discharge) is left intact. Animals scarcely show any orientation deficit after this operation

Fig. 3.10/6 Orientation of a fish to gravity with light (*L*) from the side. Left: Intact fish under normal gravity (1 G) tilted with respect to gravity by α_a. Right: After removal of the right utricle (and compensation). Under increased gravity of 2 G, the fish assumes the same tilt as before ($\alpha_b = \alpha_a$). *S* = shear. (Modified from [366])

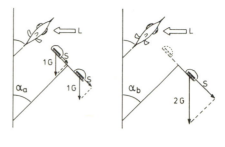

$$\alpha_a = \alpha_b$$

(shark [572], rabbit [453], crustaceans [768, 624]). The intensity of their normal response is merely halved. However, the total extirpation of an organ has a completly different aftermath. The animals are initially unable to move around in a meaningful way. They rotate around their longitudinal axis toward the defective side, fish and shrimp in the water and rabbits on the ground (crayfish [479], shrimp [768], fish [366], rabbit [543]). Immediately after removal of one labyrinth people also show falling tendencies toward the defective side.

These equilibrium disorders gradually decline due to compensation. The animals come to rest with the defective side down. But bouts of rotation continue to reappear even later when the animals are almost able to keep themselves upright and to move in a spatially ordered fashion. In the rabbit a slight tilt of the head persists, which can be seen in the skeleton as a twist of the backbone [543]. The compensation is effected by replacing the resting discharge on the defective side by a central compensation excitation (see 2.11.3). This brings the turning tendency curve back to the base line and corresponds to the situation following unilateral statolith removal. Figure 2.11/4 summarizes this mechanism. A turning tendency results from a difference between left and right excitations. The position signals from the statolith organs (as defined by the turning tendencies) are generally assumed to be based on this kind of difference mechanism [54, 596].

This entire consideration of right-left signal processing applies to sideways tilts, i.e., to position changes around the *X* axis (roll). What about the orientation of body tilt in other directions, such as pitch or diagonally?

3.10.1.1.2 Polarization Fans and Position Signals

Von Holst wrote, "The precise separation of responses to positional changes around the longitudinal and tranverse axes makes it probable that an animal has at least two kinds of turning detectors, one for the transverse and one for the longitudinal direction" [366, p. 113]. This prediction has proven true. In fact, more than two kinds of receptors have been found on the sensory surfaces of the statolith organs. The sense cells of the utricular macula are arranged so that their polarization directions form a fan-shaped pattern (fan array, Fig. 3.10/2; [532, 222, 508]).

The surface of each macula is divided into a central (= medial) zone bordered by a rim zone (Fig. 3.10/2). The hair cells of the center and the rim have opposite polarization directions. If the sensory surfaces of the left and right maculae are represented on a single disc, the polarization vectors of the center point almost radially toward the outside, and those of the rim, radially to the center (Fig. 3.10/7).

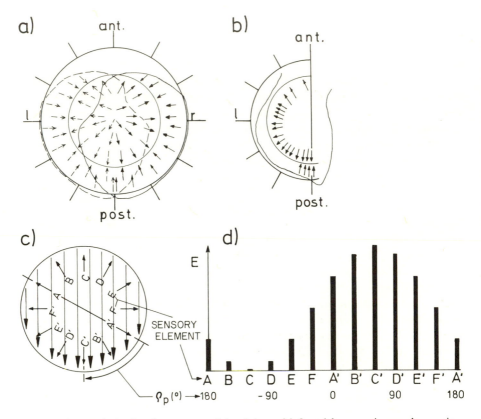

Fig. 3.10/7 a) Polarization fan pattern of the right and left utricles superimposed on a single disc with a center and rim zone (elements of the overlapping medial sectors of each side have been omitted, compare Fig. 3.10/2). b) Polarization fan pattern of the crayfish statocyst (compare legend of Fig. 3.10/8). c) A disc representing both maculae is tipped up on its side and rotated, so that C–C' is in the shear direction of the statoliths (as indicated by parallel arrows). d) Distribution of stimulus and excitation that results from the macula position shown in c). If the disc were tipped out of the plane (vertical) of the paper around the F–F' horizontal line, the excitation values would follow the shear equation. The amplitude of the curve would decrease, but its phase position would stay the same (i.e., maximum at C').

The formation of excitation differences requires pairs of opposed sensors. This condition is equally well met by pairing rim cells from opposite sides, center cells from opposite sides, or ipsilateral rim and center cells with opposite polarization directions. Since the front of each side is missing a sector of about 30°, only the posterior rim-center pairing is "complete" in the anterior-posterior direction.

The polarization directions of crustacean sense hairs are also oriented in the shape of a fan ([828], Fig. 3.10/8).

A central representation of the fan array has been found recently in the vestibular nuclei of fish (see 3.10.3).

The cells that are maximally excited are the ones whose polarization directions are the same as the shear on the statoliths (Fig. 3.10/7c, cell C'). Adjacent cells with other directions of polarization are less excited. Stimulus intensity changes as shown in Fig. 3.10/7d. The function is a sine curve. This gives rise to a distribution of stimulus and excitation on the macula with a peak at the cells that are polarized in the direction of shear.

This organization of the macula explains why neurons are often found in electrophysiological recordings that respond to tilt in several planes (Fig. 3.10/9). Recorded elements can be approximately assigned to particular regions of the macula.

In cats the polarization direction of a defined locus on the utricular macula can be correlated with the direction of eye movements released by direct electrical stimulation of that locus [227].

More precise data were provided by experiments on crayfish, in which small groups of hairs at different loci on the fan were bent with a micromanipulator [828]. Each group released direction-specific compensatory movements of both eyes (Fig. 3.10/10).

In summary, the extent of a tilt and the plane in which it occurs are coded by different systems in the gravity organs of both vertebrates and crustaceans [775, 776]. The degree of tilt in a given plane is coded by an excitation that is proportional to shear. The signal on the plane of the tilt is based on a fan-shaped array of polarization directions.

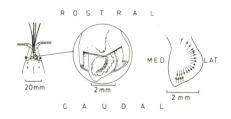

Fig. 3.10/8 Crayfish statocyst. Left: Head of a crayfish with the rostrum removed to reveal the basal segments of the antennules containing the statocysts. Middle: Dissection of the right basal segment to expose statocyst sac, which has been opened and the statolith removed. The horseshoe-shaped rows of sense hairs are partly visible. Right: The polarization fan of the hairs. Arrows indicate that excitation decreases with shear in this direction. From microscopical studies on three animals. (Modified from [828])

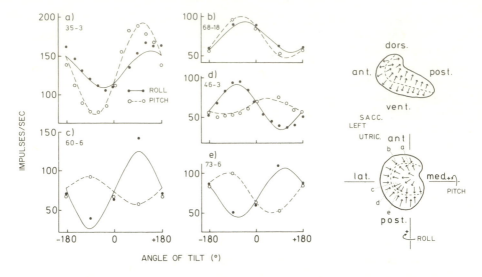

Fig. 3.10/9 Single unit recordings a)–e) from utricular fibers of the squirrel monkey, *Saimiri sciureus*, during roll and pitch permit the localization of the unit on the utricular macula as shown on the right. (Modified from [216])

Fig. 3.10/10 Crayfish eye movement during direct stimulation of small groups of sense hairs: rostral (*r*), rostral-lateral (*rl*), lateral (*l*), caudal-lateral (*cl*), and caudal (*c*). The hairs were bent 8.5° (circles), 14.5° (squares), and 20.4° (triangles). These values correspond to a tilt of the animal of 20°, 40°, and 90° (and shear forces of 0.34 G, 0.64 G, and 1.0 G). The diagram shows the ventro-dorsal components and the rostro-caudal components of the movement of the right (*RA*) and the left (*LA*) eye. Each group of hairs elicits a specific and coordinated movement of both eyes: group *l* leads to left eye upward and right eye downward; group *r*, both eyes rearward; group *c*, both eyes frontward; and groups *rl* and *cl* lead to intermediary eye movements. Each data point is the mean of 8 measurements. (Modified from [828])

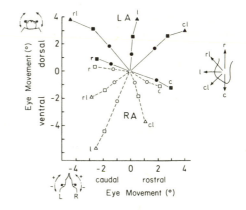

Exactly how the plane of inclination is derived from the distribution of excitations in the fan array is not yet known. The excitation peak might be calculated to give a signal corresponding to the sensor-site label of the maximally stimulated elements. The computation might resemble a vector addition such as has been described for the determination of the light intensity peak in the receptor array of the eye (2.6.2). This would furnish not only a direction (= vector direction) but also a quantity (= vector length) for the degree of tilt.

The simple model in Fig. 3.10/11 illustrates the peripheral and central processing of excitations and their transformation into "postural" responses. The two maculae are represented as a single disc. The excitations of antagonistic elements inhibit each other at the maculae, resulting in "difference" values. This might be mediated by efferent neurons in the utricles (3.10.3), as is suggested by the finding that electrical stimulation of the vestibular nuclei modulates the afferent activity of the contralateral organ [683].

The inhibition sharpens the excitation peak and improves the signal-to-noise ratio (Fig. 3.10/11b, lower diagram). The result is conveyed to the motor center, which consists of four pairs of nuclei representing the four limbs. Each pair has a nucleus for the levator and one for the depressor muscles. Inhibitory and excitatory effects of the "difference" fibers on the neurons of the nuclei bring about coordinated responses of the limbs.

The numerical example shown in Fig. 3.10/11c refers to a 90° tilt in the D–D' plane. A smaller tilt, such as 30°, would lower the shearing force so that the excitation differences would be smaller (by half, since the sine of 30° = 0.5). The consequent response would be weaker but have the same coodination pattern.

The idea of separate coding for degree and plane of tilt is supported by the results of brain stimulation experiments in cats (3.10.3.2). Electrical stimulation of a locus elicits an orientation movement in a particular plane, such as raising the head. The extent of this movement depends on the intensity of the stimulus.

It has been proposed that the excitations of macular regions are pooled for evaluation [595, 596, 54]. This is similar to the semicircular canals where the morphological division of the receptors into three primary planes "demands" such a mechanism. Signals about rotations in other planes arise through "interpolation," i.e., by a calculation of the relative contribution of each canal dependent on its plane. According to Mittelstaedt [595, 596], excitation of macula sectors could be combined in the following ways: anterior and posterior rims, anterior and posterior centers, all right, and all left. In end effect there are three pairings, anterior-posterior, right-left, and dorsal-ventral. The signals for roll, pitch, and yaw could be derived from these pairings by a crossover calculation like that in the bicomponent theory (2.6.3). The orientation of positions depends on the relative contribution of the three components. Benson and Barnes [54] subdivided the two utricular maculae into four zones. Their model corresponds roughly to the posterior half of the disc diagram shown in Fig. 3.10/7. The average excitation of each of the four sectors (right posterior rim and center, left posterior rim and center) is calculated from the vector addition of all the

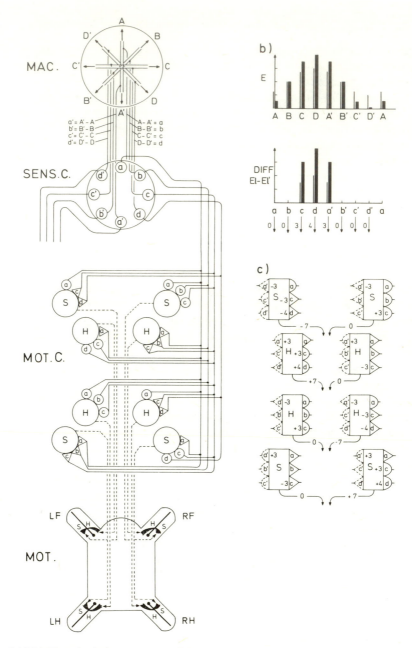

Fig. 3.10/11 Hypothetical mechanism of the transformation into an oriented response of statolith organ excitations which are proportional to shear and specific to the polarization vector. a) Excitations from antagonistic elements of the macula (*MAC.*) are subtracted; the differences are processed in the sensory center (*SENS.C.*) and distributed to the nuclei of the motor center (*MOT.C.*), where they excite (circles) or inhibit (triangles) the motor neurons of an elevator (*H*) and a depressor (*S*) system of four limbs (*LF, RF, LH, RH*). b) The upper histogram shows the distribution of excitations when shear is parallel to *D–D'*. Shear

individual excitations within a sector. This defines four diagonally pointing vectors, which can be combined according to the plane of tilt. For pitch the right and left centers are combined and compared with the right and left rim zones. For roll it is the right rim-left middle against the right middle-left rim.

In both models the wealth of directional information contained in the polarization fans is reduced and has to be extracted later by a computation involving the few basic components. They make the organization of the macula into many different directions and its central representation seem superfluous. A simple X-shaped arrangement such as that found in the ctenophores (sec 3.10.1.3) would satisfy these models. The results of experiments in which small groups of hairs in the crayfish statocyst were mechanically stimulated (Fig. 3.10/10) do not support such a pooling of fan array excitations. They indicate instead an analysis based on the direction diversity within the array.

Why have receptors for linear acceleration (maculae) developed the means to directly measure many planes, whereas those for angular acceleration (semicircular canals) are limited to three? The answer may be because the "construction" of a fan array out of canals was spatially and technically unfeasible.

3.10.1.1.3 Organization and Function of Vestibular Statolith Organs

The two utricular maculae lie approximately in the same plane (i.e., they form an angle of 180°). They are at right angles to the two saccules whose undersides face each other. In comparison, the right and left statocysts of crustaceans occupy an intermediate position (Figs. 3.10/12, 3.10/5). At the moment we can only speculate as to the possible functional significance of these differences. The following considerations are intended as an impetus for further discussion. We have already seen that gravity responses depend on bilateral excitation differences. Addition of the excitation of the two organs provides further information (Fig. 3.10/12). For example, adding the two utricular curves gives a flat horizontal curve, but superimposing the two saccular curves gives a strongly modulated curve with a maximum at 0° and a minimum at 180°. (For simplicity's sake these considerations are limited to the lower half of the saccular maculae and to the center zone of the utricles.) Because of the different orientation of the statolith organs,

---

is maximal at a tilt of 90° (bars). The thin lines indicate the excitation distribution for a 30° tilt. The lower histogram shows difference values after subtraction (= inhibition) of antagonists (negative values omitted). Note the sharpening of the peak. c) Complete circuitry of *MOT.C.* and numerical example corresponding to b). Note that "difference" fibers from the diverse sensory elements directly affect the motor nuclei. The right rear (*RH*) is raised (depressor excited and levator inhibited) and the left front (*LF*) is lowered (depressor inhibited and levator excited); left rear (*LH*) and right front (*RF*) are not changed.

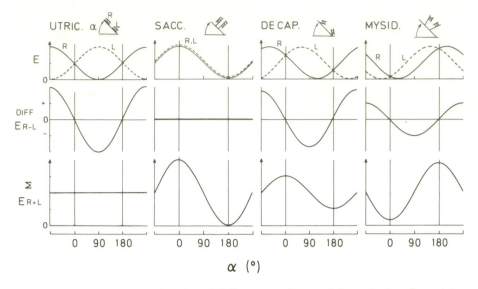

Fig. 3.10/12 Schematicized formation of differences and sums of the excitations from right and left statolith organs. From left: utricles, saccules, decapod statocysts, and mysid stato- cysts. Upper row: excitations of the right (R) and left (L) organs. Middle row: Difference = R − L. Responses correspond to the difference curve. Lower row: Sum = R + L.

the corresponding curves for crustaceans are intermediate. The difference curves have their extreme values at $+90°$ and $-90°$ (like the utricle curve); the sum curves, at $0°$ and $180°$ (like the saccule curve). This makes sum curves (from the saccule and crustaceans) well suited for distinguishing between ventral ($0°$–$90°$) and dorsal ($90°$–$180°$) positions. This distinction is not possible with difference curves (utricle and crustaceans) because positions with the same angular distance above and below $90°$ have identical values. The sum values could be compared centrally with a medium-sized constant. A sum value larger than the comparator would signal a position below $90°$ and vice versa.

All vertebrates have utricles and saccules, and all but the mammals have lagenae. The lagenae play a role in the hearing of teleost fishes [237] and of frogs [681]. Together with the utricles the lagenae of the teleost *Gym-nocorymbus* [795] and the frog [577, 126] participate in the equilibrium response. Responses to gravity stimuli can be recorded from the lagenar nerve of the ray [530]. All in all, no clear picture of the significance of the lagenae has as yet emerged.

According to a widely held rather vague notion, the perpendicular ar-rangement of the utricles to the saccules makes this complex well adapted for positional orientation in three dimensions. Analogous to the semicir-cular canals, the utricles and saccules would be assigned to the three main planes and function in the same way for each plane. Since the saccular maculae lie in the vertical plane, they would be responsible for the perceptions and responses that arise during vertical accelerations.

However, a number of differences between the utricles and the saccules cast doubt on this analogy. The perception of movement is less reliable [547] and the threshold is higher [579] for vertical accelerations than for horizontal ones (in the plane of the utricles). Electrophysiological recordings in the monkey have shown that the saccular units are less sensitive than utricular ones [216].

The saccules can be removed without noticeably impairing an animal's orientation ability. Removal of the saccules and lagenae has no effect on the equilibrium of minnows [237]. Even when blinded they are indistinguishable from normal fish in how they swim and the deft way they snap up bits of food, in short, in their whole behavior. This observation can be made right after the operation and is similar for all animals that have been studied up to now (shark [572], goldfish [552, 918], pike [871], frog [848], rabbit [879]). The saccules do, however, appear to influence compensatory eye movements (pigeon [48], dog [847], cat [227]). Since in humans eye rolling is normal even if the branch of the vestibular nerve that innervates the utricle is severed, eye movement cannot depend solely on utricular signals.

Only a small portion of the saccular fibers terminate with all the other vestibular neurons in the vestibular nuclei. The majority end in a small area next to them (cat [239], 3.10.3.1).

The significance of the saccules is still unclear [284], and the role of the utricles is in comparison much more clearly defined. The utricles are absolutely essential for normal orientation behavior. Animals missing both utricles are totally disoriented, and their movements have no meaningful relationship to gravity.

In flatfish the consequences of elimination of the utricles and the saccules is reversed. Removal of the utricles has little effect, whereas removal of the saccules strongly impairs orientation [670, 400, 772]. Since the flatfish normally lies on its side, the normal relationship of its saccules and utricles to gravity is just the opposite of that for animals in an upright body position.

3.10.1.1.4 Human Statolith Organs and Spatial Orientation

The utricle appears to be the most important statolith organ for humans, too (2.9.1.1). In the normal upright head position the utricle is tilted backward, forming an angle of about 30° with the horizontal. Thus, the "zero" position of the head is not the position of zero shear, although this (horizontal utricles) would be the most sensitive position. Figure 3.10/13 presents a possible explanation. The upright head position is not the "nor-

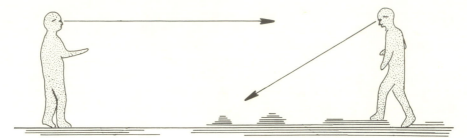

Fig. 3.10/13 A man walking on an uneven surface tips his head forward about 30° so that he can take in the ground ahead of him at a glance. This tilt brings the utricles (= dash in the head) into their most sensitive position.

mal" position for humans either at work or moving across "natural" terrain. A man walking on an uneven surface tilts his head slightly forward so he can watch his step. This brings the utricles into their most sensitive position and into the middle of their working range. (The position of the head when the utricles are horizontal is midway between the face-down position [90° forward] and the face-up position [45° backward].)

The shear hypothesis concerning the utricles has two flaws when related to human spatial orientation (see 2.9.1.1). First, the subjective vertical (SV) deviates from the shear proportionality in experiments using a centrifuge, and second, the SV curves for body tilts over 90° do not appear to correspond at all to the shear hypothesis.

The first flaw can be attributed to the effect of somatoreceptors [495]. Averaging of the signals of the two inputs (statolith organs and somatoreceptors) quantitatively accounts for the observed deviations.

The second flaw is that the SV curve continues to climb for positions in the 90°–180° range of body tilt (α) instead of falling like the sinusoidal curve required by the shear hypothesis (Fig. 3.10/14c). The curve above 90° is the mirror image of what the sinusoidal curve would have looked like (Fig. 3.10/14b). In practice this would mean that in the head-down positions (90°–180°) the sign of the shear changes (from $+G \times \sin \alpha$ to $-G \times \sin \alpha$). If this is the case, an increase in gravity should have the opposite effect on position signals in the head-down range than in the head-up range. This prediction has been borne out in experiments [786, 790]. An increase in gravity causes an overestimation of the SV angle in head-up body positions and an underestimation in head-down positions. This mechanism works as if the angle between the SV and the longitudinal body axis is adjusted relative to the 0° direction in the head-up positions and to the 180° direction in the head-down positions.

The above mechanism requires a change of sign at the 90° body position. This brings us back to the saccules, which may provide the basis for deciding

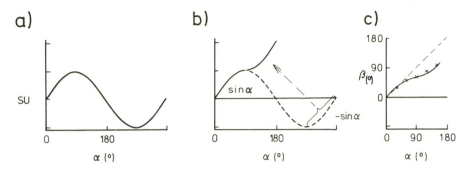

Fig. 3.10/14 Hypothetical mechanism for the perception of the subjective vertical (β) as a function of the utricle. a) The signals of the utricles (SU) are a function of the shear of its statoliths, which changes with the sine of the position angle α. b) Hypothetical transformation of sine curve of utricular signals. c) The subjective vertical (β) as a function of α. The curve is similar to that of b). The crosses are experimental data points. (Modified from [493])

between head up and head down [790, 779]. The sum values of the saccules could be compared with those of the utricles, which make ideal comparison values since they remain constant over the whole range of positions (Fig. 3.10/12). The ratio of the sum values of the saccules to those of the utricles changes at 90° from greater than 1 to less than 1.

3.10.1.2 Cephalopods (Octopus)

Shear on the statoliths is also the adequate stimulus for the octopus and other cephapods. The sense hairs of the octopus are arranged on an oval macula, so that the polarization directions form a fan (Fig. 3.10/15, [21, 22, 101]). In contrast to crustaceans and vertebrates, its gravity responses are affected only by the direction of shear and not by the intensity [101, 102, 103, 105, 781].

Figure 3.10/16 schematically compares the modes of operation of the cat and octopus statolith systems. In the octopus the shear vectors rotate in the same direction on the two maculae during roll and in opposite directions during pitch.

The compensatory eye movements depend on these stimulus processes. During a roll the octopus raises and lowers its eyes (Fig. 3.10/17). During pitch both eyes rotate in the same direction around their axes, so that they move in the plane of tilt. Eye position changes sinusoidally with body tilt, and phase difference depends on the direction of rotation (hysteresis). The responses can be accounted for by the additive superposition of the effect of each macula. Eye movements of an animal with only one statolith are half the size of those of intact animals (Fig. 3.10/17a,b) and are a

Fig. 3.10/15 Schematic representation of the statolith organs and the angular acceleration receptor system of the octopus. a) Dorsal view of the statocyst sacs containing the cone-shaped statoliths on the maculae and the horizontally directed cristae 1–6 of the angular acceleration receptor system. b) The fan of the polarization directions on the left macula. c) Arrangement of the macula and the 9 cristae in the left statocyst sac. (b and c, modified from [103, 104])

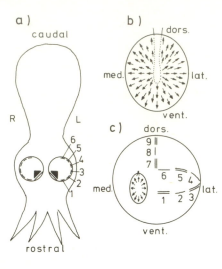

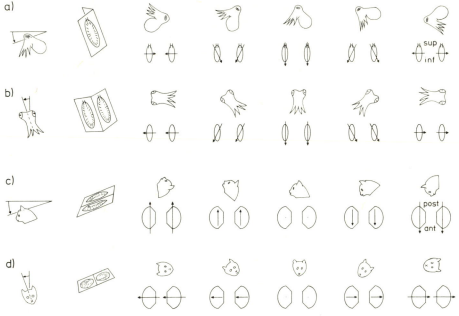

Fig. 3.10/16 Schematic representation of the stimulus processes in the statolith organs of the octopus a), b) and the cat c), d) for pitch a), c) and roll b), d). Direction and length of arrows indicate direction and intensity of the shear on the statoliths on the right and left maculae of the octopus and on the right and left utricles of the cat. In the octopus, the direction of shear rotates in opposite directions on the two maculae during pitch and in the same direction during roll. In the cat, the magnitude of shear on the macula changes in the anterior-posterior direction during pitch and in the right-left direction during roll. (Modified from [776])

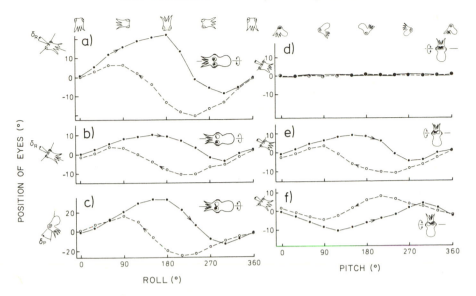

POSITION OF EYES (°)

ROLL (°)

PITCH (°)

Fig. 3.10/17 Compensatory eye movements of the octopus during roll (left) and pitch (right). The curves show the raising and lowering of the eyes (δ_R) of an intact animal a), d), of an animal with the right statolith removed b), e), and with the left statolith removed f). Note that the curves in b) have about half the amplitude of those in a). c) Eye rolling (δ_p) of an animal with no right statolith. (From [102])

superposition of raising (or lowering) and rotation of the eye (the responses to stimulation of one macula). Since the shear vector rotates the same way during roll as during pitch (e.g., on the left macula it moves from ventral to medial during a forward as well as a rightward tilt), the eyes exhibit the same movement (Fig. 3.10/17b,e).

The eye movements of intact animals can be explained by the superposition of the effects of the two maculae, which are in phase for one of the two eye movement components and in antiphase for the other. These relationships are summarized in Fig. 3.10/18.

3.10.1.3 Insects and Other Animals

First let us deal with the "other animals," which in this case are ctenophores. Their single statocyst behaves like a "minimal" model of the principle represented in vertebrates and crustaceans. The statocyst lies in a concavity in the center of the aboral (top) pole. A round statolith is surrounded by, and suspended from, four ciliated sense cells. Each of these is attached to a row of cells that bifurcates to give eight rows, which extend down the body of the animal toward its mouth. The cells in these rows bear long fused cilia

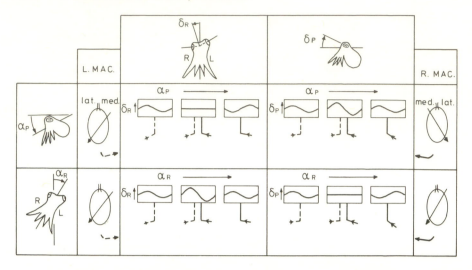

Fig. 3.10/18 The curves show the eye movements of the octopus as a function of the shear direction on the left and right maculae (*L.MAC.*, *R.MAC.*). Left: Raising and lowering of the eyes (δ_R). Right: Rolling of the eyes (δ_P). Upper row: Pitch (α_P). Lower row: Roll (α_R). The three diagrams in each block show the eye curves when only the left macula is working (left), when both are working (middle), and when only the right one is working (right). (Modified from [102])

that look like the teeth of a comb, hence their name, comb plates. The rows of comb plates beat rhythmically and propel the ctenophore through the water. The gravity orientation of this swimming is guided by the statocyst. Sense cells on opposite sides of the statocyst can be thought of as an antagonist pair that responds maximally to tilt in its plane. The statolith bends the cilia in the direction of tilt, i.e., the lower ones toward the outside and the higher ones toward the inside. This changes the firing rate of the sense cells as a function of the angle of tilt. The impulses are conducted to the comb rows where they modulate the beat frequency of the comb plates and lead to positional responses. The four sense cells form a simple cross-shaped fan array that registers the plane and degree of tilt and transforms it directly into a postural response [374].

Terrestrial insects have a completely different system. Their gravity receptors are located at the joints of the body [368]. In the bee, fields of sense hairs on the neck are stimulated by the pressure exerted by the head (Fig. 3.10/19). Another hair field is located between the thorax and the abdomen. In ants nearly all the body joints participate in gravity reception: antenna-head, head-thorax, thorax-abdomen, and thorax-legs [544, 558].

In the stick insect [913, 915] the antennal joints and the thorax-leg joints of all six legs are involved. Stick insects usually walk upward on a vertical

Fig. 3.10/19 Fields of sense hairs on the head and abdominal joints of the bee. Head and abdomen have been pulled slightly away from the thorax to expose the bristle fields. (Modified from [235])

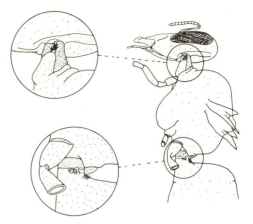

surface. After amputation of the antennae, only the pull of the body on the leg joints is critical (Fig. 3.10/20). The torque exerted on the legs by the long protruding abdomen is ineffective.

The cockroach *Arenivaga* has on each cercus two rows of plummetlike sense hairs called tricholiths, which electrophysiological studies have shown to be gravity receptors [1020]. When the cockroach is tilted, the tricholiths send signals into the two giant interneurons of the ventral nerve cord. Cercal sensilla of the cricket *Acheta* are also sensitive to gravity stimuli [1010].

In walking flies the principle for transformation of gravity signals into compensatory movements resembles that of vertebrates and crustaceans. Head movements are sinusoidally proportional to the tilt angle and linearly proportional to the weight registered by the receptors on the legs (sin α $\times$ G) [369]. Normally this weight is exerted by the body mass. In flies that were suspended from a rod attached to their backs it was exerted by a ball that the flies held between their legs. The head position relative to the thorax was found to be a function of the shearing force exerted on the legs. During roll the compensatory head movement is a sideways rotation, and during pitch, a raising or lowering of the head. These reactions must stem from the excitation patterns of the receptors on the six legs, which can be viewed in this context as a kind of array.

Water bugs take advantage of the buoyancy of air bubbles that are trapped by the hairs on their bodies and are in contact with the spiracles (*Aphelocheirus* [853]). In the water stick insect *Ranatra*, the tracheae open onto two bristle-covered, air-filled furrows on the ventral surface of its abdomen [33]. At four sites along these rows of bristles are groups of sense hairs. The group that is highest is stimulated by the expansion of the air. How these groups interact is still unknown. They might represent a simple

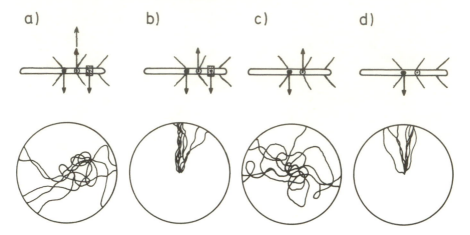

Fig. 3.10/20 Orientation of the stick insect on a vertical wall. Upper row: Experimental situations. An upward force (upward arrows) can be exerted on the body via a thread tied around the insect's pivoting point (marked by a circle). The black dot marks the body's center of gravity and the downward arrows symbolize the pull of the body weight. In a) and b) a lead collar (rectangle) with the same weight as the body is fastened to the animal in front of the pivoting point. Lower row: Examples of walks on a round vertical wall. a) When the thread is pulled upward with twice the body weight, no forces are exerted on the legs and the walks are disoriented. b) When the thread is pulled with only one body weight, the downward pull dominates and the animals walk up the wall. c) When the collar is removed, a torque is generated because the thread pulls upward in front of the body's downward pull. There is no orientation. d) Torque and body weight are normal and the animals are again oriented. Note that the animals are oriented only if there is a downward pull; torque has no effect. (Modified from [915])

kind of fan array in which pitch and roll are registered by coupling the anterior and posterior or right and left sensors.

3.10.2 Orientation to Angular Acceleration

A rotational sense based on inertia sensors has been found in vertebrates, higher molluscs, decapod crustaceans, and insects. The physical principle of stimulation is based on the inertia of a mass, e.g., semicircular canals, or of a gyroscope, e.g., halteres. A mass that can move or oscillate relative to the body resists acceleration and exerts a force on the sensory elements. Angular acceleration can be positive, as when an animal begins or speeds up a turn; or it can be negative, as when a turn is slowed down.

These sensory systems perform functions similar to those of optomotor systems. They measure and regulate turning, elicit compensatory counter-movements of the eyes, head, or other sensor-bearing appendages (1.4.3), and in general contribute to space constancy (2.10). Since these processes have already been dealt with in the general section (2.7.4, 2.9), we shall focus here on the structure and physiology of the sense organs.

3.10.2.1 Vertebrate Semicircular Canals

The word *vestibular* is often used only in the sense of semicircular canal processes, even though the statolith organs are also part of the vestibular apparatus. There is a large body of literature on this area. The physics of stimulation, the neurophysiology of the sense cells and CNS regions, balance responses, perceptual phenomena (e.g., turning dizziness, circular vection), and above all, nystagmic eye movements are catchwords that belong to this large area of research. Not the least of the reasons for the extensiveness of this area is the significance of the inner ear in medicine. Instead of citing many individual works, let us refer to the articles on the vestibular system in vol. VI of the *Handbook of Sensory Physiology* (see [52]), especially to the contributions by Cohen, Benson, Guedry, Johnson, Jongkees, Kornhuber, Mayne, and Melville Jones. A monograph by Precht [684] summarizes the present state of knowledge on the neurophysiology of the frog labyrinth.

The physics and physiology of stimulation. The semicircular canals are a system of three mutually perpendicular ring-shaped tubes that terminate in a common vestibule (Fig. 3.10/21) and that contain a fluid, the endolymph. When the head is turned suddenly, the fluid in one or more of the canals lags behind the movement of the head because of the inertia of the fluid. Thus, the canal should move past the stationary fluid, and the fluid should flow within the canals. This, however, does not occur because each semicircular canal is closed by a valve, the cupula. At its entrance to the vestibule, each canal widens out to form an ampulla. Protruding into each ampulla is a crista, a structure bearing hair tufts that, as in the statolith organs, consist of one kinocilium and several stereocilia per sense cell. The cilia project into a gelatinous mass, the cupula, which extends from one wall of the ampulla to the opposite one. Since the cupula is not very resistant to the usual histological procedures, preparations usually show it in a shrunken state fitting across the ampulla like a swinging door that doesn't quite

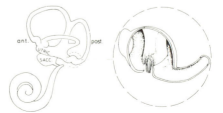

Fig. 3.10/21 Left: Left human labyrinth with the three semicircular canals (anterior, posterior, and horizontal), the utricle, the saccule, and the cochlea. Right: the ampulla of a semicircular canal with the crista, cupula, and sensory elements. (Left, modified from [918]; right, from [508, 393])

shut. For this reason it was long thought that stimulation was due to the free rotation of the endolymph in the canals, flowing past and deflecting the cupula.

Steinhausen's experiments finally demonstrated that the cupula completely fills the cross section of the ampulla and closes it tightly [833]. More recent studies even suggest that it is fixed to the ampulla wall all around [44, 978, 341]. During normal stimulation the cupula is merely distended [978, 224]. In the frog the kinocilium does not curve, but bends at its base like a rod on a hinge [223]. The cupula does not swing at its "free" end, as was originally believed, but slides across the crista at its base deflecting the sense hairs. This "shearing" process moves the hairs considerably more than a swinging door process, rendering the stimulus mechanism much more sensitive. The swinging door movement has only been observed for very strong stimuli [833, 224]. Presumably these are unphysiologically strong movements of the endolymph, which rip the top of the cupula loose. The relatively weak attachment may serve to protect the mechanism from damage [341].

In a fundamental study on the physics of stimulation van Egmond, Groen, and Jongkees [190] concluded that the semicircular canals exhibit the physical properties (dimensions, viscosity of endolymph, friction between endolymph and canal walls, elasticity of cupula) of a strongly damped torsion pendulum. Turning the head swings the pendulum, consisting of the endolymph ring and the cupula, up to its full amplitude, which depends on the intensity and duration of the stimulus. Both deflection and return are damped so that the semicircular canals in practice serve as a tachometer. They integrate the angular acceleration during the entire turn to arrive at a final angular velocity. This notion is also supported by response measurements (nystagmus, duration of turning sensation), but more recent studies [212, 263] suggest that information about both angular acceleration and velocity is available. It is not easy to get an experimental handle on these processes, and the mechanism of the semicircular canals and their signal production have yet to be fully clarified [573].

3.10.2.2 Angular Acceleration Organs of Molluscs, Crustaceans, and Insects

Molluscs. In addition to those on the macula, octopus and cuttlefish statocysts contain rows of free sense hairs [21, 969, 104] that form a band along the statocyst wall (Fig. 3.10/15). The polarization direction of these sense hairs is perpendicular to the rows. The cuttlefish has protrusions in the cavity that presumably channel the fluid flow, stimulating the hairs in an ordered fashion.

Recordings from the afferent nerves of the octopus statocyst have revealed a phenomenon that points to an effect of gravity [106]. The resting

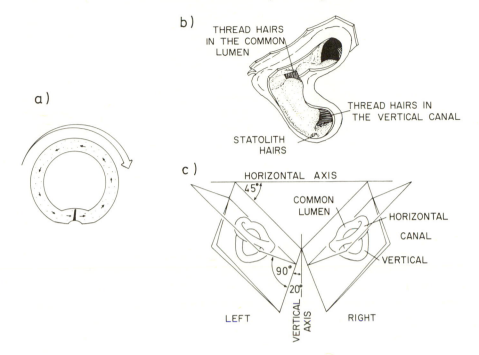

Fig. 3.10/22 Semicircular canal organs. a) Model illustrating how, as a consequence of its inertia, the canal fluid lags behind during a turn and exerts a force on the sensory hairs. b), c) Semicircular canal system of the crab *Scylla serrata*. b) Dorsal view of the right canal organ opened to reveal the interior of the horizontal canal (upper), the common lumen (middle), and the vertical canal (lower). c) Geometrical relationship of the canals to the horizontal and vertical axes (b, c, modified from [729])

discharge and the response to rotational stimuli depend on how the preparation is oriented with respect to gravity. Similar findings have been reported for crab statocysts [729] and vertebrates [529]. Whether such gravity effects have a practical meaning for the function of these systems remains to be clarified.

Crustaceans. A crab, rotated in its horizontal plane, turns in the opposite direction and shows nystagmic eye movements. Bilateral statocyst removal abolishes these responses [136]. Crab and lobster statocysts contain two types of sensory hairs, the statolith hairs and the long thread hairs, which have long been suspected of releasing the turning response [163, 165]. Sandeman [729] has thoroughly investigated the canal system of a crab (Fig. 3.10/22). The statocyst sacs have been elaborated to form two circular canals at right angles to each other. Thread hairs project across the canal lumens and detect endolymph movement.

Insects. Mittelstaedt [585] discovered an inertia sensor in the dragonfly that participates in the control of flight. When sudden gusts of wind rotate the body, the head maintains its position due to its inertia and its flexible attachment to the thorax (Fig. 3.10/23). This in turn releases counter-movements of the flight muscles. The animal can mechanically block the system by holding its head rigid with muscles.

The halteres of dipterous insects are another kind of inertia sensor [1012]. They move like a gyroscope and stabilize flight by detecting angular accelerations and releasing compensatory head and wing movements. The rows of sensilla at the base of the halteres are sensitive to their displacement.

3.10.3 Processing of Vestibular Signals in Vertebrates

3.10.3.1 Centers and Pathways

The sensory elements of the vestibular organs, the macular and cristae hair cells, are secondary sense cells (Fig. 3.10/2), which are innervated by both afferent and efferent neurons. All the fibers of the labyrinth enter the brainstem in one bundle, the vestibular (= eighth cranial) nerve, and terminate near the dorsal wall of the fourth ventricle, just beneath the base of the cerebellum, in a group of nuclei called the vestibular nuclei (Fig. 3.10/25). In mammals there are four vestibular nuclei: superior, lateral, medial, and descending.

The rostro-caudal sequence of fibers in the vestibular nerve is as follows: anterior and horizontal semicircular canals, efferent tract, posterior canal, utricle, and saccule. At the nuclei each of these tracts bifurcates into a rostral and a caudal branch, as is shown for the cat in Fig. 3.10/25. Part of the utricular fibers terminate at the same places as canal fibers. Only a small portion of the saccular fibers go to the lateral and medial nuclei. Most of them terminate in the "Y" region, which is located outside of the actual vestibular region [239].

Fig. 3.10/23 Angular acceleration sensor of the dragonfly. Above: A dragonfly in flight. A sudden turn moves the body (white arrow) with respect to the head and stimulates the sense hairs, releasing a corrective movement (black arrow). Below: The back of the head showing the V-shaped thoracic suspension around whose tip the head can turn freely. (Modified from [585])

HEAD SUSPENSION
OF THE THORAX

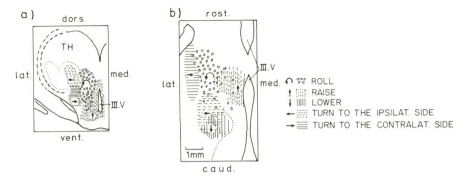

Fig. 3.20/24 Transverse section a) and horizontal section b) through the cat thalamus (*TH*) showing regions where electrical stimulation released turning. III.V denotes the third ventricle. (Modified from [413])

Recently a projection of the polarization fan of the utricular macula was found in the vestibular "nuclei" of goldfish ([747], Fig. 3.10/26). The macular map corresponds almost exactly to the ipsilateral polarization fan of the utricle in direction and proportion. The elements occupy a horizontal layer that is only a few microns thick.

The vestibular nuclei of each side are connected by direct pathways. Electrophysiologically it has been shown that the two sides can mutually excite and inhibit each other [863, 682].

The neurons of the vestibular nuclei are activated by visual and somatosensory as well as labyrinthine stimuli [682, 232].

The vestibular nuclei are directly connected to the reticular formation and to higher centers. The reticular formation also has somatosensory, visual, and acoustic input.

In the eye muscle nuclei (oculomotor, abducens, and trochlear nuclei), the labyrinthine signals feed onto the motor neurons of the eye muscles (Fig. 3.10/27a). There are only three steps in the shortest reflex pathway from the labyrinth to the eye: the sense cell, the vestibular nucleus cell, and the motor neuron in the eye muscle nucleus.

There are also vestibular effects in the diencephalon. Excitations can be recorded from thalamus neurons during eye movements elicited by labyrinthine stimulation.

The cerebellum lies directly above the vestibular nuclei and is developmentally and functionally related to them. The flocculonodular lobe and vermis of the cerebellum receive projections from the vestibular nerve and the vestibular nuclei. Cerebellar fibers synapse with vestibular and spinal fibers in the lateral nucleus (Fig. 3.10/27). The spinal fibers carry somatosensory information about limb, neck, and trunk position.

The cortex is connected to the vestibular nuclei via the thalamus. Small regions of neurons near the somatosensory fields, areas 1 and 2, respond

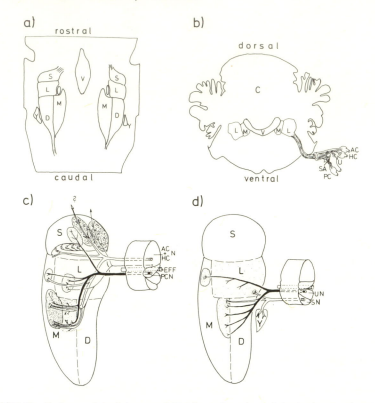

Fig. 3.10/25 Vestibular nuclei of the cat. a) Horizontal section of the brainstem showing the superior (S), lateral (L), medial (M), and descending (D) vestibular nuclei and the fourth ventricle (V). b) Cross section through the cerebellum (C), the fourth ventricle (V), and the brainstem. AC, HC, PC denote the anterior, horizontal, and posterior semicircular canals; SA, the saccule; U, the utricle. c) Right vestibular nuclei and their innervation by the semi-circular canal nerves. The nerve from the anterior (ACN) and the horizontal (HCN) canal is subdivided into a bundle of thin fibers (thin lines) and one of thick fibers. The former come from Type II hair cells; the latter, from the cup-shaped Type I hair cells (see Fig. 3.10/2). EFF denotes the efferent tract, PCN posterior canal nerve. d) Distribution of fibers from the utricular (UN) and saccular (SN) nerves. Y denotes the Y group of neurons. (a, modified from [90]; b, from [240]; c and d, from [239])

specifically to stimulation of the labyrinth receptors (Fig. 3.10/28). A few of these units also respond to somatosensory stimuli like changes in limb position. This region is connected to area 7 where signals from somato-sensory, visual, and acoustic regions converge [232].

3.10.3.2 Function of Centers

According to Kornhuber [466] the primary function of the motor cortex is the fine control of spatially oriented limb movements, especially of the

Fig. 3.10/26 Goldfish. a) Left utricular
macula with polarization directions. b) Polarization directions in the vestibular nuclei determined by electrophysiological recording before and during a horizontal
acceleration in various directions (utricular stimulation). Dots indicate recording
sites; arrows, the directions of movement
that most increased a neuron's resting activity when movement in the opposite direction decreased it; lines, directions for
neurons that were excited or inhibited by
movement in both directions. (Modified
from [747])

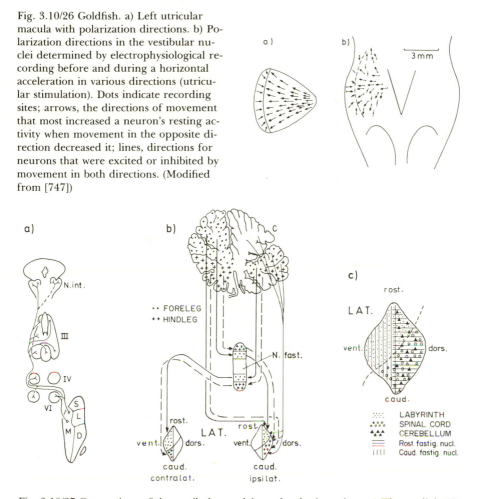

Fig. 3.10/27 Connections of the vestibular nuclei to other brain regions. a) The medial (*M*)
nucleus is connected to the eye muscle nuclei, the oculomotor (III), the trochlear (IV), and
the abducens (VI), and to the intermedial nucleus (*N.int.*). b) Connections from the cerebellum (*C*) to the lateral nucleus (*LAT*) can be direct or indirect via the fastigial nucleus
(*N.fast.*) as a relay station. The projections of the fore and hind legs are topologically organized. In the fastigial pathway, ipsilateral fibers go to the rostral part of the fastigial nucleus; contralateral, to the caudal part. (The former terminate in the dorsal region of the
lateral nucleus; the latter, in the ventral region.) The direct fibers end in the dorsal half of
the ipsilateral nucleus. c) The lateral nucleus is a relay station for fibers from the labyrinth,
spinal cord, cerebellum, and fastigial nucleus. (Modified from [90])

hands and fingers. The vestibular and somatosensory signals from the
sensory cortex furnish the spatial coordinates for the control of this movement.

Even though the thalamus, cortex, and cerebellum are activated by lab-

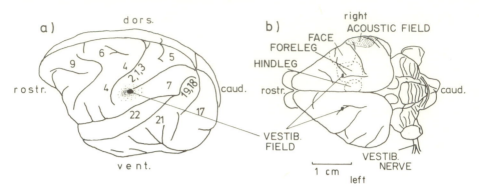

Fig. 3.10/28 Sensory fields of the cerebral cortex. Impulses can be recorded in the cortex in response to electrical stimulation of the vestibular nerves. The sites of maximum response are shown in black (vestibular field). a) Sensory regions on the left cerebral cortex of the *Rhesus* monkey. b) Dorsal view of the rabbit brain showing the cerebrum on the left and the cerebellum on the right. (Modified from [232])

yrinth stimulation, these higher centers are not necessary for simple balance reflexes. Animals whose brains have been destroyed above the brainstem and midbrain are no longer capable of spontaneous movements but can still stand and even walk if "pushed" along [543]. Thus, there must be a motor program in the brainstem that makes coordinated locomotion under vestibular control possible.

The meso-diencephalon has a special significance for brain research. W. R. Hess elicited movements and behavior patterns by electrical stimulation of this region [336, 337]. His studies instigated a new era of brain research for which he was awarded the Nobel Prize. Current was injected through a fine wire electrode inserted into particular brain regions. At the end of each experiment, the stimulus site was marked with an electrolytic lesion so that its location could be determined later.

Of the orientations dependent on the labyrinth, eye movements, as well as roll, pitch, and yaw movements of the head or the whole body, received special attention (Fig. 3.10/24). It was found that only one particular response, i.e., a turn in one body plane, could be elicited from each stimulus site. However, response intensity was a function of stimulus intensity. In a review of Hess's work, von Holst [362] wrote, "The head starts to turn towards the side at stimulus intensities below 1 V. As the stimulus is increased the body follows until the animal is rolling sideways across the ground." Apparently, the plane of tilt is determined qualitatively, e.g., by a particular nerve tract, whereas the extent of the tilt depends on the amount of excitation. In humans stimulation of the thalamus (during a brain operation) can elicit tilt and turning sensations [232].

It should not be assumed that the stimulus site is "the" center for the elicited behavior. Rather, electrical stimulation introduces signals into tracts or relay stations. In the classical experiments many of the stimulus sites lay in tracts that traversed the diencephalon and mesencephalon and that were activated during diverse behaviors. Brain stimulation experiments on chickens [365] revealed stimulus sites that released various behaviors depending on the "mood" of the animal (which could be controlled by external influences) (Fig. 3.10/29). Recording from "multimodal" neurons also does not help to locate the center for the behavior. For example, visual, acoustic, vestibular, and somaesthetic stimuli must all generate activity in the oculomotor nucleus since they all can elicit eye movements.

The excitation that occurs in a particular nucleus to sensory stimulation says nothing about where the perception of this stimulus process takes place or is released. The response of neurons in the vestibular nuclei to semicircular canal or optokinetic stimulation does not imply that the turning sensation experienced during stimulation is generated there. Such stimuli also activate a number of higher centers such as the thalamus and the cortex.

The cybernetic point of view can contribute to the understanding of results from recording and stimulation experiments. Recordings from the reticular formation of the rabbit gave unexpected results. The discharge frequency of a neuron increased when the head of a rabbit was passively

Fig. 3.10/29 Behavior of a chicken to electrical stimulation of the brainstem. a) During electrical stimulation the hen is only slightly aggressive toward a fist. b) Stimulation elicits strong aggression, shown by the spreading of the wings and the pouncing attack directed at a stuffed polecat. c) If the electrical stimulation is prolonged, the hen gets alarmed and flees. (Modified from [365])

turned, but decreased when the rabbit actively turned its head in the same direction. Neurons that were activated by raising and lowering the head behaved similarly [185]. Apparently, active and passive movements have opposite effects on the same neuron. These findings can be easily explained by feedback processes (2.4.1). The recording site must be on the output side of the system (Fig. 3.10/30, Experiment 1). During an active head movement such as a turn to the right, the recording electrode picks up the motor command for this movement. However, if the animal's head is turned passively to the right, a command for a "left turn" arrives at the recording site. This command is the corrective response of the feedback loop to the imposed movement to the right for which there was no reference value.

The vestibular nuclei are on the input side. No matter whether the movement is active or passive [739], the neurons always indicate the momentary state of stimulation of the sense organ (= position signal).

In the reticular formation when, for example, the activity of a neuron was increased by lowering of the head, electrical stimulation of the same area caused the animal to raise its head. It can be assumed that recording and stimulation sites are on the input side (Fig. 3.10/30, Experiment 2). The electrode picks up the labyrinthine signal to "lower the head," whereas electrical stimulation introduces precisely this signal. It generates a motor command for the corrective movement (= raising the head) in the processing center, since there is no reference value signal for lowering the head.

Efferent influences on the sense cells have recently received special attention (guinea pig [863], goldfish [457, 748], goldfish and rabbit [157], reviews [456, 680]). These efferent signals were recorded during turning, in some cases from the proximal stump of the cut vestibular nerve. They have three possible origins. (1) The efferent signals may be vestibular, i.e.,

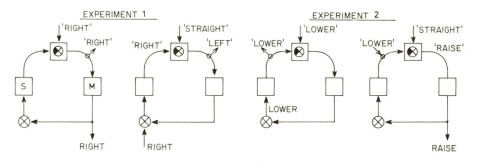

Fig. 3.10/30 Hypothetical explanation for the results of two experiments on rabbits. Experiment 1: The activity of reticular formation neurons increases during an active tilt to the right (left) and decreases during a passive tilt to the right (right). Experiment 2: In other reticular formation neurons, activity increases when the head is lowered (left). When a current is injected into the recording site, the animal raises its head (right). S = sensory, M = motor. See text for further explanation.

from the contralateral organ. This is suggested by the result of electrical stimulation in the lateral nucleus where an inhibition [729] and, in some cases, an excitation [863] from the contralateral labyrinth could be measured. (2) The efferences may be of visual origin. The excitations from optokinetic stimulation add directly to those of the semicircular canals via efferences. (3) The signals may come from motor centers [157, 680]. The efferences immediately preceding rapid eye movements may originate in motor centers that are involved in the initiation of the eye movements. Such a command center exists in the deeper layers of the tectum, which contain topological maps of the visual, acoustic, and somatosensory fields (3.1, 3.6, 3.9). Stimulation experiments reveal a corresponding motor map in which localized stimulation releases directed eye movements (3.1). During saccadic eye movements activity can also be detected in this region. Excitations are recorded just prior to an eye movement, supporting the assumption that they release it.

Efferences from the motor centers may be effective in the following way. The command center transmits not only motor commands to the muscles but also efferent signals to the labyrinth receptors. These correspond to the efference copies of the reafference principle (2.4.1) and prevent the formation of afferences. The effect of the afference is thus canceled, not centrally as in the reafference principle, but before its inception in the sense organ. The circuit diagrams shown in Fig. 3.10/31 illustrate the consequences of such a mechanism. Since the system blocks its sensors during an active movement, there is no sensory feedback for this process, i.e., it is open loop (b). The system does not "use" the sensor. Sensory input, however, is essential for the correction of disturbances, i.e., for responses to passive movements. These can and must be subject to sensory control, since the afferences are not inhibited when there is no efference copy of a motor command (c). Such a mechanism may underlie the differences between active and passive stimulation that have been found in many stimulus-response studies (2.11.4). Experiments on rotational dizziness show, for example, that when a subject in a rotating chair turns and stops himself, he feels as if he were still turning in the same direction. But, if he is passively rotated and stopped, he feels as if he were turning in the opposite direction. The latter sensation corresponds to the stimulation of the cupulae, which a sudden stop deflects in the opposite direction. Nystagmus is smaller after active rotation than after passive rotation. This might mean that the efference copy of the motor command "stop" blocks the conduction of the semicircular canal excitation caused by the stop.

This raises the questions, if the labyrinth sensors are blocked during an active movement, how does the sensation of an active movement arise? What causes the nystagmus that can also accompany active turning? There are two possibilities. Either these processes also depend on efference copies,

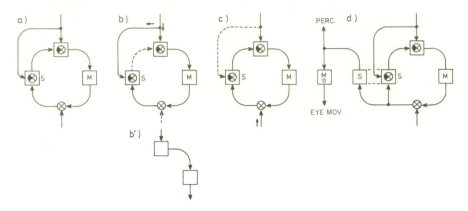

Fig. 3.10/31 Circuit diagrams illustrating how efferences may affect the sense organs of the labyrinth. a) Circuit diagram. b) A command leads to a movement via the motor apparatus (*M*), which stimulates the sensory apparatus (*S*). An efference copy of the command inhibits the sensory apparatus, canceling the excitations so that the center does not receive any feedback. The system is open loop, as shown in b'. c) A disturbance can be corrected by way of feedback, since there is no efference copy. d) Only a portion of the sensory apparatus is inhibited by the efference. The remainder can still carry signals for the perception of the movement (*PERC.*) or for eye movements (*EYE MOV.*). *MO* = motor apparatus of the eyes.

or only a portion of the sensory elements are inhibited by the efferences, and the rest can still carry the signals for the perception and the eye movement (Fig. 3.10/31d).

3.11 ORIENTATION WITHOUT EXTERNAL DIRECTING CUES

Idiothetic orientation relies on spatial information that originates within the organism. In contrast, all orientations based on external cues are allothetic (2.2.2). The term idiothetic specifies that the spatial information is endogenous, but not what kind it is. In the concept kinesthesia, on the other hand, the information comes by definition from the proprioceptors. According to Sherrington kinesthesia is the perception of posture, of active and passive movements, and of resistance to movement based on sensations arising in the muscles, joints, and bones (cited in [817]).

3.11.1 Idiothetic Information

The source of idiothetic information can be either sensory or nonsensory. The participation of the joint receptors in the perception of active movement has never been in doubt, whereas the contribution of the muscle receptors is somewhat controversial [817].

Joint receptors. In higher vertebrates (mammals have been best studied) the receptors in the capsules, tendons, and other tissues surrounding and attached to a joint are related to the cutaneous receptors (for a review, see [6]). They can be divided into three groups: (1) receptors with "flower-spray" endings like the Ruffini receptors in the joint capsules and the Golgi tendon organs, (2) receptors with encapsulated nerve endings like the Pacinian corpuscles, and (3) free nerve endings [817]. The tendon organs signal the overall stretch of the tendon. The Ruffini receptors are very sensitive to the rate and direction of joint movement. They are also affected by the state of tension and activity of the muscles attached to the tendons, which may help differentiate between active and passive movement. The Pacinian corpuscles respond to small rapid movements. The functions of these diverse receptors intermesh in the sensory (and often reflexive) control of joint movement, as well as in the generation of idiothetic signals.

Arthropods also possess several receptor types. External receptors like the joint bristles are usually arranged in discrete fields. They span the joint and are stimulated when one of the jointed segments moves relative to the other. There are also internal receptors like the stretch receptors on the elastic bands between jointed segments. Receptors embedded in the cuticle measure deformations of the cuticle that arise during movements.

Nonsensory sources of idiothetic information. It is unique to idiothetic information that it need not have a sensory origin. It may, for example, be furnished by central nervous processes underlying an animal's activity. The efferent programs for controlling the movement contain the information necessary for the spatial execution of the movement. Blest has reported on this kind of idiothetic data acquisition for the butterfly *Automeris auranthiaca* [70]. The number of rocking movements that this butterfly normally makes after a flight depends on the flight duration. Since this relationship holds even if all proprioceptors associated with flight have been blocked prior to flight, the information about flight duration must come from central nervous processes controlling the flight musculature.

Further support for the nonsensory acquisition of idiothetic information is provided by the inhibition of vestibular sensory cells by efference copy signals of eye movements (3.10.3.2). Recordings from the sense cell efferents show excitations to be correlated with eye movements. These signals occur tenths of seconds before eye muscle activity and thus cannot be due to its sensory signals.

The sensor-site label as idiothetic information. If idiothetic information is taken to mean all spatial information of endogenous origin, this also includes sensor-site and direction labels (2.3.2.3). Since an organism receives allothetic signals via its sense organs, their site and direction labels are essential for relating incoming spatial information to the body. Idiothetic is thus not a mere alternative to allothetic. Rather, idiothetic information participates in, and is a prerequisite for, every allothetic orientation.

Being idiothetic, the sensor-site and direction labels can also be sensory or nonsensory. They are sensory when the sense organ is situated on a movable carrier whose position may be monitored by proprioceptors. They are nonsensory when the sense organ is rigidly fixed to the body. In this case the sensor-site and direction labels are built into the neural circuitry.

3.11.2 Idiothetic Orientation

Idiothetic information about movements can be used to control their execution in space, i.e., to orient them. Body position serves as the spatial reference cue for idiothetic orientation. Since an idiothetic orientation can only be related to the preceding body positions, the starting position must be "right" for the orientation to be meaningful in the context of the surroundings (2.2.2).

3.11.2.1 Corrective Turning Behavior

Counterturning is a mechanism for correcting imposed course deviations and maintaining course. When an obstacle is placed in its path, a millipede is forced to abandon its course. It moves along the obstacle until it reaches the end, then swings back into its former course by making a counterturn. The size of this corrective turn depends on the deflection caused by the obstacle. Corrective turning behavior has been studied mainly in walking arthropods, insects, millipedes, and sowbugs ([10, 174, 25, 483]; for reviews see [116, 270]).

In extensive experiments [116, 601, 597], millipedes were forced to run through a jointed runway whose arms could be adjusted to any angle. The size of the counterturn that the millipede makes when it leaves the tube depends on the size of the angle and what part of the animal is forced to negotiate the bend (Fig. 3.11/1). The animal behaves as if the joint angle signals are linearly summed in a memory store, "whose maximum load determines the degree of counterturn and which during unrestrained locomotion is discharged by a counterturn" [116].

A hypothesis has been derived from the results of these experiments [597] that is useful as a model for corrective turning behavior and idiothetic course orientation (Fig. 3.11/2).

The free output of the system, the walking direction, is determined by the alignment of the head, since the coordination mechanism makes the legs of each segment step in the footsteps of the preceding ones. It is measured as the angle σ to the starting direction. This angle is a function

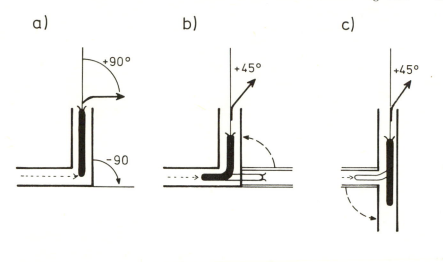

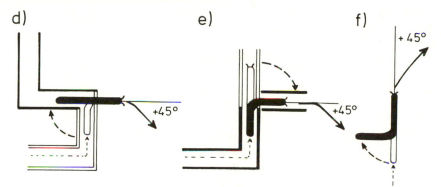

Fig. 3.11/1 Counterturning (heavy arrows) of millipedes. The white outlines indicate the position of the runway and the animal before the arm of the runway is shifted to a new position (shown by dark outlines). a) The whole millipede negotiates the bend. b) Only its posterior end makes the 90° angle. c) Only its anterior end makes the 90° angle. d) After the anterior end has carried out a turn, the posterior end is straightened out so that it does not make the counterturn. e) After the whole millipede has run through a 90° bend in the runway, a 90° counterturn is imposed on its anterior end. f) The posterior end of a free running millipede is flicked over 90° (compare with b). The counterturns appear to depend on an additive processing of the idiothetic signals. (Modified from [597])

of r, the angular velocity of the turn produced by the "head musculature" ($\int r dt$). This alignment process is simultaneously registered as the segmental joint angles κ (shown as a branch of the motor output).

The κ values are summed in "joint proprioceptors" and enter "memory" as the signal p, which is integrated over the distance and related to body length (l) to give the memory value sp. This stored value enters "hold" as

Fig. 3.11/2 Circuit diagram for the corrective turning behavior of millipedes based on a hypothetical mechanism in which the body segments automatically follow the head alignment. κ represents the angles between body segments; σ, the deviation of head alignment from the preceding walking direction; r, angular velocity of the turn; sp, memory value. See text for further explanation. (Modified from [597])

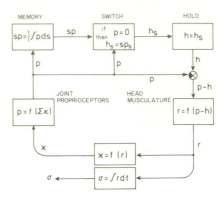

h_s via "switch" when p, the sum of all joint angles, equals zero. Thus, the content of "hold," the value h, is a function of the sum of all the preceding direction changes. It serves as the reference value for a corrective process that brings the animal back onto its original course. The circuit diagram is a feedback loop. Inequality between the actual value p and the reference value h gives rise to a turning command effecting κ, until p is equal to h and the turning command is again zero.

This behavior is not limited to the correction of detours caused by mechanical obstruction. The straight course of millipedes can be deflected by a shadow with sharp corners, and that of stick insects and cockroaches, by light or gravity. As soon as these deflecting reference stimuli are eliminated, the animals make counterturns [599].

In contrast to a mechanical obstruction, which imposes a particular direction on the animal, other deflecting stimuli may lead to compromise alignments. For example, instead of running directly toward the light, the animal takes a course intermediate to it and the previous course direction [601]. There is a similar interaction between idiothetic and gravity orientation [600].

3.11.2.2 Goal Orientation

Idiothetic goal orientation is based on an animal's having already actively covered a particular stretch. The animal uses the idiothetic data thus acquired for subsequent orientation. A simple form of this consists of repeating the exact sequence of movements, as has been described for the shrew [524, 283].

Homing involves a higher order of idiothetic orientation. In the simplest case the sequence of movements is replayed in reverse order. A more complex version is calculating the home bearing from the individual stretches of the outbound path. Startled fiddler and ghost crabs, for instance, run straight back to the entrance of their burrows (Fig. 3.11/3, [295]) even when their outbound excursion was twisted and meandering. *Uca rapax* can go straight to the entrance of its burrow from a distance of 35 cm; *Ocypode*, from 1 m. This orientation is based on vector integration of the change in direction and length for each stretch of the outbound path. Desert ants and isopods also show this kind of vector integration (2.8.2) in combination with celestial compass orientation (2.7.2).

The female gerbil *Meriones unguiculatus* searches for and retrieves "lost" young, carrying them straight back to the nest. If the nest has been moved in her absence, she returns to where it used to be. Experiments indicate that the vector integration involves only angular accelerations such as those registered by the semicircular canals but no linear accelerations [1003].

Bees may be able to idiothetically measure distance [564]. They can be trained to find an odor marker at a given distance down one arm of an X-maze. If the marker is then presented right next to the intersection, the bees run past it to the original odor site before they turn around. Assuming that there are no external reference cues, the bees can only acquire the distance values idiothetically.

Idiothetic orientation mechanisms have been very thoroughly investigated in spiders [367, 267, 269, 270, 607, 177, 178, 28]. The spider *Cupiennius salei* can orient idiothetically to a feeding site [28]. If it is chased away right after it finds a choice bit of food, it can return within 5 min from a distance of 25 cm. Its return path is not always a straight line but may contain stretches of varying length and direction. Even so, it is usually quite good at finding the right spot. Even if it has followed a circuitous

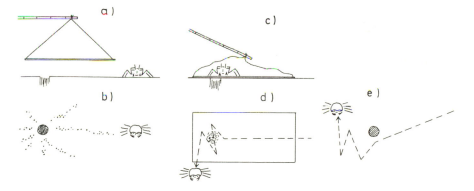

Fig. 3.11/3 Idiothetic orientation of a fiddler crab, *Uca rapax*, to its burrow entrance as seen from the side a), c) and from above b), d), e). The crab makes feeding excursions in all directions from its burrow, leaving behind tiny pellets of mud where it has been eating b). If a plate is placed over its burrow entrance, the crab runs straight to the spot above the entrance and carries out a zigzag search of the area c), d). The crab occasionally misses the entrance when it returns and has to search for it e). (Modified from [295])

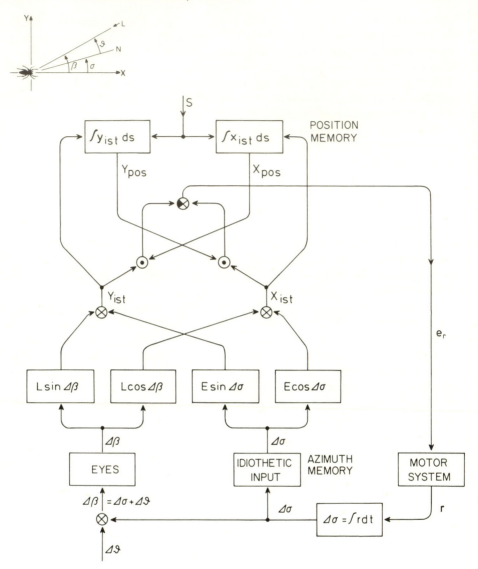

Fig. 3.11/4 Hypothetical circuit diagram of homing by a funnel web spider. β is the angle between spider and light direction; δ, the angle between light direction and web diagonal; e_r, the efferent turning command; σ, the angle between the spider and the web diagonal; L, light direction; N, web diagonal; S, the signal about the distance covered; X_{ist} and Y_{ist}, the actual values of coordinates defining the spider's position; X_{pos} and Y_{pos}, the stored position values; the dot surrounded by a circle represents a multiplication. See text for further explanation. (Modified from [597])

route to reach its prey, the funnel web spider, *Agelena labyrinthica*, returns to its retreat in a straight line. Both idiothetic and allothetic signals, like light and gravity, determine the home bearing. The processing of visual and idiothetic signals corresponds to a vector addition with weighting factors [607]. Based on the findings of Görner, Moller, and Dornfeld, Mittelstaedt has developed a hypothetical information flow pattern for this orientation system [598, 597]. Figure 3.11/4 shows a simplified version.

The motor output, the turning speed r, changes σ, the angle of the spider to the web diagonal. Whether the turn is to the left or the right depends on the sign (not shown). The idiothetic signals arising from the turns are initially stored as in the millipedes. The second input, the spider's alignment to the light (β), is affected by σ as well as by the orientation of the web to the light (δ).

The processing of the two input signals resembles that of the bicomponent theory (2.6.3). Afferent excitations, σ and β, are converted to their sine and cosine values, multiplied by weighting constants (E,L), and summed to give the actual values, X_{ist}, Y_{ist}. These represent the coordinates of the spider's position on the web at any moment in time. They are summed in two position memories and integrated over the individual stretches (S) of the spider's path. These memories hold the coordinate values (X_{pos}, Y_{pos}), which were computed on the way out from the input data. They are cross-multiplied with the actual values and their products subtracted from each other. The resulting difference determines the turning command (e_r) for the motor output r, which during its execution ($\int rdt$) changes the inputs σ and β until e_r equals zero. Normally this means that the memories are empty, and the spider has reached its retreat.

References

[1] Adam, L.-J.: Neurophysiologie des Hörens und Bioakustik einer Feldheuschrecke (Locusta migratoria). Z. vergl. Physiol. **63**, 227–289 (1969).

[2] Akert, K.: Der visuelle Greifreflex. Helv. Physiol. Acta **7**, 112–134 (1949).

[3] Altevogt, R.: Untersuchungen zur Biologie, Ökologie und Physiologie indischer Winkerkrabben. Z. Morph. Ökol. Tiere **46**, 1–110 (1957).

[4] Altevogt, R., v. Hagen, H. O.: Über die Orientierung von Uca tangeri Eydoux im Freiland. Z. Morph. Ökol. Tiere **53**, 636–656 (1964).

[5] Alverdes, F.: Stato-, Photo- u. Tangoreaktionen bei 2 Garnelenarten. Z. vergl. Physiol. **4**, 700–765 (1926).

[6] Andres, K. H., v. Düring, M.: Morphology of cutaneous receptors. In: Hdb. Sens. Physiol. II, p. 3–28. Ed.: A. Iggo. Springer Verlag, Berlin, Heidelberg, New York 1973.

[7] Angell, J. R., Fite, W.: The monaural localization of sound. Psychol. Rev. **8**, 225–246 (1901).

[8] Apter, J. T.: Eye movements following strychninization of the superior colliculus of cats. J. Neurophysiol. **9**, 73–86 (1946).

[9] Aristoteles: Politika, 1. Buch, 2. Kap.

[10] Arke, R. D.: „Correcting" behavior by insects on vertical and horizontal mazes. J. of the Kansas Entomological Soc. **37**, 169–186 (1964).

[10a] Asch, S. E., Witkin, H. A.: Studies in Space Orientation. II. Perception of the Upright with displaced Visual Fields and with Body tilted. J. exp. Psychol. **38**, 455–477 (1948).

[11] Atkin, A., Bender, M. B.: Ocular stabilization during oscillatory head movements. Vestibular system dysfunction and the relation between head and eye velocities. Arch. Neurol. (Chic.) **19**, 559–566 (1968).

[12] Aubert, H.: Eine scheinbare bedeutende Drehung von Objekten bei Neigung des Kopfes nach rechts oder links. Virchows Arch. path. Anat. **20**, 381 (1851).

[13] Autrum, H.: Über Gehör und Erschütterungssinn bei Locustiden. Z. vergl. Physiol. **28**, 580–637 (1941).

[14] Autrum, H.: Über Lautäußerungen und Schallwahrnehmungen bei Arthropoden. II. Das Richtungshören von Locusta und Versuch einer Hörtheorie für Tympanalorgane vom Locustidentyp. Z. vergl. Physiol. **28**, 326–352 (1941).

[15] Autrum, H., Schwartzkopff, J., Swoboda, H.: Der Einfluß der Schallrichtung auf die Tympanal-Potentiale von Locusta migratoria L. Biol. Zbl. **80**, 385–402 (1961).

[16] Baerends, G. P.: Fortpflanzungsverhalten und Orientierung der Grabwespe Ammophila campestris Jur. Tijdschrift voor Entomologie **84**, 69–275 (1941).

[17] Bailey, J., Thomson, P.: Acoustic orientation in the cricket Teleogryllus oceanicus (Le Guillou). J. exp. Biol. **67**, 61–75 (1977).

[18] Baldus, H.: Entfernungslokalisation der Libelle. Z. vergl. Physiol. **3**, 475–505 (1925).

[19] Banks, M. S., Aslin, R. N., Letson, R. D.: Sensitive period for the development of human binocular vision. Science **190**, 675–677 (1975).

[20] Bannan, T. E.: A plane man's guide to inertial navigation. Tech Air, July, 2–6 (1972).

[21] Barber, V. C.: The fine structure of the statocyst of Octopus vulgaris. Z. Zellforsch. mikrosk. Anat. **70**, 91–107 (1966b).

[22] Barber, V. C.: The structure of mollusc statocysts, with particular reference to cephalopods. Symp. zool. Soc. Lond. No. **23**, 37– 62 (1968).

[23] Bard, P.: Studies on the cortical representation of somatic sensibility. The Harvey Lectures Ser. **33**, p. 143, Academic Press, New York 1938.

[24] Barlow, H. B., Pettigrew, J. D.: Lack of specificity of neurones in the visual cortex of young kittens. J. Physiol. (London) **218**, 98–100 (1971).

[25] Barnwell, F. H.: An angle sense in the orientation of a millipede. Biol. Bull. **128**, 33–50 (1965).

[26] Barnwell, F. H., Brown, F. A., Jr.: Responses of planarians and snails. In: Biological Effects of Magnetic Fields, pp. 263–278, Ed.: M. F. Barnothy. Plenum Press, New York 1964.

[27] Barrós-Pita, J. C., Maldonado, H.: A fovea in the praying mantis eye. II. Some morphol. Characteristics. Z. vergl. Physiol. **67**, 79–92 (1970).

[28] Barth, F. G., Seyfarth, E.-A.: Slit sense organs and kinesthetic orientation. Z. vergl. Physiol. **74**, 306–328 (1971).

[29] Bates, H. W.: The naturalist on the river Amazonas. Vol. 2, J. Murray, London 1863.

[30] Batteau, D. W.: The role of the pinna in human localization. Proc. Roy. Soc. **158**, 158–180 (1967).

[31] Batteau, D. W.: Listening with the naked ear. In: The Neuropsychol. of spatially oriented Behavior, p. 109–133. Ed.: S. J. Freedman. Dorsey, Homewood, Ill. 1968.

[32] Baumann, F.: Experimente über den Geruchssinn und den Beuteerwerb der Viper (Vipera aspis L.). Z. vergl. Physiol. **10**, 37–119 (1929).

[33] Baunacke, W.: Studien zur Frage nach der Statocystenfunktion (Statische Reflexe bei Mollusken). Aus: Biol. Centralblatt **33**, 427–452 (1913).

[34] Baunacke, W.: Statische Sinnesorgane bei den Nepiden. Zool. Jahrb., Abt. Anatomie **24**, 190–346 (1912).

[35] Becker, G.: Ruheeinstellung nach der Himmelsrichtung, eine Magnetfeldorientierung bei Termiten. Naturwiss. **50**, 455 (1963a).

[36] Becker, G.: Magnetfeldorientierung von Dipteren. Naturwiss. **50**, 664 (1963b).

[37] Becker, G.: Reaktion von Insekten auf Magnetfelder, elektrische Felder und atmospherics. Z. angew. Entomologie **54**, 75–88 (1964).

[38] Becker, G.: Magnetfeld-Einfluß auf die Galeriebau-Richtung bei Termiten. Naturwiss. **58**, 60 (1971).

[39] Becker, G., Speck, U.: Untersuchungen über die Magnetfeldorientierung von Dipteren. Z. vergl. Physiol. **49**, 301–340 (1964).

[40] Beetsma, J., de Ruiter, L., de Wilde, J.: Possible influence of neotenine and ecdyson on the sign of phototaxis in the eyed hawk caterpillar (Smerinus ocellata L.). J. Ins. Physiol. **8**, 251–257 (1962).

[41] v. Békésy, G.: Zur Theorie des Hörens. Über das Richtungshören bei einer Zeitdifferenz oder Lautstärkenungleichheit der beiderseitigen Schalleinwirkung. Physik Z. **31**, 824–835 (1930).

[42] v. Békésy, G.: Olfactory analogue to directional hearing. J. Appl. Physiol. **19**, 369–373 (1964).

[43] v. Békésy, G.: Inhibition and the time and spatial patterns of neural activity in sensory perception. Ann. of Otology **74**, 445–462 (1965).

[44] Belanger, L. F.: Observations on the intimate structure and composition of the chick labyrinth. Anatomical Record **139**, 539–41 (1961).

[45] Belbenoit, P.: Conditionnement instrumental de l'electroperception des objets chez Gnathonemus petersii (Mormyridae, Teleostei, Pisces). Z. vergl. Physiol. **67**, 192–204 (1970).

[46] Bellrose, F. C.: Radar in orientation research. Proc. Int. Ornithol. Congr. 14th, 1966, 281–309 (1967a).

[47] Bellrose, F. C.: Orientation in waterfowl migration. Proc. Annu. Biol. Colloqu. Oregon State Univ. **27**, 73–99 (1967b).

[48] Benjamins, C. E., Huizinga, E.: Untersuchungen über die Funktion des Vestibularapparates bei Tauben II. Pflügers Arch. **221**, (1929).

[49] Bennett, M. V. L.: Electrolocation in fish. Ann. N. Y. Acad. Sci. **188**, 242–269 (1971).

[50] Bennett, M. V. L.: Mechanisms of electroreception. In: „Lateral line detectors". pp. 313–393, Ed.: P. Cahn. Indiana Univ. Press, Bloomington, Indiana 1967.

[51] Bennit, R., Dickson Merrick, A.: Migration of the proximal retinal pigment in the crayfish in relation to oxygen deficiency. Biol. Bull. **62**, 168–177 (1932).

[52] Benson, A. J.:Modification of the response to angular accelerations by linear accelerations. In: Hdb. Sens. Physiol. **VI**/2, 281–320. Ed.: H. H. Kornhuber. Springer Verlag, Berlin, Heidelberg, New York 1974.

[53] Benson, A. J.: Possible mechanisms of motion and space sickness. Proc. European Symp. Life Sci. Res. in Space. Köln-Porz. Germany, 24–26 May 1977.

[54] Benson, A. J., Barnes, G. R.,: Responses to rotating linear acceleration vectors considered in relation to a model of the otolith organs. Fifth Symp. on the role of the vestibular organs in Space exploration, 221–236. U. S. Government Printing Office, Washington 1973.

[55] Bentley, E., Sulkin, S. D.: The ontogeny of barokinesis during the zoeal development of the xanthid crab Rhithropanopeus harrisii (Gould). Mar. Behav. Physiol. 4, 275–282 (1977).

[56] Berthold, P.: Relationships between migratory restlessness and migration distances in six Sylvia species. Ibis 115, 594–599 (1973).

[57] Berthold, P., Gwinner, E., Klein, H., Westrich, P.: Beziehungen zwischen Zugunruhe und Zugablauf bei Garten- und Mönchsgrasmücke (Sylvia borin und S. atricapilla). Z. Tierpsychol. 30, 26–35 (1972a).

[58] Berthold, P., Gwinner, E., Klein, H.: Circannuale Periodik bei Grasmücken. I. Periodik der Mauser, des Körpergewichtes und der Nachtunruhe bei Sylvia atricapilla und S. borin unter verschiedenen konstanten Bedingungen. J. Ornithol. 113, 170–190 (1972b).

[59] Berthoz, A., Pavard, B., Young, L. R.: Perception of linear horizontal selfmotion induced by peripheral vision (Linearvection). Basic characteristics and visual-vestibular interactions. Exp. Brain Res. 23, 471–489 (1975).

[60] Bethe, A.: Dürfen wir den Ameisen und den Bienen psychische Qualitäten zuschreiben. Pflüg. Arch. ges. Physiol. 70, 15 (1898).

[61] van Beusekom, G.: Some experiments on the optical orientation in Philanthus triangulum fabr. Behaviour I, 3–4 (1948).

[62] Biederman-Thorson, M., Thorson, J.: Rotation-compensating reflexes independent of the labyrinth and the eye. J. comp. Physiol. 83, 103–122 (1973).

[63] Birukow, G.: Photo-Geomenotaxis bei Geotrupes silvaticus Panz. und ihre zentralnervöse Koordination. Z. vergl. Physiol. 36, 176–211 (1954).

[64] Bischof, N.: Psychophysik der Raumwahrnehmung. Hdb. d. Psychol. 1, 307–408. Hrsg.: W. Metzger. Verlag f. Psychologie, Hofgrefe, Göttingen 1966.

[65] Bischof, N.: Stellungs-, Spannungs- und Lagewahrnehmung. Hdb. d. Psychologie 1, 409–497. Hrsg.: W. Metzger. Verlag f. Psychologie, Hofgrefe, Göttingen 1966.

[66] Bischof, N.: Optic-vestibular orientation to the vertical. Hdb. Sens. Physiol. VI/2, 155–192. Ed.: H. H. Kornhuber. Springer Verlag, Berlin, Heidelberg, New York 1974.

[67] Blakemore, C.: Developmental factors in the formation of feature extracting neurons. In: The Neurosciences, III. Study program. Eds.: F. O. Schmitt, F. G. Worden. The MIT Press Cambridge, Mass., and London 1974.

[68] Blakemore, C.: Persönl. Mitteilung, 1978.

[69] Blakemore, C., Cooper, G. F.: Development of the brain depends on the visual environment. Nature 228, 477–478 (1970).

[70] Blest, A. D.: The evolution, ontogeny and quantitative control of the settling movements of some new world saturniid moths, with some comments on distance communication by honeybees. Behaviour 16, 188–253 (1960).

[71] Bogenschütz, H.: Vergl. Unters. über die optische Komponente der Gleichgewichtshaltung bei Fischen. Z. vergl. Physiol. 44, 626–655 (1961).

[72] Bossert, W. H., Wilson, E. O.: The analysis of olfactory communication among animals. J. Theoret. Biol. 5, 443–469 (1963).

[73] Braemer, W.: Verhaltensphysiologische Untersuchungen am optischen Apparat bei Fischen. Z. vergl. Physiol. 39, 374–398 (1957).

[74] Braemer, W.: Zur Gleichgewichtsorientierung schrägstehender Fische. Z. vgl. Phys. 40, 529–542 (1958).

[75] Braemer, W.: A critical review of the sun-azimuth hypothesis. Cold Spring Harb. Symp. 25, 413–427 (1960).

[76] Braemer, W., Braemer, H.: Orientation of fish to gravity. Limnology and Oceanography 3, 362–372 (1958).

[77] Braemer, W., Schwassmann, H. O.: Vom Rhythmus der Sonnenorientierung bei Fischen am Äquator. Ergebn. Biol. **26**, 278–288 (1963).

[78] Braitenberg, V.: Gehirngespinste, Neuroanatomie für kybernetisch Interessierte. 137 S., Springer Verlag, Berlin, Heidelberg, New York 1973.

[79] Braitenberg, V., Strausfeld, N. J.: Principles of the mosaic organisation in the visual system's neuropil of Musca domestica L. Hdb. Sens. Physiol. **VII**/3. Springer Verlag, Berlin, Heidelberg, New York 1973.

[80] Brandt, Th., Dichgans, J.: Circularvection, optische Pseudocoriolis-Effekte und optokinetischer Nachnystagmus: Eine vergleichende Untersuchung subjektiver und objektiver optokinetischer Nacheffekte. Albrecht v. Graefes Arch. Klin. exp. Ophthal. **184**, 42–57 (1972).

[81] Brandt, Th., Büchele, W., Arnold, F.: Arthrokinetic nystagmus and egomotion sensation. Exp. Brain Res. **30**, 331–338 (1977).

[82] Brandt, Th., Bles, W., Kapteyn, T. S., Arnold, F.: Height vertigo: a distance vertigo through visual destabilization. In: 11th World Congr. Neurol., Amsterdam, Sept. 1977. Excerpta Medica Int. Congr. Ser. **427**. Excerpta Medica, Amsterdam, Oxford 1977.

[83] Brandt, Th., Dichgans, J., Koenig, E.: Differential effects of central versus peripheral vision on egocentric and exocentric motion perception. Exp. Brain Res. **16**, 476–491 (1973).

[84] Brandt, Th., Wenzel D., Dichgans J.: Die Entwicklung der visuellen Stabilisation des aufrechten Standes b. Kind: Ein Reifezeichen in der Kinderneurologie. Arch. Psychiat. Nervenkr. **223**, 1–13 (1976).

[85] Brandt, Th., Wist, E., Dichgans, J.: Optisch induzierte Pseudocoriolis-Effekte und Circularvektion. Arch. Psychiat. Nervenkr. **214**, 365–389 (1971).

[86] Breuer, J.: Über die Funktion der Otolithen-Apparate. Pflügers Arch. ges. Physiol. **48**, 195–306 (1891).

[87] Breuer, J., Kreidl, A.: Über die scheinbare Drehung des Gesichtsfeldes während der Einwirkung einer Zentrifugalkraft. Arch. ges. Physiol. **70**, 494–510 (1898).

[88] Brickenstein, C.: Über den Netzbau der Larve von Neuredipsis bimaculata L. Abh. Bayer. Akad. d. Wiss., Math. Nat. Kl., N. F. **69**, 44 (1955).

[89] Brock, F.: Das Verhalten des Einsiedlerkrebses Pagurus arrosor Herbst während der Suche und Aufnahme von Nahrung. Z. Morph. Ökol. Tiere **6**, 415–551 (1926).

[90] Brodal, A.: Anatomy of the vestibular nuclei and their connections. In: Hdb. Sens. Physiol. **VI**/1, 239–352. Ed.: H. H. Kornhuber. Springer Verlag, Berlin, Heidelberg, New York 1974.

[91] Brodmann, K.: Vergleichende Lokalisationslehre der Großhirnrinde, in ihren Prinzipien dargestellt auf Grund des Zellenbaues. J. A. Barth, Leipzig 1909.

[92] Brown, J. L.: Orientation to the vertical during water immersion. Aerospace Med. **32**, 209–217 (1961).

[93] Brown, F. A.: Response of the Planarian, Dugesia, and the Protozoan, Paramecium, to very weak horizontal magnetic fields. Biol. Bull. **123**, 264–281 (1962).

[94] Brown, F. A.: How animals respond to magnetism. Discovery Nov. 1963.

[95] Bruderer, B.: Effects of alpine topography and winds on migrating birds. In: Animal Migration, Navigation, and homing. Symp. Univ. Tübingen, 17.–20. 8. 1977. Eds.: K. Schmidt-Koenig, W. T. Keeton. Springer Verlag, Berlin, Heidelberg, New York 1978.

[96] Brun, R.: Die Raumorientierung der Ameisen und das Orientierungsproblem im allgemeinen. Verlag Gustav Fischer, Jena 1914.

[97] Buchholtz, Ch.: Eine verhaltensphysiol. Analyse der Beutefanghandlung von Calopteryx splendens unter besonderer Berücksichtigung des Opt. AAM nach partiellen Röntgenbestr. des Protocerebrums. Verh. Dtsch. Zool. Ges. Saarbrücken, 401–412 (1962).

[98] v. Buddenbrock, W.: Über die Orientierung der Krebse im Raum. Zool. Jb. Allg. Zool. u. Physiol. **34**, 479–514 (1914).

[99] v. Buddenbrock, W.: Vergleichende Physiologie I, Sinnesphysiologie. Birkhäuser, Basel 1952.

[100] v. Buddenbrock, W., Moller-Racke, I.: Neues zur Optomotorik der Insekten. Experientia **8**, 392 (1952).

[101] Budelmann, B.-U.: The correlation between statolith action and compensatory eye movements in Octopus vulgaris. Proc. Barany Soc. 1st extraordinary Meeting Amsterdam- Utrecht 207–215 (1970).

[102] Budelmann, B.-U.: Die Arbeitsweise der Statolithenorgane von Octopus vulgaris. Z. vergl. Physiol. **70**, 278–312 (1970).

[103] Budelmann, B.-U.: Gravity receptor function in cephalopods with particular reference to Sepia officinalis. Fortschr. Zool. **23**, 84–96 (1975).

[104] Budelmann, B.-U.: Structure and function of the angular acceleration receptor systems in the statocysts of cephalopods. Symp. zool. Soc. London **38**, 309–324 (1977).

[105] Budelmann, B.-U.: The function of the equilibrium receptor systems of cephalopods. In: Proc. Neurootological and Equilibriometric Soc.. Ed.: C. F. Claussen. Edition medicin and pharmacie, Frankfurt 1978.

[106] Budelmann, B.-U., Wolff, H.-G.: Gravity response from angular acceleration receptors in Octopus vulgaris. J. comp. Physiol. **85**, 283–290 (1973).

[107] Bullock, T. H.: Evolution of neurophysiological mechanisms, 185–187. In: Behavior and evolution. Eds.: Roe, Simpson. Yale Univ. Press 1958b.

[108] Bullock, Th. H.: The origins of patterned nervous discharge. Behaviour **17**, 48–59 (1961).

[109] Bullock, T. H.: Biological sensors. In: Vistas in Sciense. Albuquerque: Univ. New Mexico Press 1968.

[110] Bullock, T.H.: General Introduction. In: Hdb. Sens. Physiol. **III**/3, Electroreceptors and other specialized receptors in lower vertebrates. Ed.: A. Fessard. Springer Verlag, Berlin, Heidelberg, New York 1974.

[111] Bullock, T. H., Barrett, R.: Radiant heat reception in snakes. Comm. Behav. Biol (A) **1**, 19–29 (1968).

[112] Bullock, T. H., Diecke, F. P. J.: Properties of an infra-red receptor. J. Physiol. London **134**, 47–87 (1965).

[113] Bullock, T. H., Fox, W.: Anatomy of the infrared sense organ in the facial pit of pit vipers. Q. J. microsc. Sci. **98**, 219–234 (1975).

[114] Bullock, T. H., Grinnell, A. D., Ikezono, E., Kameda, K., Katsuki, Y., Nomoto, M., Sato, O., Suga, N., Yanagisawa, K.: Electrophysiological studies of central auditory mechanisms in cetaceans. Z. vergl. Physiol. **59**, 117–156 (1968).

[115] Bullock, T. H., Horridge, A.: Structure and function in the nervous system I, II. W. H. Freeman & Comp. San Francisco, London 1965.

[116] Burger, M.-L.: Zum Mechanismus der Gegenwendung nach mechanisch aufgezwungenen Richtungsänderungen bei Schizophyllum sabulosum (Julidae, Diplopoda). Z. vergl. Physiol. **71**, 219–254 (1971).

[117] Burgess, P. R., Perl, E. R.: Cutaneous mechanoreceptors and nociceptors. Hdb. Sens. Physiol. **II**, Somatosens. Systems. Springer Verlag, Berlin, Heidelberg, New York 1973.

[118] Burghardt, G. M.: The primary effect of the first feeding experience in the snapping turtle. Psychon. Sci. **7**, 11 (1967).

[119] Burghardt, G. M.: Effects of early experience on food preference in chicks. Psychon. Sci. **14**, 7–8 (1969).

[120] Burghardt, G. M.: Chemical perception in reptiles In: Communication by chemical signals, p. 241–308. Eds.: J. W. Johnston Jr., D. G. Moulton and A. Turk. Appleton-Century-Crofts, N. Y. (1970).

[121] Busnel, R.-G., Dziedizic, A.: Résultats métrologiques expérimentaux de l'écholocation chez le Phocaena phocaena, et leur comparaison avex ceux de certaines chauves-souris. In: Animal Sonar Systems, 307–338, Vol. I. Ed.: R.-G. Busnel. Laboratoire de Physiologie Acoustique, Jouy-en-Josas, France 1967b.

[122] Butenandt, E.: Wirkungstheoretische Analyse der Menotaxis bei Calliphora. In: Biokybernetik, Bd. II, S. 58–63. Hrsg.: Drischl, N. Tiedt. Karl-Marx-Universität, Leipzig 1968.

[123] Büttner, U., Henn, V.: Thalamic unit activity in the alert monkey during natural vestibular stimulation. Brain Res. **103**, 127–132 (1976).

[124] Capranica, R. R.: The evoked vocal response of the bullfrog: A study of communication by sound. Research Monogr. **33**. The M.I.T. Press, Cambridge, Mass. 1965.

[125] Carlström, D.: A crystallographic study of vertebrate otoliths. Biol. Bull. **125**, 441–463 (1963).

[126] Caston, J., Precht, W., Blanks, R. H. I.: Response characteristics of frog's lagena afferents to natural stimulation. J. comp. Physiol. **118**, 273–289 (1977).

[127] Chalupa, L. M., Rhoades, R. W.: Responses of visual, somatosensory, and auditory neurones in the golden hamsters superior colliculus. J. Physiol. **270**, 595–626 (1977).

[128] Chmurzyński, J. A.: Studies on the stages of spatial orientation in females Bembex rostrata (LINNE 1758) returning to their nests (Hymenoptera, Sphegidae). Acta Biol. Exper. (Warsaw) **24**, 103–132 (1964).

[129] Chmurzyński, J. A.: Some remarks on the optics of the Bembex rostrata (L.) eye (Hymenoptera, Sphegidae). Zoologica Poloniae **13** (1963).

[130] Chmurzyński, J. A.: Preference for discontinuous shapes and patterns in the proximate orientation of female Bembex rostrata L. (Hymenoptera, Sphegidae). In: Internat. Congr. of Psychology, Ecology and Ethology in Behavioral studies. Symposium **18**, 148–150, Moskau (1966).

[131] Chung, Shin-Ho, Pettigrew, A., Anson, M.: Dynamics of the amphibian middle ear. Nature **272**, 142–147 (1978).

[132] Cloarec, A.: Interactions between different receptors involved in prey capture in Ranatra linearis (Insecta, Heteroptera). Biology of Behaviour **1**, 251–266 (1976).

[133] Cohen, B.: The vestibulo-ocular reflex arc. In: Hdb. Sens. Physiol. VI/1, 477–540. Ed.: H. H. Kornhuber. Springer Verlag, Berlin, Heidelberg, New York 1974.

[134] Cohen, B., Henn, V.: The origin of quick phases of nystagmus in the horizontal plane. In: Cerebral control of eye movements and motion perception. Bibl. ophthal. **82**, 36–55 (1972).

[135] Cohen, M. J.: The function of receptors in the statocyst of the lobster Homarus americanus. J. Physiol. **130**, 9–34 (1955).

[136] Cohen, M. J., Dijkgraaf, S.: Mechanoreception. In: The Physiology of Crustacea Vol. II, Ed.: T. H. Waterman. Academic Press, New York, London 1961.

[137] Collett, T. S.: Peering - a locust behaviour pattern for obtaining motion parallax information. J. exp. Biol. **76**, 237–241 (1978).

[138] Collett, T. S., Land, M. F.: Visual control of flight behaviour in the hoverfly, Syritta pipiens L. J. comp. Physiol. **99**, 1–66 (1975).

[139] Cotzin, M., Dallenbach, K. M.: „Facial vision": the role of pitch and loudness in the perception of obstacles by the blind. Amer. J. Psychol. **63**, 485–515 (1950).

[140] Couceiro, A., Almeida, de, D. F.: The electrogenetic tissue of some Gymnotidae. Bioelectrogenesis, Proc. of the Symp. on Comp. Bioelectrogen. 3–13 (1976).

[141] Crisp, J., Stubbings, H. G.: The orientation of barnacles to water currents. J. Anim. Ecol. **26**, 179–196 (1957).

[142] Cynader, M., Berman, N.: Receptive-field organization of monkey superior colliculus. J. Neurophysiol. **35**, 187–201 (1972).

[143] Cynader, R. C., van Sluyters, Blakemore, C.: Blakemore: Briefl. Mitteilung 1978.

[144] Czeloth, H.: Untersuchungen über die Raumorientierung von Triton. Z. vergl. Physiol. **13**, 74–163 (1930).

[145] Czihak, G., Langer, H., Ziegler, H.: Biologie (Lehrb. f. Studenten). Hrsg. G. Czihak, H. Langer, H. Ziegler. Springer Verlag, Berlin, Heidelberg, New York 1976.

[146] Dathe, H. H.: Untersuchungen zum phonotaktischen Verhalten von Gryllus bimaculatus (Insecta, Orthopteroidea). Forma et Functio **7**, 7–20 (1974).

[147] Daumer, K., Jander, R., Waterman, T. H.: Orientation of the ghost-crab Ocypode on polarized light. Z. vergl. Physiol. **47**, 56–76 (1963).

[148] Dawkins, R.: The selfish gene. Oxford University Press 1976.

[149] Daykin, P. N., Kellogg, F. E., Wright, R. H.: Host-finding and repulsion of Aedes aegypti. Can. Entomol. **97**, 239–263 (1965).

[150] Delius, J. D., Vollrath, F. W.: Rotation compensating reflexes independent of the labyrinth. J. comp. Physiol. **83** 123–134 (1973).

[151] Denny-Brown, D., Chambers, R. A.: Visuomotor function in the cerebral cortex. Arch. Neurol. Psychiat. **73**, 566 (1955).

[152] Dethier, V. G.: The role of the antennae in the orientation of carrion beetles to odors. J. N. Y. Entomol. Soc. **55**, 285–293 (1947).

[153] Dethier, V. G., Browne, L. B., Smith, C. N.: The designation of chemicals in terms of the responses they elicit from insects. J. econ. entomol. **53**, 134–36 (1960).

[154] Dichgans, J., Brandt, Th.: Visual-vestibular interaction and motion perception. Bibl. Ophthal. **82**, 327–338 (1972).

[155] Dichgans, J., Brandt, Th.: The Psychophysics of visually induced perception of self-motion and tilt. In: The Neurosciences, Eds.: F. O. Schmitt, F. G. Warden. M. I. T. Press, Cambridge, Mass. 1974.

[156] Dichgans, J., Brandt, Th., Held, R.: The role of vision in gravitational orientation. In: Mechanisms of spatial perception and orientation as related to gravity. Ed.: H. Schöne. Fortschr. Zool. **23**, 255–263 (1975a).

[157] Dichgans, J., Schmidt, C. L., Wist, E. R.: Frequency modulation of afferent and efferent unit activity in the vestibular nerve by oculomotor impulses. Progress in Brain Res. **37**, 449–456 (1972).

[158] Dichgans, J., Held, R., Young, L. R., Brandt, Th.: Moving visual scenes influence the apparent direction of gravity. Science **178**, 1217–1219 (1972).

[159] Dijkgraaf, S.: Over een merkwaardige functie van den gehoorzin bij vleermuizen. Verslagen Nederlandsche Akademie van Wetenschappen Afd. Naturkunde, **52**, 622–627 (1943).

[160] Dijkgraaf, S.: Die Sinneswelt der Fledermäuse. Experientia **2**, 438–48 (1946).

[161] Dijkgraaf, S.: Über die Reizung des Ferntastsinnes bei Fischen und Amphibien. Experientia **3**, 206 (1947).

[162] Dijkgraaf, S.: Spallanzani und die Fledermäuse. Experientia **5**, 90 (1949).

[163] Dijkgraaf, S.: Rotationssinn nach dem Bogengangsprinzip bei Crustaceen. Experientia **11**, 407 (1955a).

[164] Dijkgraaf, S.: Die Augenstielbewegungen der Languste (Palinurus vulgaris). Experientia **11**, 329 (1955b).

[165] Dijkgraaf, S.: Kompensatorische Augenstieldrehungen und ihre Auslösung bei der Languste (Palinurus vulg.). Z. vergl. Physiol. **38**, 491–520 (1956a).

[166] Dijkgraaf, S.: Elektrophysiologische Untersuchungen an der Seitenlinie von Xenopus laevis. Experientia **12**, 276 (1956b).

[167] Dijkgraaf, S.: Über die kompensatorischen Augenstielbewegungen bei Brachyuren. Pubbl. Staz. Zool. Napoli **28**, 341–358 (1956c).

[168] Dijkgraaf, S.: Structure and functions of the statocyst in crabs. Experientia **12**, 394 (1956d).

[169] Dijkgraaf, S.: Spallanzani's unpublished experiments on the sensory basis of objects perception in bats. Ibis **51**, 1, 163 (1960).

[170] Dijkgraaf, S.: Biological significance of the lateral line organs. In: Lateral Line Detectors, 83–95. Ed.: P. Cahn. Univ. Press, Indiana 1967.

[171] Dijkgraaf, S., Hessels, H. G. A.: Über Bau und Funktion bei der Schnecke Aplysia limacina. Z. vergl. Physiol. **62**, 38–60 (1969).

[172] Dijkgraaf, S., Kalmijn, A. J.: Untersuchungen über die Funktion der Lorenzinischen Ampullen an Haifischen. Z. vergl. Physiol. **47**, 438–456 (1963).

[173] Dijkgraaf, S., Kalmijn, A. J.: Versuche zur biologischen Bedeutung der Lorenzinischen Ampullen bei den Elasmobranchiern. Z. vergl. Physiol. **53**, 187–194 (1966).

[174] Dingle, H.: Further observations on correcting behaviour in Boxelder bugs. Animal Behaviour **12**, 116–124 (1964).

[175] Dingle, H.: Turn alternation by bugs on causeways as a delayed compensatory response and the effects of varying visual inputs and length of straight path. Animal Behaviour **13**, 171–177 (1964).

[176] Doane, B. K., Mahatoo, W., Heron, W., Scott, T. H.: Changes in perceptual function after isolation. Canad. J. Psychol. **13**, 210–219 (1959).

[177] Dornfeldt, K.: Die Bedeutung der Haupt- und Nebenaugen für das Heimfindevermögen der Trichterspinne Agelena labyrinthica (Clerck) mit Hilfe einer Lichtquelle. Dissertation Berlin 1972.

[178] Dornfeldt, K.: Eine Elementaranalyse des Wirkungsgefüges des Heimfindevermögens der Trichterspinne Agelena labyrinthica (CL.). Z. Tierpsychol. **38**, 267–293 (1975b).

[179] Dräger, U. C., Huber, D. H.: Responses to visual stimulation and relationship between visual, auditory, and somatosensory inputs in mouse superior colliculus. J. Neurophysiol. **38**, 690–713 (1975).

[180] Dräger, U. C., Hubel, D. H.: Topography of visual and somatosensory projections to mouse superior colliculus. J. Neurophysiol. **39**, 91–101 (1976).

[181] Duelli, P.: Orientierung ohne richtende Außenreize bei Reptilien (Hemidactylus frenatus Gekkonidae). Z. Tierpsychol. **38**, 324–328 (1975a).

[182] Duelli, P.: A fovea for E-vector orientation in the eye. J. comp. Physiol. **102**, 43–56 (1975b).

[183] Duelli, P., Wehner, R.: The spectral sensitivity of polarized light orientation in Cataglyphis bicolor (Formicidae, Hymenoptera). J. comp. Physiol. **86**, 37–53 (1973).

[184] Duensing, F.: Die Erregungskonstellation im Rautenhirn des Kaninchens bei den Labyrinthstellreflexen. Naturwiss. **22**, 681–690 (1961).

[185] Duensing, F., Schaefer, K. P.: Die Aktivität einzelner Neurone der Formatio reticularis des nicht gefesselten Kaninchens bei Kopfwendungen und vestibulären Reizen. Arch. Psychiat. Nervenkr. **201**, 97–122 (1958).

[186] Duncker, K.: Über induzierte Bewegung. Psychol. Forsch. **12**, 180 (1929).

[187] Edrich, W.: The waggle dance of the honey bee; a new formulation. Fortschr. Zool. **23**, 20–29 (1975).

[188] Edrich, W.: Interaction of light and gravity in the orientation of the waggle dance of honey bees. Anim. Behav. **25**, 342–363 (1977).

[189] Edwards, A. S.: Body sway and vision. J. exp. Psych. **36**, 526–535 (1946).

[190] van Egmond, A. A. J., Groen, J. J., Jongkees, L. B.W.: The mechanics of the semicircular canal. J. Physiol. **110**, 1–17 (1949).

[191] Eibl-Eibesfeldt, I.: Grundriß der vergleichenden Verhaltensforschung, Ethologie. Piper, München 1967.

[192] Elsner, N., Huber, F.: Neurale Grundlagen artspezifischer Kommunikation bei Orthopteren. Fortschr. Zool. **22**, 1–48 (1973).

[193] Emlen, S. T.: Migratory orientation in the Indigo Bunting, Passerina cyanea. Part I. Evidence for use of celestial cues. Auk **84**, 309–342 (1967a).

[194] Emlen, S. T.: Migratory orientation in the Indigo Bunting, Passerina cyanea. Part II. Mechanism of celestial orientation. Auk **84**, 463–489 (1967b).

[195] Emlen, S. T.: Problems in identifying bird species by radar signature analyses: intraspecific variability. In: „The biological aspects of the bird/aircraft collision problem", p. 509–524. Ed.: S. Gauthreaux. Air Force Office of Scientific Research, Clemsen, North Carolina, 1974.

[196] Emlen, S. T.: Migration: Orientation and navigation. In: Avian Biology Vol. V. Eds.: D. S. Farner, J. R. King. Academic Press, Inc. New York, San Francisco, London 1975.

[197] Enright, J. T.: Lunar orientation of Orchestoidea corniculata Stoub (Amphipoda). Biol. Bull. **120**, 148–156 (1961).

[198] Erulkar, S. D.: Comparative Aspects of spatial localization of sound. Physiol. Rev. **52**, 237–360 (1972).

[199] Evans, E. F.: Neural processes for the detection of acoustic patterns and for sound localization. The Neurosciences, Third Study Programm, p. 131–145. Eds.: F. O. Schmitt, F. G. Worden. The M.I.T. Press Cambridge, Mass., and London 1974.

[200] Evans, W. E.: Echolocation by marine delphinids and one species of fresh water dolphin. J. acoust. Soc. Amer. **54**, 191 (1973).

[201] Evans, W. E., Dreher, J. J.: Observations on scouting behavior and associated sound production by the Pacific bottlenosed porpoise (Tursiops gilli Dall). Bull. Sth. Calif. Acad. Sci. **61**, 217–226 (1962).

[202] Ewert, J.-P.: Quantitative Analyse von Reiz-Reaktionsbeziehungen bei visuellem Auslösen der Beutefang-Wendereaktion der Erdkröte (Bufo bufo L.). Pflügers Arch. **308**, 225–243 (1969).

[203] Ewert, J.-P.: Lokalisation und Identifikation im visuellen System der Wirbeltiere. Fortschr. Zool. **21**, 307–333 (1973).

[204] Ewert, J.-P.: The neural basis of visually guided behavior. Sci. Amer. **230**, 34–42 (1974).

[205] Ewert, J.-P.: Neuro-Ethologie. Einführung in die neurophysiologischen Grundlagen des Verhaltens. Springer Verlag, Berlin, Heidelberg, New York 1976.

[205a] Ewert, J.-P., Borchers, H.-W.: Reaktionscharakteristik von Neuronen aus dem Tectum opticum und subtectum der Erdkröte Bufo bufo (L.). Z. vergl. Physiol. **71**, 165–189 (1971).

[206] Ewert, J.-P.: The visual system of the toad: behavioral and physiological studies on a pattern recognition system. From: The Amphibian Visual System. A Multidisciplinary approach. Academic Press, INC. New York, San Francisco, London 1976.

[207] Ewer, D. W., Bursell, E.: A note on the classification of elementary behaviour patterns. Behaviour 3, 40–47 (1950).

[208] Ewert, J.-P., Hock, F. J., v. Wietersheim, A.: Thalamus, Praetectum, Tectum: Retinale Topographie und physiologische Interaktionen bei der Kröte Bufo bufo (L.). J. comp. Physiol. 92, 343–356 (1974).

[209] Fabre, J.: Souvenirs entomologiques. Série 1, 2, 3, 4. Paris, 23e éd. (1919–1922).

[210] Farkas, S. R., Shorey, H. H.: Mechanisms of orientation to a distant pheromone source. In: Pheromones, pp. 81–95. Ed.: M. C. Birch. North-Holland, Amsterdam 1974.

[211] Feinleib, M. E., Curry, G. M.: The nature of the photoreceptor in phototaxis. Hdb. Sens. Physiol. I, Receptor mechanisms. Ed.: W. Loewenstein. Springer Verlag, Berlin, Heidelberg, New York 1971.

[212] Fernandez, C., Goldberg, J. M.: Physiology of peripheral neurons innervating semicircular canals of the squirrel monkey, Part II. Response to sinusoidal stimulation and dynamics of peripheral vestibular system. J. Neurophysiol. 34, 661–675 (1971).

[213] Fernandez, C., Goldberg, J. M.: Physiology of peripheral neurons innervating otolith organs of the squirrel monkey. I. Response to static tilts and to long-duration centrifugal force. J. Neurophysiol. 39, 970 (1976a).

[214] Fernandez, C., Goldberg, J. M.: Physiology of peripheral neurons innervating otolith organs of the squirrel monkey. II. Directional selectivity and force-response relations. J. Neurophysiol. 39, 985–995 (1976b).

[215] Fernandez, C., Goldberg, J. M.: Physiology of peripheral neurons innervating otolith organs of the squirrel monkey. III. Response Dynamics. J. Neurophysiol. 39, 996 (1976c).

[216] Fernandez, C., Goldberg, J. M., Abend W. K.: Response to static tilts of peripheral neurons innervating otolith organs of the squirrel monkey. J. Neurophysiol. 35, 978–997 (1972).

[217] Fischer, M. H.: Messende Untersuchungen über die Gegenrollung der Augen und die Lokalisation der scheinbaren Vertikalen bei seitlicher Neigung des Gesamtkörpers bis zu 360°. II. Mitteilung: Untersuchungen an Normalen. Graef. Arch. 123, 476–508 (1930a).

[218] Fischer, M. H.: Mess. Untersuchungen über die Gegenrollung der Augen und der Lokalis der scheinbaren Vertikalen bei seitl. Neigung des Körpers, Kopfes u. Stammes. III. Mitteilung: Untersuchungen an einem Ertaubten mit Funktionsuntüchtigkeit beider Vestibularapparate und einem einseitig Labyrinthlosen. Graef. Arch. 123, 509–531 (1930b).

[219] Fischer, M. H., Kornmüller, A. E.: Der Schwindel. In: Hdb. norm. path. Physiol. 15/1, 422–494. Hrsg.: A. Bethe. G. v. Bergmann, G. Embden, A. Ellinger. Springer Verlag, Berlin, Heidelberg, New York 1930.

[220] Fischer, M. H., Kornmüller, A. E.: Egozentrische Lokalisation 2. Mitt. Optische Richtungslokalisation beim vestibulären Nystagmus. J. Psychol. Neurol. 41, 383 (1930/31).

[221] Fitger, C.: Tactile-Kinesthetic Space estimation. The Influence of gravity. Psychol. Res. 39, 113–135 (1976).

[222] Flock, Åke: Structure of the macula utriculi with special reference to directional interplay of sensory responses as revealed by morphological polarization. J. Cell Biol. 22, 413–431 (1964).

[223] Flock, Å., Flock, B., Murray E.: Studies on the sensory hairs of receptor cells in the inner ear. Acta Oto-laryngol. 83, 85–91 (1977).

[224] Flock, Å., Goldstein, M. H.: Cupular movement and nerve impulse response in the isolated semicircular canal. Brain Res. 157, 11–19 (1978).

[225] Fitger, C.: persönliche Mitteilung, unveröffentl. Daten (1977).

[226] Flügge, Ch.: Geruchliche Raumorientierung von Drosophila melanogaster. Z. vergl. Physiol. 20, 464–499 (1933/34).

[227] Fluur, E., Mellström, A.: Utricular stimulation and oculomotor reactions. The Laryngoscope 80, 1701–1712 (1970).

[228] Fluur, E., Mellström, A.: Saccular stimulation and oculomotor reactions. The Laryngoscope 80, 1713–1721 (1970).

[229] Foley, J. M.: Primary distance perception. In: Hdb. Sens. Physiol. **VIII**, 181–213. Eds.: R. Held, H. W. Leibowitz, H.-L. Teuber. Springer Verlag, Berlin, Heidelberg, New York 1978.

[230] Fraenkel, G. S., Gunn, D. L.: The orientation of animals. Oxford University Press, 1940. 2nd. Ed.: Dover Publ., Inc. New York 1961.

[231] Franzisket, L.: Untersuchungen zur Spezifität und Kumulierung der Erregungsfähigkeit und zur Wirkung einer Ermüdung in der Afferenz bei Wischbewegungen des Rückenmarksfrosches. Z. vergl. Physiol. **34**, 525–538 (1953).

[232] Fredrickson, J. M., Kornhuber, H. H., Schwarz, D. W. F.: Cortical projections of the vestibular nerve. In: Hdb. of Sensory Physiol. **VI**/1, 565–582. Ed.: H. H. Kornhuber. Springer Verlag, Berlin, Heidelberg, New York 1974.

[233] v. Frisch, K.: Über den Gehörsinn der Fische. Biol. Rev. **11**, 210–246 (1936).

[234] v. Frisch, K.: Gelöste und ungelöste Rätsel der Bienensprache. Naturwiss. **35**, 12-23, 38–43 (1948).

[235] v. Frisch, K.: Tanzsprache und Orientierung der Bienen. Springer Verlag, Berlin, Heidelberg, New York 1965.

[236] v. Frisch, K., Lindauer, M.: Über die „Mißweisungen" bei den richtungsweisenden Tänzen der Bienen. Naturwiss. **18**, 585–594 (1961).

[237] v. Frisch, K., Stetter, H.: Untersuchungen über den Sitz des Gehörsinnes bei der Elritze. Z. vergl. Physiol. **17**, 697–797 (1932).

[238] Fromme, H. G.: Untersuchungen über das Orientierungsvermögen nächtlich ziehender Kleinvögel, Erithacus rubecula, Sylvia communis. Z. Tierpsychol. **18**, 205–220 (1961).

[239] Gacek, R. R.: The course and central termination of first order neurons supplying vestibular endorgans in the cat. Acta Oto-laryngol. Suppl. **254**, 1–66 (1969).

[240] Gacek, R. R.: Morphological Aspects of the Efferent Vestibular System. In: Hdb. Sens. Physiol. **VI**/14. Ed.: H. H. Kornhuber. Springer Verlag, Berlin, Heidelberg, New York 1974.

[241] Galambos, R., Griffin, D. R.: The supersonic cries of bats. Anat. Rec. **78**, 95 (1940).

[242] Galambos, R., Griffin, D. R.: Obstacle avoidance by flying bats; the cries of bats. J. Exp. Zool. **89**, 475–90 (1942).

[243] Gaze, R. M.: The representation of the retina on the optic lobe of the frog. Quarterly J. Exp. Physiol. **43**, 209–214 (1958).

[244] Gaze, R. M.: The formation of nerve connections. Academic Press, London, New York 1970.

[245] Gaze, R. M., Jacobson, M.: The projection of the binocular visual field on the optic tecta of the frog. J. Exp. Physiol. **47**, 273–280 (1962).

[246] Gerhardt, H. C., Rheinlaender, J.: Accuracy of Sound Localization in a miniature dendrobatic frog. Am. Nat. submitted 1979.

[247] Gertz, W.: Geruchsdressuren und Reizschwellenbestimmungen an Tritonen. Z. vergl. Physiol. **25**, 389–426 (1938).

[248] Geuze, J. J.: Observations on the function and the structure of the statocysts of Lymnaea stagnalis (L.). Netherl. J. Zool. **18**, 155–204 (1968).

[249] Gewecke, M.: Die Wirkung von Luftströmung auf die Antennen und das Flugverhalten der Blauen Schmeißfliege (Calliphora erythrocephala). Z. vergl. Physiol. **54**, 121–164 (1967).

[250] Gewecke, M.: Bewegungsmechanismus und Gelenkrezeptoren der Antennen von Locusta migratoria L. (Insecta, Orthoptera). Z. Morph. Tiere **71**, 128–149 (1972a).

[251] Gewecke, M.: Antennen und Stirn-Scheitelhaare von Locusta migratoria L. als Luftströmungs-Sinnesorgane bei der Flugsteuerung. J. comp. Physiol. **80**, 57–94 (1972b).

[252] Gewecke, M.: The antennae of insects as aircurrent sense organs and their relationship of the control of flight. In: Exp. Analysis of Insect Behaviour. p. 100–113. Ed.: L. Barton Browne. Springer Verlag, Berlin, Heidelberg, New York 1974.

[253] Gewecke, M.: The influence of the air-current sense organs on the flight behaviour of Locusta migratoria. J. comp. Physiol. **103**, 79–95 (1975).

[254] Gewecke, M.: Control of flight in relation to the air in Locusta migratoria (Insecta, Orthoptera). J. Physiol., Paris, **73**, 581–592 (1977).

[255] Gewecke, M., Philippen, J.: Control of the horizontal flightcourse by air-current sense organs in Locusta migratoria. Physiol. Entomol. **3**, 43–52 (1978).

[256] Gewecke, M., Woike, M.: Breast feathers as an air-current sense organ for the control of flight behaviour in a songbird (Carduelis spinus). Z. Tierpsychol. **47**, 293–298 (1978).

[257] Gibson, J. J.: The perception of the visual world. Ed.: L. Carmichael, Houghton Mifflin Company, Boston; The Riverside Press Cambridge, Mass. 1950.

[258] Gibson, J. J.: The senses considered as perceptual systems. Houghton Mifflin Company, Boston, New York, Atlanta, Geneva (III.), Dallas, Palo Alto (1966). Die Sinne und der Prozess der Wahrnehmung. Übers.: J. und E. Köhler, H. Huber, Bern, Stuttgart, Wien 1973.

[259] Gibson, J. J., Mowrer, O. H.: Determinants of the perceived vertical and horizontal. Psychol. Rev. **45**, 300 (1938).

[260] Giesen, M., Klinke, R.: Die Richtcharakteristik primärer Afferenzen des Otolithenorgans bei intakter efferenter Innervation. Acta Oto-laryngol. **67**, 49–56 (1969).

[261] Glenn, J. H.: Pilot's flight report. Results of the first U.S. manned orbital space flight, Febr. 20, 1962. Manned Spacecraft Center National Aeronautics and Space Administration Government Printing Office, Washington 1962.

[262] Goldberg, J. M., Brown, P. B.: Functional organization of the dog superior olivary complex: an anatomical and electrophysiological study. J. Neurophysiol. **31**, 639–656 (1968).

[263] Goldberg, J. M., Fernandez, C.: Physiology of peripheral neurons innervating semicircular canals of the squirrel monkey. Part I. Resting discharge and response to constant angular acceleration. II. Variations among units in their discharge properties. J. Neurophysiol. **34**, 635–661, 676–684 (1971).

[264] Gordon, B. J.: Receptive fields in deep layers of cat superior colliculus. J. Neurophysiol. **36**, 157–178 (1973).

[265] Goris, R. C., Nomoto, M.: Infrared reception in oriental crotaline snakes. Comp. Biochem. Physiol. **23**, 879–892 (1967).

[266] Goris, R. C., Terashima, Shin-Ichi: Central response to infra-red stimulation of the pit receptors in a crotaline snake, Trimeresurus flavoviridis. J. Exp. Biol. **58**, 59–76 (1973).

[267] Görner, P.: Die optische und kinästhetische Orientierung der Trichterspinne Agelena labyrinthica (Cl.). Z. vergl. Physiol. **41**, 111–153 (1958).

[268] Görner, P.: Untersuchungen zur Morphologie und Elektrophysiologie des Seitenlinienorgans vom Krallenfrosch (Xenopus laevis Daudin). Z. vergl. Physiol. **47**, 316–338 (1963).

[269] Görner, P.: Über die Koppelung der optischen Orientierung und kinästhetischen Orientierung bei den Trichterspinnen Agelena labyrinthica (Clerck) und Agelena gracilens C. L. Koch. Z. vergl. Physiol. **53**, 253–276 (1966).

[270] Görner, P.: Beispiele einer Orientierung ohne richtende Außenreize. Fortschr. Zool. **21** (1973).

[271] Görner, P.: Source localization with labyrinth and lateral line in the clawed toad (Xenopus laevis). From: Sound reception in fish. Eds.: A. Schuijf and A. D. Hawkins. Elsevier Sci. Publ. Comp. Amsterdam, Oxford, New York 1976.

[272] Görner, P., Andrews, P.: Trichobothrien, ein Ferntastsinnesorgan bei Webespinnen. Z. vergl. Physiol. **64**, 301–317 (1969).

[273] Gould, J. L., Henery, M., Mac Leod, M. C.: Communication of direction by the honey bee. Science **169**, 544–554 (1972).

[274] Graybiel, A., Clark, B.: Perception of the horizontal or vertical with the head upright, on the side, and inverted under static conditions, and during exposure to centripetal force. Aerospace Med. **33**, 147–155 (1962).

[275] Graybiel, A., Kellogg, R. S.: The inversion illusion in parabolic flight: Its probable dependence on otolith function. Aerospace Med. **38**, 1099–1102 (1967).

[276] Graybiel, A., Miller, E. F. II, Newsom, B. D., Kennedy, R. S.: The effect of water immersion on perception of the oculogravic illusion in normal and labyrinthine-defective subjects. Acta otolaryngol. **65**, 599–610 (1968).

[277] Griffin, D. R.: Bird navigation. Biol. Rev. **27**, 359 (1952).

[278] Griffin, D. R.: Listening in the dark. Yale Univ. Press, Inc. (1958). 2nd Ed.: Dover Publications, New York 1974.

[279] Griffin, D. R.: Echo-Ortung der Fledermäuse, insbesondere beim Fangen fliegender Insekten. Naturwiss. Rdschau **15**, 169–173 (1962).

[280] Griffin, D. R.: The physiology and geophysics of bird navigation. Quart. Rev. Biol. **44**, 255 (1969).

[281] Grimsehl-Tomaschek: Lehrbuch der Physik, II. B. G. Teubner, Leipzig, Berlin 1943.

[282] Groot, C.: On the orientation of young sockeye salmon (Oncorhynchus nerka) during their seaward migration out of lakes. Behaviour Suppl. **14**, 1–198 (1965).

[283] Grünwald, A.: Untersuchungen zur Orientierung der Weißzahnspitzmäuse (Soricidae, Crocidurinae). Z. vergl. Physiol. **65**, 191–217 (1969).

[284] Guedry, F. E.: Psychophysics of vestibular sensation. In: Hdb. Sens. Physiol. **VI**/2, 3–154. Ed.: H. H. Kornhuber. Springer Verlag, Berlin, Heidelberg, New York 1974.

[285] Guedry, F. E., Mortensen, C. E., Nelson, J. B., Correia, M. J.: A comparison of nystagmus and turning sensations generated by active and passive turning. In: Vestibular Mechanisms in Health and Disease, p. 317–325. Ed.: J. D. Hood. Academic Press, London, New York, S. Francisco 1978.

[286] Gunn, D. L., Comment on Koehler, O.: Die Analyse der Taxisanteile instinktartigen Verhaltens. In: Physiol. Mechanisms in animal behaviour, 269-304. Symp. Soc. exp. Biol. **4**, Cambridge, Univ. Press 1950.

[287] Gunn, D. L.: The meaning of the term 'Klinokinesis'. Anim. Behav. **23**, 409–412 (1975).

[288] Gurnee, H.: Thresholds of vertical movement of the body. J. exp. Psychol. **17**, 270–285 (1934).

[289] Gwinner, E.: Wirkungen des Mondlichts auf die Nachtaktivität von Zugvögeln. Lotsenversuche an Erithacus rubecula und Ph. phoenicurus. Experientia **23**, 227 (1967).

[290] Gwinner, E.: Endogenous timing factors in bird migration. In Animal Orientation and Navigation, 321–38. Eds.: S. R. Galler et al. NASA, Washington, DC. 1971.

[291] Gwinner, E.: Orientierung. In: E. Schüz, Grundriß der Vogelzugskunde, pp. 299–348, Parey, Berlin, Hamburg 1971.

[292] Gwinner, E.: Circannual rhythms in bird migration. Ann. Rev. Ecol., Syst. **8**, 381–405 (1977).

[293] Gwinner, E., Biebach, H.: Endogene Kontrolle der Mauser und der Zugdisposition bei südfinnischen und südfranzösischen Neuntötern (Lanius collurio). Die Vogelwarte **29**, 1077: 56–63 (1977).

[294] Gwinner, E., Wiltschko, W.: Endogenously controlled changes in migratory direction of the garden warbler, Sylvia borin. J. comp. Physiol. **125**, 267–273 (1978).

[294a] van Haaften, J. L., Verwey, J.: The role of water currents in the orientation of Marine Animals. Extrait Arch. Neerl. Zool. **13**, 493–499 (1960).

[295] v. Hagen, O.: Nachweis einer kinästhetischen Orientierung bei Uca rapax. Z. Morph. Ökol. Tiere **58**, 301–320 (1967).

[296] Hahn, E.: Ferntastsinn und Strömungssinn beim augenlosen Höhlenfisch Anoptichthys jordani im Vergleich zu anderen Teleostiern. Dissertationsschrift 1960.

[297] Hand, W. G., Davenport, D.: The experimental analysis of phototaxis and photokinesis in flagellates. In: Photobiology of microorganisms, p. 253–383. Ed.: P. Halldal. Wiley, London 1970.

[298] Hangartner, W.: Spezifität und Inaktivierung des Spurpheromons von Lasius fuliginosus Latr. und Orientierung der Arbeiterinnen im Duftfeld. Z. vergl. Physiol. **57**, 103–136 (1967).

[299] Hangartner, W.: Structure and variability of the individual odor trail in Solenopsis geminata Fabr. (Hymenoptera, Formicidae). Z. vergl. Physiol. **62**, 111–120 (1969).

[300] Hans, H., Thorsteinson, A. J.: The influence of physical factors and host plant odour on the induction and termination of dispersal flights in Sitona cylindricollis Fahr. Entomol. exp. appl. **4**, 165–177 (1961).

[301] Hara, T. J.: Chemoreception. In: Fish Physiology, Eds.: W. S. Hoar and D. J. Randall. Vol. V. Sensory systems and electric organs. Academic Press, New York, London 1971.

[302] Harden Jones, F. R.: Fish migration. London: Edward Arnold Ltd. 1968.

[303] Harrison, J. M., Howe, M. E.: Anatomy of the afferent auditory nervous system of mammals. In: Hdb. of Sensory Physiol. **V**/1, 283–336. Eds.: W. D. Keidel and W. D. Neff. Springer Verlag, Berlin, Heidelberg, New York 1974.

[304] Hartwick, R., Kiepenheuer, J., Schmidt-Koenig, K.: Further experiments on the olfactory hypothesis of pigeon homing. In: Animal Migration, Navigation, and Homing. Symp. Univ. Tübingen, 17.–20. 8. 1977. Eds.: K. Schmidt-Koenig, W. T. Keeton. Springer Verlag, Berlin, Heidelberg, New York 1978.

[305] Haskell, P. T., Paskin, M. W. J., Moorhouse, J. E.: Laboratory observations on factors affecting the movements of hoppers of the desert locust. J. Insect. Physiol. **8**, 53–78 (1962).

[306] Hasler, A. D.: Underwater Guideposts Homing of Salmon. The University of Wisconsin Press Madison, Milwaukee, and London 1966.

[307] Hasler, A. D., Scholz, A. T.: Olfactory imprinting in Coho Salmon (Oncorhynchus kisutch). In: Animal Migration, Navigation and Homing. Symp. Univ. Tübingen, 17.–20. 8. 1977. Eds.: K. Schmidt-Koenig & W. T. Keeton, Springer Verlag, Berlin, Heidelberg, New York 1978.

[308] Hassenstein, B.: Ommatidienraster und afferente Bewegungsintegration. Z. vergl. Physiol. **33**, 301–326 (1951).

[309] Hassenstein, B.: Abbildende Begriffe. Verh. Dtsch. Zool. Ges. Tübingen 197–202 (1954).

[310] Hassenstein, B.: Über die Wahrnehmung der Bewegung von Figuren und unregelmäßigen Helligkeitsmustern. Z. vergl. Physiol. **40**, 556–92 (1958).

[311] Hassenstein, B.: Optokinetische Wirksamkeit bewegter periodischer Muster. Z. Naturforsch. **14b**, 659–74 (1959).

[312] Hassenstein, B.: Kybernetik und biologische Forschung. Akad. Verlagsges. Athenaion Frankfurt/Main 1966.

[313] Hassenstein, B., Reichardt, W.: Systemtheoretische Analyse der Zeit-, Reihenfolgen- und Vorzeichenauswertung bei der Bewegungsperzeption des Rüsselkäfers Chlorophanus. Z. Naturforsch. **11b**, 513–24 (1956).

[314] Hatai, S., Abe, N.: The responses of the catfish, Parasilurus asotus, to earthquakes. Proc. imp. Acad. Japan **8**, 375–378 (1932).

[315] Hatai, S., Kokubo, S., Abe, N.: The earth currents in relation to the responses of catfish. Proc. imp. Acad. Japan **8**, 478–481 (1932).

[316] Hediger, H., Heusser, H.: Zum „Schießen" des Schützenfisches, Taxotes jaculatrix. Natur und Volk **91**, 237–243 (1961).

[317] Heiligenberg, W.: „Electromotor" response in the electric fish Eigenmannia (Rhamphichthyidae, Gymnotoidei). Nature **243**, 301–302 (1973).

[318] Heiligenberg, W.: Principles of electrolocating and jamming avoidance in electric fish. Studies of Brain Function **1**, Springer Verlag, Berlin, Heidelberg, New York 1977.

[319] Hein, A., Held, R.: Dissociation of the visual placing response into elicited and guided components. Science **158**, 390–392 (1967).

[319a] Heisenberg, M., Wolf, R.: On the Fine Structure of Yaw Torque in Visual Flight Orientation of Drosophila Melanogaster. J. comp. Physiol. **130**, 113–130 (1979).

[320] Held, R.: Two modes of processing. Spatially distributed visual stimulation. In: The Neurosciences, II. Study program, Ed.: F. O. Schmitt. The Rockefeller Univ. Press, New York 1970.

[321] Held, R., Bauer, J. A.: Visually guided reaching in infant monkeys after restricted rearing. Science **155**, 718–720 (1967).

[322] Held, R., Bossom, J.: Neonatal deprivation and adult arrangement. J. Comp. and Physiol. Psychol. **54**, 33–37 (1961).

[323] Held, R., Dichgans, J., Bauer, J.: Characteristics of moving visual scenes influencing spatial orientation. Vision Res. **15**, 357–365 (1975).

[324] Held, R., Freedman, S. J.: Plasticity in human sensorimotor control. Science **142**, 455–462 (1963).

[325] Held, R., Hein, A.: Movement-produced stimulation in the development of visually guided behaviour. J. Comp. and Physiol. Psychol. **56**, 872–876 (1963).

[326] v. Helmholtz, H.: Hdb. d. physiologischen Optik. Hamburg, Leipzig 1896.

[327] v. Helversen, O., Edrich, W.: Der Polarisationsempfänger im Bienenauge: ein Ultraviolettrezeptor. J. comp. Physiol. **94**, 33–47 (1974).

[328] Hemmings, C. C.: Olfaction and vision in fish schooling. J. Exp. Biol. **45**, 499–464 (1966).

[329] Henke, K.: Forschung und Lehre heute. Zum 70. Geb. von A. Kühn. In: A. Kühn, 5. Biol. Jahresheft, Hrsg.: G. Grasse, Verband Dtsch. Biologen e. V. Iserlohn 1972.

[330] Heran, H., Lindauer, M.: Windkompensation und Seitenwindkorrektur der Bienen beim Flug über Wasser. Z. vergl. Physiol. **47**, 39–55 (1963).

[331] Heron, W., Doane, B. K., Scott, T. H.: Visual disturbances after prolonged perceptual isolation. Canad. J. Psychol. **10**, 13–18 (1956).

[332] Herrnkind, W. F.: Orientation in shore-living Arthropods, especially the sand fiddler crab. In: Behav. Mar. Anim. 1–59. Ed.: H. E. Winn and B. C. Olla 1972.

[333] Herrnkind, W., Kanciruk, P.: Mass migration of spiny lobster, Panulirus argus (Crustacea: Palinuridae): Synopsis and orientation. In: Animal Migration, Navigation and Homing, p. 430–439. Symp. Univ. Tübingen, 17.– 20. 8. 1977. Eds.: K. Schmidt-Koenig, W. T. Keeton. Springer Verlag, Berlin, Heidelberg, New York 1978.

[334] Herter, K.: Tierphysiologie. I. Stoffwechsel und Bewegung. Sammlung Göschen. Das Wissen d. Welt. Walter de Gruyter & Co., Berlin, Leipzig 1927.

[335] Hess, E. H.: Space perceptions in the chick. Scient. Amer. **195**, 71–76 (1956).

[336] Hess, W. R.: Diencephalon; Autonomic and Extrapyramidal Functions. Grune & Stratton, New York 1954.

[337] Hess, W. R., Bürgi, S. Bucher, V.: Motorische Funktion des Tektal- und Tegmentalgebietes. Psychiatrie u. Neurol. **112**, 1–52 (1946).

[338] Heusser, H.: Den Taxien gleichende Spontanwendungen. Z. Tierpsychol. **26**, 623–28 (1969).

[339] Hill, K. G.: Carrier frequency as a factor in phonotactic behaviour of female crickets (Teleogryllus commodus). J. comp. Physiol. **93**, 7–18 (1974).

[340] Hill, K. G., Boyan, G. S.: Sensitivity to frequency and direction of sound in the auditory system of crickets (Gryllidae). J. comp. Physiol. **121**, 79–97 (1977).

[341] Hillman, D. E.: Cupular structure and its receptor relationship. Brain Behav. Evol. **10**, 52–68 (1974).

[342] Hingston, R. W. G.: Instinct and intelligence. McMillan & Co., New York 1929.

[343] Hixson, W. C., Niven, J. I., Correia, M. J.: Kinematics nomenclature for psychological accelerations, Monogr. **14**, Pensacola, Fla.: Naval Aerospace Medical Institute 1969.

[344] van der Hoeve, J., De Kleijn, A.: Tonische Labyrinthreflexe auf die Augen. Pflügers Arch. ges. Physiol. **169**, 241–262 (1917).

[345] Hoffmann, G.: Experimentelle u. theoretische Analyse eines adaptiven Orientierungsverhaltens: Die „optimale" Suche der Wüstenassel Hemilepistus reaumuri, Audouin und Savigny (Crustacea, Isopoda, Oniscoidea) nach ihrer Höhle. Dissertation, vorgelegt am 9. 3. 1978. Würzburg 1978.

[346] Hofmann, F. B.: Die Lehre vom Raumsinn des Auges. Aus: Hdb. d. gesamten Augenheilkunde (Graefe/Saemisch). 2. Aufl. Bd. III (Physiologische Optik), Kap. XIII - Teil 1 (1920) u. Teil 2 (1925) Verl. J. Springer, Berlin. Reprint: Springer Verlag, Berlin, Heidelberg, New York 1970.

[347] Hoffmann, K.: Versuche zu der im Richtungsfinden der Vögel enthaltenen Zeitschätzung. Z. Tierpsychol. **11**, 453–475 (1954).

[348] Hölldobler, B.: Recruitment behavior in Camponotus socius (Hym. Formicidae). Z. vergl. Physiol. **75**, 123–142 (1971).

[349] Hölldobler, B.: Chemische Strategie beim Nahrungserwerb der Diebsameise (Solenopsis fugax Latr.) und der Pharaoameise (Monomorium pharaonis L.) Oecologia (Berl.) **11**, 371–380 (1973a).

[350] Hölldobler, B.: Zur Ethologie der chemischen Verständigung bei Ameisen. Nova Acta Leopoldina **37**, 259–292 (1973b).

[351] Hölldobler, B.: Recruitment behavior, home range orientation and territoriality in Harvester ants, Pogonomyrmex. Behav. Ecol. Sociobiol. **1**, 3–44 (1976a).

[352] Hölldobler, B.: Communication in social Hymenoptera. In: How animals communicate. Ed.: Th. A. Sebeok. Indiana Univ. Press, Bloomington 1976b.

[353] Hölldobler, B., Möglich, M., Maschwitz, U.: Communication by tandem running in the ant Camponotus sericeus. J. comp. Physiol. **90**, 105–127 (1974).

[354] Hölldobler, B., Stanton, R. C., Markl, H.: Recruitment and food-retrieving behavior in Novomessor (Formicidae, Hymenoptera) I. Chemical Signals. Behav. Ecol. Sociobiol. **4**, 163–181 (1978).

[355] Hölldobler, B., Wilson, E. O.: Colony-specific territorial pheromone in the african weaver ant Oecophylla longinoda (Latreille). Proc. Natl. Acad. Sci. USA **74**, 2072–2075 (1977).

[356] v. Holst, E.: Über den Lichtrückenreflex bei Fischen. Pubbl. Staz. Zool. Napoli **15**, 143–158 (1935).

[357] v. Holst, E.: Vom Wesen der Ordnung im Zentralnervensystem. Naturwiss. **25**, 625–631, 641–647 (1937).

[358] v. Holst, E.: Quantitative Messung von Stimmungen im Verhalten der Fische. Symp. Soc. Exp. Biol. **4**, 143–172. Anim. Behav. (1950a).

[359] v. Holst, E.: Die Tätigkeit des Statolithenapparats im Wirbeltierlabyrinth. Naturwiss. **12**, 265–272 (1950b).

[360] v. Holst, E.: Einfluß der nichtbelichteten Retina auf das Gleichgewichtsverhalten von Fischen. Naturwiss. **41**, 507–508 (1954).

[361] v. Holst, E.: Neue Gedanken und Versuche zur Sensomobilität. Aeta Neurovegetativa **12**, 337–345 (1955).

[362] v. Holst, E.: ZNS: Die Funktionsstruktur des Zwischenhirns (ZH). Fortschr. Zool. **2**, (1958).

[363] v. Holst, E., Mittelstaedt, H.: Das Reafferenzprinzip (Wechselwirkungen zwischen ZNS und Peripherie). Naturwiss. **37**, 464–476 (1950).

[364] v. Holst, E., Schoen, L.: Der Einfluß mechanisch veränderter Augenstellungen auf die Richtungslokalisation bei Fischen. Z. vergl. Physiol. **36**, 433–442 (1954).

[365] v. Holst, E., v. St. Paul, U.: Vom Wirkungsgefüge der Triebe. Naturwiss. **47**, 409–422 (1960).

[366] v. Holst, E., Kaiser, H., Schoen, L., Roebig, G., Göldner, G.: Die Arbeitsweise des Statolithenapparates bei Fischen. Z. vergl. Physiol. **32**, 60–120 (1950).

[367] Holzapfel, M.: Die nicht-optische Orientierung der Trichterspinne Agelena labyrinthica (CL.). Z. vergl. Physiol. **20**, 55–116 (1934.)

[368] Horn, E.: The contribution of different receptors to gravity orientation in insects. Fortschr. Zool. **23**, 1–17 (1975).

[369] Horn, E., Lang, H.-G.: Positional head reflexes and the role of the prosternal organ in the walking fly, Calliphora erythrocephala. J. comp. Physiol. **126**, 137–146 (1978).

[370] Horn, E., Rayer, B.: Compensation of vestibular lesions in relation to development. Naturwiss. **65**, 441 (1978).

[371] v. Hornbostel, E. M., Wertheimer, M.: Über die Wahrnehmung der Schallrichtung. Akad. Wiss. Berlin, 388–396 (1920).

[372] Hornby, A. S., Gatenby, E. V., Wakefield, H.: The advanced learner's dictionary of current English. Oxford Univ. Press, London 1970.

[373] Horridge, G. A.: Relations between nerves and cilia in ctenophores. Amer. Zoologist **5**, 357–375 (1965).

[374] Horridge, G. A.: Primitive examples of gravity receptors and their evolution. In: Gravity and the organism, 203–222. Eds.: S. A. Gordon & M. J. Cohen. The University of Chicago Press, Chicago and London 1971.

[375] Horridge, G. A., Boulton, P. S.: Prey detection by Chaetognatha via a vibration sense. Proc. Roy. Soc. Lond. Ser. B **168**, 413–19 (1967).

[376] Howard, I. P., Templeton, W. B.: Human spatial orientation. Wiley, New York 1966.

[377] Howland, H. C.: Semicircular canal and otolithic organ function in free-swimming fish. In: Gravity and the organism, 283–291. Eds.: S. A. Gordon & M. J. Cohen. The Univ. of Chicago Press, Chicago and London 1971.

[378] Hubel, D. H.: The visual cortex of the brain. Scient. Amer. **168**, Nov. 1963.

[379] Hubel, D. H., Wiesel, T. N.: Receptive fields, binocular interaction and functional architecture in the cat's visual cortex. J. Physiol. **160**, 106–154 (1962).

[380] Hubel, D. H., Wiesel, T. N.: Shape and arrangement of columns in cat's striate cortex. J. Physiol. **165**, 559–568 (1963).

[381] Hubel, D. H., Wiesel, T. N.: Receptive field studies in the visual system of newborn and monocular deprived kitten. Acta Psychol. **23**, 304–306 (1964).

[382] Hubel, D. H., Wiesel, T. N.: Receptive fields and functional architecture in two nonstriate visual areas (18 and 19) of the cat. J. Neurophysiol. **28**, 229–289 (1965).

[383] Hubel, D. H., Wiesel, T. N.: The period of susceptibility to the physiological effects of unilateral eye closure in kittens. J. Physiol. **206**, 419–436 (1970).

[384] Hubel, D. H., Wiesel, T. N.: Stereoscopic vision in macaque monkey. Nature **225**, 41–42 (1970).

[385] Huber, F.: Sitz und Bedeutung nervöser Zentren für Instinkthandlungen beim Männchen von Gryllus campestris L. Z. Tierpsychol. **12**, 12–48 (1955).

[386] Huber, F.: Untersuchungen über die Funktion des Zentralnervensystems und insbesondere des Gehirns bei der Fortbewegung und der Lauterzeugung der Grillen. Z. vergl. Physiol. **44**, 60–132 (1960).

[387] Huber, F.: Nervöse Grundlagen der akustischen Kommunikation bei Insekten. Aus: Rheinisch-Westf. Akad. Wiss. Westdeutscher Verlag Opladen (1970).

[388] Humphrey, N. K.: What the frog's eye tells the monkey's brain. Brain, Behavior & Evol. **3**, 324–337 (1970).

[389] Humphrey, N. K., Weiskrantz, L.: Vision in monkeys after removal of the striate cortex. Nature **215**, 595–597 (1967).

[390] van Iersel, J. J. A.: On the orientation of Bembix rostrata L. Trans. Ninth. Int. Congr. Ent. **1**, 384–393 (1952).

[391] van Iersel, J. J. A., van den Assem, J.: Aspects of orientation in the diggerwasp Bembix rostrata. Anim. Behav. **1**, 145–162 (1966).

[392] van Iersel, J. J. A.: The extension of the orientation system of Bembix rostrata as used in the vicinity of its nest. In: Function and Evolution in Behaviour. Eds.: Baerends, Beer, Manning. Clarendon Press, Oxford 1975.

[393] Igarashi, M.: Dimensional study of the vestibular end organ apparatus. Sec. Symp. on the role of the vestibular organs. Moffet Field 1966, Nat. Aeron. Space Administr., Washington 1966.

[394] Ioalé, P., Papi, F., Fiaschi, V., Baldaccini, N. E.: Pigeon navigation: effects upon homing behaviour by reversing wind direction at the loft. J. comp. Physiol. **128**, 285–295 (1978).

[395] Ilse, D.: Über den Farbensinn der Tagfalter. Z. vergl. Physiol. **8**, 658–692 (1929).

[396] Ishay, J., Sadeh, D.: Geotropism of hornet comb construction under persistent acceleration. Behav. Ecol. Sociobiol. **2**, 119–129 (1977).

[397] Istomina-Tsvetkova, K. P.: Contribution to the study of trophic relations in adult worker bees. XVII. Internat. Beekeeping Congr. Bologna-Roma 1958, **2**, 361–368 (1960).

[398] Ito, T., Sanada, Y.: Location of receptors for righting reflexes acting upon the body in primates. Jap. J. Physiol. **15**, 235–242 (1965).

[399] Jacobs-Jessen, U. F.: Zur Orientierung der Hummeln und einiger anderer Hymenopteren. Z. vergl. Physiol. **41**, 597–641 (1959).

[400] Jakobs, W.: Über das Labyrinth der Pleuronectiden. Zool. Jahrb. Allg. Zool. **44**, 523–574 (1928).

[401] Jander, R.: Die optische Richtungsorientierung der roten Waldameise (Formica rufa L.). Z. vergl. Physiol. **40**, 162–238 (1957).

[402] Jander, R.: Menotaxis und Winkeltransponieren bei Köcherfliegen (Trichoptera). Z. vergl. Physiol. **43**, 680–686 (1960).

[403] Jander, R.: Grundleistungen der Licht- und Schwereorientierung von Insekten. Z. vergl. Physiol. **47**, 381–430 (1963).

[404] Jander, R.: Die Hauptentwicklungsstufen der Lichtorientierung bei den tierischen Organismen. Naturwiss. Rndsch. **18**, 318–324 (1965).

[405] Jander, R.: Ein Ansatz zur modernen Elementarbeschreibung der Orientierungshandlung. Z. Tierpsychol. **27**, 771–778 (1970).

[406] Jeffress, L. A.: A place theory of sound localization. J. comp. Physiol. Psychol. **41**, 35–39 (1948).

[407] Jennings, H. S.: Das Verhalten der niederen Organismen unter natürlichen und experimentellen Bedingungen. B. G. Teubner, Leipzig u. Berlin 1910.

[408] Johnson, C. G.: Migration and dispersal of insects by flight. Methuen, London 1969.

[409] Johnson, W. H., Jongkees, L. B. W.: Motion sickness. Part 1. Aetiology and Autonomic effects. Part 2. Some sensory aspects. In: Hdb. Sens. Physiol. **VI**/2, 389–411. Ed.: H. H. Kornhuber. Springer Verlag, Berlin, Heidelberg, New York, 1974.

[410] Jongkees, L. B. W.: Some remarks on the function of the vestibular organ. J. Laryngol. and Otol. **2**, 1–10 (1952).

[411] Jongkees, L. B. W., Groen, J. J.: On directional hearing. J. Laryngol. Otol. **61**, 494–504 (1946).

[412] Julesz, B.: Global stereopsis: Cooperative phenomena in stereoscopic depth perception. In: Hdb. Sens. Physiol. **VIII**, 215–256. Eds.: R. Held, H. W. Leibowitz, H.-L. Teuber. Springer Verlag, Berlin, Heidelberg, New York 1978.

[413] Jung, R., Hassler, R.: The extrapyramidal motor system. Hdb. Physiol.-Neurophysiol. II, Springer Verlag, Berlin, Heidelberg, New York 1960.

[414] Kaiser, W.: A preliminary report on the analysis of the optomotor system of the honey bee – single unit recordings during stimulation with spectral lights. In: Inform. Proc. in the Visual Systems of Arthropods, 167–70. Ed.: R. Wehner 1972.

[415] Kaiser, W.: The relationship between visual movement detection and colour vision in insects. In: The compound eye and vision of insects, 359–377. Ed.: G. A. Horridge. Oxford, Clarendon 1975.

[416] Kaiser, W., Liske, E.: Die optomotorischen Reaktionen von fixiert fliegenden Bienen bei Reizung mit Spektrallichtern. J. comp. Physiol. 89, 391–408 (1974).

[417] Kaiser, W., Seidl, R., Vollmar, J.: The participation of all three colour receptors in the phototactic behaviour of fixed walking honeybees. J. comp. Physiol. 122, 27–44 (1977).

[418] Kalmijn, A. J.: Electro-perception in sharks and rays. Nature 212, 1232–1233 (1966).

[419] Kalmijn, A. J.: The detection of electric fields from inanimate and animate sources other than electric organs. In: Hdb. Sens. Physiol. 3/3, 148–200. Ed.: A. Fessard. Springer Verlag, Berlin, Heidelberg, New York 1974.

[420] Kalmijn, A. J.: The electric and magnetic sense of sharks, skates, and rays. Oceanus 20, 45 (1977).

[421] Kalmijn, A. J.: Experimental evidence of geomagnetic orientation in elasmobranch fishes. In: Animal Migration, Navigation, and Homing. Symp. Univ. Tübingen, 17.–20.8.1977. Eds.: K. Schmidt-Koenig, W. T. Keeton. Springer Verlag, Berlin, Heidelberg, New York 1978.

[422] Kalmijn, A. D., Kolba, C. A., Kalmijn, V.: Orientation of catfish (Ictalurus nebulosus) in strictly uniform electric fields: I. Sensitivity of response. Biol. Bull. 151, 415 (1976).

[423] Kalmijn, V., Kolba, C. A., Kalmijn, A. D.: Orientation of catfish (Ictalurus nebulosus) in strictly uniform electric fields: II. Spatial discrimination. Biol. Bull. 151, 415–416 (1976).

[424] Kalmring, K.: The afferent auditory pathway in the ventral cord of Locusta migratoria (Acrididae). I. Synaptic connectivity and information processing among the auditory neurons of the ventral cord. J. comp. Physiol. 104, 103–141 (1975).

[425] Kalmring, K., Rheinlaender, J., Römer, H.: Akustische Neuronen im Bauchmark von Locusta migratoria. J. comp. Physiol. 80, 325–352 (1972).

[426] Kathariner, L.: Versuche über die Art der Orientierung der Honigbiene. Biol. Zbl. 22, 646 (1903).

[427] Keeton, W. T.: Effects of magnets on pigeon homing. In: Animal orientation and navigation, 579–594. Eds.: Galler, S. R., et al. NASA SP-262, U. S. Govt. Printing Office, Washington, D. C. 1972.

[428] Keeton, W. T.: Magnets Interfere with pigeon homing. Proc. Nat. Acad. Sci. 68, 102–106 (1971).

[429] Keeton, W. T.: Release-site bias as a possible guide to the „map" component in pigeon homing. J. comp. Physiol. 82, 1–16 (1973).

[430] Keeton, W. T.: The orientational and navigational basis of homing in birds. Advances in the study of behavior 5, Acad. Press, New York, San Francisco, London 1974.

[431] Keidel, W. D.: Räuml. Hören, 518-555. Hdb. Psychol. Bd. Allg. Psychologie. I. Der Aufbau des Erkennens, 1. Halbband: Wahrnehmung u. Bewußtsein. Hrsg.: W. Metzger, H. Erke. Verl. f. Psychol., Hogrefe, Göttingen 1966.

[432] Keller, H. U., Wilkinson, P. C., Abercrombie, M., Becker, E. L., Hirsch, J. G., Miller, M. E., Scott Ramsey, W., Zigmond, S. H.: A proposal for the definition of terms related to locomotion of leucocytes and other cells. Clin. exp. Immunol. 27, 377–380 (1977).

[433] Kellogg, W. N., Kohler, R.: Responses of the porpoise to ultrasonic frequencies. Science, 116, 250–252 (1952).

[434] Kellogg, W. N., Kohler, R., Morris, H. N.: Porpoise, sounds as sonar signals. Science, 117, 239–243 (1953).

[435] Kennedy, J. S.: The visual responses of flying mosquitoes. Proc. Zool. Soc., Ser. A, Vol. 109, 221–242 (1940).

[436] Kennedy, J. S.: Classification and nomenclature of animal behaviour. Nature, Lond. 155, 178–179 (1945a).

[437] Kennedy, J. S.: Classification and nomenclature of animal behaviour. Nature, Lond. 156, 754 (1945b).

[438] Kennedy, J. S.: The migration of the desert locust (Schistocerca gregaria Forsk.) I. The behaviour of swarms, II. A Theory of long-range migrations. Phil. Trans. Roy. Soc. Lond. **235**, 163–290 (1951).

[439] Kennedy, J. S.: Behavior as physiology. In: Insects and physiology, 249–265. Eds.: J. W. L. Beament, J. E. Treherne. Oliver & Boyd, Edinburgh and London 1967.

[440] Kennedy, J. S.: Olfactory responses to distant plants and other odor sources. In: Chemical control of Insect behavior: Theory and Application. Eds.: H. H. Shorey, J. J. McKelvej, Jr.. Wiley & Sons, London, New York, Sidney, Toronto 1977.

[441] Kennedy, J. S.: The concepts of olfactory „arrestment" and „attraction". Physiol. Entomology **3**, 91–98 (1978).

[442] Kennedy, J. S.: Brief vom 12. Januar 1979 (a).

[443] Kennedy, D., Davis, W. J.: Organization of invertebrate motor systems. In: Hdb. of Physiology, Sect. I, vol. I, part 2, pp. 1023–1087; Amer. Physiol. Soc., Bethesda, Md. 1977.

[444] Kennedy, J. S., Marsh, D.: Pheromone-regulated anemotaxis in flying moths. Science **184**, 999–1001 (1974).

[445] Kinne, O.: Mammals: Orientation in Space. In: Marine Ecol. II, p. 709–916. Ed.: O. Kinne. J. Wiley & Sons, London, New York, Sydney, Toronto 1975.

[446] Kirmse, W., Lässig, P.: Strukturanalogie zwischen dem System der horizontalen Blickbewegungen der Augen beim Menschen und dem System der Blickbewegungen des Kopfes bei Insekten mit Fixationsreaktionen. Biol. Zentralblatt **90**, 175–193 (1971).

[447] Kirschfeld, K.: Die notwendige Anzahl von Rezeptoren zur Bestimmung der Richtung des elektrischen Vektors linear polarisierten Lichtes. Z. Naturforsch. **276**, 578–579 (1972a).

[448] Kirschfeld, K.: The visual system of Musca: Studies on optics, structure and function. In: Information processing in the visual system of arthropods. Ed.: R. Wehner. Springer Verlag, Berlin, Heidelberg, New York 1972b.

[449] Kirschfeld, K.: Das neurale Superpositionsauge. Fortschr. Zool. **21**, 229–257 (1973).

[450] Kirschfeld, K., Lindauer, M., Martin, H.: Problems of menotactic orientation according to the polarized light of the sky. Z. Naturforsch. **30**, c, 88–90 (1975).

[451] Kleerekoper, H.: Some effects of olfactory stimulation on locomotor patterns in fish. In: Olfaction and Taste II. Pergamon Press, Oxford, New York 1967a.

[452] Kleerekoper, H.: Some aspects of olfaction in fishes with special reference to orientation. Am. Zool. **7**, 385–395 (1967b).

[453] de Kleijn, A., Versteegh, C.: Näheres über die Auslösestellen der Labyrinthreflexe im peripheren Labyrinth. Acta oto-laryngol. (Stockh.) **22**, 327-337 (1935).

[454] Kleint, H.: Versuche über die Wahrnehmung. Z. Psychol. **138**, 1–3 (1936).

[455] Klensch, H.: Die Lokalisation des Schalles im Raum. Naturwiss. **36**, 145–149 (1949).

[456] Klinke, R., Galley, N.: Efferent innervation of vestibular and auditory receptors. Physiological Rev. **54**, 316 (1974).

[457] Klinke, R., Schmidt, C. L.: Efferent influence on the vestibular organ during active movements of the body. Pflüg. Arch. **318**, 325–332 (1970).

[458] Koehler, O.: Beiträge zur Sinnesphysiologie der Süßwasserplanarien. Z. Vergl. Physiol. **16**, 606–754 (1932).

[459] Koehler, O.: Die Analyse der Taxisanteile instinktartigen Verhaltens. Symp. Soc. Exp. Biol. **4**, 269–304, Anim. Behav. (1950).

[460] Kogan, A. B.: The effect of a constant magnetic field on the movement of Paramecia. Biofizika **10**, 322 (1965).

[461] Kohler, I.: Über Aufbau und Wandlungen der Wahrnehmungswelt. Insbesondere über ‚bedingte Empfindungen'. Sitzgsber. Österr. Akad. Wissensch., Phil.-hist. Kl. **227**, (1951).

[462] Kohler, I.: Die Zusammenarbeit der Sinne und das allgemeine Adaptationsproblem. In: Hdb. d. Psychol., Allgem. Psychol. I., Hrsg. W. Metzger, Hofgrefe, Göttingen 1966.

[463] Kokubo, S.: On the behaviour of catfish in response to galvanic stimuli. Sci. Rep. Tohoku Univ. Biol. **9**, 87–96 (1934).

[464] Kolb, E.: Untersuchungen über zentrale Kompensationen und Kompensationsbewegungen einseitig entstateter Frösche. Z. vergl. Physiol. **37**, 136–160 (1955).

[465] Konishi, M.: How the owl tracks its pray. Amer. Scient. **61**, 414–424 (1973).

[466] Kornhuber, H. H.: The vestibular system and the general motor system. In: Hdb. Sens. Physiol. **VI**/2, 581–620. Ed.: H. H. Kornhuber. Springer Verlag. Berlin. Heidelberg. New York 1974.

[467] Koshland, D. E., Jr.: Chemotaxis as a model for sensory systems. Fed. Eur. Biochem. Soc. Lett. **40** (Suppl.): S 3–S 9 (1974).

[468] Kramer, E.: Orientation of the male silkmoth to the sex attractant Bombykol. Olfaction & Taste **V**, 329–335. Academic Press, New York, San Francisco, London (1975).

[469] Kramer, E.: The orientation of walking honey-bees in odour fields with small concentration gradients. Physiol. Entomol. **1**, 27–37 (1976).

[470] Kramer, G.: Sinnesleistung der Seitenlinie von Xenopus. Zool. Jb., Allg. Zool. u. Physiol. **52**, 629–676 (1935).

[471] Kramer, G.: Orientierte Zugaktivität gekäfigter Singvögel. Naturwiss. **37**, 188 (1950).

[472] Kramer, G.: Weitere Analyse der Faktoren, welche die Zugaktivität des gekäfigten Vogels orientieren. Naturwiss. **37**, 377–378 (1950).

[473] Kramer, G.: Experiments on bird orientation and their interpretation. Ibis **99**, 196–227 (1957).

[474] Kramer, G., v. Saint Paul, U.: Stare (Sturnus vulgaris L.) lassen sich auf Himmelsrichtungen dressieren. Naturwiss. **37**, 526–527 (1950).

[475] Krebs, J. R., Davies, N. B. (Eds.): Behavioural Ecology. Blackwell Scientific Publications, Oxford, London, Edinburgh, Melbourne 1978.

[476] Kreidl, A.: Beiträge zur Physiologie des Ohrlabyrinths auf Grund von Versuchen an Taubstummen. Pflügers Archiv **51**, 119–120, 133–150 (1892).

[477] Kreidl, A.: Versuche an Krebsen. Sitzgsber. österr. Akad., Math.-naturwiss. Kl., 3. Abh. **102** (1893).

[478] Kruger, L., Stein, B. E.: Primordial sense organs and the evolution of sensory systems. In: Hdb. of Perception **III**, p. 63–87, Eds.: E. C. Carterette, M. P. Friedman. Academic Press, New York 1973.

[479] Kühn, A.: Versuche über die reflektorische Erhaltung des Gleichgewichts bei Krebsen. Verh. Dtsch. Zool. Ges. Freiburg, 262–277 (1914).

[480] Kühn, A.: Die Orientierung der Tiere im Raum. Gustav Fischer Verlag, Jena 1919.

[481] Kühn, A.: Phototropismus und Phototaxis der Tiere. Hdb. norm. u. path. Physiol. **12**, 17–35 (1929).

[482] Kühn, A.: Autobiographie (bis 1937). Nova Acta Leopoldina **21**, 143, 274–280 (1959).

[483] Kupfermann, I.: Turn alternation in the pill bug (Armadillidium vulgare). Anim. Behav. **14**, 68–72 (1966).

[484] Lackner, J. R.: Induction of illusory self-rotation and nystagmus by a rotating sound-field. Aviation, Space & environ. Med. **48**, 129–131 (1977).

[485] Land, M. F.: Mechanisms of orientation and pattern recognition by jumping spiders (Salticidae). Inform. Proc. in the Visual Systems of Arthropods, Ed.: R. Wehner. Springer Verlag, Berlin, Heidelberg, New York 1972.

[486] Land, M. F.: A comparison of the visual behavior of a predatory arthropod with that of a mammal. In: The Neurosciences, Third Study Program, p. 411–418. Eds.: F. O. Schmitt, F. G. Worden. The M.I.T. Press, Cambridge, Mass., London 1974.

[487] Lang, H.-J.: Über das Lichtrückenverhalten des Guppy (Lebistes reticulatus) in farbigen und farblosen Lichtern. Z. vergl. Physiol. **56**, 296–340 (1967).

[488] Larking, R. P.: Radar observations of behavior of some migrating birds in response to sound broadcast from the ground. In: Animal Migration, Navigation, and Homing. Symp. Univ. Tübingen, 17.–20.8.1977, Eds.: K. Schmidt-Koenig, W. T. Keeton. Springer Verlag, Berlin, Heidelberg, New York 1978.

[489] Larsen, O. N., Michelsen, A.: Biophysics of the ensiferan ear III. The cricket ear as a four-input system. J. Comp. Physiol. **123**, 217–227 (1978).

[490] Lauer, J., Lindauer, M.: Die Beteiligung von Lernprozessen bei der Orientierung. Fortschr. Zool. **21**, 349–370 (1973).

[491] Laverack, M. S.: Responses of cuticular sense organs of the lobster, Homarus vulg. (Crustacea) I. Hairpeg organs as water current receptors. Comp. Biochem. Physiol. **5**, 319–325 (1962).

[492] Laverack, M. S.: Responses of cuticular sense organs of the lobster, Homarus vulg. III. Acticity invoked in sense organs of the carapace. Comp. Biochem. Physiol. **10**, 261–272 (1963).

[493] Lechner-Steinleitner, S.: Interaction of labyrinthine and somatoreceptor inputs as determinants of the subjective vertical. Psychol. Res. **40**, 65–76 (1978).

[494] Lechner-Steinleitner, S., Schöne, H.: Hysteresis in orientation to the vertical (the effect of time of preceding tilt on the subjective vertical). From: Vestibular Mechanisms in Health and Disease. VI. Extraordinary meeting of the Barany Soc. Ed.: J. D. Hood. Academic Press, London, New York, San Francisco 1978.

[495] Lechner-Steinleitner, S., Schöne, H., Wade, N. J.: Perception of the Visual Vertical: Utricular and Somatosensory Contributions. Psychol. Res. **40**, 407–414 (1979).

[496] Lee, K. J., Woolsey, T. A.: A proportional relationship between peripheral innervation density and cortical neuron number in the somatosensory system of the mouse. Brain Res. **99**, 349–353 (1975).

[497] Leibowitz, H., Dichgans, J.: Zwei verschiedene Seh-Systeme. Neue Untersuchungsergebnisse zur Raumorientierung. Umschau **77**, 353 (1977).

[498] Lestienne, F., Berthoz, A., Mascot, J.-C., Koitcheva, V.: Effets posturaux induits par une scène visuelle en mouvement linéaire. III. Symp. internat. de posturographie, Paris, 23.–26. 9. 1975, Agressology **17**, C, 37–46 (1976).

[499] Lestienne, F., Soechting, J., Berthoz, A.: Postural readjustments induced by linear motion of visual scenes. Exp. Brain Res. **28**, 363–384 (1977).

[500] Levin, L., Maldonado, H.: A fovea in the praying mantis eye. III. The centring of the prey. Z. vergl. Physiol. **67**, 93–101 (1970).

[501] Lewis, D. B.: The physiology of the tettigoniid ear. 4. A new hypothesis for acoustic orientation behaviour. J. exp. Biol. **60**, 861–869 (1974).

[502] Lewis, D. B.: Persönl. Mitteilung 1979.

[503] Lindauer, M.: Allgemeine Sinnesphysiologie. Orientierung im Raum. Fortschr. Zool. **16**, 58–140 (1963).

[504] Lindauer, M.: Kompaßorientierung. Erg. Biol. **26**, 158–180 (1963).

[505] Lindauer, M.: The effective information contents of the dance of the honey bee. Fortschr. Zool. **23**, 31–33 (1975).

[506] Lindauer, M., Kerr, W.: Die gegenseitige Verständigung bei den stachellosen Bienen. Z. vergl. Physiol. **41**, 405–434 (1958).

[507] Lindauer, M., Martin, H.: Die Schwereorientierung der Bienen unter dem Einfluß des Magnetfeldes. Z. vergl. Physiol. **60**, 219–243 (1968).

[508] Lindeman, H. H.: Studies on the morphology of the sensory regions of the vestibular apparatus. Erg. Anat. Entw. gesch. **42**, 1–113 (1969).

[509] Linsenmair, K. E.: Anemomenotaktische Orientierung bei Skorpionen (Chelicerata, Scorpiones). Z. vergl. Physiol. **60**, 445–449 (1968).

[510] Linsenmair, K. E.: Die Windorientierung laufender Insekten. Fortschr. Zool. **21**, 59–79 (1973).

[511] Linsenmair, K. E.: Anemomenotaktische Orientierung bei Tenebrioniden und Mistkäfern (Insecta Coleoptera). Z. vergl. Physiol. **64**, 154–211 (1969).

[512] Linsenmair-Ziegler, Ch.: Vergleichende Untersuchungen zum photo-geotaktischen Winkeltransponieren pterygoter Insekten. Z. vergl. Physiol. **68**, 229–262 (1970).

[513] Lissmann, H. W.: Continous electrical signals from the tail of a fish, Gymnarchus niloticus Cuv. Nature **167**, 201 (1951).

[514] Lissmann, H. W.: On the function and evolution of electric organs in fish. J. exp. Biol. **35**, 156–191 (1958).

[515] Lissmann, H. W., Machin, K. E.: The mechanism of object location in Gymnarchus niloticus and similar fish. J. exp. Biol. **35**, 451–486 (1958).

[516] Lissmann, H. W., Machin, K. E.: Electric receptors in a non-electric fish (Clarias). Nature (Lond.) **199**, 88–89 (1963).

[517] Loe, P. R., Tomko, D. L., Werner, G.: The neural signal of angular head position in primary afferent vestibular nerve axons. J. Physiol. **230**, 29–50 (1973).

[518] Loeb, J.: Über Geotropismus bei Tieren. Pflügers Arch. **49**, 175–189 (1891).

[519] Loeb, J.: Die Tropismen. Hdb. d. vergl. Physiol. Bd. **IV**, 451–511. Hrsg.: H. Winterstein. Gustav Fischer, Jena 1913.

[520] Loeb, J.: Forced movements, Tropisms and Animal conduct, pp. 209, Philadelphia, London 1918.

[521] Loewenstein, O.: Experimentelle Untersuchungen über den Gleichgewichtssinn der Elritze (Phoxinus laevis L.). Z. vergl. Physiol. **17**, 833–849 (1932).

[522] Loftus-Hills, J. J., Johnstone, B. M.: Auditory function, communication, and the brain-evoked response in Anuran Amphibians. J. acoust. Soc. Amer. **47**, 1131–1138 (1969).

[523] Lorenz, K. Z.: Über die Bildung des Instinktbegriffes. Naturwiss. **25** (1937).

[524] Lorenz, K. Z.: Die angeborenen Formen möglicher Erfahrung. Z. Tierpsychol. **5**, 235–409 (1943).

[525] Lorenz, K. Z.: The comparative method in studying innate behavior patterns. In: Physiol. mechanisms in animal behavior. Symp. Soc. Exp. Biol. 4. Anim. Behav., Cambridge Univ. Press 1950.

[526] Lorenz, K. Z.: Die instinktiven Grundlagen menschlicher Kultur. Naturwiss. **54**, 377–388 (1967).

[527] Lorenz, K. Z.: Vergleichende Verhaltensforschung. Grundlagen der Ethologie. Springer, Wien, New York 1978.

[528] Lorenz, K., Tinbergen, N.: Taxis und Instinkthandlung in der Eirollbewegung der Graugans. Z. Tierpsychol. **2**, 1–29 (1938).

[529] Lowenstein, O. E.: Comparative Morphology and Physiology. In: Hdb. Sens. Physiol. **VI**/1, 75–120. Ed.: H. H. Kornhuber. Springer Verlag, Berlin, Heidelberg, New York 1974.

[530] Lowenstein, O., Roberts, D. M.: The equilibrium function of the otolith organs of the Thornback ray (Raja clavata). J. Physiol. **110**, 392–415 (1950).

[531] Lowenstein, O., Wersäll, J.: A functional interpretation of the electron-microscopic structure of the sensory hairs in the cristae of the Elasmobranch Raja clavata in terms of directional sensitivity. Nature **184**, 1807–1808 (1959).

[532] Lowenstein, O., Osborne, M. P., Wersäll, J.: Structure and innervation of the sensory epithelia of the labyrinth in the Thornback ray (Raja clavata). Proc. Roy. Soc. B, **160**, 1–12 (1964).

[533] Lubbock, I. (Lord Avebury): Ants, Bees and Wasps. (1st Ed. 1881) 7th Ed. IInd Impr., London 1906.

[534] Lüling, K. H.: Morphologisch-anatomische und histologische Untersuchungen am Auge des Schützenfisches Toxotes Jaculatrix (Pallas 1766) (Toxotidae), nebst Bemerkungen zum Spuckgehaben. Z. Morph. u. Ökol. Tiere **47**, 529–610 (1958).

[535] Lüling, K. H.: The archer fish. Scientific American **209**, 100–106 (1963).

[536] Lyons, J., Thomas, D. R.: Influence of postural distortion on the perception of visual vertical in pigeons. J. exp. Psychol. **76**, 120–124 (1968).

[537] Mach, E.: Über den Gleichgewichtssinn. Sitz. Ber. Österr. Akad. Wiss. Wien (Math.-Naturw. Kl.) **69**, 44 (1874).

[538] Mach, E.: Grundlinien der Lehre von den Bewegungsempfindungen. Engelmann, Leipzig 1875.

[539] MacKay, D. M.: Towards an information-flow model of human behaviour. Brit. J. Psychol. **47**, 30–43 (1956).

[540] MacKay, D. M.: Theoretical models of space perception. In: Aspects of the Theory of Artificial Intelligence, 83–104. Plenum Press, 1962.

[541] MacKay, D. M.: Visual stability and voluntary eye movements. Hdb. Sens. Physiol. **VII**/3, p. 307–331 (1973).

[542] MacKay, D. M.: The dynamics of perception. In: Cerebral Correlates of Conscious Experience, p. 53–68. Eds.: P. A. Busher, A. Rougeul-Buser. Elsevier, Amsterdam 1978.

[542a] Mackintosh, J. H.: Factors affecting the recognition of territory boundaries by mice (Mus musculus). Anim. Behav. **21**, 464–470 (1973).

[543] Magnus, R.: Körperstellung. Springer, Berlin 1924.

[544] MacKay, D. M., Gardiner, M. F.: Two strategies of information processing. In: Auditory processing of biologically significant sounds. Eds.: F. F. Worden, R. Galambos. Neurosci. Res. Prog. Bull. **10**, 77–78 (1972).

[545] MacKay, D. M., Mittelstaedt, H.: Visual stability and motor control (reafference revisited). Aus: Kybernetik und Bionik 5. Kongr. Dtsch. Ges. f. Kybernetik, Nürnberg, 28.–30.3.1973. R. Oldenbourg, München, Wien 1974.

[546] Macnab, R., Koshland, D. E.: The gradient-sensing mechanism in bacterial chemotaxis. Proc. Natl. Acad. Sci. USA **69**, 2509–2512 (1972).

[547] Malcolm, R., Melvill Jones, G.: A quantitative study of vestibular adaptation in humans. Canadian Forces Institute of Environmental Medicine, 69-RO-1, pp. 37 (May 1969). Acta Oto-laryngol. (Stockh.) **70**, 126–135 (1970).

[548] Malcolm, R., Melvill Jones, G.: Erroneous ception of vertical motion by humans seated in upright position. Acta Oto-laryngol. (Stockh.) **77**, 274–283 (1974).

[549] Maldonado, H., Barròs-Pita, J. C.: A fovea in the praying mantis eye. I. Estimation of the Catching Distance. Z. vergl. Physiol. **67**, 58–78 (1970).

[550] Maldonado, H., Benko, M., Issern, M.: Study of the Role of Binocular Vision in Mantids to Estimate long Distances. Z. vergl. Physiol. **68**, 72–83 (1970).

[551] Maldonado, H., Levin, L., Barròs-Pita, J. C.: Hit distance and the predatory strike of the praying mantis. Z. vergl. Physiol. **56**, 237–257 (1967).

[552] Manning, F. B.: Hearing in the goldfish in relation to the structure of the ear. J. exp. Zool., Philadelphia **41**, 5–20 (1924).

[553] Marais, E.: Die Seele des Affen. Symposion-Verlag, Esslingen 1973. (engl. Original: „The soul of the ape"; Human and Rousseau, 1969).

[554] Markl, H.: Borstenfelder an den Gelenken als Schweresinnesorgane bei Ameisen und anderen Hymenopteren. Z. vergl. Physiol. **45**, 475–569 (1962).

[555] Markl, H.: Die Verständigung durch Stridulationssignale bei Blattschneiderameisen. I. Die biologische Bedeutung der Stridulation. Z. vergl. Physiol. **57**, 299–330 (1967).

[556] Markl, H.: Die Verständigung durch Stridulationssignale bei Blattschneiderameisen. III. Die Empfindlichkeit für Substratvibrationen. Z. vergl. Physiol. **69**, 6–37 (1970).

[557] Markl, H.: Leistungen des Vibrationssinnes bei wirbellosen Tieren. Fortschr. Zool. **21**, 100–120 (1973).

[558] Markl, H.: The perception of gravity and of angular acceleration in invertebrates. In: Hdb. Sens. Physiol. **VI**/1, p. 17-74. Ed.: H. H. Kornhuber. Springer Verlag, Berlin, Heidelberg, New York 1974.

[559] Markl, H., Lang, H., Wiese, K.: Die Genauigkeit der Ortung eines Wellenzentrums durch den Rückenschwimmer Notonecta glauca L. J. comp. Physiol. **86**, 359–364 (1973).

[560] Markl, H., Fuchs, S.: Klopfsignale mit Alarmfunktion bei Roßameisen (Camponotus, Formicidae, Hymenoptera). Z. vergl. Physiol. **76**, 204–225 (1972).

[561] Marme-Karelse, A. M., Bles, W.: Circular vection and human posture. II. Does the auditory system play a role? Agressologie **18**, 329–333 (1977).

[562] Marsh, D., Kennedy, J. S., Ludlow, A. R.: An analysis of anemotactic zigzagging flight in male moths stimulated by pheromone. Physiol. Entomol. **3**, 221–240 (1978).

[563] Martin, H.: Zur Nahorientierung der Biene im Duftfeld zugleich ein Nachweis für die Osmo-Tropotaxis bei Insekten. Z. vergl. Physiol. **48**, 481–533 (1964).

[564] Martin, H.: Leistungen des topochemischen Sinnes bei der Honigbiene. Z. vergl. Physiol. **50**, 254–292 (1965).

[565] Martin, H., Lindauer, M.: Orientierung im Erdmagnetfeld. Fortschr. Zool. **21**, 211–228 (1973).

[565a] Maschwitz, U., Hölldobler, B., Möglich, M.: Tandemlaufen als Rekrutierungsverhalten bei Bothroponera tesserinoda Forel (Formicidae: Ponerinae). Z. Tierpsychol. **35**, 113–123 (1974).

[566] Mason, P. R.: Chemo-klino-kinesis in planarian food location. Animal Behav. **23**, 460–469 (1975).

[567] Mast, S. O.: Light and the behaviour of organisms. 410 pp., Wiley, New York 1911.

[568] Mast, S. O.: Factors involved in the process of orientation of lower organisms in light. Biol. Rev. **13**, 186–224 (1938).

[569] Matthews, G. V. T.: Sun navigation in homing pigeon. J. exp. Biol. **30**, 243–267 (1953).

[570] Matthews, G. V. T.: The astronomical bases of „nonsense" Orientation. Proc. 13th Internat. Ornithol. Congr. 415–429 (1963).

[571] Matthews, G. V. T.: Vogelflug. W. Goldmann, München 1971.

[572] Maxwell, S. S.: Labyrinth and equilibrium. J. B. Lippincott Company, Philadelphia, London 1923.

[573] Mayne, R.: A systems concept of the vestibular organs. In: Hdb. Sens. Physiol. **VI**/2, 493–580. Ed.: H. H. Kornhuber. Springer Verlag, Berlin, Heidelberg, New York 1974.

[574] Mayr, E.: Teleologisch und teleonomisch: eine neue Analyse. Aus: [575] Kap. 11, das in leicht veränderter Form übernommen wurde aus: Teleological and teleonomic: a new analysis. Boston Studies in the Philosophy of Science **14**, 91–117 (1974).

[575] Mayr, E.: Evolution und die Vielfalt des Lebens. Springer Verlag, Berlin, Heidelberg, New York 1979.

[576] McNally, W. J., Tait, J.: Some results of section of particular nerve branches to the ampullae of the four vertical semicircular canals of the frog. Quart. J. exp. Physiol. **23**, 147–196 (1933).

[577] McNaughton, I. P. J., McNally, W. J.: Some experiments which indicate that frog's lagena has equilibrial function. J. Laryng. **61**, 204–14 (1946).

[578] Melvill Jones, G.: The functional significance of semicircular canal size. In: Hdb. Sens. Physiol. **VI**/1, 171–184. Ed.: H. H. Kornhuber. Springer Verlag, Berlin, Heidelberg, New York 1974.

[579] Melvill Jones, G., Young, L. R.: Subjective detection of vertical acceleration: A velocity-dependent response? Acta Otolaryngol. **85**, 45–53 (1978).

[580] Merkel, F. W., Fromme, H. G., Wiltschko, W.: Nicht-visuelles Orientierungsvermögen bei nächtlich zugunruhigen Rotkehlchen. Die Vogelwarte **22**, 168–173 (1964).

[581] Merkel, F. W., Wiltschko, W.: Magnetismus und Richtungsfinden zugunruhiger Rotkehlchen (Erithacus rubecula). Die Vogelwarte **23**, 71–77 (1965).

[582] Michelsen, A., Larsen, O. N.: Biophysics of the Ensiferan Ear. I. Tympanal vibrations in bushcrickets (Tettigoniidae) studied with Laser vibrometry. J. comp. Physiol. **123**, 193–203 (1978).

[583] Mitchell, D. E., Griffin, F., Muir, D.: Behavioural compensation of cats after early rotation of one eye. Exp. Brain Res. **25**, 109–113 (1976).

[584] Mittelstaedt, H.: Telotaxis und Optomotorik von Eristalis bei Augeninversion. Naturwiss. **36**, 90 (1949).

[585] Mittelstaedt, H.: Physiologie des Gleichgewichtssinnes bei fliegenden Libellen. Z. vergl. Physiol. **32**, 422–463 (1950).

[586] Mittelstaedt, H.: Regelung und Steuerung bei der Orientierung der Lebewesen. Regelungstechnik **2**, 226 (1954a).

[587] Mittelstaedt, H.: Regelung in der Biologie. Regelungstechnik **2**, 177–200 (1954b).

[588] Mittelstaedt, H.: Prey capture in mantids. Recent Advances in Invertebrate Physiology, Univ. of Oregon Publ. 51–71 (1957).

[589] Mittelstaedt, H.: The analysis of behaviour in terms of control systems. In: Group Processes, Transact. 5th Conf., Oct. 1958, 45–84. Ed.: B. Schaffner. The Josiah Macy Foundation, New York 1958.

[590] Mittelstaedt, H.: Die Regelungstheorie als methodisches Werkzeug der Verhaltensanalyse. Naturwiss. **48** (8), 246–254 (1961).

[591] Mittelstaedt, H.: Probleme der Kursregelung bei freibeweglichen Tieren. In: Aufnahme und Verarbeitung von Nachrichten durch Organismen, 138–147, Hirzel Verlag, Stuttgart 1961.

[592] Mittelstaedt, H.: Bikomponenten-Theorie der Orientierung. Ergeb. Biol. **26**, 253–258 (1963).

[593] Mittelstaedt, H.: Basic control patterns of orientational homeostasis. In: Homeostasis and Feedback Mechanisms. 8. Symp. Soc. Exp. Biol. Cambridge **18**, 365–385 (1964).

[594] Mittelstaedt, H.: Reafferenzprinzip - Apologie und Kritik. Erlanger Physiologentagung 1970, Ed.: W. D. Keidel, K.-H. Plattig. Springer Verlag, Berlin, Heidelberg, New York 1971.

[595] Mittelstaedt, H.: Kybernetik der Schwereorientierung. Verh. Dtsch. Zool. Ges. **65**, 185 (1972).

[596] Mittelstaedt, H.: On the processing of postural information. Fortschr. Zool. **23**, 128–141 (1975).

[597] Mittelstaedt, H.: Kurs- und Lageregelung, Kybernetische Analyse von Orientierungsleistungen. Kybernetik 1977. 6. Kongr. d. Dtsch. Ges. f. Kybernetik, München, 30. 3. bis 1. 4. 1977, R. Oldenbourg Verlag, München, Wien 1978.

[598] Mittelstaedt, H., Mittelstaedt-Burger, M.-L.: Mechanismen der Orientierung ohne richtende Außenreize. Fortschr. Zool. **21**, 46–58 (1973).

[599] Mittelstaedt-Burger, M.-L.: Idiothetic course control and visual orientation. In: Inform. Proc. in the Visual Systems of Arthropods, p. 275-279. Ed.: R. Wehner. Springer Verlag, Berlin, Heidelberg, New York 1972.

[600] Mittelstaedt, M.-L., Mittelstaedt, H., Mohren, W.: Interaction of gravity and idiothetic course control in Millipedes. J. comp. Physiol. **133**, 267–281 (1979).

[601] Mittelstaedt, M.-L.,Mittelstaedt, H., Mohren, W.: Das Zusammenwirken von geotaktischer und idiothetischer Kursregelung bei Spirostreptus. Verh. Dtsch. Zool. Ges. **69**, 270 (1976).

[602] Mletzko, H.: Orientierungsrhythmen von Carabidae (Abtl. Entomol. Staatsuniv. Moskau). Z. obsc. Biol. **30**, 232–233 mit dtsch. Zus.fass. 1969.

[603] Möglich, M., Hölldobler, B.: Communication and orientation during foraging and emigration in the ant Formica fusca. J. comp. Physiol. **101**, 275–288 (1975).

[604] Möglich, M., Maschwitz, U., Hölldobler, B.: Tandem calling: A new kind of signal in ant communication. Science **186**, 1046–1047 (1974).

[605] Möhres, P.: Fledermausorientierung. Z. vergl. Physiol. **34**, 547–588 (1953).

[606] Moiseff, A., Pollack, G. S., Hoy, R. R.: Steering responses of flying crickets to sound and ultrasound: mate attraction and predator avoidance. Proc. Natl. Acad. Sci. USA **75**, 4052–4056 (1978).

[607] Moller, P.: Die systematischen Abweichungen bei der optischen Richtungsorientierung der Trichterspinne Agelena labyrinthica. Z. vergl. Physiol. **66**, 78–106 (1970).

[608] Mörchen, A., Rheinlaender, J., Schwartzkopff, J.: Latency shift in insect auditory nerve fibers. Naturwiss. **65**, 656 (1978).

[609] Mrosovsky, N.: Orientation mechanisms of marine turtles. In: Animal Migration, Navigation and Homing. Symp. Univ. Tübingen, 17.–20. 8. 1977. Eds.: K. Schmidt-Koenig, W. T. Keeton. Springer Verlag, Berlin, Heidelberg, New York 1978.

[610] Müller, G. E.: Über das Aubert'sche Phänomen. Z. Sinnesphysiol. **49**, 109–246 (1916).

[611] Müller, J.: Beiträge zur vergleichenden Physiologie des Gesichtsinnes. Leipzig 1826.

[612] Müller, J.: Elements of Physiology, Book V, Vol. II, pp. 1059–1087, translated by W. Baly. Taylor and Walton, London 1842. Reproduced in Visual Perception: the Nineteenth Century, pp. 35–69. Ed.: W. Dember. J. Wiley & Sons, London, New York 1964.

[613] Murphey, R. K.: Sensory aspects of the control of orientation to prey by the waterstrider, Gerris remigis. Z. vergl. Physiol. **72**, 168–185 (1971).

[614] Murphey, R. K.: Motor control of orientation to prey by the waterstrider, Gerris remigis. Z. vergl. Physiol. **72**, 150–167 (1971).

[615] Murphey, R. K.: Mutual inhibition and the organization of a non-visual orientation in Notonecta. J. comp. Physiol. **84**, 31–40 (1973).

[616] Murphey, R. K., Mendenhall, B.: Localization of receptors controlling orientation to prey by the back swimmer Notonecta undulata. J. comp. Physiol. **84**, 19–30 (1973).

[617] Murphey, R. K., Zaretsky, M. D.: Orientation to calling song by female crickets, Scapsipedus marginatus (Gryllidae). J. exp. Biol. **56**, 335–352 (1972).

[618] Murray, R. W.: The ampullae of Lorenzini. Hdb. Sens. Physiol. **III**/3, p. 125-146. Ed.: A. Fessard. Springer Verlag, Berlin, Heidelberg, New York 1974.

[619] Murr-Danielczick, L.: Über den Geruchssinn der Mehlmottenschlupfwespe Habrobracon Juglandis Ashmead. Z. vergl. Physiol. **11**, 210–269 (1930).

[620] Mygind, S. H.: Functional Mechanism of the Labyrinthine Epithelium, I. Arch. Otolaryngol. **82**, 450–461 (1965).

[621] Mygind, S. H.: Functional Mechanism of the Labyrinthine Epithelium, II, III. Arch. Otolaryngol. **82**, 579 (1965), **83**, 29 (1966).

[621a] Mykytowycz, R.: Territorial marking by rabbits. Sci. Amer. **218**, 116–126 (1968).

[622] Napier, J. R., Walker, A. C.: Vertical clinging and leaping in living and fossil primates. In: Neue Ergebnisse der Primatologie (Int. Congress) 65–69 (1967).

[623] Nauta, J. H., Karten, H. J.: A General Profile of the Vertebrate Brain, with Sidelights on the Ancestry of Cerebral Cortex. In: The Neurosciences, II. Study Program, p. 7-26. Ed.: F. O. Schmitt. The Rockefeller University Press, New York 1970.

[624] Neil, D. M.: The mechanism of statocyst operation in the mysid shrimp Praunus flexuosus. J. exp. Biol. **62**, 685–700 (1975a).

[625] Neil, D. M.: The control of eyestalk movements in the mysid shrimp Praunus flexuosus. J. exp. Biol. **62**, 487–504 (1975b).

[626] Neil, D. M.: Statocyst control of eyestalt movements in mysid shrimps. Fortschr. Zool. **23**, 98–108 (1975c).

[627] Neil, D. M.: The optokinetic responses of the mysid shrimp Praunus flexuosus. J. exp. Biol. **62**, 505–518 (1975d).

[628] Neil, D. M., Schöne, H.: Reactions of the spiny lobster, Palinurus vulgaris to substrate tilt (II). Input-output analysis of eyestalk responses. J. exp. Biol. **79**, 59–67 (1979).

[629] Neil, D. M., Schöne, H., Scapini, F.: Leg resistance reaction as an output and an input. Reactions of the spiny lobster, Palinurus vulgaris to substrate tilt (VI). J. comp. Physiol. **129**, 217–221 (1979).

[630] Nelson, D. R.: Hearing thresholds, frequency discrimination and acoustic orientation in the lemon shark, Negaprion brevirostris (Poey). Bull. mar. Sci. **17**, 741–768 (1967).

[631] Nelson, D. R., Gruber, S. H.: Sharks: attraction by low-frequency sounds. Science **142**, 975–977 (1963).

[632] Nelson, J. R., House, W. F.: Ocular countertorsion as an indicator of otolith function: Effects of unilateral vestibular lesions. Trans. Amer. Acad. Ophthal. Otolaryngol. **75**, 1313–21 (1971).

[633] Neuweiler, G.: Echoortung. Aus: Biophysik - Ein Lehrbuch. Hrsg. W. Hoppe, W. Lohmann, H. Markl, H. Ziegler. Springer Verlag, Berlin, Heidelberg, New York 1977.

[634] Nisbet, I. C. T.: Atmospheric turbulence and bird flight. Brit. Birds **48**, 557–559 (1955).

[635] Noble, C. E.: The perception of the vertical: III. The visual vertical as a function of centrifugal and gravitational forces. J. exp. Psychol. **39**, 839–850 (1949).

[636] Noble, G. K., Schmidt, A.: The structure and function of the facial and labial pits of snakes. Proc. Amer. Phil. Soc. **77**, 263–288 (1937).

[637] Nocke, H.: Physical and physiological properties of the tettigoniid („Grasshopper") ear. J. comp. Physiol. **100**, 25–57 (1975).

[638] Norris, K. S., Prescott, J. H., Asa-Dorian, P. V., Perkins, P.: An experimental demonstration of echo-location behavior in the porpoise, Tursiops truncatus (Montagu). Biol. Bull. **120**, 163–176 (1961).

[639] Nyborg, H.: A method for analysing performance in the rod-and-frame test. I. Scand. J. Psychol. **15**, 119–123 (1974).

[640] Nyborg, H., Isaksen, B.: A method for analysing performance in the rod-and-frame test. II. Test of the statistical model. Scand. J. Psychol. **15**, 124–126 (1974).

[641] Nyborg, H.: Light intensity in the rod-and-frame test reconsidered. Scand. J. Psychol. **15**, 236–237 (1974).

[642] Nyborg, H.: The rod-and-frame test and the field dependence dimension: some methodological, conceptual, and developmental considerations. Univer. of Aarhus, Psychol. Inst. Tryk, Aarhus 1976.

[643] Oelke, H., Schüz, E.: III. · Forschungsmethoden. In: Grundriß der Vogelzugskunde. Eds.: E. Schüz, P. Berthold, E. Gwinner, H. Oelke. Paul Parey, Berlin, Hamburg 1971.

[644] Orr, R. T.: Animals in Migration. MacMillan, New York 1970.

[645] Osborne, G. O., Hoyt, C. P.: Phenolic resins as chemical attractants for males of the grass grub beetle, Costelytra zealandica. Ann. Entomol. Soc. Am. **63**, 1145–1147 (1970).

[646] Otto, E.: Untersuchungen zur Frage der geruchlichen Orientierung bei Insekten. Zool. Jb. Allgem. Zool. u. Physiol. **62**, 65–92 (1951).

[647] Ozhigova, A. P., Ozhigov, J. E.: Constant magnetic field effect on paramecium movement. Biofizika **11**, 1026–1033 (russisch) (1966).

[648] Palmer, J. D.: Organismic spatial orientation in very weak magnetic fields. Nature (Lond.) **198**, 1061–1062 (1963).

[649] Papi, F.: Orientation by night: the moon. Cold Spring Harbor Symp. on Quant. Biol. **25**, 457–480 (1960).

[650] Papi, F., Fiore, L., Fiaschi, V., Benvenuti, S.: Olfaction and homing in pigeons. Monitore Zool. Ital. **6**, 85–95 (1972).

[651] Papi, F., Keeton, W. T., Brown, A. I., Benvenuti, S.: Do American and Italian pigeons rely on different homing mechanisms? J. comp. Physiol. **128**, 303–317 (1978).

[652] Pardi, L.: Über die Orientierung von Tylos latreilli (Auch. und Sav.) (Isopoda terrestria). Z. Tierpsychol. **11**, 175–181 (1954b).

[653] Pardi, L.: Innate components in the solar orientation of littoral amphipods. Cold Spring Harbor Symp. on Quantit. Biol. **25**, 395–401 (1960).

[654] Pardi, L., Papi, F.: Ricerche sull'orientamento di Talitrus saltator (MONTAGU) (Crustacea-Amphipoda) I. L'orientamento durante il giorno in una popolazione del litorale tirrenico. Z. vergl. Physiol. **35**, 459–489 (1953).

[655] Pardi, L., Papi, F.: Kinetic and tactic responses. In: The Physiology of Crustacea, Vol. II, pp. 365–393. Ed.: T. H. Watermann. Academic Press, New York 1961.

[656] Patten, B. M.: A quantitative determination of the orienting reaction of the blowfly Larva (Calliphora erythrocephala Meigen). J. Exp. Zool. **17**, 213–280 (1914).

[657] Payne, R. S., Drury, W. H.: Marksman of the darkness. Natural History, **67**, 316–323 (1958).

[658] Payne, R. S.: How the barn owl locates prey by hearing. The Living Bird, 1. Annual Cornell Lab. Ornithol., 151–159 (1962).

[659] Payne, R. S.: Acoustic location of prey by barn owls (Tyto alba). J. exp. Biol. **54**, 535–537 (1971).

[660] Pennycuick, C. J.: The physical basis of astro-navigation in birds: theoretical considerations. J. exp. Biol. **37**, 573–593 (1960).

[661] Perdeck, A. C.: Two types of orientation in migrating starlings, Sturnus vulgaris L. and chaffinches, Fringilla coelebs L., as revealed by displacement experiments. Ardea **56**, 1–37 (1958).

[662] Perttunen, V.: The reversal of positive phototaxis by low temperatures in Blastophagus piniperda L. Ann. Ent. Fenn. **24**, 12–18 (1958).

[663] Perttunen, V.: Effect of the temperature on the light reactions of Blastophagus piniperda L. Ann. Ent. Fenn. **25**, 65–71 (1959).

[664] Perttunen, V., Kangas, E., Oksanen, H.: The mechanisms by which Blastophagus piniperda (Coleoptera: Scolytidae) reacts to the odour of an attractant fraction isolated from pine phloem. Ann. Entomol. Fennici **34**, 205–222 (1968).

[664a] Peters, R. P., Mech, L. D.: Scent marking in wolves. Am. Sci. **63**, 628–637 (1975).

[665] Pettigrew, J. D.: The Neurophysiology of binocular vision. Sci. Amer. **227**, 84 (1972).

[666] Pettigrew, A., Shin-Ho Chung, Anson, M.: Neurophysiological basis of directional hearing in amphibia. Nature **272**, 138–142 (1978).

[667] Pfeffer, W.: Lokomotorische Richtungsbewegungen durch chemische Reize. In: Unters. a. d. bot. Inst. Tübingen, **1**. Hrsg. W. Pfeffer. W. Engelmann, Leipzig 1881–1885.

[668] Pierce, G. W., Griffin, D. R.: Experimental determination of supersonic notes emitted by bats. J. Mammal. **19**, 454–455 (1938).

[669] Pittendrigh, C. S.: Adaptation, natural selection, and behavior. In: Behavior and evolution. Eds.: A. Roe, G. G. Simpson. Yale University Press, New Haven 1958.

[670] Platt, C.: Central control of postural orientation in flatfish. I. Postural change dependence on central neural changes. J. exp. Biol. **59**, 491–521 (1973).

[671] Platt, C.: Central control of postural orientation in flatfish. II. Optic-vestibular efferent modification of gravistatic input. J. exp. Biol. **59**, 523–541 (1973).

[672] Poggio, T., Reichardt, W.: Visual control of orientation behaviour in the fly. Part II. Towards the underlying neural interactions. Quart. Rev. Biophysics **9**, 377–438 (1976).

[673] Poggio, T., Reichardt, W.: Nonlinear interactions underlying visual orientation behaviour of the fly. Cold Spring Harb. Symp. quant. Biol. **40** (1976).

[674] Pommerville, J.: Analysis of Gamete and Zygote Motility in Allomyces. Exp. Cell Res. **113**, 161–172 (1978).

[675] Popov, A. V., Shuvalov, V. F.: Phonotactic behavior of crickets. J. comp. Physiol. **119**, 111–126 (1977).

[676] Popov, A. V., Shuvalov, V. F., Svetlogorskaya, I. D., Markovich, A. M.: Acoustic behaviour and auditory system in insects. In: Symp. Mechanoreception. Ed.: J. Schwartzkopff. Rhein. Westf. Akad. Wiss. **53**, 281–300 (1974).

[677] Popov, A. V., Shuvalov, V. F., Markovich, A. M.: The spectrum of the calling signals phonotaxis, and the auditory system in the cricket (Gryllus bimaculatus). Transl. from Zhurnal Evolyutsionnoi Biokhimii i Fiziologii **11**, 453–460 (1975).

[678] Pöppel, E., Held, R., Frost, D.: Residual visual function after brain wounds involving the central visual pathways in man. Nature **243**, 295 (1973).

[679] Precht, H.: Das Taxisproblem in der Zoologie. Z. wiss. Zool. **156**, 1–128 (1942).

[680] Precht, W.: Cerebellar influences on eye movements. Basic mechanisms of ocular motility and their clinical implications. Eds.: G. Lennerstrand, P. Bach-Y-Rita. Pergamon Press, Oxford, New York 1975.

[681] Precht, W.: Physiology of the peripheral and central vestibular systems. In: Frog Neurobiology. Eds.: R. Llinás u. W. Precht, Springer Verlag, Berlin, Heidelberg, New York 1976.

[682] Precht, W.: Physiological aspects of the efferent vestibular system. In: Hdb. Sens. Physiol. **VI**/1, 221–236. Ed.: H. H. Kornhuber. Springer Verlag, Berlin, Heidelberg, New York 1974a.

[683] Precht, W.: The Physiology of the vestibular nuclei. In: Hdb. Sens. Physiol. **VI**/1, 353–416. Ed.: H. H. Kornhuber. Springer Verlag, Berlin, Heidelberg, New York 1974b.

[684] Precht, W.: Neuronal operations in the vestibular system. In: Studies of brain function **2**. Ed.: V. Braitenberg. Springer Verlag, Berlin, Heidelberg, New York 1978.

[685] Quix, F. H.: Die Otolithenfunktion in der Otologie. Z. Hals-Nasen und Ohrenheilkunde **8**, 517–537 (1924).

[686] Quix, F. H., Eijsvogel, M. H. P. M.: Experimente über die Funktion des Otolithenapparates beim Menschen. Z. Hals-, Nasen- u. Ohrenheilkunde **23**, 68–96 (1929).

[687] Rabaud, E.: Acquisition des habitudes et repères sensorielles chez les guepes. Bull. biol. Fr. Belg. **60**, 313 (1926).

[688] Rádl, E. M.: Untersuchungen über den Phototropismus der Tiere. Verlag W. Engelmann, Leipzig 1903.

[689] Reason, J. T., Benson, A, J.: Voluntary movement control and adaptation to cross-coupled stimulation. Aviation, Space & Environmental Med. Nov. 1978.

[690] Regen, J.: Über die Anlockung des Weibchens von Gryllus campestris L. durch telephonisch übertragene Stridulationslaute des Männchens. Pflügers Arch. Physiol. **155**, 193–200 (1913).

[691] Rehbein, H.: Auditory neurons in the ventral cord of the locust: morphological and functional properties. J. comp. Physiol. **110**, 233–250 (76).

[692] Reichardt, W., Roggio, T.: Visual control of orientation behaviour in the fly. Part I. A quantitative analysis neural interactions. Quart. Rev. Biophysics **9**, 311–375 (1976).

[693] Reichardt, W., Wenking, H.: Optical detection and fixation of objects by fixed flying flies. Naturwiss. **56**, 424–425 (1969).

[694] Reinig, H.-J., Uhlemann, H.: Über das Ortungsvermögen des Taumelkäfers Gyrinus substriatus Steph. (Coleoptera, Gyrinidae). J. comp. Physiol. **84**, 281–298 (1973).

[695] Rheinlaender, J.: Transmission of acoustic information at three neuronal levels in the auditory system of Decticus verrucivorus (Tettigoniidae, Orthoptera). J. comp. Physiol. **97**, 1–53 (1975).

[696] Rheinlaender, J.: Das phonotaktische Orientierungsverhalten beim Laubfrosch Hyla cinerea. Verh. Dt. Zool. Ges. Konstanz, **71**, 178 (1978).

[697] Rheinlaender, J., Gerhardt, H. C., Yager, D. P., Capranica, R. R.: Accuracy of Phonotaxis by the greenfrog (Hyla). J. comp. Physiol. **133**, 247–255 (1979).

[698] Rheinlaender, J., Kalmring, K., Popov, A. V., Rehbein, H.: Brain projections and information processing of biologically significant sounds by two large ventralcord neurons of Gryllus bimaculatus DeGeer (Orthoptera, Gryllidae). J. comp. Physiol. **110**, 251–269 (1976).

[699] van Rhijn, F. A.: Optic orientation in hatchlings of the sea turtle, Chelonia mydas. Marine Behav. & Physiol., **6**, 105–122 (1979).

[700] Rice, A. L.: The responses of certain mysids to changes in hydrostatic pressure. J. exp. Biol. **38**, 391–401 (1961).

[701] Rice, A. L.: Observations on the effects of changes of hydrostatic pressure on the behavior of some marine animals. J. mar. biol. Ass. U. K. **44**, 163–175 (1964).

[702] Richards, W.: Visual space perception. Hb. of Perception **5**. Eds.: E. C. Carterette & M. P. Friedman; Acad. Press, New York, San Francisco, London 1975.

[703] Riegert, P. W.: Humidity reactions of Melanoplus bivittatus (Say) and Camnula pellucida (Schudd.) (Orthoptera, Acrididae): reactions of normal grasshoppers. Canadian Entomologist **91**, 35–40 (1959).

[704] Risler, H.: Das Gehörorgan der Männchen von Anopheles stephensi LISTON (Culicidae). Zool. Jb. Anat. **73**, 165–186 (1953).

[705] Robert, P.: Les migrations orientees du hanneton commune Melolontha melolontha. Ergeb. Biol. **26**, 134–145 (1963).
[706] Robinson, D.: Eye movements evoked by collicular stimulation in the alert monkey. Vision Res. Vol. **12**, 1795–1808 (1972).
[707] Roeder, K. D.: Electric activity in nerves and ganglia. In: Insect Physiology. Ed. K. D. Roeder. J. Wiley & Sons, London 1953.
[708] Roeder, K. D.: Spontaneous activity and behavior. Scient. Monthly **80**, 362–370 (1955).
[709] Roeder, K. D.: The behaviour of free flying moths in the presence of artificial ultrasonic pulses. Anim. Behav. **10**, 300–304 (1962a).
[710] Roeder, K. D.: Neural mechanisms of animal behavior. Am. Zoologist, **2**, 105–115 (1962b).
[711] Roeder, K. D.: Nerve cells and Insect Behavior. Harvard University Press, Cambridge, Mass. 1963.
[712] Roeder, K. D.: Turning tendency of moth exposed to ultrasound while in stationary flight. J. Insect Physiol. **13**, 873–888 (1966).
[713] Roeder, K. D.: Interaction of moths and bats. Kybernetik Kongress München 1968, Oldenbourg Verlag, München, Wien 1969.
[714] Roeder, K. D., Treat, A. E.: Ultrasonic reception by the tympanic organ of noctuid moths. J. exper. Zool. **134**, 127–157 (1957).
[715] Roeder, K. D., Treat, A. E.: The reception of bat cries by the tympanic organ of noctuid moths. Sensory communication, pp. 545–560, Ed.: W. Rosenblith. M. J. T. Technology Press, Boston 1961a.
[716] Roeder, K. D., Treat, A. E.: An acoustic sense in some hawkmoths (Choerocampinae). J. Insect Physiol. **16**, 1069–1086 (1970).
[717] Roeder, K. D., Treat, A. E., Vande Berg, J. S.: Distal lobe of the Pilifer: an ultrasonic receptor in Choerocampine Hawkmoths. Science **170**, 1089–1099 (1970).
[718] Rohlf, F. J., Davenport, D.: Simulation of simple models of animal behavior with a digital computer. J. Theoret. Biol. **23**, 400–424 (1969).
[719] Romanes, G. J.: Die geistige Entwicklung im Tierreich. Ernst Günthers Verlag, Leipzig 1885.
[720] Rose, J. E., Gross, N. B., Geisler, C. D., Hind, J. E.: Some neural mechanisms in the inferior colliculus of the cat which may be relevant to localization of a sound source. J. Neurophysiol. **29**, 288–314 (1966).
[721] Rosengren, R.: Route fidelity, visual memory and recruitment behaviour in foraging wood ants of the genus Formica (Hymenoptera, Formicidae). Acta Zool. Fennica **133**, 1–106 (1971).
[722] Roth, A.: Electroreception in the catfish, Amiurus nebulosus. Z. vergl. Physiol. **61**, 196–202 (1968).
[723] Roth, A.: Elektrische Sinnesorgane beim Zwergwels Ictalurus nebulosus (Amiurus nebulosus). Z. vergl. Physiol. **65**, 368–388 (1969).
[724] Roth, A.: Wozu dienen die Elektrorezeptoren der Welse? J. comp. Physiol. **79**, 113–135 (1972).
[725] Rudolph, P.: Zum Ortungsverfahren von Gyrinus substriatus Steph. (Taumelkäfer). Z. vergl. Physiol. **56**, 341–375 (1967).
[726] de Ruiter, L., v. d. Horn, I. J.: Changes in phototaxis during the larva life of the eyed hawk moth. Nature **179**, 1027 (1957).
[727] Rupprecht, R.: Das Trommeln von Plecopteren. Z. vergl. Physiol. **59**, 38–71 (1968).
[728] Sala, O.: The efferent vestibular system. Acta Oto-laryngol. (Stockh.) (Suppl.) **197**, 1–34 (1965).
[729] Sandeman, D. C.: Dynamic receptors in the statocysts of crabs. Fortschr. Zool. **23**, 185–191 (1975).
[730] Sandeman, D. C.: Compensatory eye movements in crabs. From: Identified neurons and behavior of Arthropods. Ed.: Graham Hoyle. Plenum Publ. Corp. 1977.
[731] Sandeman, D. C., Okajima, A.: Statocyst-induced eye movements in the crab Scylla serrata. III. The anatomical projections of sensory and motor neurones and the responses of the motor neurones. J. Exp. Biol. **59**, 17–38 (1973).
[732] Santschi, F.: Observations et remarques critiques sur le mecanisme de l'orientation. Rev. Suisse de Zoologie **19**, 303–338 (1911).

[733] Sauer, F.: Zugorientierung einer Mönchsgrasmücke (Sylvia atricapilla L.) unter künstlichem Sternenhimmel. Naturwiss. **43**, 231–232 (1956).

[734] Sauer, F.: Astronavigatorische Orientierung einer unter künstlichem Sternenhimmel verfrachteten Klappergrasmücke (Sylvia c, Curruca L.). Naturwiss. **44**, 71 (1957).

[735] Sauer, F., Sauer, E.: Zur Frage der nächtlichen Zugorientierung von Grasmücken. Rev. Suisse Zool. **62**, 250–259 (1955).

[736] Sauer, F., Sauer, E.: Star navigation of nocturnal migrating birds. Cold Spring Harb. Symp. Quant. Biol. **25**, 463–473 (1960).

[737] Scapini, F.: Orientation of Talitrus saltator Montagu (Crustacea Amphipoda) in fresh, sea and diluted sea water. Monitore zool. Ital. (N. S.) **13** (1979).

[738] Scapini, F., Neil, D. M., Schöne, H.: Leg-to-body geometry determines eyestalk reactions to substrate tilt. Substrate Orientation in Spiny lobsters (IV). J. comp. Physiol. **126**, 287–291 (1978).

[739] Schaefer, K.-P., Schott, D., Meyer, D. L.: On the organization of neuronal circuits involved in the generation of the orientation response (Visual graspreflex). Fortschr. Zool. **23**, 199–211 (1975).

[740] Scharstein, H.: Diskussionsbeitrag, p. 49. In: Mechanisms of spatial perception and orientation as related to gravity. Int. Symp. Köln, 1973, Hrsg. H. Schöne. Fortschr. Zool. **23** (1975a).

[741] Scharstein, H.: Der Mechanismus der Sollwertvorstellung bei der Kursregelung der roten Waldameise (Formica polyctena). Dissertation, München 1975b.

[742] Scheich, H., Bullock, T. H.: The detection of electric fields from electric organs. In: Hdb. Sens. Physiol. **III**/3, p. 201–256. Ed.: A. Fessard. Springer Verlag, Berlin, Heidelberg, New York 1974.

[743] Schevill, W. E., McBride, A. F.: Evidence for echo-location by cetaceans. Deep Sea Res. **3**, 153–154 (1956).

[744] Schiller, P. H., Koerner, F.: Discharge characteristics of single units in superior colliculus of the alert Rhesus monkey. J. Neurophysiol. **34**, 920–936 (1971).

[745] Schlichte, H.-J. Schmidt-Koenig, K.: Zum Heimfindevermögen der Brieftaube bei erschwerter optischer Wahrnehmung. Naturwiss. **58**, 329–330 (1971).

[746] Schmid, B.: Über die Ermittlung des menschlichen und tierischen Individualgeruches durch den Hund. Z. vergl. Physiol. **22**, 524–538 (1935).

[747] Schmidt, C. L.: Manuskript über Ableitungen aus den Vestibulariskernen beim Goldfisch, 1979.

[748] Schmidt, C. L., Wist, E. R., Dichgans, J.: Efferent frequency modulation in the vestibular nerve of Goldfish correlated with saccadic eye movements. Exp. Brain Res. **15**, 1–14 (1972).

[749] Schmidt-Koenig, K.: Die Sonne als Kompass im Heim-Orientierungssystem der Brieftauben. Z. f. Tierpsychol. **18**, 221–244 (1961).

[750] Schmidt-Koenig, K.: Current problems in bird orientation. Advances in the study of behavior **1**, 217–278 (1965).

[751] Schmidt-Koenig, K.: Ein Versuch, theoretisch mögliche Navigationsverfahren von Vögeln zu klassifizieren und relevante sinnesphysiologische Probleme zu umreißen. Verh. Dtsch. Zool. Ges. **64**, 243–245 (1970).

[752] Schmidt-Koenig, K.: Migration and homing in animals. Springer Verlag, Berlin, Heidelberg, New York 1975.

[753] Schmidt-Koenig, K., Keeton, W. T.: Sun compass utilization by pigeons wearing frosted contact lenses. The Auk **94**, 1. (1977).

[754] Schmidt-Koenig, K., Phillips, J. B.: Local anesthesia of the olfactory membrane and homing in pigeons. In: Animal Migration, Navigation, and Homing. Symp. Tübingen, 17.–20. 8. 1977. Eds.: K. Schmidt-Koenig, W. T. Keeton. Springer Verlag, Berlin, Heidelberg, New York 1978.

[755] Schmidt-Koenig, K., Walcott, Ch.: Flugwege und Verbleib von Brieftauben mit getrübten Haftschalen. Naturwiss. **60**, 108–109 (1973).

[756] Schneider, D.: Beitrag zu einer Analyse des Beute- und Fluchtverhaltens einheimischer Anuren. Biol. Zbl. **73**, 225–282 (1954).

[757] Schneider, D.: Die Arbeitsweise tierischer Sinnesorgane im Vergleich zu technischen Meßgeräten. Arbeitsgemeinschaft für Forschung. Nordrhein-Westf. 1967.

[758] Schneider, D.: Insect olfaction: Deciphering system for chemical messages. Am. Ass. Advancement Sci. **163**, 1031–1037 (1969).

[759] Schneider, F.: Unters. über die optische Orientierung der Maikäfer sowie über die Entstehung von Schwärmbahnen und Befallskonzentrationen. Mitt. Schweiz. Entomol. Ges. **25**, 269–340 (1952).

[760] Schneider, F.: Die Fernorientierung des Maikäfers während seiner ersten Fraßperiode und beim Rückflug in das alte Brutgebiet. Verh. Schweiz. Naturforsch. Ges. Neuenbg., 95–96 (1957).

[761] Schneider, F.: Der experimentelle Nachweis einer magnetischen und elektrischen Orientierung des Maikäfers. Verh. Schweizer. Naturforsch. Ges. Kanton Aargau, 132–134 (1960).

[762] Schneider, F.: Ultraoptische Orientierung des Maikäfers in künstlichen elektrischen und magnetischen Feldern.Ergeb. Biol. **26**, 147–157 (1963).

[763] Schneider, G. E.: Contrasting visuomotor functions of tectum and cortex in the golden hamster. Psychol. Forsch. **31**, 52–62 (1967).

[764] Schnitzler, H.-U.: Die Ultraschall-Ortungslaute der Hufeisen-Fledermäuse (Chiroptera-Rhinolophidae) in verschiedenen Orientierungssituationen. Z. vergl. Physiol. **57**, 376–408 (1968).

[765] Schnitzler, H.-U.: Die Echoortung der Fledermäuse und ihre hörphysiologischen Grundlagen. Fortschr. Zool. **21**, 136–189 (1973).

[766] Schöne, H.: Die Lichtorientierung der Larven von Acilius sulcatus L. und Dytiscus marginalis L. Z. vergl. Physiol. **33**, 63–98 (1951a).

[767] Schöne, H.: Die Regulation der Fehlbewegungen einseitig geblendeter Dytiscuslarven. Z. f. Naturforsch. **5b**, 283–386 (1951b).

[768] Schöne, H.: Statozystenfunktion und statische Lageorientierung bei dekapoden Krebsen. Z. vergl. Physiol. **36**, 241–260 (1954).

[769] Schöne,H.: Kurssteuerung mittels der Statocysten (Messungen an Krebsen). Z. vergl. Physiol. **39** 235–40 (1957).

[770] Schöne, H.: Optisch gesteuerte Lageänderungen (Versuche an Dytiscidenlarven zur Vertikalorientierung). Z. vergl. Physiol. **45**, 590–604 (1962a).

[771] Schöne, H.: Über den Einfluß der Schwerkraft auf die Augenrollung und auf die Wahrnehmung der Lage im Raum. Z. vergl. Physiol. **46**, 57–87 (1962b).

[772] Schöne, H.: Über die Arbeitsweise der Statolithenapparate bei Plattfischen. Jahresh. d. Verb. Dtsch. Biol. **4**, 135–156 (1964a).

[773] Schöne, H.: On the role of gravity in human spatial orientation. Aerosp. Med. **35**, 764–72 (1964b).

[774] Schöne, H.: Gravity receptors and gravity orientation in Crustacea. In: Gravity and the organism, 223–235. Eds.: S. A. Gordon, M. J. Cohen. Univ. of Chicago Press, Chicago, London 1971.

[775] Schöne, H.: Raumorientierung, Begriffe und Mechanismen. Fortschr. Zool. **21**, 1–19 (1973).

[776] Schöne, H.: On the transformation of the gravity input into reactions by statolith organs of the „fan" type. Fortschr. Zool. **23**, 120–126 (1975a).

[777] Schöne, H.: The „weight" of the gravity organ's signal in the control of perceptual and reflex type orientation at different body positions. Fortschr. Zool. **23**, 274–283 (1975b).

[778] Schöne, H.: Spatial orientation in animals. In: Marine Ecology, Vol. II, 499–533. Ed.: O. E. Kinne. John Wiley & Sons, London 1975c.

[779] Schöne, H.: Orientation of perceived vertical as a function of the inputs from statolith organs and somesthetic system. Cybernetics 1977. Proc. 6th Congr. Dtsch. Ges. f. Kybernetik, held at Munich 30.3.–1. 4. 1977. Hrsg.: G. Hauske, E. Butenandt. Oldenbourg Verlag, München, Wien 1978.

[780] Schöne, H.: Die Beuteorientierung der Larven der Wasserkäfer Acilius sulcatus und Dytiscus marginalis. Unveröffentl. Untersuchungen 1949.

[781] Schöne, H., Budelmann, B.-U.: The function of the gravity receptor of Octopus vulgaris. Nature **226**, 864–865 (1970).

[782] Schöne, H., Lechner-Steinleitner, S.: The effect of preceding tilt on the perceived vertical. Hysteresis in perception of the vertical. Acta Oto-laryngol. **85**, 68–73 (1978a).

[783] Schöne, H., Neil, D. M.: The integration of leg position-receptors and their interaction with statocyst inputs in spiny lobsters (Reactions of Palinurus vulgaris to substrate tilt III.). Mar. Behav. Physiol. **5**, 45– 59 (1977).

[784] Schöne, H., Neil, D. M., Scapini, F.: The influence of substrate contact on gravity orientation. Substrate orientation in spiny lobsters V. J. comp. Physiol. **126**, 293–295 (1978).

[785] Schöne, H., Neil, D. M., Stein, A., Carlstead, M. K.: Reactions of the spiny lobster, Palinurus vulgaris, to substrate tilt I. J. comp. Physiol. **107**, 113–128 (1976).

[786] Schöne, H., Parker, D. E.: Inversion of the effect of increased gravity on the subjective vertical. Naturwiss. **54**, 288–289 (1967b).

[787] Schöne, H., Parker, D. E., Mortag, H. G.: Subjective vertical as a function of body position and gravity magnitude. Naturwiss. **54**, 288 (1967a).

[788] Schöne, H., Schöne, Hedwig: Integrated function of statocyst and antennular proprioceptive organ in the spiny lobster. Naturwiss. **54**, 289 (1967c).

[789] Schöne, H., Steinbrecht, R. A.: Fine structure of statocyst receptor of Astacus fluviatilis. Nature **220**, 184–186 (1968a).

[790] Schöne, H., Udo de Haes, H. A.: Space orientation in humans with special reference to the interaction of vestibular, somaesthetic and visual inputs. In: Biokybernetik III, Materialien 2. Internat. Sympos. Biokybernetik, 172–191. Ed.: H. Drischel u. N. Tiedt. VEB Gustav Fischer Verl., Jena, 1971a.

[791] Schöne, H., Wade, N. J.: The influence of force magnitude on the perception of body position II. Effect of body posture. Br. J. Psychol. **62**, 347–352 (1971b).

[792] Schoen, L.: Quantitative Untersuchungen über die zentrale Kompensation nach einseitiger Utriculusausschaltung bei Fischen. Z. vgl. Physiol. **32**, 121–150 (1950).

[793] Schoen, L.: Das Zusammenspiel beider Augen als Gleichgewichtsorgan der Fische. Verh. Dtsch. Zool. Ges., Wilhelmshaven, 191–195 (1951).

[794] Schoen, L.: Mikroableitungen einzelner zentraler Vestibularisneurone von Knochenfischen bei Statolithenreizen. Z. vgl. Physiol. **39**, 399–417 (1957).

[795] Schoen, L., v. Holst, E.: Das Zusammenspiel von Lagena und Utriculus bei der Lageorientierung der Knochenfische. Z. vgl. Physiol. **32**, 552–571 (1950).

[796] Schüz, E.: Grundriß der Vogelzugskunde. Paul Parey, Berlin, Hamburg 1971.

[797] Schwalb, H. H.: Beiträge zur Biologie einheimischer Lampyriden (L. noctiluca und Phausis splendidula) und experimentelle Analyse ihres Beutefang- und Sexualverhaltens. Zool. Jb. Syst. **88**, 399–550 (1960).

[798] Schwartz, E.: Bau und Funktion der Seitenlinie des Streifenhechtlings Aplocheilus lineatus. Z. vergl. Physiol. **50**, 55–87 (1965).

[799] Schwartz, E.: Die Ortung von Wasserwellen durch Oberflächenfische. Z. vergl. Physiol. **74**, 64–80 (1971).

[800] Schwartz, E.: Zur Lokalisation akustischer Reize von Fischen und Amphibien. Fortschr. Zool. **21**, 121–135 (1973).

[801] Schwartz, E.: Lateral-line mechano-receptors in fishes and amphibians. In: Hdb. Sens. Physiol. **III**/3, 257–278. Ed.: A. Fessard. Springer Verlag, Berlin, Heidelberg, New York 1974.

[802] Schwartzkopff, J.: Vergleichende Physiologie des Gehörs und der Lautäußerungen. Fortschr. Zool. **15**, 214–336 (1962).

[803] Schwartzkopff, J.: Die akustische Lokalisation bei Tieren. Ergeb. Biol. **25**, 136–171 (1962).

[804] Schwartzkopff, J.: Principles of signal detection by the auditory pathway of invertebrates and vertebrates. In: Mechanoreception, Symp. Bochum 1973. Ed.: J. Schwartzkopff. Wiss. Abh. Rhein.-Westf. Akad. Wiss. 1974.

[805] Schwink, I.: Experimentelle Unters. über Geruchssinn und Strömungswahrnehmung in der Orientierung bei Nachtschmetterlingen. Z. vergl. Physiol. **37**, 19–56 (1954).

[806] Segui-Goncalves, L.: A study of orientation information given by one trained bee dancing. J. Apicult. Res. **3**, 113–132 (1969).

[807] Seydel, A., Schöne, H.: Über die Einstellung nach zwei Lichtern von Astacus fluviatilis. Unveröff. Ergebnisse 1959.

[808] Seymour, C., Lewis, B., Larsen, O. N., Michelsen, A.: Biophysics of the ensiferan ear II. The steady-state gain of the hearing trumpet in bushcrickets. J. comp. Physiol. **123**, 205–216 (1978).

[809] Shaw, E. A. G.: The external ear. In: Hdb. Sens. Physiol. **V**/1, 455–490. Ed.: W. D. Keidel, W. D. Neff. Springer Verlag, Berlin, Heidelberg, New York 1974.

[810] Shorey, H. H., Farkas, S. R.: Sex pheromones of lepidoptera. 42. Terrestrial odor-trail following by pheromone-stimulated males of Trichoplusia ni. Ann. Entomol. Soc. Amer. **66**, 1213–1214 (1973).

[811] Shuvalov, V. F., Popov, V. A.: Reaction of females of the domestic cricket Acheta domestica to sound signals and its changes in ontogenesis. Translated from Zhurnal Evolyutsionnoi Biokhimii i Fiziologii 7, 612– 616 (1971).

[812] Simmons, J. A.: Acoustic radiation patterns for the echolocating bats Chilonycteris rubiginosa and Eptesicus fuscus. J. Acoust. Soc. America, 46, (4) Part 2, 1054–1056 (1969).

[813] Simmons, J. A., Vernon, J. A.: Echolocation: Discrimination of targets by the bat, Eptesicus fuscus. J. Exp. Zoology 176, 315–328 (1971).

[814] Simmons, J. A., Brock Fenton, M., O'Farrell, M. J.: Echolocation and pursuit of prey by bats. Science 203, 16–21 (1979).

[815] Singer, S.: Zur Kenntnis der motorischen Funktionen des Lendenmarks der Taube. S.-B. Akad. Wiss. Wien, math.-nat. Kl. 89, 167–185 (1884).

[816] Singer, W., Zihl, J., Pöppel, E.: Subcortical control of visual thresholds in humans: evidence for modality specific and retinotopically organized mechanisms of selective attention. Exp. Brain Res. 29, 173–190 (1977).

[817] Skoglund, S.: Joint receptors and kinaesthesis. Hdb. Sens. Physiol., Somatosens. System II, 111–127, Springer Verlag, Berlin, Heidelberg, New York 1973.

[818] Spallanzani, L.: Opere de Lazzaro Spallanzani. 5 vols. Ulrico Heopli, Milan 1932.

[819] Sperry, R. W.: The effect of crossing nerves to antagonistic muscles in the hind limb of the rat. J. comp. Neurol. 45, 1–19 (1941).

[820] Sperry, R. W.: Effect of 180 degree rotation of the retinal field on visuomotor coordination. J. exp. Zool. 92, 263–279 (1943).

[821] Sperry, R. W.: Neural basis of the spontaneous optokinetic response produced by visual inversion. J. comp. Physiol. Psychol. 43, 482–489 (1950).

[822] Sperry, R. W.: Mechanisms of neural maturation. In: Hdb. exp. Psychology, Ed.: S. S. Stevens, Wiley & Sons, New York, Chapman & Hall, London 1951.

[823] Sperry, R. W.: Physiological Plasticity and Brain Circuit Theory. In: Biol. Biochem. Bases of Behaviour, 401–424. Eds.: H. F. Harlow, C. N. Woolsey. Univ. Wisc. Press, Madison 1958.

[824] Spiegel, E. A., Demetriades, S. D.: Die zentrale Kompensation des Labyrinthverlustes. Pflügers Arch. ges. Physiol. 210, 215–222 (1925).

[825] Sprague, J. M., Berlucchi, G., Rizzolatti, G.: The role of the superior colliculus and pretectum in vision and visually guided behavior. In: Hdb. Sens. Physiol. VII/3, Central Processing of Visual Information, part B, p. 90–101. Ed.: R. Jung. Springer Verlag, Berlin, Heidelberg, New York, 1973.

[826] Stange, G.: Die zentralnervöse Verrechnung optischer Afferenzen bei der Gleichgewichtshaltung von Fischen. J. comp. Physiol. 80, 95–118 (1972).

[827] Stasko, A. B., Sullivan, Ch. M.: Responses of planarians to light: an examination of klino-kinesis. In: Animal Behav. Monogr. Eds.: J. M. Cullen, C. G. Beer.4/2, 47–124 (1971).

[828] Stein, A.: Attainment of positional information in the crayfish statocyst. Fortschr. Zool. 23, 109–118 (1975).

[829] Stein, A., Schöne, H.: Über das Zusammenspiel von Schwereorientierung und Orientierung zur Unterlage beim Flußkrebs. Verh. Dtsch. Zool. Ges. 65, 225–229 (1972).

[830] Stein, B. E., Magalhaes-Castro, B., Krüger, L.: Relationship between visual and tactile representations in cat superior colliculus. J. Neurophysiol. 39, 401–419 (1976).

[831] Steiner, G.: Zur Duftorientierung fliegender Insekten. Naturwiss. 40, 514–515 (1953).

[832] Steiner, G.: Über die Geruchs-Fernorientierung von Drosophila melanogaster in „ruhender Luft". Naturwiss. 41, 287 (1954).

[833] Steinhausen, W.: Über den Nachweis der Bewegung der Cupula in der intakten Bogengangsampulle des Labyrinthes bei der natürlichen, rotatorischen und calorischen Reizung. Pflügers Arch. ges. Physiol. 228, 322 (1931).

[834] Stempell, W.: Zoologie im Grundriss. Gebrüder Borntraeger, Berlin 1935.

[835] Stone, R. W., Jr., Letko, W.: Some observations during weightlessness simulation with subject immersed in a rotating water tank. Nat. Aeronautics and Space Administration, Washington D. C. 1964.

[836] Stone, J., Freeman, R. B.: Neurophysiological mechanisms in the visual discrimination of form. Hdb. Sens. Physiol. VII/3, Central Processing of visual information, part A, p. 154–207, Ed.: R. Jung. Springer Verlag, Berlin, Heidelberg, New York 1973.

[837] Strausfeld, N. J.: Atlas of an insect brain. Springer Verlag, Berlin, Heidelberg, New York 1976.

[838] Stresemann, E.: Exkursionsfauna (Wirbellose II/2). Hrsg. E. Stresemann. Volk und Wissen, Volkseigener Verlag, Berlin 1974.

[839] Sulkin, S. D.: Depth regulation of crab larvae in the absence of light. J. exp. mar. Biol. Ecol. **13**, 73–82 (1973).

[840] Sulkin, S. D.: The influence of light in the depth regulation of crab larvae. Biol. Bull. **148**, 333–343 (1975).

[841] Suthers, R. A.: Acoustic Orientation by Fish-catching Bats. J. exp. Zool. **158**, 319 (1965).

[842] Szabo, T.: Sense organs of the lateral line system in some electric fish of the Gymnotidae, Mormyridae and Gymnarchidae. J. Morph. **117**, 229–250 (1965).

[843] Szabo, T.: Orientierungsmechanismen bei elektrischen Fischen. Fortschr. Zool. **21**, 190–210 (1973).

[844] Szabo, T.: Anatomy of the specialized lateral line organs of electroreception. In: Hdb. Sens. Physiol. **III**/3, 13–58. Ed.: A. Fessard. Springer Verlag, Berlin, Heidelberg, New York 1974.

[845] Szabo, T.: 15. Elektrorezeption und Ortung im elektrischen Feld. Aus: Biophysik, ein Lehrb., Hrsg. W. Hoppe, W. Lohmann, H. Markl, H. Ziegler. Springer Verlag, Berlin, Heidelberg, New York 1977.

[846] Szabo, T., Fessard, A.: Physiology of Electroreceptors. In: Hdb. Sens. Physiol. **III**/3, p. 59–124. Ed.: A. Fessard. Springer Verlag, Berlin, Heidelberg, New York 1974.

[847] Szentàgothai, J.: Die Rolle der einzelnen Labyrinthrezeptoren bei der Orientierung von Augen und Kopf im Raum. Akadèmiai Kiado, Budapest 1952.

[848] Tait, J., McNally, W. J.: V. Some features of the action of the utricular maculae (and of the associated action of the semicircular canals) of the frog. Phil. Trans, Roy. Soc. B **224**, 241–288 (1934).

[849] Terashima, Shin-Ichi, Goris, R. C.: Tectal organization of pit viper infrared reception. Brain Res. **83**, 490–494 (1975).

[850] Tesch, F.-W.: Migratory behaviour of displaced homing yellow eels (Anguilla anguilla) in the North Sea. Helgoländer wiss. Meeresunters. **27**, 190–198 (1975).

[851] Thomas, D. R., Lyons, J.: Visual field dependency in pigeons. Anim. Behav. **16**, 213–218 (1968).

[852] Thomas, D. R., Lyons, J.: Further evidence of a sensory-tonic interaction in pigeons. J. of. exp. Analysis of Behavior **11**, 167–171 (1968).

[853] Thorpe, W. H., Crisp, D. J.: Studies on plastron respiration III. The orientation responses of Aphelocheirus (Hemiptera, Aphelocheiridae, Naucoridae) in relation to plastron respiration; together with an account of specialized pressure receptors in aquatic insects. J. exp. Biol. **24**, 310–328 (1947).

[854] Tinbergen, N.: Über die Orientierung des Bienenwolfes (Philanthus triangulum Fabr.). Z. vergl. Physiol. **16**, 305–334 (1932).

[855] Tinbergen, N.: Über die Orientierung des Bienenwolfes (Philanthus triangulum Fabr.). II. Die Bienenjagd. Z. vergl. Physiol. **21**, 699–716 (1935).

[856] Tinbergen, N.: The study of instinct, Clarendon Press, Oxford 1951. Instinktlehre, Übs.: O. Koehler. Parey, Berlin, Hamburg 1952.

[857] Tinbergen, N., Kruyt, W.: Über die Orientierung des Bienenwolfes (Philanthus triangulum Fabr.). III. Die Bevorzugung bestimmter Wegmarken. Z. vergl. Physiol. **25**, 292–334 (1938).

[858] Tinbergen, N., van der Linde, R. J.: Über die Orientierung des Bienenwolfes (Philanthus triangulum Fabr.) IV. Heimflug aus unbekanntem Gebiet. Biol. Zbl. **58**, 425–435 (1938).

[859] Tischner, H.: Über den Gehörsinn von Stechmücken. Acustica **3**, 335–343 (1953).

[860] Tischner, H., Schief, A.: Fluggeräusch und Schallwahrnehmung bei Aedes aegypti L. (Culicidae). Verh. Dtsch. zool. Ges. Tübingen, 453–460 (1954).

[861] Trendelenburg, W.: Über die Bewegungen der Vögel nach Durchschneidung der Rückenmarkwurzeln. Arch. Anat. Physiol. **1906**, 1–126 (1906).

[862] Trevarthen, C. B.: Two mechanisms of vision in primates. Psychol. Forsch. **31**, 299–337 (1968).

[863] Trincker, D.: Analyse des afferenten Informationsflusses von Labyrinth-Receptoren, seiner Stabilisierung durch Rückkoppelung und der Kriterien für Konstanz der Raum- und Zeitkoordinaten zentraler Datenverarbeitung. Biokybernetik II. In: Materialien I. Int. Symp. „Biokybernetik" Leipzig, 19.– 22. 9. 1967. Hrsg.: H. Drischel, N. Tiedt; Karl-Marx-Univ. Leipzig 1968.

[864] Trott, T. I., Dimock, R. V.: Intraspecific Trail, following by the mud Snail Ilyanassa obsoleta. Mar. Behav. Physiol. **5**, 91–101 (1978).

[865] Tsang, N., Macnab, R., Koshland, D. E.: Common mechanisms for repellents and attractants in bacterial chemotaxis. Science (N. Y.) **181**, 60–63 (1973).

[866] Tschermak, A, Schubert, G.: Über Vertikalorientierung im Rotatorium und im Flugzeuge. Pflügers Arch. ges. Physiol. **228**, 234–256 (1931).

[867] Udo de Haes, H. A.: Stability of apparent vertical and ocular countertorsion as a function of lateral tilt. Perception & Psychophysics **8**, 137–142 (1970).

[868] Udo de Haes, H. A., Schöne, H.: Interaction between statolith organs and semicircular canals on apparent vertical and nystagmus (Investigations on the effectiveness of the statolith organs). Acta Oto-laryngol. (Stockh.) **69**, 25–31 (1970).

[869] Ulagaraj, S. M., Walker, T. J.: Phonotaxis of Crickets in Flight: Attraction of Male and Female Crickets to Male Calling Song. Science **182**, 1278–1279 (1973).

[870] Ulagaraj, S. M., Walker, T. J.: Response of flying mole crickets to three parameters of synthetic songs broadcast outdoors. Nature **253**, 530–31 (1975).

[871] Ulrich, H.: Die Funktion der Otolithen, geprüft durch direkte mechanische Beeinflussung am lebenden Hecht. Pflügers Arch. ges. Physiol. **235**, 548–553 (1935).

[872] Ulyott, P.: The behaviour of Dendrocoelum lacteum. I. Responses at light-and-dark boundaries, II. Responses in non-directional gradients. J. exp. Biol. **13**, 253–278 (1936).

[873] Vannini, M.: Researches on the coast of Somalia. The shore and the dune of Sar Uanle. 4. Orientation and anemotaxis in the land hermit crab, Coenobita rugosus Milne Edwards. Monit. zool. Ital. (N. S.) **6**, 57–90 (1975).

[874] Vannini, M.: Researches on the coast of Somalia. The shore and the dune of Sar Uanle. 7. Field observations on the periodical transdunal migrations of the hermit crab, Coenobita rugosus Milne Edwards. Monit. Zool. Ital. (N. S.), Suppl. **VII**, 145–185 (1976).

[875] Verheijen, F. J.: The mechanisms of the trapping effect of artifical light sources upon animals. Extrait Arch. Neerl. Zool. **13**, 1–107 (1958).

[876] Verheijen, F. J.: Sky radiance features representing orientational cues to birds. Paper read on 14th Int. Etholog. Conf. Parma, Italy 1975.

[877] Verheijen, F. J.: Orientation based on directivity, a directional parameter of the animal's radiant environment. In: Animal Migration, Navigation, and Homing. Eds.: K. Schmidt-Koenig, W. T. Keeton. Springer Verlag, Berlin, Heidelberg, New York 1978.

[878] Verheijen, F. J., Wildschut, J. T.: The photic orientation of hatchling sea turtles during water finding behaviour. Netherlands J. Sea Res. **7**, 53–67 (1973).

[879] Versteegh, C.: Ergebnisse partieller Labyrinthexstirpation bei Kaninchen. Acta Oto-laryngol. **11**, 393–408 (1927).

[880] Verwey, J., van Haaften, J. L.: s. [294a].

[880a] Vinnikov, Ya. A., Gasenko, O. G., Titova, L. K., Bronstein, A. A., Tsirulis, T. P., Pevznier, R. A., Govardovskii, N. A., Gribakin, F. G., Aronova, M. Z., Tchekhonadskii, N. A.: The balance receptor. The evolution of its structural, cytochemical and functional organization. In: Problems in Space Biology, 12. Ed.: V. N. Tchernigovskii. NAUKA, Leningrad. (Russisch) 1971.

[881] Vleugel, D. A.: Über die wahrscheinlichste Methode der Windorientierung ziehender Buchfinken (Fringilla coelebs). Ornis Fenn. **36**, 78–88 (1959).

[882] Vleugel, D. A.: Über nächtlichen Zug von Drosseln und ihre Orientierung. Vogelwarte **21**, 307–313 (1962).

[883] Wade, N. J.: Visual orientation during and after lateral head, body, and trunk tilt. Perception and Psychophysics, **3**, 215–219 (1968).

[884] Wade, N. J., Day, R. H.: Tilt and centrifugation in changing the direction of body-force. Am. J. Psychol. **53**, 637–639 (1967).

[885] Wade, N. J., Schöne, H.: The influence of force magnitude on the perception of body position. I. Effect of Head Posture. Br. J. Psychol. **62**, 157–163 (1971).

[886] Waespe, W., Henn, V.: Neuronal activity in the vestibular nuclei of the alert monkey during vestibular and optokinetic stimulation. Exp. Brain Res. **27**, 523–538 (1977).

[887] Wagner, G.: Topography and pigeon orientation. In: Animal Orientation and Navigation, p. 259–273. Eds.: Galler et al. NASA SP-262, U. S. Gov. Print. Off., Washington 1972.

[888] Walcott, C.: A spider's vibration receptor: Its anatomy and physiology. Am. Zoologist **9**, 133–144 (1969).

[889] Walcott, C., Green, R.: Orientation of homing pigeons altered by a change in the direction of an applied magnetic field. Science **184**, 180– 182 (1974).

[890] Walcott, C., Schmidt-Koenig, K.: The effect on pigeon homing of anesthesia during displacement. Auk **90**, 281–286 (1973).

[891] Waldvogel, J. A., Benvenuti, S., Keeton, W. T., Papi, F.: Homing pigeon orientation influenced by deflected winds at home loft. J. comp. Physiol. **128**, 297–301 (1978).

[892] Wallace, G. K.: Visual scanning in the desert locust Schistocerca gregaria Forskal. J. exp. Biol. **36**, 512–525 (1959).

[893] Wallraff, H. G.: Über das Heimfindevermögen von Brieftauben mit durchtrennten Bogengängen. Z. vergl. Physiol. **50**, 313–330 (1965).

[894] Wallraff, H. G.: Das Navigationssystem der Vögel. Ein theoretischer Beitrag zur Analyse ungeklärter Orientierungsleistungen. R. Oldenbourg Verl., München, Wien 1974.

[895] Wallraff, H. G.: Proposed principles of magnetic field perception in birds. Oikos **30**, 188–194 (1978).

[896] Walton, A. S., Herrnkind, W. F.: Hydrodynamic orientation of spiny lobster, Panulirus argus (Crustacea: Palinuridae): Wave surge and unidirectional currents. Proc. Ann. Northeastern Mtg. Animal Behav. Soc. 1977, Plenary Papers. Memorial Univ. of New Foundland. Marine Sci. Res. Lab, Tech. Report No. 20 (1977).

[897] Wapner, S., Werner, H.: Perceptual development. An investigation within the framework of sensory-tonic field theory. Worcester, Mass. 1957.

[898] Watson, J. B., Lashley K. S.: Homing and related activities of birds: Publ. 211, Carnegie Institution, Washington 1915.

[899] Wehner, R.: Die Konkurrenz von Sonnenkompaß- und Horizontmarken-Orientierung bei der Wüstenameise Cataglyphis bicolor (Hymenoptera, Formicidae). Verh. Dtsch. Zool. Ges. **63**, 238–242 (1970).

[900] Wehner, R.: Das Koordinatensystem des Sehfeldes bei Arthropoden. Fortschr. Zool. **21**, 258–293 (1973).

[901] Wehner, R.: Space constancy of the visual world in insects. Fortschr. Zool. **23**, 148–160 (1975).

[902] Wehner, R.: Polarized-light navigation by insects. Scient. Amer. **235**, 106–114 (1976a).

[903] Wehner, R.: Structure and function of the peripheral visual pathway in Hymenopterans. In: Neural Principles in vision. Eds.: F. Zettler, R. Weiler. Springer Verlag, Berlin, Heidelberg, New York 1976b.

[904] Wehner, R., Labhart, Th.: Perception of the geomagnetic field in the fly Drosophila melanogaster. Experientia **26**, 967–968 (1970)

[905] Wehrhahn, C., Reichardt, W.: Visually induced height orientation of the fly Musca domestica. Biol. Cybernetics **20**, 37–50 (1975).

[906] Weis-Fogh, T.: An aerodynamic sense organ stimulating and regulating flight in locusts. Nature, London **164**, 873–874 (1949).

[907] Weis-Fogh, T., Jensen, M.: Biology and physics of locust flight I.–IV. Phil. Trans. Roy. Soc. London B **239**, 415–585 (1956).

[908] Weiss, P.: Self-Differentiation of the basic patterns of coordination. Comp. Psychol. Monographs **17**/4, 1–96 (1941a).

[909] Weiss, P.: Autonomous versus reflexogenous activity of the central nervous system. Proc. Amer. Philos. Soc. **84**, 53–64 (1941b).

[910] Wellington, W. G., Sullivan, C. R., Henson, W. R.: The light reactions of Larvae of the spotless fall webworm, Hyphantria textor Harr. (Lepidoptera: Arctiidae). Canad. Entomol. **86**, 529–542 (1954).

[910a] Wells, M. J.: Nerve structure and function. Advanc. Sci. Lond. **57**, 449–57 (1958).

[911] Wells, M. J.: The orientation of Octopus. In: Orientierung der Tiere (Animal Orientation). Symp. in Garmisch-Partenkirchen 17.–21. 9. 1962. Ed.: H. Autrum. Erg. Biol. **26**, 40–54 (1963).

[912] Wells, M. J., Wells, J.: The function of the brain of octopus in tactile discrimination. J. exp. Biol. **34**, 131–142 (1957).

[913] Wendler, G.: Laufkoordination und Regelung der Beinstellung bei der Stabheuschrecke Carausius morosus. Proc. XII Int. Congr. Ent. London, 1964 (1965).

[914] Wendler, G.: Über einige Modelle in der Biologie. Studium Generale **18**, 284–290 (1965).

[915] Wendler, G.: Physiology and systems analysis of gravity orientation in two insect species (Carausius morosus, Calandra granaria). Fortschr. Zool. **23**, 33–46 (1975).

[916] Wenner, A. M., Johnson, D. L.: Reply to v. Frisch: Honey bees: Do they use direction and distance information provided by their dances. Science **158**, 1076–1077 (1967).

[917] Wensler, R. J. D.: The effect of odors on the behavior of adult Aedes aegypti and some factors limiting responsiveness. Can. J. Zool. **50**, 415–420 (1972).

[918] Werner, C. F.: Das Gehörorgan der Wirbeltiere und des Menschen. Verlag Georg Thieme, Leipzig 1960.

[919] Werner, G.: The topology of the body representation in the somatic afferent pathway. In: The Neurosciences, Second Study Programm, p. 605–617. Ed.: F. O. Schmitt. The Rockefeller Univ. Press, N. Y. 1970.

[920] Werner, G.: Neural information processing with stimulus feature extractors. In: The Neurosciences, Third study program, 171–183. Eds.: F. O. Schmitt, F. G. Worden. The M.I.T. Press Cambridge, Mass. u. London 1974.

[921] Werner, G., Whitsel, B. L.: The topology of dermatomal projection in the medial lemniscal system. J. Physiol. **192**, 123–144 (1967).

[922] Werner, G., Whitsel, B. L.: Topology of the body representation in somatosensory area I of primates. J. Neurophysiol. **31**, 856–69 (1968).

[923] Werner, G., Whitsel, B. L.: Functional organization of the somatosensory cortex. Hdb. Sens. Physiol. II. Somatosens. System, p. 625–636, 665–687. Springer Verlag, Berlin, Heidelberg, New York 1973.

[924] Wersäll, J.: Electron micrographic studies of vestibular hair cell innervation. In: Neural Mechanisms of the auditory and vestibular systems, 247–257. Eds.: G. L. Rasmussen, W. F. Windle. Thomas, Springfield, Ill. 1960.

[925] Wersäll, J., Lundqvist, P.-G.: Morphological polarization of the mechanoreceptors of the vestibular and acoustic systems. In: Sec. Symp. on the Role of the Vestibular Organs in Space Exploration, 57–72. NASA SP-115, U. S. Gov. Print. Off. Washington 1966.

[926] Wersäll, J., Bagger-Sjöbäck, D.: Morphology of the vestibular sense organ. In: Hdb. Sens. Physiol. VI/1, p. 123–170. Ed.: H. H. Kornhuber. Springer Verlag, Berlin, Heidelberg, New York 1974.

[927] West, G. S.: On the sensory pit of the crotalinae. Quart. Journ. Micr. Sci. **43**, 49–58 (1900).

[928] Whitfield, I. C.: ‚Auditory space’ and the role of the cortex in sound localization. Psychophysics and Physiology of Hearing. Eds.: E. F. Evans, J. P. Wilson. Academic Press, London 1977.

[929] Whitfield, I. C., Cranford, J., Ravizza, R., Diamond, I. T.: Effects of unilateral ablation of auditory cortex in cat on complex sound localization. J. Neurophysiol. **35**, 718–731 (1972).

[930] Wiener, N.: Cybernetics. New York 1948, 2. Aufl. The M.I.T. Press and J. Wiley & Sons. Inc., New York, London 1961.

[931] Wiersma, C. A. G., Yanagisawa, K.: On types of interneurons responding to visual stimulation present in the optic nerve of the rock lobster, Panulirus interruptus. J. Neurobiol. **2**, 291–309 (1971).

[932] Wiersma, C. A. G.: Space constancy in crustacean optic interneurons. Fortschr. Zool. **23**, 143–147 (1975).

[933] Wiese, K.: Das mechanorezeptorische Beuteortungssystem von Notonecta. I. Die Funktion des tarsalen Scolopidialorgans. J. comp. Physiol. **78**, 83–102 (1972).

[934] Wiese, K.: The mechanoreceptive system of prey localization in Notonecta II. The priniciple of prey localization. J. comp. Physiol. **92**, 317–325 (1974).

[935] Wiesel, T. N., Hubel, D. H.: Effects of visual deprivation on morphology and physiology of cells in the cat's lateral geniculate body. J. Neurophysiol. **26**, 978–993 (1963).

[936] Wiesel, T. N., Hubel, D. H.: Single-cell responses in striate cortex of kittens deprived of vision in one eye. J. Neurophysiol. **26**, 1004–17 (1963).

[937] Wigglesworth, V. B.: The sensory physiology of the human louse Pediculus humanus corporis de Geer (Anoplura). Parasitology **33**, 67–109 (1941).

[938] de Wilde, J., Hille Ris Lambers-Suverkropp, K., van Tol, A.: Responses to air flow and airborne plant odour in the Colorado beetle. Neth. J. Pl. Path. **75**, 53–57 (1969).

[939] Williams, C. B.: Insect migration. The New Naturalist, Collins, London 1958.

[940] Wilson, E. O.: Source and possible nature of the odor trail of fire ants. Science **129**, 643–644 (1959).

[941] Wilson, E. O.: The insect societies. Harvard University Press 1971.

[942] Wilson, E. O.: Sociobiology: the new synthesis. Harvard University Press 1975.

[943] Wilson, E. O., Bossert, W. H.: Chemical communication among animals. Rec. Prog. Horm. Res. **19**, 673 (1963).

[944] Wiltschko, W.: The influence of magnetic total intensity and inclination on directions preferred by migrating European Robins (Erithacus rubecula). Symp. Anim. Orient. and Navigation. NASA SP-262. U. S. Gov. Printing Off. Washington D. C. 1972b.

[945] Wiltschko, W.: Der Magnetkompaß der Gartengrasmücke (Sylvia borin). J. Ornithol. **115**, 1–7 (1974).

[946] Wiltschko, W., Gwinner, E.: Evidence for an Innate Magnetic Compass in Garden Warblers. Naturwiss. **61**, p. 406 (1974).

[947] Wiltschko, W., Wiltschko, R.: Magnetic compass of european robins. Science **176**, 62–64 (1972a).

[948] Wiltschko, W., Wiltschko, R.: The interaction of stars and magnetic field in the orientation system of night migrating birds. Z. Tierpsychol. **39**, 265–282 (1975a).

[949] Wiltschko, W., Wiltschko, R.: The interaction of stars and magnetic field in the orientation system of night migrating birds. I. Autumn experiments with European Warblers (Gen. Sylvia). Z. Tierpsychol. **37**, 337–355 (1975b).

[950] Wiltschko, W., Wiltschko, R.: Interrelation of magnetic compass and star orientation in night-migrating birds. J. comp. Physiol. **109**, 91–99 (1976a).

[951] Wiltschko, W., Wiltschko, R.: Die Bedeutung des Magnetkompasses für die Orientierung der Vögel. J. Ornithologie **117**, 362–387 (1976b).

[952] Witkin, H. A.: The nature and importance of individual differences in perception. J. Personality **18**, 145–170 (1949).

[953] Witkin, H. A.: Sex differences in perception. Trans. New York Acad. Sci. **12** (1949).

[954] Witkin, H. A.: Perception of body position and of the position of the visual field. Psychol. Monogr. **63**/7, 1–63 (1949).

[955] Witkin, H. A.: Visual factors in the maintenance of upright posture. Amer. J. Psychol. **63**, 31–50 (1950).

[956] Witkin, H. A.: Perception of the upright when the direction of the force acting on the body is changed. J. exp. Psychol. **43**, 93 (1952).

[957] Witkin, H. A.: The perception of the upright. Sci. Amer. Febr., 1–8 (1959).

[958] Witkin, H. A., Asch, S. E.: Studies in space orientation. III. Perception of the upright in the absence of a visual field. J. exp. Psychol. **38**, 603–614 (1948).

[959] Witkin, H. A., Asch, S. E.: Studies in space orientation. IV. Further experiments on perception of the upright with displaced visual fields. J. exp. Psychol. **38**, 762–782 (1948).

[960] Witkin, H. A., Dyk, R. B., Faterson, H. F., Goodenough, D. R., Karp, S. A.: Psychological differentiation. Wiley, New York 1962.

[961] Witkin, H. A., Lewis, H. B., Hertzman, M., Machover, K., Meissner, P. B., Wapner, S.: Personality through perception. Harper, New York 1954.

[962] Wolff, H. G.: Statische Orientierung bei Mollusken. Fortschr. Zool. **21**, 80—99 (1973).

[963] Wolff, H. G.: Statocysts and geotactic behaviour in gastropod molluscs. Fortschr. Zool. **23**, 63–84 (1975).

[964] Woolsey, T. A.: Somatosensory, auditory and visual cortical areas of the mouse. John Hopkins Hospital Bull. **121**, 91–112 (1967).

[965] Woolsey, C. N., Fairman, D.: Contralateral, ipsilateral and bilateral representation of cutaneous receptors in somatic areas I and II of the cerebral cortex of pig, sheep and other mammals. Surgery **19**, 684–702 (1946).

[966] Wright, R. H.: The science of smell. Basic Books, Inc., Publishers. George Allen & Unwin Ltd., New York 1964.

[967] Wurtz, R. H., Goldberg, M. E.: Activity of superior colliculus in behaving monkey. III. Cells discharging before eye movements. J. Neurophysiol. **35**, 575–586 (1972).

[968] Würdinger, I.: Vergleichend morphologische Untersuchungen zur Jugendentwicklung von Anser- und Branta-Arten. J. Ornithol. **116**, 65–86 (1975).

[969] Young, J. Z.: The anatomy of the nervous system of Octopus vulgaris. Clarendon Press, Oxford 1971.

[970] Young, L. R.: The current status of vestibular system models. Automatica **5**, 369–383 (1969).

[971] Young, L. R.: Developments in modelling visual-vestibular interactions. Aerospace. Med. Res. Lab. Rept. AMRL -71-14 Wright Patterson Airforce Base, Ohio 1971.

[972] Young, L, R., Meiry, J. L., Yao, T. Li: Control engineering approaches to human dynamic space orientation. In: Sec. Symp. on the Role of the Vestibular Organs in Space Exploration. NASA SP-115, U. S. Print. Off. Washington 1966.

[973] Young, L. R., Dichgans, J., Murphy, R., Brandt, Th.: Interaction of optokinetic and vestibular stimuli in motion perception. Acta Otolaryng. **76**, 24–31 (1973).

[974] Young, L. R., Henn, V. S.: Nystagmus produced by pitch and yaw rotation of monkeys about non-vertical axes (1). Fortschr. Zool. **23**, 235–246 (1975).

[975] Young, L. R., Oman, C. R.: Model for vestibular adaptation to horizontal rotations. Aerosp. Med. **40**, p. 1076–1080 (1969).

[976] Young, L. R., Oman, C. M., Dichgans, J. M.: Influence of head orientation on visually induced pitch and roll sensation. Aviation, Space and Environmental Medicine **46**, 264–269 (1975).

[977] Zacharias, G. L., Young, L. R.: Manual control of yaw motion with combined visual and vestibular cues. In: 13. Ann. Conf. on Manual Control, Mass. Inst. Techn., June 1977. p. 389–402, 1977.

[978] Zalin, A.: On the function of the Kinocilia and Stereocilia with special reference to the phenomenon of directional preponderance. J. Laryng., Otol. **81**, p. 119–135 (1967).

[979] Zaretsky, M. D.: Specificity of the calling song and short term changes in the phonotactic response by female crickets (Scapsipedus marginatus, Gryllidae). J. comp. Physiol. **79**, 153–172 (1972).

[980] Zee, D. S., Yee, R. D., Robinson, D. A.: Optokinetic responses in labyrinthine defective human beings. Brain Res. **113**, 423–428 (1976).

[981] Zeuner, F.: The prothoracic tracheal apparatus of Saltatoria (Orthoptera). Proc. Roy. Ent. Soc. A **11**, 11–21 (1936).

SUPPLEMENTARY REFERENCES

[982] Aristotle: Politics, Book 1, Ch. 2. Trans. by J.E.C. Weldon. London (1883).

[983] Baker, R. R.: The evolutionary ecology of animal migration. Hodder and Stoughton, London, Sydney, Aukland, Toronto 1978.

[984] Baker, R. R.: Goal orientation by blindfolded humans after long-distance displacement: Possible involvement of a magnetic sense. Science **210**, 555–557 (1980).

[985] Barth, F. G.: Strain detection in the arthropod exoskeleton. In: Sense organs, pp. 112–141. Eds.: M. S. Laverack, P. J. Cosens. Blackie, Glasgow 1981.

[986] Blakemore, R. P., Frankel, R. B.: Magnetic navigation in bacteria. Sci. Amer. **245**, 42–49 (1981).

[987] Bles, W.: Stepping around: circular vection and coriolis effects. In: Attention and performance IX, pp. 48-61. Eds.: J. B. Long, A. D. Baddeley. Lawrence Erlbaum Associates, Hillsdale, N.J. 1981.

[988] Camhi, J. M.: The escape system of the cockroach. Sci. Amer. **243**, 144–156 (1980).

[989] Edrich, W.: Honey bees: Photoreceptors participating in orientation behaviour to light and gravity. J. Comp. Physiol. **133**, 111–116 (1979).

338 — References

[990] Foster, K. W., Smyth, R. D.: Light antennas in phototactic algae. Microbiol. Rev. **44**, 572–630 (1980).
[991] Frömel, G.: Extraction of objects from structured backgrounds in the cat superior colliculus. Part II. Biol. Cybernetics **38**, 75–83 (1980).
[992] Gerhardt, H. C., Rheinlaender, J.: Accuracy of sound localization in a miniature dendrobatid frog. Naturwiss. **67**, 362–363 (1980).
[993] Gonshor, A., Melville Jones, G. M.: Postural adaptation to prolonged optical reversal of vision in man. Brain Res. **192**, 239–248 (1980).
[994] Havukkala, I.: Klinokinetic and klinotactic humidity reactions of the beetles Hylobius abietis and Tenebrio molitor. Physiol. Entomol. **5**, 133–140 (1980).
[995] Hölldobler, B., Traniello, J.: Tandem running pheromone in ponerine ants. Naturwiss. **67**, 360 (1980).
[996] Ioalè, P., Albonetti, E.: Effects of differentially shielded lofts on pigeon homing. Naturwiss. **68**, 209–210 (1981).
[997] Johnson, P. B., Hasler, A. D.: The use of chemical cues in the upstream migration of Coho salmon, Oncorhynchus kisutch Waldbaum. J. Fish Biol. **17**, 67–73 (1980).
[998] Knudsen, E. I.: Sound localization in birds. In: Comparative studies of hearing in vertebrates, pp. 289–322. Eds.: A. N. Popper, R. R. Fay. Springer Verlag, Berlin, Heidelberg, New York 1980.
[999] Labhart, T.: Specialized photoreceptors at the dorsal rim of the honeybee's compound eye: Polarizational and angular sensitivity. J. Comp. Physiol. **141**, 19–30 (1980).
[1000] Larkin, R. P.: Transoceanic bird migration: Evidence for detection of wind direction. Behav. Ecol. Sociobiol. **6**, 229–232 (1980).
[1001] Mather, J. G., Baker, R. R.: Magnetic sense of direction in woodmice for route-based navigation. Nature **291**, 152–155 (1981).
[1002] Midgley, G. C., Tees, R. C.: Orienting behavior by rats with visual cortical and subcortical lesions. Exp. Brain Res. **41**, 316–328 (1981).
[1003] Mittelstaedt, M.-L., Mittelstaedt, H.: Homing by path integration in a mammal. Naturwiss. **67**, 566–567 (1980).
[1004] Murlies, J., Jones, C. D.: Fine-scale structure of odour plumes in relation to insect orientation to distant pheromone and other attractant sources. Physiol. Entomol. **6**, 71–86 (1981).
[1005] Newman, E. A., Hartline, P. H.: Integration of visual and infrared information in bimodal neurons of the rattlesnake optic tectum. Science **213**, 789–791 (1981).
[1006] Pals, N.: Local geo-electric fields at the bottom of the sea and their relevance for electro-sensitive fish. Proefschrift. De Rijksuniversiteit te Utrecht, 11. Jan. 1982. Durkkerij Elinkwijk BV, Utrecht 1982.
[1007] Quinn, T. P.: Evidence for celestial and magnetic compass orientation in lake migrating sockeye salmon fry. J. Comp. Physiol. **137**, 243–248 (1981).
[1008] Rollo, C. D., Wellington, W. G.: Environmental orientation by terrestrial mollusca with particular reference to homing behaviour. Can. J. Zool. **59**, 225–239 (1981).
[1009] Roucoux, A., Gnitton, D. Crommelinck, M.: Stimulation of the superior colliculus in the alert cat. II. Eye and head movements evoked when the head is unrestrained. Exp. Brain Res. **39**, 75–85 (1980).
[1010] Rozhkova, G. I.: Effect of body orientation in the gravitational field on directional sensitivity of the cercal system of neurons in crickets. J. Neurophysiol. **12**, 397–403 (1980).
[1011] Sandeman, D. C.: Angular acceleration, compensatory head movements and the halteres of flies (Lucilia serricata). J. Comp. Physiol. **136**, 361–367 (1980).
[1012] Sandeman, D. C., Markl, H.: Head movements in flies (Calliphora) produced by deflexion of the halteres. J. Exp. Biol. **85**, 43–60 (1980).
[1013] Scapini, F., Pardi., L.: Nuovi dati sulla tendenza direzionale innata nell'orientamento solare degli anfipodi litorali. Accademi Nazionale dei lincei. Classe di Scienze fisiche, matematiche e naturali. Ser. 8, **64**, 592–597 (1979).

[1014] Singer, W., Freeman, B., Rauschecker, J.: Restriction of visual experience to a single orientation affects the organization of orientation columns in cat visual cortex. Exp. Brain Res. **41**, 199–215 (1981).

[1015] Tusa, R. J., Palmer, L. A.: Retinotopic organization of areas 20 and 21 in the cat. J. Comp. Neur. **193**, 147–164 (1980).

[1016] Tusa, R. J., Palmer, L. A., Rosenquist, A. C.: The retinotopic organization of area 17 (striate cortex) in the cat. J. Comp. Neur. **177**, 213–236 (1978).

[1017] Tusa, R. J., Rosenquist, A. C., Palmer, L. A.: Retinotopic organization of areas 18 and 19 in the cat. J. Comp. Neur. **185**, 657–678 (1979).

[1018] Walcott, C.: Magnetic orientation in homing pigeons (invited). IEEE Transactions of Magnetics **16**, 1008–1013 (1980).

[1019] Wallraff, H. G.: Olfaction and homing in pigeons: Nerve-section experiments, critique, hypotheses. J. Comp. Physiol. **139**, 209–224 (1980).

[1020] Walthall, W. W., Hartman, H. B.: Receptors and giant interneurons signaling gravity orientation information in the cockroach Arenivaga. J. Comp. Physiol. **142**, 359–369 (1981).

[1021] Weber, T., Thorson, J., Huber, F.: Auditory behavior of the cricket. I. Dynamics of compensated walking and discrimination paradigms on the Kramer treadmill. J. Comp. Physiol. **141**, 215–232 (1981).

[1022] Wehner, R.: Spatial vision in arthropods. In: Hdb. Sens. Physiol. **VII**/6C, pp. 287–616. Ed.: H. Autrum. Springer Verlag, Berlin, Heidelberg, New York 1981.

[1023] Wehner, R.: The perception of polarized light. In: Biology of photoreceptors. Symp. Soc. Exp. Biol. Eds.: D. Cosens, D. Vince-Prue. Cambridge Univ. Press, Cambridge 1982.

[1024] Wehner, R.: The bee's celestial map—a simplified model of the outside world. Proc. IUSSI. Neurophysiology and Behaviour of Social Insects. Boulder, Colorado 1982.

[1025] Wehner, R., Srinivasan, M. V.: Searching behaviour of desert ants, genus Cataglyphis (Formicidae, Hymenoptera). J. Comp. Physiol. **142**, 315–338 (1981).

[1026] Wendler, G., Dambach, M., Schmitz, B., Scharstein, H.: Analysis of the acoustic orientation behavior in crickets (Gryllus campestris L.). Naturwiss. **67**, 99–100 (1980).

[1027] Wiltschko, W., Gwinner, E., Wiltschko, R.: The effect of celestial cues on the ontogeny of non-visual orientation in the garden warbler (Sylvia borin). Z. Tierpsychol. **53**, 1–8 (1980).

[1028] Wolf. R., Heisenberg, M.: On the fine structure of yaw torque in visual flight orientation of Drosophila melanogaster. II. A temporally and spatially variable weighting function for the visual field ('Visual Attention'). J. Comp. Physiol. **140**, 69–80 (1980).

Index

accommodation, 42
Acilius sulcatus, 72, 77-79, 142, 168
actual value, 50
afferent, 32
allothetic orientation, 26, 294
ampullae of Lorenzini, 182, 187, 195
ampullary organs, 182-184
angular acceleration orientation, 280-284. *See also* inertial navigation
angular light distribution (ALD), 73-74, 153
ants. See also *Cataglyphis bicolor*; gravity receptors, 278; landmark orientation, 162, 163; light-gravity orientation, 86; olfactory orientation, 40, 84, 198-202, 203; sun compass orientation, 71, 83, 157, 163; vibration orientation, 237
array organ, 36, 142-143, 154
arrestant, 65
arrow worm, 235-236
astrocompass orientation. *See* star compass orientation
astrotaxis, 62
attractant, 65
Aubert phenomenon, 115-116, 137
auditory cortex, 210, 212
autotropotaxis, 59
azimuth, sun, 101, 103

bacteria, 41, 66-67, 190-191
balance (body position), 13, 251, 258, 288
barnacle, 240
bat, 215-220
beach flea, 14, 21-22, 140
bees, color vision, 151, 154, 170; eye, 170-171; goal orientation, 28, 111; gravity orientation, 82, 86, 278; idiothetic orientation, 297; landmark orientation, 162, 163; olfactory orientation, 34, 197, 204; orientation of comb to magnetic field, 190; orientation in wind, 242, 244; polar-

ized light orientation, 157; sun compass orientation, 12, 29, 100, 157, 163; waggle dance, 88-89, 190, 246
beetles. *See also* type of beetle; heat orientation, 175; light orientation, 21; magnetic field orientation, 165, 189, 190; olfactory orientation, 66, 203, 204; orientation to wind, 82, 240; vibration orientation, 233-234
behavior, 4; interaction with environment, 4-5, 17; physiology of, 17-19
bicomponent theory, 82-83
bicoordinate navigation, 107-109
bioelectric field, 179-181
bisensor system, compensation of sensory perturbation, 143-145; for determining gradient direction, 39-40, 65; for determining incident direction, 36-38, 65
blind people, echolocation, 43, 221; orientation by hearing and touch, 141; perception of movement, 175
blindness, from sensory deprivation, 139
block diagram. *See* circuit diagram
body alignment, course-constant, 12, 98-99; space-constant, 12-13, 98-99
body axes, 7-8, 10
brain, electrical stimulation, 269, 288-289; insect, 169-170; vertebrate, 149-151
brainstem, 151, 288
butterfly, 6-7, 14, 21, 293

caddis fly, 24, 240
Cartesian coordinates. *See* coordinate systems
cat, auditory central nervous system, 212; gravity orientation, 144, 267, 269, 275; perturbation of visual development, 139-140, 146, 147
Cataglyphis bicolor (desert ant), homing to polarized light, 107, 154-156, 297; land-

Library of Congress Cataloging in Publication Data

Schöne, Hermann.
  Spatial orientation.

  Translation of: Orientierung im Raum.
  Bibliography: p.
  Includes index.
  1. Spatial orientation (Psychology). 2. Human
behavior.   3. Animal behavior.   I. Title.
QP443.S3613 1984   152.1′882   84-42561
ISBN 0-691-08363-0
ISBN 0-691-08364-9 (pbk.)